Technological innovation

Technological innovation

Oversights and foresights

Edited by

Raghu Garud
Praveen Rattan Nayyar
Zur Baruch Shapira
New York University

CAMBRIDGE
UNIVERSITY PRESS

Published by the Press Syndicate of the University of Cambridge
The Pitt Building, Trumpington Street, Cambridge CB2 1RP
40 West 20th Street, New York, NY 10011-4211, USA
10 Stamford Road, Oakleigh, Melbourne 3166, Australia

First published 1997

Printed in the United States of America

Library of Congress Cataloging-in-Publication Data

Technological innovation : oversights and foresights / edited by Raghu
  Garud, Praveen Rattan Nayyar, Zur Baruch Shapira.
      p.   cm.
    ISBN 0-521-55299-0 (hbk.)
    1. Technological innovations.   2. Decision-making.   I. Garud
  Raghu.   II. Nayyar, Praveen Rattan.   III. Shapira, Zur Baruch.
  HD45.S394   1997
  338'.064—dc20   96-29121
                                                             CIP

A catalog record for this book is available from the British Library

ISBN 0-521-55299-0 hardback

Contents

Contributors   *page* vii

Foreword   ix

Preface   xiii

Section I   Introduction

1   Technological innovation: Oversights and foresights   3
    Raghu Garud, Praveen Nayyar, and Zur Shapira

Section II   Learning to flip coins

2   On flipping coins and making technology choices: Luck as an
    explanation of technological foresight and oversight   13
    Jay B. Barney

3   Technological choices and the inevitability of errors   20
    Raghu Garud, Praveen Nayyar, and Zur Shapira

4   Rational entrepreneurs or optimistic martyrs? Some
    considerations on technological regimes, corporate entries,
    and the evolutionary role of decision biases   41
    Giovanni Dosi and Dan Lovallo

Section III   Tailoring fits

5   Cognition and capabilities: Opportunities seized and missed in
    the history of the computer industry   71
    Richard N. Langlois

6   Changing the game of corporate research: Learning to thrive in
    the fog of reality   95
    John Seely Brown

7   Environmental determinants of work motivation, creativity, and
    innovation: The case of R&D downsizing   111
    Teresa M. Amabile and Regina Conti

Section IV   Remembering to forget

8 Local rationality, global blunders, and the boundaries of
   technological choice: Lessons from IBM and DOS   129
   Joseph F. Porac

9 On the dynamics of forecasting in technologically complex
   environments: The unexpectedly long old age of
   optical lithography   147
   Rebecca Henderson

10 Three faces of organizational learning: Wisdom, inertia,
   and discovery   167
   Daniel Levinthal

11 Organizational entrepreneurship in mature-industry firms:
   Foresight, oversight, and invisibility   181
   Mariann Jelinek

12 Minimizing technological oversights: A marketing research
   perspective   214
   Jehoshua Eliashberg, Gary L. Lilien, and Vithala R. Rao

Section V   (S)Top management and culture

13 Firm capabilities and managerial decision making: A theory of
   innovation biases   233
   Janet E. L. Bercovitz, John M. de Figueiredo, and David J. Teece

14 Organization responsiveness to environmental shock as an
   indicator of organizational foresight and oversight: The role
   of executive team characteristics and organizational context   260
   Johann Peter Murmann and Michael L. Tushman

15 Technological innovation, learning, and leadership   279
   Andrew H. Van de Ven and David N. Grazman

16 Risky lessons: Conditions for organizational learning   306
   Baruch Fischhoff, Zvi Lanir, and Stephen Johnson

17 Exploiting enthusiasm: A case study of applied theories
   of innovation   325
   Gideon Kunda

Section VI   Clearing the fog

18 Beating the odds: Towards a theory of technological innovation   345
   Raghu Garud, Praveen Nayyar, and Zur Shapira

Author Index   355

Subject Index   361

Contributors

Teresa Amabile   Harvard University, Boston, MA

Jay Barney   Ohio State University, Columbus, OH

Janet E. L. Bercovitz   University of California, Berkeley, CA

John Seely Brown   Xerox Corporation, PARC, Palo Alto, CA

Regina Conti   Brandeis University, Waltham, MA

Giovanni Dosi   University of Rome, "La Sapienza," Rome, Italy

Jehoshua Eliashberg   University of Pennsylvania, Philadelphia, PA

John M. de Figueiredo   University of California, Berkeley, CA

Baruch Fischhoff   Carnegie Mellon University, Pittsburgh, PA

Raghu Garud   New York University, New York, NY

David N. Grazman   University of Southern California, Los Angeles, CA

Rebecca Henderson   Massachusetts Institute of Technology, Cambridge, MA

Mariann Jelinek   College of William and Mary, Williamsburg, VA

Stephen Johnson   Decision Research, Eugene OR

Gideon Kunda   Tel Aviv University, Ramat Aviv, Israel

Richard Langlois   University of Connecticut, Storrs, CT

Zvi Lanir   Institute for Strategic Thought and Practice, Tel Aviv, Israel

Dan Levinthal   University of Pennsylvania, Philadelphia, PA

Gary Lilien   Pennsylvania State University, University Park, PA

Daniel Lovallo   University of Pennsylvania, Philadelphia, PA

James G. March   Stanford University, Stanford, CA

Johann Peter Murmann   Columbia University, New York, NY

Praveen Nayyar   New York University, New York, NY

Joseph Porac   University of Illinois, Champaign, IL

Vithala Rao   Cornell University, Ithaca, NY

Zur Shapira   New York University, New York, NY

David Teece   University of California, Berkeley, CA

Michael L. Tushman   Columbia University, New York, NY

Andrew H. Van de Ven   University of Minnesota, Minneapolis, MN

Foreword

James G. March

This book is about technological innovations. It is set against a background of contemporary technological turbulence and numerous attempts to describe the genesis of various changes in technology that have been observed. It represents an attempt to make sense of the technological dynamism that appears to be endemic to the times and to provide some plausible suggestions for managing it.

The task is not an easy one. In particular, it is a task that is complicated by the conspicuous importance of technological innovation to modern life. There is no shortage of stories of innovation. They fill biographies, the popular press, and the after-hours conversations of participants. These stories have certain similarities. Changes in technologies, practices, and products are characteristically described in terms of the triumph of the new over the old. Initially, a new idea, institution, or practice is introduced into a small part of the system. Ultimately, it becomes pervasive. The stories use the powers of retrospection to identify individual and organizational genius in this triumph of good over evil.

The obvious difficulty with these stories is not so much that they can be demonstrated unambiguously to be false as it is that *even if they were false* we would nevertheless construct and repeat them. The market for stories of individual and collective triumph is insatiable, and anthropomorphic biases in human storytelling and comprehension are legendary. As a result, the fact that the tales of innovation that are told seem to have a consistent structure is hardly compelling evidence for their validity.

The present book tries to bring a certain open-mindedness to those stories, an open-mindedness that is skeptical about received truths but willing to entertain the possibility that there is some connection between popular stories and a serious theory of innovation. It focuses more attention than is usual on the failures of innovation, exploring the theoretical and engineering implications of the fact that the process of innovation generates failures much more frequently than it does successes. The contributors examine the extent to which it is possible to use ideas drawn from a contrast between innovative failure and innovative success as a basis for increasing the frequency of success. They differ a bit on whether such an increase is possible, but those differences are probably less significant in the long run than are the ways in which the studies illuminate our thinking about learning, discovery, and knowledge.

Many of the chapters can be seen as variations on a theme of organizational learning and its problems, particularly two central complications in adaptation through learning. The first is the difficulty of specifying the optimal allocation of resources between exploiting and developing what is already known and exploring what might come to be known. Defining an optimum involves trade-offs across time and space that are exceptionally difficult to calibrate. The second is the difficulty of avoiding dynamic imbalances between exploitation and exploration. Experiential learning processes, for example, tend to drive out exploration. Much of the richness of the book lies in the careful delineation of the many considerations involved in understanding and managing that balance. The chapters describe various forms of a dialectic between discipline and imagination that is reminiscent not only of Schumpeterian economics but also of theories of creativity in art and poetry.

It would, however, be a mistake to locate the book exclusively in a context of contemporary technology and contemporary economic organizations. Stories of innovation are not unique to studies of technological change. They are also characteristic of histories of ideologies, political systems, technologies, scientific knowledge, and breakfast cereals. And although the things that are specific to specific technologies and particular times are clearly important, so also are the things that inform our interests in history more generally.

As a result, the book is also a book in pursuit of a theory of history. Historians are notorious for their inclination to quarrel over what a theory of history should comprise, indeed over whether such a thing is imaginable; but there is little disagreement over the proposition that the world changes. History records numerous transformations of cultures, political and economic systems, organizations, and groups. The study of history is concerned with recording, interpreting, and understanding those changes.

The present contributors, for the most part, share with most other modern students of history a perspective on historical change that is broadly evolutionary. That is, the meanderings of history are assumed to have three central attributes: First, they are strongly inertial. Many of the processes of historical development reproduce existing structures, beliefs, and practices. Second, they produce a modest flow of experiments with deviant structures, beliefs, and practices. Third, any successful substitution of a new structure, belief, or practice for an old one is more likely to improve a culture's match with its current environment than it is to degrade that match. Within that broad frame there is plenty of room for disagreement, particularly over such things as the extent to which the process ever approaches an

equilibrium, whether the equilibrium is uniquely implicit in the environment, and whether the environment is similarly developing at the same
time.

The weakest part of historical theories within this variation–selection–retention tradition is the treatment of variation. In classical Darwinian versions, mutations are treated essentially as inexplicable, random curiosities,
some extremely small fraction of which turn out to provide some survival
advantage. Some of the contributors to this volume, along with some of
their colleagues not represented here, are (more or less) Darwinian in the
sense that they see no serious evidence that any process that generates innovations has any capability for prescreening them intelligently. Put another
way, they see the processes that produce those few innovative ideas that
subsequently thrive to be essentially indistinguishable from the processes
that produce those many innovative ideas that subsequently disappear. The
difference between madness and genius is in the unpredictable certification
of history.

For this group of contributors, there is no question of improving the innovative yield of the processes of history. They argue that the powerful
vividness of their experiences with innovative success blinds participants
and observers to the fact that "truly" innovative success is associated with
changes that appear crazy to any well-informed person ex ante, thus with
changes that will be eliminated by any attempt to introduce deliberate management of innovative change. From this perspective, it is possible to vary
the amounts of resources and energy that are devoted to craziness and thus
to vary the rate of innovation; but any attempt to improve the yield is coun-
terproductive.

Most of the contributors to this volume, on the other hand, are (more or
less) Lamarckian in the sense that they see innovations and history as attributable to willful human action and possibly susceptible to some degree of
intentional management. They try to understand what makes an innovation
successful (or alternatively what leads an organization to discover or create
an innovation that will be successful). In more general terms, they reflect
somewhat greater optimism than their colleagues about the possibilities for
shaping and predicting historical change.

The conflict between the Darwinian Tolstoys and the Lamarckian Carlyles of the world is not resolved here. Rather, these two poles are used to
inform a more textured view of change; one that is filled with the concrete
realities of specific situations and with a conception of the possibilities for
meaningful engineering intervention without necessarily being able to predict historical development.

So, the book, as advertised, is about technological innovations; and it can
be read with profit by anyone interested in how such innovations can be understood and shaped. From a rich base of empirical cases and theoretical
frames, the authors produce a portrait of modern technology and its development in a (predominately) democratic political system and a (predomi-

nately) market economy. But the book is simultaneously a book about history, particularly about the ways conscious actions, intentions, luck, and knowledge affect the course of history. Many of the ideas could as easily be used to talk about the development of religious movements, political institutions, or scientific paradigms.

Preface

Ideas beget ideas. This adage captures both the genesis of this book and its central theme. It all began when Avijit Ghosh, then Director of the Center for Entrepreneurial Studies at the Stern School of Business, New York University, called to ask if we would be interested in exploring entrepreneurship using a technology lens. Having already spent time exploring the notion of oversights and foresights, we quickly decided that exploring entrepreneurship through a technology lens would be a fruitful endeavor, especially if it were to be a cross-disciplinary one.

Deciding to put together a collection of thought-provoking ideas on this subject, we contacted many leading thinkers from several disciplines. We were gratified by the overwhelmingly enthusiastic response. Rather than ask each author to contribute independently, we concluded that it would be productive to organize a workshop where ideas could generate ideas.

To emphasize the multidisciplinary nature of the phenomenon, we organized the workshop by major "disciplines" that we had identified (technology, marketing, decision making, organizational processes and strategy). Our strategy was to bring together leading thinkers in each of these disciplines and ask them to present their ideas at the workshop so that contributors could get a more holistic perspective. We wanted each participant to have an opportunity to benefit from this cross-pollination process. Consequently, we decided to hold each presentation sequentially. In addition to the presenters, each session had a chairperson and a discussant. We requested discussants to address papers contained in each session both individually and collectively. We kept the task of integrating the papers across disciplines to ourselves.

Ideas generated ideas at the workshop. Each paper pointed to a facet of the phenomenon that was different yet complementary. Discussants' comments were invaluable in pointing out how papers could be modified to enhance their value, both individually and collectively. Conversations between participants offered an additional means for the exchange of ideas. Some of these ideas were solidified in an after-dinner speech by John Seely Brown who shared the practical aspects of dealing with oversights and foresights.

After the workshop, we decided to divide the editorial work. Each contributor was assigned an editor from amongst the three of us. Besides discussants' comments, we also offered authors feedback on (1) literature and comments that could be used to enhance the value of each manuscript, (2) modifications that would tie the manuscripts together with respect to the overall theme of the book, and (3) a synopsis of the core propositions contained in other manuscripts so that authors could modify their own manuscripts to create a truly interdisciplinary book.

Even as we offered feedback, we began realizing the limitations of a book on innovation organized by disciplines. Such an organizing scheme, we found, created more of an artificial disciplinary barrier to a phenomenon that is truly interdisciplinary. Consequently, we began trying different ways of organizing the book. For instance, we tried to organize the book by "levels" of analyses, but then soon found that many papers, and indeed the phenomenon of interest, cuts across levels. The current scheme, although committing a "procrustean transformation" in its own way, represents to us the elements of a theory of innovation.

As we experimented with the arrangement of the chapters in the book, we simultaneously experimented with its title. At first, we chose the title "Technological Oversights and Foresights." We soon discovered that this title, by itself, suggested that we and our contributors were looking at technological outcomes that, only in hindsight, could be defined as oversights or foresights. After experimenting with a few more titles including one that had entrepreneurship in it, we finally settled on the title "Technological Innovation: Oversights and Foresights."

In the title, as in the rest of the book, we use "innovation" to suggest that it is as much of a process as it is an outcome. Such a dual meaning for innovation is similar in intent to the dual meanings associated with words such as "building," "construction," and "work," designating both a process and its finished product (Dewey, 1934). As Dewey explains, for these words, "Without the meaning of the verb that of the noun remains blank" (Dewey, 1934, p. 51).

In a similar vein, although innovation is often thought of only as an outcome, we use the word to mean process as well. In particular, learning can render technological innovation a process that is systematic, enacted, unconstrained, and manageable. Without learning, however, ideas do not foster ideas, and, innovation remains an outcome of technological choices similar to outcomes associated with the flip of a coin.

In reaching this central theme, we have made many demands on our patient contributors, some of whom have revised their chapters more than once. These are the "visible" colleagues in this book. The discussants and chairpersons who made valuable contributions are the "invisible" ones. The discussants were Linda Argote, Frances Milliken, James Utterback, and Sidney Winter. The chairpersons were John Dutton, Charles Fombrun, Avijit Ghosh, George Smith, and Jon Turner. In inaugurating the workshop, George Daly set the stage for the discussions to follow. Others who contributed at the workshop include Meg Graham, Dorothy Leonard-Barton, Joseph Litterer, Mike Rappa, Bill Starbuck, and Sarah Tabler. We thank them.

Of course, there were many others whose ideas, commitment, and energy made this book possible. Prime among them are Patricia Edwards and Loretta Poole of the Center for Entrepreneurial Studies who took it upon themselves to orchestrate the entire workshop. Besides the services of Pat and Loretta, the Center also generously extended financial support, making the workshop and the book possible. Our immediate colleagues Roger Dunbar and Arun Kumaraswamy have influenced us immensely in the way we have thought about these issues. The editor at Ampersand, Paul Schwartz, deserves a special word of thanks, as do Rebecca Gallin, Harry Wang, and Joy Turnheim of NYU for helping with the editorial work and the cover design. Karen Angelillo, Gia Pangilinan, and Alaine Robertson also gave freely of their time.

There were many at Cambridge University Press who believed in our project and actively and patiently cheered our progress. We thank them, especially Julia Hough.

Reference

Dewey, J. (1934). *Art as Experience*. New York: Minton, Balch, p. 51

New York   Raghu Garud
December, 1996   Praveen Rattan Nayyar
                                                   Zur Shapira

Section I
Introduction

1 Technological innovation: Oversights and foresights

Raghu Garud, Praveen R. Nayyar, and Zur Shapira

Technological changes offer firms some of the most important opportunities for maintaining corporate vitality. Indeed, there are many well known cases of firms capitalizing on technological opportunities. For instance, Sun Microsystems was among the first few firms in the computer industry to initiate the development of RISC chips that are now revolutionizing the computer industry (Alster, 1987). 3M has reaped benefits from its Post-it Notes as has Sony from its Walkman (Nayak & Ketteringham, 1986). There are many other instances of such "technological foresights."

There are also several instances of firms failing to capitalize on technological opportunities. For instance, RCA, a recognized leader in broadcasting, chose not to invest in FM technology (Hughes, 1989). Xerox Corporation was among the first few firms to develop many of the elements of the personal computer that we now use but was unable to reap commercial benefits from its efforts (Smith & Alexander, 1988). There are many other instances of such "technological oversights."

Why do such technological oversights and foresights occur? One view is that oversights and foresights are inevitable[1] because technological outcomes are *uncertain* and *contingent* upon a match between the internal capabilities of a firm and its external environments, and because technological choices are *complex* and *constrained* by the past. These are the challenges that the chapters in this book attempt to address in an effort to develop a theory of technological innovation.

Challenges to the creation of a theory of technological innovation

Uncertainty

The uncertainty challenge is richly illustrated by Barney (chapter 2, this volume) in his use of a coin-flipping analogy to suggest "luck" as an explanation of technological oversights and foresights. This challenge is all the more acute in the case of technological innovation wherein outcomes are less certain than the outcomes from the flip of a fair coin. By some accounts, only two out of 10 innovations succeed (Mansfield, 1981; Cooper & Kleinschmidt, 1990; Van de Ven, 1986; Rosenberg, 1994). Indeed, pushing this perspective a bit further, oversights and foresights cannot be determined ex-ante and are constructs that can only be applied post-hoc.

Contingency

Coins are flipped knowing ex-ante whether heads or tails constitutes a positive outcome. However, judging outcomes of technological innovation as successes or as failures is more difficult. This is because whether or not an endeavor leads to a positive or negative outcome is contextually determined (Langlois, chapter 5, this volume). Oversights and foresights, from this perspective, are contingent upon a match between internal competencies and external environments, the connections between which are often tenuous and emergent (March & Sproull, 1990). Moreover, these environments do not remain static. As these environments change, previous successes may be viewed as failures or vice versa. Thus, success or failure may only be determined post-hoc, although actions have to be taken ex-ante.

Constraints

In addition, choices made in the present are constrained by choices of the past. Successive investments in an approach, whether they be cognitive, behavioral, or economic, result in increasing momentum in a particular direction, thereby creating a "trajectory" (Dosi, 1982; Porac, chapter 8, this volume; Henderson, chapter 9, this volume). Such path dependencies (Arthur, 1988; David, 1985; Powell, 1991) can result in an escalation of commitment to a course of action that may be at odds with a different, larger emerging "reality" (Garud & Rappa, 1994; Levitt & March, 1988). Here again, outcomes of a technological choice made in the present are considered as oversights or as foresights only in hindsight (Utterback, 1994).

Complexity

To complicate matters, technology practitioners who make decisions in the present are subject to a number of biases (Bercovitz, Figueiredo, & Teece, chapter 13, this volume). Even if it did matter, human judgment is limited at best and biased as well. These limits and biases apply all the more so to situations involving complex decisions, as is usually the case with technological choices. These limits and biases result in technological choices that are viewed as foresights or oversights only in hindsight.

Given these challenges, it appears that Barney's coin-flipping analogy may be too generous a metaphor when it comes to describing outcomes of technological innovations. In other words, innovations are not just "chancy," but are constrained by the past as well, even as humans with their limited cognitive resources make complex decisions in a changing contextualized world. If we were to flip an unbiased coin, we might have a 50/50 chance of success. Outcomes from technological innovation appear to be bleaker. Under these conditions, only hindsight is 20/20.

Beating the odds: Towards a theory of technological innovation

To construct a theory of technological innovation, we must suggest how it is possible to enhance the slim odds of technological success, which can be known only in the future, by adopting practices in the present, given (and despite) our pasts. Specifically, we must identify ways to deal with the complexities associated with technological choices to systematically influence outcomes. We must demonstrate how it is possible for us to escape our past in order to create a new future. Moreover, we must establish that practitioners actively try to tailor a fit between their "external" environments and "internal" competencies.

Learning to flip coins

Chapters in the next section address the challenge arising from uncertainty. The section begins with Barney's chapter, which suggests that technological foresights and oversights are simply lucky outcomes of a random process. One way to address this challenge is to aggregate outcomes across units and time, to learn from each "experiment" so that the odds of success may increase across units and time. This is what we (Garud, Nayyar, and Shapira) propose in chapter 3. Dosi and Lovallo (chapter 4) suggest that even if learning does not occur, individual experiments create alternatives to choose from (see also Levinthal, chapter 10, this volume).

Tailoring fits

The third section addresses the contingent nature of outcomes. Beginning with a chapter by Langlois (chapter 5) that articulates the problem, the section continues with a chapter by Brown (chapter 6) that suggests why and how fits can be tailored by firms as they enact their realties. Similar to Weick's (1979) notion of enactment and March's (1991) notions of exploration, Brown suggests that "Our jobs is to be there as markets evolve, to learn to recognize them even before they recognize themselves, because we can't afford to wait for the clarity of hindsight as we construct linkages between emerging markets and emerging technologies. We allow technologies to shape markets and the markets to shape the technologies." Amabile and

Conti's chapter (chapter 7) also explores this issue, but by examining the context for fostering creativity within organizations. They argue that many of the downsizing efforts currently underway in organizations can adversely affect employee motivations to engage in innovative activities. Amabile and Conti then offer several suggestions as to how this negative facet of downsizing may be overcome.

Remembering to forget

Chapters in the fourth section explore how it might be possible to attenuate the links with the past to reduce its constraining effects. The challenge is articulated by Porac (chapter 8) who argues that technological trajectories are "sticky" in the sense that past actions and choices constrain the present and the future. Henderson (chapter 9), too, offers insights on how past beliefs about the potentials of a technology might constrain its limits. Reflecting on similar issues, Levinthal (chapter 10) points out that the codification of past experiences, considered as "wisdom" in stable environments, acts as inertial forces in changing environments. Consequently, Levinthal argues that unlearning may be required for "discovery." Jelinek (chapter 11) too is mindful of the need to create new initiatives in mature industries. She suggests that substantial entrepreneurship is required on the part of members who perform organizationally "unnatural" and "illegitimate" acts. She suggests that such "unnatural" and "illegitimate" acts can be cultivated through the pervasive sharing of managerial tasks and responsibilities, mindful alertness to anomalies, and ambiguity absorption by means of mutual support. Eliashberg, Lilien, and Rao (chapter 12) point out that the use of many market research tools may accentuate the problems of the past when technology practitioners extrapolate from them. These authors offer tools that are appropriate to probe the future rather than the past

(S)top management and culture

The fifth section addresses the role of top management in dealing with complexity. Bercovitz, Figueiredo, and Teece (chapter 13) articulate the challenge of complexity. Specifically, they highlight the biases inherent in making decisions on complex issues. Murmann and Tushman (chapter 14) illustrate how the collective mobilization of innovation intelligence through the presence of a diversity of perspectives in top-management teams is fundamental to dealing with the complexities associated with innovation. Van de Ven and Grazman (chapter 15) have a similar message. They suggest that it is important to put in place dialectical processes to overcome the potential myopia that might develop during technological innovations. However, Fischhoff, Lanir, and Johnson (chapter 16) and Kunda (chapter 17) caution that top-management intervention can create unintended side effects. Specifically, top-management intervention may decrease the possibility of autonomous innovation (Fischhoff, Lanir & Johnson, chapter 16, this volume), or might create a subtle cultural context in which innovating members "burn" themselves out in the quest of a task that by its very nature can never be completed (Kunda, chapter 17, this volume).[2]

In sum, the challenges to a theory of innovation stem from the fact that technological outcomes are uncertain and contingent upon a match between firms' internal capabilities and external environments, even as technological activities are complex and constrained. These are powerful ideas. The underpinnings to a theory of technological innovation lie in an equally enticing set of ideas. Specifically, technological outcomes can be systematically enacted to overcome constraints of the past by managing complexity in the present.

Learning makes the difference

By themselves, the terms technological oversights and foresights focus attention on innovation as outcomes. Such a focus creates a roadblock to the construction of a theory of technological innovation. Focusing on outcomes alone can result in "functional" thinking, wherein we begin rationalizing how and why oversights and foresights may have occurred only in hindsight.

To gain potency, oversights and foresights as outcomes have to be part of a larger process. Indeed, learning is a key process that distinguishes technological innovation as a game of chance from one that is a game that involves skill as well. Without learning (or unlearning as the case might be) technological choices are indeed just "coin flips." With the introduction of learning, however, technological innovation becomes an activity that possess the potential to be systematic, enacted, unconstrained, and manageable.

Indeed, each chapter in this book has several implications for the notion of learning as applied to technological choices over a period of time, though their meanings and applications differ. For instance, the notion of learning, associated with the organizing theme in the second section, results from repeated choices that are made possible by aggregating across time and entities. In contrast, the notion of learning implicit in the theme of the third section has to do with the recognition and creation of a match between an external environment (that is not fully in a firm's control) and internal capabilities (that create a certain cognitive mind-set). Most interestingly, the notion of learning is inextricably intertwined with notions of unlearning for chapters in the fourth section. Learning results in the creation of a stock of knowledge that might need to be abandoned to create a "launching ground" for new learning in an attempt to accumulate contemporary useful knowledge. Learning, from the perspective of the fifth section, has to do with a combination of the above approaches as practitioners attempt to manage technological innovations in a complex and messy world.

Each chapter is a richer mosaic of ideas about learning and unlearning than we have attributed to them. The important point to note is that if we have to create a useful theory of technological innovation, the notion of learning, in its various forms, is fundamental. We (Garud, Nayyar, and Shapira) return to these issues once again in the conclusion of the book (chapter 18) in which we provide our readers a way to integrate the various themes in this book. In doing so, we take the first steps towards creating a theory of technological innovation that entertains the proposition that it is possible to "beat the odds."

Acknowledgments

We acknowledge financial and organizational support from the Center for Entrepreneurial Studies, Stem School of Business, New York University. We thank Sanjay Jain and Arun Kumaraswamy for their comments on an earlier version of this chapter.

Notes

1 See Utterback (1994), he uses the metaphor of innovation as a game of "chutes and ladders" to suggest that oversights and foresights are inevitable.
2 These chapters are richer than the conceptual "boxes" that we have put them into. Indeed, it is important to note that these boxes emerged inductively as we experimented with various combinations and approaches to the organization of the book. When we first conceptualized this book, we had the various contributors organized by disciplines (technology, marketing, decision making, organizational processes, and strategy). We found that such an organizing scheme created artificial disciplinary barriers to a phenomenon that is truly interdisciplinary. We then tried to organize the book by "levels" of analyses. We soon discovered that many chapters cut across levels. The current scheme, although committing a "procrustean transformation" of its own, nevertheless represents elements of a theory of technological innovation.

References

Alster, N. (1987). How Intel and Motorola missed the Sun rise. *Electronic Business*, 13(21), 32–34.
Arthur, B. (1988). Self-reinforcing mechanisms in economics. in P. Anderson et al., *The Economy as an Evolving Complex System*. Reading, MA: Addison-Wesley.
Cooper, R. G. and Kleinschmidt, E. J. (1990). New product success factors: A comparison of "kills" versus successes and failures. *R&D Management*, 20, 1, 47–63.
David, P. (1985). Clio and the economics of QWERTY, *Economic History*, 75: 227–332.
Dosi, G (1982). Technological paradigms and technological trajectories. *Research Policy*, 11: 147–162.
Garud, R. and Rappa, M. (1994). A socio-cognitive model of technology evolution. *Organization Science* 5, 3: 344–362.
Hughes, T. P. (1989). *American Genesis: A Century of Invention and Technological Enthusiasm, 1870–1970*. New York: Viking.

Levitt, B. and March, J. G. (1988). Organizational learning. *Annual Review of Sociology,* 14, 319–340.

Mansfield, E. (1981). How economists see R&D. *Harvard Business Review,* November–December, 98–106.

March, J. G. and Sproull, L. S. (1990). Technology, management, and competitive advantage. In P. S. Goodman, L. S. Sproull, and Associates (eds.), *Technology and Organizations.* San Francisco: Jossey-Bass, 144–173.

March, J. G. (1991). Exploration and exploitation in organizational learning. *Organization Science,* 2(1), 71–87.

Nayak, P. and Ketteringham, J. (1986). *Breakthroughs.* New York: Rawson Associates.

Powell, W. W. (1991). Expanding the scope of institutional analysis. In W. W.Powell and P. J. DiMaggio (eds.), *The New Institutionalism in Organizational Analysis.* Chicago: University of Chicago Press, 183–203.

Rosenberg, N. (1994). *Exploring the Black Box: Technology, Economics, and History.* New York: Cambridge University Press.

Smith, D. and Alexander, R. (1988). *Fumbling the Future: How Xerox Invented, Then Ignored, the First Personal Computer.* New York:William Morrow.

Utterback, J. M. (1994). *Mastering the Dynamics of Innovation.* Boston: Harvard Business School Press.

Van de Ven, A. H. (1986). Central problems in the management of innovation. *Management Science,* 32(5), 590–607.

Weick, K. (1979). *The Social Psychology of Organizing.* Reading, MA: Addison-Wesley.

Wilson, T. L. and Hiavacek, J. D. (1984). Don't let good ideas sit on the shelf. *Research Management,* 27 (3), 27–34.

Section II
Learning to flip coins

2 On flipping coins and making technology choices: Luck as an explanation of technological foresight and oversight

Jay B. Barney

The ad was unusually bold for the *Wall Street Journal*. The headline read, "A Chance to Earn Big Bucks." The fine print went on to describe a contest to be held the next week at a large auditorium in New York City. The contest was going to be simple one, with simple rules. Upon arrival, each contestant would be given a quarter. In the first round of the contest, all contestants would flip their coins. Contestants who flipped a "head" would continue in the contest; those who flipped a "tail" would be eliminated. The contest would continue through a series of coin flipping rounds, until there was only one person left. This person would then collect all the quarters from all the contestants. To ensure that there would be a single winner, if all those in the contest flipped "tails" in a particular round, they would all be allowed to continue in the contest. The ad described only one requirement for those seeking to enter this contest: they must be either highly educated, or have a great deal of experience, in the management of technology.

Of course, this ad created a great stir among the business and technological elite in the nation. The Internet was full of people discussing the contest, arguing about whether or not they should attend, and debating the relative merits of alternative coin-flipping methodologies. As the day of the contest approached, it became clear that the number of people who wanted to be in the contest was larger than what could be safely accommodated in an auditorium, and the contest organizers moved the contest from the auditorium to the Meadowlands stadium, in New Jersey.

The day of the contest dawned bright and clear, and contestants began to arrive in New Jersey. As the appointed time drew closer, the stands at the Meadowlands began to fill. Then, the chairs that had been placed on the playing field began to fill, as over 80,000 technology-management experts anticipated the first round. While they waited, many individuals worked on their own coin-flipping skills—honing those skills to a fine edge.

Finally, the time for the contest arrived. All the contestants arose, and, as the signal was given, flipped their coins. About half were "heads," about half were "tails." The groans of those who had flipped "tails" were drowned out by the cheers of those who flipped "heads." The crowd hushed as the signal for the second round was given. About half were "heads," and half were "tails." Twenty-thousand round two winners shouted in delight, while 20,000 second-round losers sat quietly and contemplated their losses. Then the third round began. About half were "heads" and half were "tails." Ten thousand contestants had defied the odds and had flipped heads three times in a row!

The next several rounds went quickly, and whittled the number of contestants down from 10,000, to 5,000, to 2,500, to 1,250, to 625, to 312, to 156. One hundred and fifty six people had flipped heads nine times in a row! The contest organizers decided to take a short break. During this time, contestants who had gone out of the contest in earlier rounds sought out the special 156 who were still in the game. These early losers, in anticipation of another contest to be held sometime in the future, wanted to learn the coin-flipping secrets from these special 156. Of course, these 156 were willing to share their secrets—for a modest fee. Indeed, several of these 156, in anticipation of this opportunity, had already set up times for "coin-flipping seminars." Despite fees up to $5,000 per seminar, demand was solid and sales brisk.

After the break, the contest continued. The special 156 flipped their coins. About half were "heads," about half were "tails." Rounds 11 through 17 continued until there were only two contestants left. One was a college drop-out software engineer from the northwestern part of the United States; the other was a hardware engineer who ran a well-known computer company headquartered just north of New York City. All 80,000 contestants watched with a mixture of excitement, awe, and jealously as these two contestants began to flip their coins. In the end, the software engineer from the northwest flipped a head and the hardware engineer from New York flipped a tail. The crowd surged forward, lifted the winner on their shoulders, and carried him to the organizer's platform. On the platform, in front of the cheering and adoring crowd, this engineer received over 80,000 quarters—over $20,000. Together with the money he had made on his coin-flipping seminars, he was able to continue to invest in his software company. His company was ultimately very successful. Later, he was both hailed as one of the great minds of this century and vilified as an evil monopolist. But it all began because he won the coin-flipping contest held in the Meadowlands.

This story is, of course, fiction. However, its message is clear. The observed differences in performance between the software engineer from the Northwest and everyone else who was involved in this contest cannot be taken as definitive proof that this engineer was somehow "better," "more efficient," or "more able" than these others. In this contest, he was simply lucky.

In the same way, observed differences among firms in their ability to anticipate and exploit technological changes cannot be taken as definitive proof that some firms are somehow "better," "more efficient," or "more able" in anticipating and exploiting these changes than others. Rather, it may simply be the case that some firms are lucky in their technology choices and others are unlucky.

All this does not imply that real differences in the ability to anticipate and exploit technological changes do not exist. Indeed, many of the chapters in this volume describe in some detail what some of these real differences might be. However, while much of this work is suggestive and intriguing, most of it fails to reject what might be called the ultimate alternative hypothesis: that observed differences among firms along these dimensions reflect chance events and luck. Rejecting this ultimate alternative hypothesis is a difficult challenge, but one that those who study technological foresight and oversight must accept.

Luck in explanations of firm performance

Of course, this is not the first time that "luck" has been suggested as an explanation of performance differences across firms. While little of this work has focused directly on the role of luck in understanding technological foresight and oversight, the logic of this previous work is, in many ways, directly applicable to this technology-management question. For example, in 1950 Armen Alchian suggested that, under conditions of uncertainty, differences between successful and unsuccessful firms can often be attributed to luck. Alchian (1950, p. 214) argues:

Assume that thousands of travelers set out from Chicago, selecting their roads completely at random and without foresight. Only [an] "economist" knows that on but one road are there any gasoline stations. He can state categorically that travelers will *continue* to travel only on that road; those on other roads will soon run out of gas. Even though each one selected his route at random, we might have called those travelers who were so fortunate as to have picked the right road wise, efficient, foresighted, etc. Of course, we would consider them the lucky ones. If gasoline supplies were now moved to a new road, some formerly luckless travelers would again would be able to move.

Also, in an article titled "Causes of Interfirm Profitability Differences." Mancke (1974) argued that luck may be a more parsimonious explanation of differences in firm performance than any of the then popular industrial-organization explanations. While Mancke acknowledged that differences in firm performance may be due to monopoly power, economies of scale, or other reasons, he showed, through a series of simulations, that these differences can also be explained using a random-chance model. Mancke's challenge for those interested in understanding why some individuals or firms are able to anticipate and exploit technology changes while others are not is direct:

Empirical evidence that firm profit rates are positively correlated with size, market share, and past growth can neither confirm nor deny the popular hypotheses that these firm attributes are positively correlated with either monopoly power or scale economies. (Mancke, 1974, pp. 190–191)

Alchian and Mancke are not alone in arguing that luck can be an important determinant of differences in firm performance. In the field of strategic management, similar arguments have been developed by Rumelt and Wensley (1981), Lippman and Rumelt (1982), Barney (1986), and Reed and DiFillippi (1990). Also, most evolutionary models, in both economics (Nelson & Winter, 1982) and organization theory (Hannan & Freeman, 1977), recognize the importance of luck in determining firm performance.

Objections to luck explanations

Of course, these luck explanations of firm performance have not gone unchallenged. For example, Caves, Gale, and Porter (1977), in a reply to Mancke, suggest that while luck may be a *partial* explanation of differences in firm performance, it is possible to discover that amount of firm performance that is attributable to luck, and that amount that is attributable to nonluck factors. Indeed, these authors propose and execute an empirical approach for examining this question, an approach that Mancke (1977) finds singularly unconvincing.

Others have also attempted to empirically estimate the role of luck and nonluck factors in determining firm performance. In their study of the relationship between market share and firm performance, Rumelt and Wensley (1981) go to great lengths to examine this issue. Unfortunately, at least for Caves, Gale, and Porter (1977), Rumelt and Wensley conclude that once random shocks are included in the analysis, the relationship between market share and profits is no longer statistically significant. In other words, Rumelt and Wensley suggest that virtually all the observed positive correlation between market share and firm performance can be explained as a manifestation of random events and chance.

Perhaps the most consistent objection to luck explanations of differences in firm performance concerns the prescriptive implications of such explanations (Caves, Gale, & Porter, 1977). At a societal level, luck explanations suggest that government regulations that reduce concentration in an industry can be misguided. Since differences in the market shares of firms in an industry is primarily a matter of some firms being lucky and other firms being unlucky, it seems to make little sense to "punish" larger firms. This would be like punishing the winner of our coin-flipping contest solely because he won the contest. While a lucky firm might subsequently engage in anticompetitive behavior, the simple existence of large market share cannot be taken as a clear indicator of anticompetitive behavior (Demsetz, 1973).

At the level of the individual firm, the prescriptive limitations of luck explanations of differences in firm performance are even more problematic.

For example, if observed differences between the ability of firms to anticipate and exploit technological changes reflect the fact that some firms may
have been lucky in their technology choices and others may have been unlucky, what prescriptive advice can be given to managers—that they should
"be lucky"?

Rejecting the luck hypothesis

As suggested earlier, simply because luck can be an explanation of the different abilities firms have to anticipate and exploit technological change, it
does not follow that luck is the only explanation of such differences. The
challenge facing researchers is to develop rigorous methods for rejecting the
luck alternative in favor of some other explanation of these differences.

As is shown by Caves, Gale, and Porter (1977) and Rumelt and Densely
(1981), this can be a difficult task. Simply observing real differences between
technologically foresighted and other firms is not proof that these differences led to technological foresight. Moreover, even standard statistical
techniques cannot be used, by themselves, to reject this alternative hypothesis. For example, when one runs a multiple regression and obtains estimates
of regression coefficients, the traditional null hypothesis is that this coefficient is equal to zero. However, by rejecting this null hypothesis, one does
not reject the possibility that the underlying process that led to a statistically
significant coefficient was essentially stochastic in nature. As Mancke (1974)
and others have shown, purely random processes can generate statistically
significant results.

One way to resolve this problem would be to rely on prediction: rather
than focusing only on observed differences at a given point in time, examine how those differences affect the ability of firms to anticipate and exploit
technological changes in the future. One could imagine a model that is able
to divide a sample of firms in an industry into two types: high-foresight
firms and low-foresight firms. By observing whether or not high-foresight
firms are able to anticipate and exploit future technological change better
than low-foresight firms, the underlying model that was used to classify
firms could be put at risk.

Of course, this kind of research is difficult to do. A sufficiently precise
model for assigning firms to "high-foresight" and "low-foresight" categories would have to be developed. Certainly, much of the work in this volume could be instrumental in the development of such a model. Moreover,
the researcher would also have to observe the behavior of all these firms
over a long period of time, to see how different firms react to different technological changes in the environment.

Despite its power to test nonluck explanations of technological foresight
and oversight, this quasiexperimental design does have at least one important limitation: firms that were lucky in making their technology choices
early in this quasiexperiment may gain first-mover advantages that will

give them advantages in subsequent technological choices (Lieberman & Montgomery, 1988). This will confound the researcher's ability to distinguish between luck and nonluck explanations of subsequent technological choices.

Consider, for example, the winner of our coin-flipping contest. Because this individual was lucky and won this contest, he earned at least $20,000 and was able to continue to invest in his firm. Ultimately, this firm was enormously successful. However, would it have been as successful if this individual had not been lucky in the first place? Put differently, how much of this firm's ultimate success can be attributed to the fact that its founder was lucky in the coin-flipping contest and how much to nonluck factors? Even if a model could be developed to rigorously assign individuals and firms to "high-foresight" and "low-foresight" categories, first-mover advantages attributable to lucky technology choices may enable some firms to appear to have high foresight, when, in fact, they are simply enjoying some continuing benefits of their lucky choices.

The attributes of high-foresight firms

Despite the significant challenges associated with testing luck and nonluck explanations of technological foresight and oversight, it is possible – at least at a general level – to describe the kinds of firm attributes that could distinguish between "high-foresight" and "low-foresight" firms. In particular, we know that whatever the differences between these types of firms, it must be difficult for firms without "high-foresight" attributes to obtain them (Barney, 1991). We know this is the case because if it was easy for "low-foresight" firms to understand and imitate the attributes that enabled "high-foresight" firms to have "high-foresight," then there would be no "low-foresight" firms left.

Recent developments in the Resource-Based View of the Firm in strategic management suggest the kinds of firm attributes that are not easy to understand and not easy to imitate (Barney, 1986; 1991). In general, when the ability to exercise technological foresight builds on resources and capabilities that have developed over long periods of time, that were acquired or developed during unique periods of history, around which significant causal ambiguity exists, or that are based on socially complex relationships among individuals and groups of individuals in a firm, then firms without these attributes will face significant cost disadvantages in developing them. Many of the explanations of differences in technological foresight in this volume build on these kinds of organizational resources and capabilities. In this sense, this work represents an important step in the development of a more rigorous approach to understanding why some firms are able to anticipate and exploit technological changes, while others are not.

References

Alchian, A. (1950). Uncertainty, evolution, and economic theory. *Journal of Political Economy*, 58, 211–221.

Barney, J. B. (1986). Strategic factor markets: Expectations, luck, and business strategy. *Management Science*, 32, 1231–1241.

Barney, J. B. (1991). Firm resources and sustained competitive advantage. *Journal of Management*, 17, 99–120.

Caves, R. E., Gale, B. T., and Porter, M. E. (1977). Interfirm profitability and differences: Comment. *Quarterly Journal of Economics*, 91, 667–676.

Demsetz, H. (1973). Industry structure, market rivalry, and public policy. *Journal of Law and Economics*, 16, 1–9.

Hannan. M. T. and Freeman, J. (1977). The population ecology of organizations. *American Journal of Sociology*, 82, 929–964.

Lieberman, M. and Montgomery, D. B. (1988). First mover advantages. *Strategic Management Journal*, 9, Special Issue, 41–58.

Lippman, S. and Rumelt, R. (1982). Uncertain imitability: An analysis of interfirm differences in efficiency under competition. *Bell Journal of Economics*, 13, 418–438.

Mancke, R. B. (1974). Causes of interfirm profitability differences: A new interpretation of the evidence. *Quarterly Journal of Economics*, 88, 181–193.

Mancke, R. B. (1977). Interfirm profitability differences: Reply. *Quarterly Journal of Economics*, 95, 677–680.

Nelson, R. and Winter, S. (1982). *An Evolutionary Theory of Economic Behavior*. Cambridge, MA: Harvard University Press.

Reed, R. and DiFillippi, R. (1990). Causal ambiguity, barriers to imitation, and sustainable competitive advantage. *Academy of Management Review*, 15, 88–102.

Rumelt, R. and Wensley, R. (1981). In search of the market share effect. *Proceedings of the Academy of Management Meetings, 1981*, 2–6.

3 Technological choices and the inevitability of errors

Raghu Garud, Praveen R. Nayyar, and Zur Shapira

It seemed like a marvelous idea at the time: Grocery shoppers would use an ID card that, combined with the electronic scanners at the checkout line, would tell marketers exactly who bought what. . . . But six years later, the effort looks as if it could turn out to be one of Citicorp's biggest follies. The POS (for point-of-sale) Information Services unit has spent about $200 million, generated just $20 million in revenue at best and made a mess of relationships with many grocery chains and consumer goods producers.

Other direct marketers . . . saved millions of dollars in being able to see where Citicorp went wrong. (Bleakley, 1991)

My biggest mistake was failing to get Data General into the PC business. (Mr. de Castro, Chairman and cofounder of Data General Corp., quoted in Wilke, 1990)

Technology is a double-edged sword. While it can create wealth, it can also consume and destroy it. This duality strikes at the very heart of strategic management because technological changes offer firms some of the most important opportunities for revitalization. Entire industries can emerge from new technologies, as illustrated by the overnight delivery and video games businesses. At the same time, however, technological changes can threaten firms' very existence. New technologies can make products offered by incumbent firms obsolete, as illustrated by the audio cassette recorder's superiority over phonograph records.[1]

Despite the importance of technological change for corporate vitality, there are several instances of decision makers failing to recognize and capitalize on technological opportunities and of decision makers failing to recognize technological threats. For instance, RCA, a recognized leader in broadcasting, chose not to invest in FM technology, which was successful later (Hughes, 1989). Xerox developed the first personal computer in 1976 but decided not to commercialize it (Smith & Alexander, 1988). Sony chose not to adopt the ultimately successful VHS format for video tape recorders (Nayak & Ketteringham, 1986).[2] In contrast, there are also several examples of firms exploiting technological opportunities. For instance, Sun Microsystems was among the first few firms in the computer industry to initiate the development of RISC chips that are now revolutionizing the computer industry (Alster, 1987; Wilke, 1992). The 3M Corporation has reaped benefits from Post-It notes as has Sony from its Walkman, despite gloomy forecasts (Nayak & Ketteringham, 1986).

These specific instances are symptomatic of a more general phenomena that we label as technological "oversights" and "foresights." A technological oversight occurs when a firm adopts a technology that is eventually unsuccessful (for example, the unsuccessful VideoDisc developed by RCA) or when a firm does not adopt a technology that is eventually successful (such as the CT scanner that was invented yet spurned by EMI). In contrast, a technological foresight occurs when a firm adopts a technology that is eventually successful (Xerox's decision to commercialize xerography) or when it does not adopt a technology that is eventually unsuccessful (several banks chose not to invest in the apparently unsuccessful point-of-sale information systems adopted by Citicorp).[3]

We treat oversights and foresights as consequences of choices by firms to invest, or withhold investment, in a particular technology. Investment decision making is a complicated, protracted process of gathering and processing data to make, accept or reject decisions under conditions of uncertainty (Ali, Kalwani & Kovenock, 1993; Amit & Schoemaker, 1993; Galai & Shapira, 1985). Under such conditions, *there is only a partial correlation between actions and outcomes*. The likelihood of success of an investment in a project can be only partially predicted. Hence, one of two errors is likely to occur. First, some projects selected will turn out to be failures. Second, in retrospect it can be determined that some rejected projects would have actually been successful.[4]

How should strategic management theories deal with these two errors? Uncertainty about future outcomes cannot be eliminated, only reduced. Therefore, these two errors can never be completely eliminated when decisions are undertaken under conditions of uncertainty. In fact, whether an error has been made is only revealed ex-post. However, it is possible to improve predictive validity (within certain limits) to aid investment decisions ex-ante. In addition, as discussed later, reducing one type of error without improving the predictive validity of project-selection mechanisms will increase the other type of error. Existing strategic-management paradigms (for example, resource-based and industry-structure views) do not address this dilemma as they ignore cognitive elements implicit in every resource-allocation process. Yet, these elements are particularly relevant in contemporary environments characterized by rapid technological change, wherein complex technologies place tremendous cognitive demands on decision makers.

We develop our argument by first offering a brief description of the extant literature on technological choices. To extend this literature, we next introduce a selection model that has previously been applied in different contexts to explore the relationships between false positives and false negatives. Next, we discuss limits to improvements in the predictability of technological outcomes and therefore the inevitability of errors. As an example of how firms may deal with the inevitability of errors, we discuss how incentives should be designed to accomplish two outcomes. First, incentives can be designed to encourage innovation-team members to learn from their mistakes and improve predictability. Second, incentives can be designed to ensure that the appropriate type of error (Type I or Type II) is minimized.

Technological choice

Technology-choice issues are becoming increasingly important in contemporary environments characterized by rapid technological change. In such environments, the notion of sustainable advantage is inextricably linked with a firm's ability to introduce new products. No longer can decision makers sit on their laurels by creating defensible niches through first-movement. Instead, they must continually choose between technologies. This task is made all the more difficult because of the complexity associated with modern technologies (Weick, 1990) and the rapidity with which decisions have to be made (Eisenhardt, 1989).

We suggest that the technology-choice literature can broadly be classified into three interrelated streams—the *technological*, the *economic* and the *institutional*. The technological perspective focuses on technical determinants—how well a technology performs in comparison to others (for example, Farrell, 1993), its future potentials (for example, Foster, 1986), and the interrelationships between form and function (for example, Petroski, 1992). Consistent with this perspective is the "technology-push" hypothesis (for example, Comroe & Dripps, 1976), which suggests that advances in science and technology will lead to superior technologies that will most likely be adopted.

The marketing and economics perspective focuses not so much on scientific determinants but on economic ones. This perspective suggests that there are a number of strong economic issues that encourage the acceptance of certain technologies over others. These economic issues include: (1) the extent to which resources are available for any technology (for example, Kay, 1979), (2) potential returns from an investment (Bower, 1970; Brealey & Myers, 1984), and (3) the reluctance to adopt new technologies that cannibalize earlier investments (for example, Connor, 1988). Consistent with this perspective is the "market-pull" hypothesis that suggests that customer needs will shape technological choices.

Appreciating the polar extremes for the genesis of these two perspectives, many have adopted a techno-economic perspective to guide technological choices (for example, White & Graham, 1978; Freeman, 1986; Cooper, 1986). Others, who have adopted an institutional perspective, offer other social, cognitive, and political forces that shape the evolution and adoption of technologies that develop in a path-dependent, cumulative manner (David, 1985; Arthur, 1988; Powell, 1991). This perspective recognizes that institutionalized rules and practices create a context that shapes the cognition of technology champions (Garud & Rappa, 1994). Those operating within such a professionalized field choose within a set of institutional beliefs, not simply because they are the best, but because conformance confers legitimacy (Scott, 1987). Consequently, the "best technology" may not necessarily be chosen.

These viewpoints are not mutually exclusive. Technological, economic and institutional forces are all-important in determining technology assessment and adoption. We choose technologies that work, but within a "choice set" prescribed by institutionalized fields (Scott, 1991). Economic forces play a role, but have power to dislodge entrenched trajectories only occasionally (Rosenberg, 1982). Together, these forces create what have been labeled as technological trajectories (Dosi, 1982). Trajectories represent paths along which a technology develops based on previous choices and on future expectations (Dosi, 1982; Nelson & Winter, 1982). These paths build up in a cumulative manner as initial choices dictate future opportunities; some or all of the investments are irreversible and may not be easily deployed to pursue other approaches. Moreover, these paths require distinct institutionalized practices that emerge through a socio-political process.

Thus, there are significant technological, economic, and institutional forces that compels innovation members to persist with a technological trajectory. This "stickiness" associated with these trajectories places a premium on how, what, and when we choose. An inappropriate choice of technological trajectory will result in the expenditure of considerable resources leading to an "oversight by commission." One may argue that such an oversight by commission could be eliminated by deciding not to choose any technology at all—in itself a choice decision. But then, in this age of rapid technological change, such a course would increase "oversight by omission." Somewhere between these two extremes we must be able to create choice rules that allows us to trade off between these two types of errors. To understand these issues, we first discuss a choice model.

False negatives and false positives in technology choices

The importance of analyzing the effects of judgmental processes and cognitive biases on strategic management has been examined by several authors (Amit & Schoemaker, 1993; Hoskisson, Hitt, & Hill, 1991; Schwenk, 1984; Zajac & Bazerman, 1991). While part of the effects stem from the underlying structure and features of the human judgmental system (Tversky & Kahneman, 1974), other potential determinants of "biased" decisions are the incentives and penalties associated with the outcomes of strategic decisions. Executive's decisions in situations of uncertainty appear to be affected more by attempts to avoid failure rather than by attempts to pursue risky alternatives whose potential success can be described as only probabilistic (Shapira, 1993). When faced with the need to make decisions on risky projects, managers are worried about making one of two errors. They may accept a project that should have been rejected, or reject a project that should have been accepted.

Decision makers involved with technology choices are aware of the two potential errors and their implications for risk-taking. On the one hand there is a tendency for decision makers to behave in a risk-averse manner. Pursuing this avenue is manifested by attempts to continue building on alternatives that proved successful in the past without exploring new avenues through innovation. However, firms operating in dynamic environments soon discover that avoiding the challenge of dealing with innovations may prove dangerous. As March (1991) noted, firms often get caught in a conflict between the need to *explore* new opportunities and the tendency to *exploit* existing resources.

Consistent with March's focus, the framework of aspirations and resources may be used to analyze intrafirm decisions as well. Following the analysis of risk perceptions and attitudes in a large sample of managers, March and Shapira (1987, 1992) developed a model that relates risk tendencies to resources and attention to a target such as an aspiration level. If decision makers perceive their resources to be below their aspiration level, their consequent behavior is likely to be risk seeking. If, on the other hand, they perceive their resources to be above their aspiration level, their behavior is likely to be risk averse.[5]

Suppose these decision makers consider investing in a particular project. They face an accept-or-reject decision that may lead them either to success or failure. This decision situation is best exemplified by the selection model depicted in Figure 3.1. In this project-selection decision, a critical value x_c for a predictor variable is determined such that if the ex-ante evaluation of a project yields a value x where $x \geq x_c$, the project is accepted. A project is rejected if $x < x_c$. After the project is complete, its performance is measured against a critical value, y_c. If the ex-post realized value is equal to or greater than y_c, the project is considered a success. Otherwise, the project is classified a failure. The degree to which the ex-post realization of a project is predicted by a selection criterion is referred to as the predictive validity of the model and is described by the correlation coefficient R_{xy}. The ellipse in Figure 3.1 is an illustration of the boundary surrounding actual data points (x_i, y_j) where x_i is the measure of the project on the predictor variable while y_j is its subsequent performance level.

Figure 3.1 describes the four potential categories that may result from a selection decision. Two categories designate success ("positive hits" and "negative hits") and the other two designate failure. The latter two regions,

y (performance)

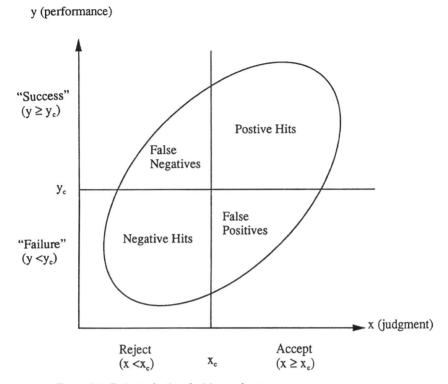

Figure 3.1. Project selection decision and outcomes.

labeled as "false positives" and "false negatives," are the most problematic for decision makers. The former designates the failure of a project that had been accepted while the latter describes the success (eventually elsewhere) of a project that had been rejected. "False positives" and "false negatives" are called Type I and Type II errors, respectively, in the statistical-inference literature.[6]

As Figure 3.1 suggests, the only way to minimize both types of errors is by increasing the predictive validity of the model. In the limit, when $R_{xy} = 1$, the ellipse turns into a straight line and both errors are eliminated. At the other end, when $R_{xy} = 0$, the ellipse becomes a perfect circle and predictability vanishes. In most personnel-selection studies, it has been found that R_{xy} does not exceed 0.5 (Cascio, 1991), as illustrated by the elliptical boundary surrounding the data points in Figure 3.1. This limit to the improvement of predictability is illustrated by the fact that even 3M Corporation, which is an exemplar of continual innovation, is unable to perfectly predict the outcomes of its technological choices.

Managers who are driven primarily by concerns about failure may put a greater emphasis on minimizing Type I errors (i.e., false positives), since they are visible. In contrast, Type II errors (i.e., false negatives) are often not visible, since rejected projects may not be pursued by anyone. Consequently, decision makers may choose to commit Type II errors even though these errors may be more detrimental to firms than Type I errors due to opportunity costs. Decision makers' risk tendencies are, in fact, determined by the utilities of the two errors. Important to firms are the costs associated with the two errors. At times, the costs of committing Type I errors may be more salient, since shareholders may be troubled with investments in "white elephants." However, consistent with March's (1991) notion of exploration, reducing Type II error (while increasing Type I error) may be the right avenue in many situations characterized by rapid change and innovation.

Minimizing Type I error can be achieved by putting a higher hurdle on the decision criteria. This is exemplified by the line labeled x_{ci} (where $x_{ci} > x_c$) in Figure 3.2. By shifting x_c to the right of its position in Figure 3.1, the area designated "false positives" is smaller but the area representing "false negatives" is larger in comparison to the same areas in Figure 3.1. Similarly, Type H errors would be reduced if x_c is moved to the left of its position in Figure 3.1. However, note that the area depicting the sum of Type I and Type II errors does not decrease by mere changes in the value of x_c. Shifting

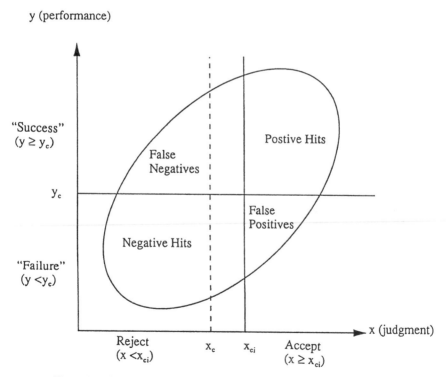

Figure 3.2. Project selection and variations in decision criteria.

x_c changes only the relative frequencies of the two errors, namely, following a shift in x_c, one error goes down but the other goes up.

It is not possible, therefore, to reduce both errors by merely changing the decision criteria, x_c. It should also be noted that simply restricting the range on the predictor variable (x) by considering a narrow range of projects will also not reduce errors. The probability of committing either a Type I or a Type II error is a function of the area that falls into the false-positive or false-negative regions, respectively, *relative* to the total area of the ellipse. Thus, reducing the total area of the ellipse does not necessarily decrease the relative area of the two errors. On the contrary, since predictive validity is measured by the correlation coefficient R_{xy}, restricting the range of x (for example, by constraining the set of projects being considered) will result in a lower R_{xy}. This is due to the fact that correlation is actually a standardized co-variation measure. If the variance of one of the variables is reduced, covariation is reduced as well. This phenomenon is labeled "restriction of range" and may actually lead to more (rather than less) error.

This discussion should not be confused with the desire to reduce variance for better measurement. In the selection model, an observed score is a combination of a true score and an error term. Reducing the variance of the error term is highly desirable. However, merely restricting the range of the observed score will not reduce error variance. In the extreme case, if all projects get exactly the same score (that is, variance is zero), the correlation between project scores and any other measure is zero. In sum, the only way to reduce both errors is by increasing the predictive validity of the model (R_{xy}). This can be achieved by collecting data and refining the measures used, not by arbitrary moves of the decision criterion x_c.

Applying the model

Several considerations are important in applying the model in technology-choice decisions. Appropriate measures are required to discriminate between projects that should be accepted from those that should be rejected. Similarly, appropriate measures are required to discriminate between success and failure.[7] While it may be easier to employ a common measure across time, the realities of the technology-development process compel decision makers to choose measures that are different across time. This is because selection measures are used to help in resource allocation among competing technologies. Later, other measures are often used to gauge the success of a project in comparison to competition. For example, net present value (NPV) and internal rate of return (IRR) are well accepted selection measures for evaluating projects (Brealey & Myers, 1984). In contrast, return on investment (ROI), profitability, and market share are widely used measures of success.

In addition to choosing measures, decision makers need to choose an appropriate criterion for each measure to discriminate between the accept and reject regions and between success and failure. Since decision makers seek to increase their ability to choose technologies that are likely to be successful, they also need to establish the relationship between selection criteria and indicators of success.

In the context of evaluating technological projects in organizations, decision makers frequently lack ex-ante criteria that are valid predictors of future success. Confronting this challenge, decision makers frequently employ the *same* criterion that they would use to measure the success of the project ex-post, and make an estimation of the projects' performance in the future to make accept-or-reject decisions. This practice is inappropriate for two reasons: judgmental and political. First, it is problematic vis-à-vis the nature of the selection model. In this model, we proposed identifying predictors that can be used to predict future success. By using estimates of future ROI, we rely on the judgment of the persons making the estimate. Their estimate is based on some other underlying variables (such as expertise and reputation of the project team). In a sense, they are integrating information on these variables to produce the estimate. However, it has been shown (Dawes & Corrigan, 1974) that humans do a poor job of information integration (and hence of forecasting). Therefore, using the actual underlying variables may be a more reliable way of establishing a selection measure. If, however, a single selection criterion is needed, the ranking of projects by a few evaluators could be more reliable than ROI estimates.

Second, using the same criterion ex-ante and ex-post may lead to political games between top management and project sponsors. Decision makers and project proposers may represent the value of a project differently (Bower, 1970; Williamson, 1975). For instance, project proposers may be overly optimistic and aggressive in promoting the benefits of their project while being blind to or silent about the potential costs involved. In anticipation of this possibility, those who evaluate projects for funding may discount claims made by project proposers. The traditional way to accomplish this is by placing higher hurdles on the selection criteria (Brealey and Myers, 1984).

However, there are situations in which it is beneficial to have relaxed selection criteria. These are situations in which an individual project proposal would by itself appear nebulous and be unattractive on any criterion. But a collectivity of such nebulous proposals may lead to the creation of significant technological breakthroughs. As Nelson (1959) pointed out, this is frequently the case when considering advances in basic science. The problem here is one of motivating researchers to pursue activities that individually would not meet overall corporate-investment criteria. Under these conditions, setting selection criteria that are less strict than success criteria would increase the flow of proposals.

The practice of encouraging "bootlegging" among researchers at firms such as 3M and Hitachi illustrates how these criteria may be chosen to foster innovation. These firms have implicitly set $x_c = 0$ for a portion of each researcher's time. For instance, researchers at 3M are permitted to pursue any project they desire for up to 15% of their time. The success of 3M at introducing a stream of new and innovative products attests to the value of such a strategy.

Limits to predictability and the inevitability of errors

Realizing that errors are inevitable, decision makers may undertake two initiatives. First, they may try to learn from their mistakes to reduce the number of errors in the future. Second, they may trade off one type of error at the expense of the other, depending upon the technology context they confront. We discuss these two initiatives in greater detail below.

Learning from mistakes

The sum of the two errors can be reduced by increasing the predictive validity of the criterion chosen to accept or reject projects. To accomplish this, decision makers need to establish a relationship between selection criteria (for example, NPV or IRR) and measures of success (for example, ROI or market share). Once this is accomplished, decision makers can be more confident in their ability to accept or reject a project based on an estimate of NPV or IRR, as the case may be. Ideally, of course, selection measures should be perfectly correlated with measures of success. Since this is seldom the case in practice, decision makers should collect historical data on previous accept-or-reject decision criteria and the outcomes of projects funded and not funded.[8] If there were insufficient historical data, decision makers could conduct experiments using different values of the selection criteria to establish the level of correlation between selection and success measures in their experience.

Such experimentation may seem unusual to an uninformed observer and it may suggest a somewhat arbitrary decision-making process, since decision criteria would appear to shift idiosyncratically. To ensure that such experiments are not perceived as reflecting an arbitrary decision-making process, it is important to clarify that experiments will be undertaken to gather data to improve the decision-making process.[9] By this means, the predictive validity of selection criteria could be improved.

As we are dealing with decisions in situations where there is considerable uncertainty, improving predictability may not be easy. Most likely, the conflict between the two risk tendencies (risk seeking versus risk averse) and the two judgmental errors (Type I versus Type II) may be present most of the time, highlighting the dual nature of technology-development decisions. However, since we advocate a dynamic framework, learning from the past becomes important. Collecting data and experimenting may be necessary to counteract the tendencies to search for confirming evidence only (Einhom & Hogarth, 1978), and to fall prey to reasoning by hindsight (Fischhoff, 1975). Data on all four quadrants of Figure 3.1 are needed for learning and for improving predictability. Obviously, there are other variables that can confound learning. For instance, a project that is selected may get considerable funding it would otherwise not have received, thereby increasing the chances for its success beyond what would be predicted by the model. This may lead to what Einhorn and Hogarth (1978) called a "treatment effect," which may hinder our ability to improve judgmental predictability. For instance, Hirsch (1972) demonstrated that predicting successful records in the music-publishing industry is extremely difficult, since records that get selected initially are given tremendous publicity (a treatment effect). Nevertheless, in this industry, Type II errors cannot be ignored, since rejected records often get produced by other firms and, therefore, become visible.

Trade-offs between errors

Decision makers can make trade-offs between Type I and Type II errors through their choice of decision criteria and incentive schemes. This trade-off depends upon the technological context surrounding choices. For instance, several scholars suggest two broad technological contexts — an *era of ferment*, wherein multiple technological approaches exist, and an *era of incremental change*, wherein technological activities take on the form of product elaboration and improvements (Anderson & Tushman, 1990; Utterback & Abernathy, 1975). The era of ferment is characterized by the presence of a number of alternative trajectories (Dosi, 1982), each one of which could eventually be successful. Each trajectory incorporates designs that emphasize certain dimensions of technological merit while compromising on others (Tushman & Rosenkopf, 1992).

Since information about these technological trajectories increases over time, it might be argued that decision makers within firms could postpone their technology adoption decisions. There are, however, other aspects of technological change that drive firms to choose from technological trajectories even during the presence of multiple trajectories that offer conflicting benefits. First, technology develops in a cumulative fashion, making it increasingly difficult over time for a firm to enter into a technology race begun by others. Second, technological opportunities dwindle over time as technology options become fewer and as cospecialized assets required for the successful commercialization of the technology are foreclosed (Teece, 1987). As a result, postponing technology-adoption decisions may lock out a firm from a technological field (Cohen & Levinthal, 1990; Ghemawat, 1991).

Thus, the timing of technology-choice decisions is a key issue. Very early choices may not provide the opportunity to generate organizational intelligence about alternative trajectories, thereby locking in the firm to a trajectory early in the development of a technology. Very late choices, on the other hand, may lock out a firm. Consequently, there is a window of opportunity within which firms must decide on the specific technological trajectory they wish to pursue. During this window of opportunity, the firm may wish to generate information about various trajectories so as to make an informed choice. This requires that managers encourage researchers to take risks in order to explore alternative paths, even though only one of them will eventually be chosen. Besides enhancing organizational intelligence, exploring alternative paths also hedges the firm's bets by creating options that it might pursue in the future when information about trajectories increases. In the context of our framework, this implies minimizing Type II errors—encouraging risk taking and exploration

For example, in supercomputing, IBM and Cray Research are both actively developing three different technologies: vector machines, massively parallel processors, and workstation clusters. Seymour Cray, the founder of Cray Research, believed, however, that "his company's decision to bet on MPP simply "diluted" its support for future vector-processor machines" (Mitchell, 1993, pp. 80–90). In new audio recording and playback technologies, Sony has hedged its bets by licensing Philips' Digital Compact Cassette technology and by promising to sell digital cassettes even as it continues to develop its own Mini Disc technology (Therrien, 1992). In the development of the videotape recorder, "the successive heads of RCA research for years had to orchestrate a competition between several videoplayer technologies inside the Laboratories, unsure which one would, or should, win out . . . each element of the system could be approached in several possible ways" (Graham, 1986, pp. 5–15).

An era of incremental change follows the era of ferment. During this era, the direction of technical change is relatively more predictable. For firms, a challenge during the era of incremental technological change is one of appropriating the benefits that a technology offers (Ghemawat, 1991; Teece, 1987). Although a firm may have "picked the winner," its ability to benefit from a technology may be compromised if rival firms enter the industry with substitute products. Firms confront this challenge by engaging in activities that improve product performance and process efficiencies. Technological choices now are between alternative courses of action *within a path* that improve its performance and quality and reduce its cost. That is, there is inadequate knowledge of how path-specific outcomes can be accomplished.

A part of this technological uncertainty is stochastic and cannot be reduced through experimentation (Nelson & Winter, 1977). However, another part of this technological uncertainty represents preliminary ignorance that can be reduced by trial-and-error learning. Trial-and-error learning is an adaptive process wherein researchers generate information that guides their future actions. As cost reduction is important during this stage of technology development, an important consideration during this trial-and-error learning process is to avoid alternatives that consume more resources than they save. This suggests that the type of decisions made during the era of incremental change would be different from those made during the era of ferment. In particular, during the era of incremental change, most of a firm's resources should be allocated to exploit its relative advantage. In the context of our framework, this implies creating sequential hurdles for the chosen technology (so as to arrive at the best design). This would mean, in general, minimizing Type I errors.

In practice, determining the technological context when making a choice is a big challenge. There are many indicators—such as the presence or absence of multiple technological trajectories and the emergence of a dominant design—to help make this determination. However, this determination is not only difficult but also dangerous. Misjudging the technological context could lead to an inappropriate trade-off between Type I and Type II errors, resulting in greater technological oversights and fewer foresights.

Fortunately, we do not need clear cut-off points in time during the evolution of a technology in order to apply the proposed model. In the presence of multiple technological trajectories, the model suggests that firms must first create options by exploring alternative technological trajectories. As information about each of the alternative technological trajectories unfolds, firms can begin prioritizing and focusing their resources. Rather than selecting specific trajectories to pursue, this process is one that progressively rejects those trajectories that clearly appear not to be worth pursuing, thereby eventually narrowing a firm's options to those that are more likely to be viable in the future.

For instance, George Poste, chairman of pharmaceutical research at SmithKline Beecham PLC, noted that "there's a limit to how many (medical research programs) any company, no matter how large, can afford to be in" (Moore, 1992, p. B5). The company has decided to reallocate funds previously spent on gastrointestinal research among five different priority therapeutic areas. Similarly, Honda is reported as "putting 67 percent of its R&D budget into improving gas engines, 28 percent for electric vehicles, and the remaining 5 percent for more far-off possibilities, such as hydrogen and methanol" (Miller, 1992, p. 46).

Role of incentives

A contemporary view is that incentives are needed because the interests of principals and agents are often not aligned. Therefore, incentives are designed to align interests. If alignment cannot be achieved, controls are instituted to prevent any opportunistic behavior on the part of agents. These controls often take the form of indirect and direct supervision. Further, it has been widely recognized that appropriate incentives and control systems must be instituted to encourage risk-seeking and innovation. For instance, a lack of formal structure, and extrinsic and intrinsic rewards in the form of autonomy, recognition, special compensation, and dual ladders have been suggested (Galbraith & Kazanjian, 1986). Consistent with this advice, General Electric selectively rewards innovators and entrepreneurs who try and fail (Aguilar & Hammermesh, 1985). However, it appears that most managers reduce Type I errors by instituting incentive schemes that carry a more direct link to compensation (Shapira, 1994).

The literature on the role of incentive and control systems, however, does not consider which type of error should be minimized at the expense of the other through the reward system. Specifically, the conditions under which different types of risk taking should be encouraged is not addressed. Thus, to foster innovation, firms are only advised to institute systems to encourage risk taking. The model developed in this chapter shows, however, that one type of error should be encouraged while the other discouraged, depending upon the technological context. This observation has important implications for the design of appropriate incentives. For example, as Galai and Shapira (1985) have shown, it is more appropriate to seek a balance between Type I and Type II errors, namely between investment and opportunity losses, to foster a more rational approach to risk taking.

Further, not discriminating between error types may lead to some unfortunate consequences. Type I errors are visible and they are often punished. In other words, risk-seeking behavior is penalized. Witness, for example, the recent firing of three senior executives of Maytag's Hoover unit in the United Kingdom for perceived errors in designing a sales-promotion program (Miller, 1993). In contrast, Type II errors are invisible and they often go unpunished, thereby inappropriately rewarding risk-averse behavior, as is illustrated by the long tenures of several senior managers who appear to have missed opportunities (Andrews, 1990; Wilke, 1990).

One way to try to affect executives' strategic decisions is by structuring their incentives (and penalties) in a flexible way in terms of minimizing Type I and Type II errors. Minimizing one error versus the other may lead to differential strategies in line with the exploration and exploitation strategies. We do not argue for the advantage of one strategy over the other. Instead, our analysis suggests that the choice of strategy and the related incentive schemes depend on the technological context.

Specifically, during the era of ferment, when a number of alternative technologies are competing for predominance, decision makers need to encourage the exploration of all alternatives. In other words, Type II errors are to be reduced so that consideration of potentially promising technologies is not prematurely foreclosed. To this end, relatively greater autonomy to pursue research, and recognition for reaching-out, should be provided. In addition, incremental innovations to existing technologies should not be emphasized and may even be discouraged.

During the era of incremental change, decision makers need to encourage many incremental innovations. In other words, Type I errors are to be reduced so that corporate resources are not misdirected towards trying to develop alternatives to the already dominant technology. To this end, relatively less autonomy to pursue research is appropriate, and autonomy should be centered around the dominant technology. In addition, recognition should be provided for achieving improvements in existing technologies that result in improved performance measured by, say, market share or return on investment.

Conclusion

Strategic-management theories focus on the creation and sustenance of wealth. New technologies, if successful, provide some of the most important sources of wealth. However, if not successful, new technologies can drain firms of their valuable resources. In this way, new technologies can act as both a source and a sink.

To explore this duality, this chapter attempts to link risk taking by decision makers to the context of technological development. First, we explored Type I and Type II decision errors and pointed out the trade-offs that exist between them. Next, we argued that decision makers can reduce the sum of the two errors. Paradoxically, this requires making errors with a view to improving the predictive validity of project-selection measures, a process that Einhorn (1986) called "accepting error to make less error." An inadequate consideration of this fact may lead to certain dysfunctional actions that detract from learning through innovation. For instance, a propensity to automatically ascribe blame for performance below expectations may stifle creativity.

Considering the conflict between exploration and exploitation, there are many forces in firms that push for exploitation rather than exploration. Amongst them are the nonrational escalation of commitment (Staw, 1981) and the inertial tendencies not to engage in cannibalization of existing technologies. However, cannibalization is often required for innovation or for preventing a competitor from innovation that may render the firm's technology obsolete (Conner, 1988).[10] In this context, we suggested that decision makers may want to reduce one type of error even at the expense of increasing the other depending upon the stage of technology development. Specifically, exploration requires that decision makers reduce Type II errors, while exploitation requires that they reduce Type I errors.

These technology-choice issues are becoming increasingly important in contemporary environments characterized by rapid change. The increasing pace of technological change and the associated complexity places a premium on understanding how decisions are made and what can be done to improve them. This requires that behavioral aspects of decision making should be included in any theory of strategic management (Zajac & Bazerman, 1991). However, decision makers are missing in many theories of strategic management that have focused on positioning or inimitability. For instance, the structure–conduct–performance paradigm (see, for example, Porter, 1980) has been articulated at the firm and industry levels, thereby precluding an analysis of decision makers and decision-making processes. Moreover, this paradigm does not explicitly incorporate the time dimension in its construction, a facet that is critical to understanding how firms can create and sustain a competitive advantage through the choice of technologies.

The resource-based view is another perspective that does not include decision makers in its formulation (see Peteraf, 1993 for a recent review). This perspective has examined how firms might develop a sustainable competitive advantage through the creation of inimitable resources. However, this perspective has largely ignored how these resources can entrap firms in the past even as new technologies make old inimitable resources worthless. In this context, Elster (1983) pointed out that through their choices, humans can avoid being trapped by the past Therefore, they can escape the inevitability of the future.

This paper is one effort to accomplish the task of bringing the decision maker back into a theory of strategic management. By focusing on decision makers and coupling them with their changing technological context, our framework suggests new avenues of inquiry. For instance, a key question for strategic management pertains to the creation of organizational intelligence. Variability and errors in outcomes usually evoke negative reactions from managers. We tend to penalize people for errors and attempt to eliminate variability in outcomes. However, variability and errors are the very attributes that make learning possible in the context of innovation. As Walter Wriston, former CEO of Citibank, noted, "good judgment comes from experience; experience comes from bad judgment" (Kearns & Nadler, 1992, p. 267). Variability and errors help us to learn and develop valid predictors of successful innovations, thereby creating organizational intelligence. Without this organizational intelligence, the process of innovation cannot be institutionalized (Schumpeter, 1975). Whether we explore or exploit, errors are inevitable. We must learn from, reduce, and make appropriate trade-offs between errors. Strategic management theories must grapple with these issues.

Acknowledgment

We acknowledge financial assistance from the Center for Entrepreneurial Studies, New York University.

Notes

1   As Graham noted, "R&D is still an enigma. . . . But R&D's strangeness and remoteness to the rest of the organization affects not only its effectiveness as a support function, but its credibility as a generator and implementor of strategic opportunities. . . . The need for general managers to concern themselves with R&D is becoming more compelling. . . . When R&D allocates its resources and assigns priorities to one area of research over another, it is inevitably predetermining corporate strategy" (1986, pp. 220–229).

2   Buderi noted that "corporate histories are replete with good ideas that lan-

guished on the shelf. . . . Such oversights are to some extent unavoidable, if only because once an industry matures there's a tendency to think the big inventions have already been made and to focus instead on small improvements" (1993, p. 80). Europe's EUREKA program, encompassing 650 projects, is expected to cost $15 billion, but only 17% of corporate participants claim that it has helped improve competitiveness; the ESPRIT program, expected to cost nearly $10 billion, has a hit rate of only 50% in 915 projects; only one-third of 1130 projects in the $3.2 billion BRITE program have shown any commercial value (Levine, 1993). Quiana, a synthetic silk introduced by Du Pont, cost about $200 million to develop and market. It was abandoned for natural fibers and died. Electronic imaging businesses have cost Du Pont over $600 million since the mid-60s yet have yielded only red ink. After 10 years and $1 billion, Du Pont officials admit that pharmaceuticals take longer and cost more to develop and market than they anticipated (McMurray, 1992).

3   The saga of the initial development of xerography and personal computers is well known. Markoff (1991) chronicles 13 technologies conceived at Xerox's Palo Alto Research Center that were rejected by Xerox and later successfully developed by other firms. However, not surprisingly, data on the extent of such occurrences is rarely collected.

In the motion picture production industry, about two-thirds of the top-100 wide-release films (those released simultaneously in more than 500 theaters in the U.S.) during 1985–1991 had below average gross box-office receipts. Interestingly, some studios such as Paramount and 20th Century Fox had significantly better "hit rates." Sixty percent of Paramount's releases had above average gross box-office receipts, whereas 50% of 20th Century Fox's were above average. In contrast, Disney and Warner Brothers had only 33% of their releases grossing above-average receipts (*Movie Stats*, 1991).

In industries such as oil and gas exploration, the occurrence of outcomes that in retrospect may be considered to be oversights or foresights seems almost taken for granted because of the low success rates. About a third of all wells drilled in the United States during the period 1986–1990 yielded neither oil nor gas (American Petroleum Institute, 1990).

In consumer goods, new product introductions are singularly unsuccessful. For example, a noted annual industry survey reported that of all products introduced into the market in 1991, only 17% met their business objectives. In other words, the failure rate after product introduction was 83% (Group EFO Limited, 1992). A study by Arthur D. Little found that only 8% of new cereals introduced succeed (Zangwill, 1993). Given such low odds for success, it is a wonder that firms still try at all.

4   Graham noted that "during the mid-1970s, RCA's decision not to stick with Magtape was received by the press and the industry as a healthy focusing of the company's effort on a product with higher potential. Only later, when it would become apparent that RCA's decision had in effect determined that no American company would be able to compete with the Japanese in manufacturing videotape recorders, would the press, in its customary fickle way, ask how such a thing could have happened. How could RCA, the American consumer electronics industry's traditional pioneer, fail to produce a magnetic tape player of its own making?" (1986, p. 149).

5   March and Shapira (1992) do recognize that at a "survival" point, firms will exhibit risk-seeking behavior (exploration) irrespective of whether performance is

below or above aspiration levels. Firms with few resources but high aspirations may also engage in exploration to compete with rivals possessing greater resources.

6 A similar model is frequently used in the psychometric literature and has been adopted for the study of individual decision making by Einhorn and Hogarth (1978).

7 Note that although we developed the model using a single measure, decision makers may, in fact, employ multiple measures. This may introduce trade-offs among measures.

8 Collecting data on the outcomes of projects that were funded may be relatively easy. Collecting data on the outcomes of projects that were not funded by the firm but were, perhaps, funded by competitors is possible, but is rarely done. In fact, seldom are any records maintained of alternatives that were considered and not funded. To improve predictive validity, however, such data must be collected and analyzed.

9 Experimentation is possible in established firms that confront several technology choice decisions over time. By creating a database on successes and failures, decision makers in established firms may create organizational intelligence that start-up firms do not have.

10 Torres noted that professional investors favor firms that still "possess the savage entrepreneurial appetite with which they were founded. They want companies willing to innovate. They want cannibals that will cheerfully destroy the past in order to feed the future. . . . Intel is a model cannibal, some pros say" (1992, p. CI).

References

Aguilar, F. and Hammermesh, R. (1985). *General Electric, 1984*. Case 9-385-315, Harvard Business School.

Ali, A., Kalwani, M. U., and Kovenock, D. (1993). Selecting product development projects: Pioneering versus incremental innovation strategies. *Management Science*, 39(3), 255–274.

Alster, N. (1987). How Intel and Motorola missed the Sun rise. Electronic Business, 13(21), 32–34.

American Petroleum Institute. (1990). *Monthly Completion Report*. September.

Amit, R. and Schoemaker, P. J. H. (1993). Strategic assets and organizational rent. *Strategic Management Journal*, 14(1), 33–46.

Anderson, P. and Tushman, M. L. (1990). Technological discontinuities and dominant designs: A cyclical model. *Administrative Science Quarterly*, 35(4), 604–633.

Andrews, E. L. (1990). The illogical process of invention. *New York Times*, May 5.

Arthur, B. (1988). Self-reinforcing mechanisms in economics. In P. Anderson et al., *The Economy as an Evolving Complex System*. Reading, MA: Addison-Wesley.

Bleakley, F. R. (1991). Citicorp's folly? How a terrific idea for grocery marketing missed its targets. *Wall Street Journal*, April 3, A1.

Bower, J. L. (1970). *The Resource Allocation Process*. Cambridge, MA: Harvard University Press.

Brealey, R. and Myers, S. (1984). *Principles of Corporate Finance*. New York: McGraw-Hill.

Buderi, R. (1993). American inventors are reinventing themselves. *Business Week*, January 18, 78–82.

Cascio, W. (1991). *Applied Psychology in Personnel Management*. Englewood Cliffs, NJ: Prentice-Hall.

Cohen, W. M. and Levinthal, D. A. (1990). Absorptive capacity: A new perspective on learning and innovation. *Administrative Science Quarterly*, 35(1), 128–152.

Comroe, J. H. and Dripps, R. D. (1976). Scientific basis for the support of biomedical science. *Science*, 192, 105–111.

Conner, K. R. (1988). Strategies for product cannibalism. *Strategic Management Journal*, 9, 9–26.

Constant, E. W. (1987). The social locus of technological practice: Community, system, or organization? In W. E. Bijker, T. P. Hughes and T. J. Pinch (eds.), *The Social Construction of Technological System: New Directions in the Sociology and History of Technology*. Cambridge, MA: MIT Press. pp. 223–242.

Cooper, R. G. (1986). *Winning at New Products*. Reading, MA: Addison-Wesley.

David, P. (1985). Clio and the economics of QWERTY. *American Economic Review*, 75(2), 332–337.

Dawes, R. M. and Corrigan, B. (1974). Linear models in decision making. *Psychological Bulletin*, 81, 95–106.

Dosi, G. (1982). Technological paradigms and technological paths. *Research Policy*, 11(3), 147–162.

Einhorn, H. J. (1986). Accepting error to make less error. *Journal of Personality Assessment*, 50, 387–395.

Einhorn, H. J. and Hogarth, R. M. (1978). Confidence in judgement: Persistence of the illusion of validity. *Psychological Review*, 85(5), 395–416.

Eisenhardt, K. (1989). Making fast strategic decisions in high-velocity environments. *Academy of Management Journal*, 32(3), 543–576.

Elster, J. (1983). *Explaining Technical Change: A Case Study in the Philosophy of Science*. New York: Cambridge University Press.

Farrell, C.(1993). Survival of the fittest technologies. *New Scientist*, February 6, 35–39.

Fischhoff, B. (1975). Hindsight and foresight: The effect of outcome knowledge on judgment under uncertainty. *Journal of Experimental Psychology: Human Perception and Performance*, 1, 288–299.

Foster, R. N. (1986). *Innovation: The Attacker's Advantage*. New York: Summit Books.

Freeman, C. (1986). *The Economics of Industrial Innovation*. Cambridge MA: MIT Press.

Galai, D. and Shapira, Z. (1985). Project selection, errors, compensation and incentives. Paper presented at the 10th SPUDM Research Conference, Helsinki.

Galbraith, J. R. and Kazanjian, R. K. (1986). *Strategy Implementation: Structure, Systems and Process*. New York: West Publishing.

Garud, R. and Rappa, M. (1994). A socio-cognitive model of technology evolution. *Organization Science*, 5, 3, 344–362.

Ghemawat, P. (1991). *Commitment: The Dynamic of Strategy*. New York: The Free Press.

Graham, M. B. W. (1986). *RCA and the VideoDisc: The Business of Research*. New York: Cambridge University Press.

Group EFO Limited. (1992). *The 1992 Innovation Survey*. Weston, CT: .

Hirsch, P. (1972). Processing fads and fashions: An organizational set analysis of cultural industry systems. *American Journal of Sociology*, 77, 639–659.

Hoskisson, R. E., Hitt, M. A., and Hill, C. W. L. (1991). Managerial risk taking in diversified firms: An evolutionary perspective. *Organization Science*, 2(3), 296–314.

Hughes, T. P. (1989). *American Genesis: A Century of Invention and Technological Enthusiasm, 1870–1970.* New York: Viking Press.

Kay, N. M. (1979). *The Innovating Firm: A Behavioral Theory of Corporate R&D.* New York: St. Martin Press.

Kearns, D. T. and Nadler, D. A. (1992). *Prophets in the Dark: How Xerox Reinvented Itself and Beat Back the Japanese.* New York: HarperCollins.

Levine, J. B. (1993). How Europe swings the big science tab. *Business Week,* March 22, 62–64.

March, J. G. (1991). Explorations and exploitation in organizational learning. *Organization Science,* 2(1), 71–87.

March, J. G. and Olsen, J. P. (1976). Organizational learning and the ambiguity of the past. *European Journal of Political Research,* 3, 141–171.

March, J. G. and Shapira, Z. (1987). Managerial perspectives on risk and risk taking. *Management Science,* 33(11), 1404–1418.

March, J. G. and Shapira, Z. (1992). Variable risk preferences and the focus of attention. *Psychological Review,* 99(1), 172–183.

Markoff, J. (1991). And not a personal computer in sight. *New York Times,* October 6, 3(1).

McMurray, S. (1992). Changing a culture: Du Pont tries to make its research wizardry serve the bottom line. *Wall Street Journal,* March 27, A1.

Miller, K. L. (1992). Honda sets its sights on a different checkered flag. *Business Week,* August 45–46.

Miller, J. P. (1993). Maytag U.K. Unit finds promotion is too successful. *Wall Street Journal,* March 31, 1993, A7.

Mitchell, R. (1993). In supercomputing, superconfusion. *Business Week,* March 22, 89–90.

Moore, S. D. (1992). SmithKline realigns research program. *Wall Street Journal,* September 2, B5.

Movie Stats. (1991). Paul Kagan Associates, Inc., Carmel, CA, July 31.

Naj, A. K. (1991). Firms to decide if supersonic jet will fly. *Wall Street Journal,* February 8, B 1.

Nayak, P. and Ketteringham, J. (1986). *Breakthroughs.* New York: Rawson Associates.

Nelson, R. R. (1959). The simple economics of basic scientific research. *Journal of Political Economy,* 67(3), 297–306.

Nelson, R. R. and Winter, S. G. (1977). In search of a useful theory of innovation. *Research Policy,* 6, 36–76.

Nelson R. R. and Winter, S. G. (1982). *An Evolutionary Theory of Economic Change.* Cambridge, MA: Harvard University Press.

Petroski, H. (1992). *The Evolution of Useful Things.* New York: Alfred A. Knopf.

Peteraf, M. (1993). The cornerstones of competitive advantage: A resource-based view. *Strategic Management Journal,* 14(3), 179–191.

Porter, M. (1980). *Competitive Strategy.* New York: Free Press.

Powell, W. W. (1991). Expanding the Scope of Institutional Analysis. In W. W. Powell and P. J. DiMaggio (eds.), *The New Institutionalism in Organizational Analysis.* Chicago: University of Chicago Press, 183–203.

Rosenberg, N. *Inside the Black Box: Technology and Economics.* (1982). Cambridge: Cambridge University Press.

Schumpeter, J. A. (1975). *Capitalism, Socialism and Democracy.* Reading, MA: Addison-Wesley.

Schwenk, C. R. (1984). Cognitive simplification processes in strategic decision making. *Strategic Management Journal*, 5, 111–128.

Scott, W. R. (1987). The Adolescence of Institutional Theory. *Administrative Science Quarterly* 32, 493–511.

Scott, W. R. Unpacking Institutional Arguments. In W. W. Powell and P. J. DiMaggio (eds.), *The New Institutionalism in Organizational Analysis*. Chicago: University of Chicago Press, 164–182.

Shapira, Z. (1993). Risk-sharing incentive contracts: On setting compensation policy for expatriate professionals in a foreign operation. In Y. Aharoni (ed), *Coalitions and Competition: The Globalization of Professional Business Services*, London: Routledge, 153–161.

Shapira, Z. (1994). *Risk Taking: A Managerial Perspective*. New York: Russell Sage Foundation.

Smith, D. and Alexander, R. (1988). *Fumbling the Future: How Xerox Invented, then Ignored, the First Personal Computer*. New York: William Morrow.

Staw, B. M. (1981). The escalation of commitment to a course of action. *Academy of Management Review*, 6, 577–587.

Teece, D. J. (1987). Profiting from technological innovation: Implications for integration, collaboration, licensing and public policy. In D. J. Teece (ed.), *The Competitive Challenge: Strategies for Industrial Innovation and Renewal*. Cambridge, MA: Ballinger. 185–219.

Therrien, L. (1992). The sound and the fury at Sony and Philips. *Business Week*, June 15, 42.

Torres, C. (1992). For technology winners, seek out cannibals. *Wall Street Journal*, August 31, C 1.

Tushman, M. L. and Anderson, P. (1986). Technological Discontinuities and Organizational Environments. *Administrative Science Quarterly*, 31, 439–465.

Tushman M. and Rosenkopf, L. (1992). Organizational determinants of technological change: Toward a sociology of technological evolution. In B. Staw and L. Cummings, (eds.), *Research in Organizational Behavior, Vol. 14*. Greenwich, CT: JAI Press.

Tversky, A. and Kahneman, D. (1974). Judgment under uncertainty: Heuristics and biases. *Science*, 185, 1124–1131.

Utterback, J. M. and Abernathy, W. J. (1975). A dynamic model of process and product innovation. *OMEGA*, 3, 639–656.

Weick, K. (1990). Technology as equivoque: Sense-making in new technologies. In P. Goodman and L. Sproull (eds.), Technology and organizations. San Francisco. Jossey Bass, 1–44.

Wilke, J. R. (1980). Data General board ousts co-founder. *Wall Street Journal*, December 13, B7.

Wilke, J. R. (1952). Workstation unveilings today underscore competition. *Wall Street Journal*, November 10, B4.

Williamson, O. E. (1975). *Markets and Hierarchies*. New York: The Free Press.

Zajac, E. J. and Bazerman, M. H. (1991). Blind spots in industry and competitor analysis: Implications of interfirm (mis)perceptions for strategic decisions. *Academy of Management Review*, 16(1), 37–56.

Zangwill, W. I. (1993). When customer research is a lousy idea. *Wall Street Journal*, March 8, A 12.

4 Rational entrepreneurs or optimistic martyrs? Some considerations on technological regimes, corporate entries, and the evolutionary role of decision biases

Giovanni Dosi and Dan Lovallo

I. Introduction

This is a rather conjectural report on the evolutionary role of decision biases—at both the level of individuals and of organizations—and, in particular, on their importance to the processes of corporate entry and the evolution of industrial structures. A growing and quite robust body of evidence highlights the pervasiveness of various types of biases in individual decision making, which accounts for systematic departures from predictions of the canonical model of rational choice (see, for example, Kahneman & Tversky, 1973, 1986, Shafir & Tversky, 1992). For our purposes, we will mainly concern ourselves with *overconfidence* or optimism, which frequently leads to bold forecasts of the consequences of one's own actions. Also, by way of example, we will examine risk seeking in the domain of losses, which often yields escalating commitments in the face of failures. Interestingly, these biases appear to carry over from the level of individuals to that of groups and organizations and, indeed, might even be amplified in the latter circumstances (see, for example, Kahneman & Lovallo, 1993, Lovallo, 1996a, and the literature discussed there). In this respect, a challenging domain of investigation – with vast ramifications into the analyses of the nature of entrepreneurship, technological change, and industrial dynamics – is that of corporate entry into an industry.

Numerous studies have shown that the vast majority of entrants fail (see, for example, Dunne, Roberts, & Samuelson, 1988). Furthermore, there are significant interindustry differences in failure rates. Evidence of high-level firm failure rates appears to be consistent with experimental data showing that, typically, people are unrealistically optimistic, exhibit illusions of control in even modestly complex environments, and systematically neglect the statistics of previously observed performances.

In this study, we report some preliminary results and conjectures from an ongoing investigation of corporate entry, postentry performances, and the collective outcome of innovative successes and failures. First, we propose that persistent *intra*industry differences in firm performances are the joint outcome of a) heterogeneous patterns of organizational learning and b) cognitive mechanisms such as unrealistic optimism and "competitive blind spots" – areas where agents insufficiently consider the contingent decisions of their opponents.

Second, we suggest some hypotheses on *inter*industry differences in relative entry rates and postentry performances using a taxonomy of technological and market regimes. The basic idea is that knowledge and learning – concerning new products, new techniques, and new markets – are specific to distinct production activities. In turn, "technological paradigms" map expectations and corporate behaviors into diverse patterns of entry behaviors that are at least partly independent of the standard measures of profitability and risk. Of course, were we to find robust corroboration of this conjecture, it would be witness against any naive "rational-expectation" hypothesis on entrepreneurial behavior.

Our third conjecture takes this argument a step further. We propose that *micro "irrationalities"* – in terms of unrealistic optimism, etc – *are likely to be a fundamental ingredient in the collective development of new knowledge bases and new industries.* The development of new technological paradigms and the related emergence of new industries and new "technological communities" might be intimately associated with seemingly wasteful mistakes, rough search heuristics, and even "irrational" hubris, rather than sober forecasts.

Our empirical evidence is diverse. We will draw both on a few experimental studies, on the growing evidence on the economics of innovation, and on what we know from some statistical surveys and longitudinal samples of firms in manufacturing industries in various countries. (Research aimed at testing the foregoing conjectures, in collaboration with John Balwin, Statistics Canada, is currently underway).

In sections II to IV we briefly review the relevant evidence from behavioral decision research, identify analogous biases in organizational decision patterns, and present some experimental evidence on entry decisions. Section V discusses the evidence on corporate entry, postentry performances, exit, and the puzzles that all this entails. In section VI we outline some elements of an evolutionary interpretation and suggest some promising links with complementary exercises in evolutionary modeling as well as some possible further developments.

II. From individual biases to organizational errors

In economics, the use of psychological assumptions other than rationality to make predictions about organizational behavior is relatively rare, although the company is quite good – including John Maynard Keynes, Herbert Simon, Richard Nelson, Oliver Williamson, and Sidney Winter, among others. Certainly, from an empirical point of view, there is massive evidence that individuals do deviate from the behavioral patterns prescribed by rational models. Furthermore, these deviations are systematic – the errors tend to be in the same direction – which implies that nonrational behavior is often not random but predictable.

However, one of the major hurdles to incorporating alternative psychological assumptions into economic models is a healthy skepticism about how individual decision biases are likely to "scale up" to organizational outcomes. While it is beyond the scope of this work to examine the vast literature on individual and organizational decision making, there are good reasons to believe that organizations, in many instances, reinforce rather than mitigate individual decision biases (see, for example, March & Shapira, 1987, Kahneman & Lovallo, 1993, and Lovallo, 1996a). "Escalation" situations are a very good example of the consistency of psychological phenomena in various contexts and at widely different units of analysis (ranging from individual choices under experimental conditions all the way to enormous collective tragedies such as the Vietnam War). Two basic psychological principles lay at the foundation of "escalation phenomena," at the level of *both* individuals and organizations, namely: (i) people respond to changes rather than absolute levels, and, (ii) they exhibit diminishing sensitivity to quantities of various items, including money.

As is known, drawing on these two principles, Kahneman and Tversky (1979) constructed *prospect theory*, a descriptive theory of risk taking, in which individuals, due to diminishing sensitivity for absolute quantities, are both risk averse for gains and risk seeking in the domain of losses. Risk-seeking preferences for losses imply that when people have not made peace with their losses they are likely to place lower than expected value bets in order to break even. On average, these bets will fail and lead to even greater losses. Fox and Staw (1979) show that considering an important aspect of social context – the need for accountability – enhances individual willingness to "throw good money after bad." Using managers as subjects, Bateman and Zeithami (1989) also observe escalation behavior. Finally, Bazerman et al (1984) find that groups escalate less frequently but more dramatically than individuals. At each point along the path from individual-choice behavior to individual choice embedded in a social context to group decision making, there is reason to suspect that economic organizations will also escalate commitments to *losing courses of action*. The consistency of the findings mentioned above and others (for example, the cases that Janis, 1982 and Ross and Staw, 1986) recount of the Vietnam War and the Vancouver World Fair) indicate that these suspicions are valid.

Quite similar considerations apply to the widespread phenomena of overconfidence and "framing effects" in the interpretation of the available information. For example, March and Shapira (1987) suggest that managers tend to interpret uncertainty simply in terms of "challenges" to their abilities and commitments to the pursuit of their goals. "Groupthink" has been identified as a cause of organizational optimism (Janis, 1982). Moreover, groups are prone to use "representative heuristics" – the tendency to formulate probabilities on uncertain events based on the similarity of the event itself with some salient property of its parent population (Kahneman & Tversky, 1973, Argote, Seabright & Dyer, 1986).

There is extensive literature on overoptimism in project evaluation (for example, Merrow et al., 1981) and with regard to R&D (see discussion in Freeman, 1982). Grossly optimistic errors are especially likely if the project involves new technology or otherwise places the firm in an unfamiliar territory. In an interesting discussion of the cause of failure in capital investment projects, Arnold (1986) finds:

> Most companies support large capital expenditure programs with a worst case analysis that examines the projects' loss potential. But the worst case forecast is almost always too optimistic. . . . When managers look at the downside they generally describe a mildly pessimistic future rather than the worst possible future.

Standard operating procedures and decision methods, ranging from discounted cash flows and net present value methods in investment evaluation to cost accounting, often involve framing effects, overconfidence, preference for confirming evidence (for a discussion, especially with regard to technological innovation, see Schoemaker and Marais, 1995).

More generally, the acknowledgment of the specificities of technological and organizational competences embodied in each firm (Teece et al., 1994, Dosi & Marengo (1993) also entails the recognition of specific heuristics, problem-framing, and, ultimately, of diverse collective structures of cognition defining what the organization can do, how it does it, and where and how it can search for novel technologies and products. Clearly, competence specificity, other things being equal, will tend to strengthen an *inside view* in forecasts and decisions. That view – as detailed in Kahneman and Tversky (1979) and Kahneman and Lovallo (1993) – draws on knowledge of the case at hand and constructs an ideal history of the future conditional on the sequences of actions by the decision makers. (In contrast, an "outside view" is statistical and comparative, drawing from past experiences of analogous cases.)

In brief, organizational decision making in general, and, a fortiori, relatively unique "strategic" activities concerning innovation, diversification, and entry – grounded in firm-specific knowledge – is often likely to involve biased assessments of one's own technological and competitive abilities (stemming from overconfidence, the "inside view," and illusion of control), and inertial and escalating commitments (with neglect of potentially relevant information and "sunk-cost fallacies"). We suggest that entrepreneurial decisions of entry are no exception. In particular, it is worth reporting some experiments by one of us (Lovallo) indicating how "inside-view" thinking is likely to lead to excess entry. We refer to the prediction that there will be excess entry as the *optimism hypothesis*. The experiments reported below serve three purposes. First, one would like to test whether the relative optimism that we see in noncompetitive environments survives in the face of competitive interaction. Second, the controlled environment allows us to unpack the effects that various types of inside-view thinking have on entry. Third, these experiments may provide clearer insights into the psychology of competition, which would lead to more informative field surveys of entrants.

III. Experimental design

The isomorphism between the experiment and the industrial activity that we model is illustrated in Figure 4.1. It is reasonable to assume that one of the first steps towards entry is for a firm to undertake some kind of market assessment in order to determine if there is sufficient opportunity in terms of probability and the size of a market to warrant entry. In the experiments, subjects are provided with information about the market capacity – the number of entrants that can earn positive amounts of money in any given period. The next step in the entry process is competitor analysis. In an industrial setting, this procedure involves multiple dimensions including estimating the likely number and quality of potential entrants. In these experiments we explicitly ask subjects to estimate the number of entrants they expect to enter in each period. Implicitly, they make their entry decision, which is the next step in the process. Finally, in both environments there is competition and diverse performances that result in differential payoffs based on relative skills.

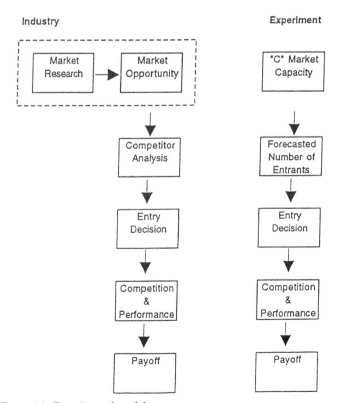

Figure 4.1. Experimental model.

Given this broad overview of the experimental model, let us be more specific about particular experiments where we manipulate several factors in the competitive environment. One of the most important manipulations is whether subjects self-selected themselves into a particular experiment or not. In some experiments, subjects are recruited to participate in entry games and no particular information is given about the dimension on which the subjects will compete. In other experiments, we explicitly ask for subjects who consider themselves to be above the median in terms of their knowledge of sports or current events. The subjects share common knowledge about the method in which they were recruited. In addition to the self-selection manipulation, the entry games occur in three different competitive environments: simultaneous entry without feedback, simultaneous entry with feedback, and sequential entry. In the simultaneous-entry condition, all of the subjects make their entry decisions at the same time. The feedback that the subjects receive is about the number of entrants that entered in the previous period. In the sequential-entry condition, each subject is given an entry order number that remains constant throughout the experiment. For example, the subject with entry order number one makes his entry decision first, subject two goes second, etc. All of the entry decisions are public knowledge.

In all of the experiments, we use an identical payoff table (Table 4.1). The amounts listed are the payoffs for the successful entrants for each market capacity. Unsuccessful entrants always lose $10. Consider the following example. If market capacity is two, then the highest-ranked entrant receives $33, the second-highest-ranked entrant receives $17, and anyone else that enters the market loses $10. In any case, the maximum total possible profit in the market is $50. This means that if five more entrants in excess of market capacity enter, the total profit in the market will be $0. For example, if there are seven entrants when the market capacity is two, the total profit for the entrants as a group will be $0, since the two top-ranked entrants will split $50 according to the payoff table and the third-through-seventh-

Table 4.1. *Payoff for sucessful entrants as a function of* C *(market capacity)*

Rank	C			
	2	4	6	8
1	33	20	14	11
2	17	15	12	10
3		10	10	8
4		5	7	7
5			5	6
6			2	4
7				3
				2

ranked entrants will each lose $10. If there were eight entrants when the market capacity was two total profits would be –$10.

In each experiment there, are two different ranking procedures: random rank and skill-based rank. In the random-rank procedure, subjects' ranks are predetermined by a random-number generator. Subjects do not know their ranks prior to making their entry decisions. After all the entry decisions have been made, a tournament starts, to be played for real money. It is only at that point subjects learn of their randomly assigned ranks. In the skill-based rank condition, subjects are shown examples of the types of questions on which their ranks will be based. However, they do not answer the questions until all of the entry decisions have been made. Then, subjects are given a quiz and their ranks are based on the number of questions they answer correctly. The purpose of the random-ranked condition is to control for risk preferences. In games with asymmetric payoff functions, such as the one described here, there is no way ex-ante to determine the equilibrium number of entrants without knowing subjects' risk preferences. Since the subjects not change across the different versions of the experiment, if we assume that their risk preferences do not change from one condition to the next, the only reason for greater entry in the skill-ranked condition is that subjects have more sanguine views of their probability of success than in the random-ranked condition. It is the difference in the number of entrants in the two conditions that will be the primary measure of interest throughout the experiments. Table 4.2 contains an example of the actual form subjects use to record their responses.

If, for example, there are 12 periods in each condition, balls numbered 1–24 will be placed in a bingo cage at the end of the experiment; the period corresponding to the chosen ball will be played for real money. The experimental procedure is summarized below.

1. Read instructions aloud
2. Comprehension test on the payoff
3. Explanation of the two types of ranking
4. Subjects are shown examples of the skill question
5. Subjects are informed that one period will be played for real money
6. Subjects make their forecasts and entry decisions in the random-rank condition
7. Subjects make their forecasts and entry decisions in the skill-rank condition
8. After all of the entry decisions are made, subjects take the quiz
9. A randomly drawn period is chosen to be played
10. Subjects' earnings are computed and immediately paid

IV. Summary of the results

Without going into too much detail, which can be found in Lovallo (1996b), this section summarizes the results from the experiments. There are four findings that are of interest. First, it is clear that there is excess entry in the

Table 4.2. *Market experiment A—random rank*

NAME _____   DATE _____

Payoff for Successful Entrants as a function of C

			C	
Rank	2	4	6	8
1	33	20	14	11
2	17	15	12	10
3		10	10	8
4		5	7	7
5			5	6
6			2	4
7				3
8				2

How much would you earn if $C = 6$, you entered, and your rank was 5 among the entrants? _____

How much would you earn if $C = 2$, you entered, and your rank was 4 among the entrants? _____

Round	C	Expected number of entrants	Enter	Not enter	Number of entrants
1					
2					
3					
4					
5					
6					
7					
8					
9					
10					
11					
12					

skill condition as compared to the risk-controlling, random-rank condition. This was true in each and every experiment. Furthermore, the expected value of entering in the random-rank condition was significantly positive in all of the experiments, while it was significantly negative in all of the skill-ranked conditions. Second, the excess entry that we observe in these experiments is not caused by "blind spots" – on average, subjects' forecasts of the number of entrants are accurate. This means that subjects in the skill condition are saying, "I realize that on average people are going to lose money in this market, but I'm not. I'm in!"

The next finding is the most surprising. In experiments without self-selection, we find a significant divergence between the number of entrants in the skill-versus random-rank conditions. However, this divergence is dwarfed by the magnitude of the divergence in markets with self-selection. This suggests that a large amount of excess entry is caused by reference-group neglect (Lovallo 1996a), rather than some variant of optimism. Reference-group neglect refers to the tendency of people to underappreciate the group with which they are competing. It is a competitive manifestation of inside-view thinking. For example, suppose that you are a phenomenally good cook and you are thinking of opening a restaurant. If you are asked to evaluate yourself as a cook in comparison to the general population, you might say that you are in the top 5%, and you might be right. However, a more pertinent question is how good of a cook are you in comparison to others in the restaurant business, almost all of whom consider themselves to be, and probably are, in the top of 5% of cooks. Reference group neglect implies that you will insufficiently regress your prediction of your relative ability in this more competitive group.

Finally, it is useful to point out that the effect that we are discussing is robust across many different types of competitive environments. The effect is significant with feedback and without self-selection and is even more robust without feedback and with self-selection. Furthermore, the effect works in both simultaneous- and sequential-entry games. Indeed, there is no significant difference between the effect in these two environments, which is rather astonishing. This means that in a sequential-entry environment, people are making a decision to enter knowing with probability one that the value of the game to the player as a group is already negative!

Our general conjecture is that this experimental evidence on cognitive and decision-biased entry also bears important implications for the understanding of *actual* entry processes of new firms in industry. In order to argue the point, let us begin by considering some available evidence on corporate entry and entrants' performances.

V. Patterns of entry, post-entry performance, and exit in manufacturing

Geroski (1991) identifies four major "stylized facts" on the entry process. First, "many firms attempt to enter each year, but [. . .] few survive for more than a year or two. The average entrant is, it seems, basically a tourist and not an immigrant, enjoying a life that is often nasty, brutish, and, above all, short" (p. 283). Second, "different measures of entry (net and gross entry measures, entry based on sales or on number of firms) are not very highly related to each other" (p. 287). Third, "there are a range of different types of entrants, and some are more successful at penetrating markets or surviving than others" (p. 290). Fourth, "the effects of entry [on market performance] – like the lives of most entrants – are fairly modest" (p. 293).

Dunne et al. (1988) examine the patterns of firm entry, growth, and exit of different types of firms over the period 1963–1982, using plant-level data from the U.S. Census of Manufacturers. For the 1967 entrant cohort, 63.8% of all new-firm, new-plant entrants exited within 5 years, while 49.6% of all diversifying-firm, new-plant entrants exited. The difference in failure rates is similar to the cohort's age. Within 15 years, 87.9% of the new-firm, new-plant entrants exited, whereas 74.6% of the diversifying-firm, new-plant entrants exited. The differences between de novo and diversifier exit rates are substantial for all the cohorts in the sample at any of the time periods measured.

The high mortality of entrants is corroborated by longitudinal studies on industrial life cycles (see Hannan and Freeman, 1989, Carroll and Swaminathan, 1992, Klepper, 1992), and so are the differences in post-entry performances according to different types of entrants and the timing of entry.

Consider, for example, Lane's investigation of ATM manufacturers (Lane, 1989). The ATM market began shortly before 1969. The first firm to enter the market was Money Machine Inc. in 1967. An interesting pattern of entry develops over the life cycle of this industry. The earliest entrants into the industry were almost all de novo entrants; the next group of entrants were the diversifying firms; the final wave of entry came from foreign firms. The average entry date for the three groups of firms were 1970, 1975, and 1979, respectively. The reasonably distinct partition between the entry dates for the three entrant types suggests that there is a systematic difference between the firm types that drive entry behavior. De novo firms, obviously, are start-up firms without any prior production experience. All of the diversifying firms that entered this industry had prior production experience in a related domestic industry. Specifically, diversifying firms had production experience in either cash-handling products, security products (safes and vaults), or computers. The foreign firms all had prior experience producing ATMs abroad prior to entering the U.S. market, although the degree to which they were selling other products in the U.S. market varied. (The question of whether prior U.S. market experience is a significant contributor to success is an interesting one that is not addressed in the Lane study.)

Docutel, a de novo entrant, was the dominant firm in the early years of the industry. However, as time went on, the de novo entrants lost market share to the diversifying entrants. In the middle to late 1970s, Diebold, an early diversifier became the dominant firm and held that position until the end of the sample period, 1986. The rise of Diebold coincided with the period when the overall size of the ATM market grew most rapidly. Eventually, in October

1986 when Docutel exited, all of the de novo entrants were a memory. Furthermore, the average life span for all of the de novo and diversifying firms that entered after the median entry date for their respective groups, except for the lone surviving firm (Concord), was less than 2.5 years. Whether these firms made or lost money cannot be determined from the available data. However, given that sunk costs play a significant role in this industry, it does not seem likely that such a brief visit would be profitable.

The big winners in this market in terms of market share were Diebold, NCR, and IBM – all early diversifying entrants. The experience that these firms had in safes and computers appeared to provide production advantages that increased market share and the likelihood of survival. Firm-wide production experience unrelated to the ATM industry did not confer an advantage either in terms of market share or survival. Furthermore, previous safe and computer experience with banks has greater advantages for survival and market share than nonbank-related safe and computer experience.

A somewhat similar story emerges from Mitchell's account of the medical diagnostic imaging industry (Mitchell 1989, 1991, 1993): one observes waves of new entrants (both de novo and diversifying entrants) linked with the introduction of new major technologies (nuclear imaging scanners, ultrasound equipment, etc.), mortality rates especially high among new comers, and incumbents regaining relatively quickly their dominant market shares. In fact, newcomer market share fell to 10% or less by 1988 in all of the subfields except for ultrasound. Even in ultrasound, where newcomers are a majority, their market share was less than 50% in 1988. In the subfields there have been waves of fluctuations in newcomer market share associated with newcomer product innovations. However, in all but the most recent upsurge of newcomer share in the ultrasound segment, incumbents recovered their market position.

Incumbents were also much more likely to survive (84%) in comparison to diversifying (44%) and de novo firms (29%) as of 1988. The method of exit also differs systematically between the firm types. 70% of the de novo firms that exit do so by closing down, whereas 70% of the diversifying or incumbent firms sell their business when they exit. Even the early newcomers to industries, one of the first three newcomers in each subfield, performed relatively poorly. Only two of 15 early newcomers still existed in 1990 and neither of these firms was in the top three in market share. This performance stands in sharp contrast to the early incumbent entrants – ten of 15 survived until 1990 and five of the 10 survivors were market-share leaders in 1988. In the medical diagnosis imaging industry it seems that de novo and diversifying firms' innovations contribute more to the evolution of the industry than to these firms' own success.

Other industries, however, suggest quite different patterns. In semiconductors (Dosi, 1984, and Malerba, 1985), some de novo entrants have indeed become the industry leaders while most diversifiers from seemingly related industries have failed. Likewise, in the computer-communication industry, the main actors have been new firms (Pelkey, 1993). Somewhat similarly, in photolithographic alignment equipment, incumbents have fared rather poorly, and each reconfiguration of product technologies has been associated with the emergence of new industry leaders (Henderson, 1988, 1993, Henderson & Clark, 1990).

At broader levels of description – often 2- to 4-digit industries – some intersectoral regularities in the process of entry, growth, and mortality appear to emerge. So, for example, entry, while being a very pervasive phenomenon, appears to be positively correlated with the number of incumbents and the growth of shipments in the industry and its variability, whereas there seems to be little correlation with industry profitability. Entry in concentrated industries seems to be lower in terms of number of firms but entrants tend to be bigger and have a higher life expectancy. The probability of survival of new small firms appear to be lower in capital-intensive and innovation-intensive industries. Hazard rates do not appear to be affected by scale economies in low-tech industries but they are in high-tech ones. The instantaneous effect of entry on output in terms of shares is generally low, but the medium-term one (of those surviving) is quite significant.[1] Moreover, hazard rates and post-entry performances seem to be significantly influenced by the nature of the entrant (whether de novo start-up or diversifying from other sectors). Finally, other more detailed traits of the entrants (such as educational attributes of the founders and the organizational strategies) seem to influence survival probabilities (Brüderl, Preisendorfer, & Ziegler, 1992).

What do we make of all this evidence on entry, performance, and mortality? How do we relate it to the cognitive and decision biases discussed in the previous section? And what is the importance of these biases for technical change and industrial dynamics?

VI. An evolutionary view of knowledge and biases in economic change

There are three major building blocks in our argument. First, cognitive biases are widespread attributes of adaptation and discovery in complex and evolving environments. Second, the nature of such biases – or, more generally of decision rules – can be inferred to a large extent from the characteristics of the knowledge upon which agents draw. This applies also to entry decisions. Third, at least with regard to entry, biases might often have a positive collective effect, in that they might be necessary to trigger exploratory behaviors, contribute to the development of commonly shared "technological paradigms," and ultimately foster the establishment and diffusion of new knowledge and new organizational forms.

Learning, competence traps, and biases

One of the remarkable features of most of the evidence discussed in sections II to IV is that biases are also prone to emerge in circumstances where the decision problem is sufficiently transparent to allow the unequivocal identification of "rational" decision procedures. A fortiori, one can expect them to emerge in more opaque and changing environments. Of course, an interpretation of such phenomena could be simply in terms of human fallibility, due, for example, to some underlying computational limitation, attention economizing, and inertial reinforcement of past behavioral responses. Far from denying that all these factors are at work, the line of inquiry that we want to pursue here is that, more fundamentally, these biases might be an unavoidable corollary of the ways agents form their interpretative models of the world and their behavioral routines in evolutionary environments.

It seems to us that a growing number of contributions from different camps – evolutionary economics, organization theory, cognitive psychology, and artificial intelligence sciences – are starting to converge in their analyses of learning processes in all circumstances when the environment continuously changes or in any case is sufficiently complex to entail some *competence gap* between the skills notionally required for decision and those "naturally" available to the agents (Heiner, 1983, 1988). It is clearly a perspective that goes back to the research program of Simon, Cyert, March, Nelson, and Winter on the nature and implications of "bounded rationality" and has been recently enriched by experimental evidence and computer-simulated models. To make a long story very short, this perspective implies a radical shift in the object of analysis: rather than focusing on the signals that the environment delivers to the unit of decision, it emphasizes the inner features of the response mechanism of the unit itself and the ways internal representations of the world are constructed.[2]

There are some quite general implications that come out of this perspective. First, facing an essential ambiguity in the relationships between events actions and outcomes,[3] agents are bound to search for appropriate categories that frame cognition and actions. Second, action rules often take the form of relatively event-invariant routines, which are nonetheless "robust," in the sense that they apply to entire classes of seemingly analogous problems. Third, adaptive learning, involving interrelated units of knowledge (that is, some sort of cognitive system), tend to lead to lock-in phenomena. For example, Dosi and Egidi (1991) discuss these learning dynamics in the simple case of the Rubik cube, and Dosi et al. (1994) show, in a simulated model of adaptive learning, the emergence of economic rules such as mark-up prices. Levinthal (1993) studies organizational adaptation on a "rugged landscape" (a selection environment characterized by interdependent and nonlinear contributions of various organizational attributes to the "fitness" of the organization). He shows the adaptive emergence of a few archetypes of organizations and behavioral patterns which, depending on the interdependence among traits, tend to lock organizational evolution even when the external environment changes in ways that are unfavorable to the existing setups. Marengo (1992) presents a model of co-evolution between organizational representations of the environment and its behavioral responses in a changing environment.

For our purposes here, what is important to notice is that by switching the analytical emphasis from agents as "information processors" to agents as "imperfect explorers" and "problem-solvers," it is easy to appreciate the widespread emergence of cognitive frames and decision routines. They are, in a sense, the inevitable outcome of imperfect adaptation to ever-changing and potentially surprising environments, even if they appear as "biases" whenever the environment is simple enough as to notionally allow more re-fined and orthodox rational decision procedures. All this applies, we sug-gest, to individuals and even more so, to organizations. But seeing organi-zations as problem solvers naturally leads to acknowledgement of the role of their internal knowledge, competences and "visions" as prime determi-nants of their behaviors. As Levinthal puts it

The ability of firms to evaluate and utilize outside knowledge is a function of their level of prior related knowledge. [The latter] confers an ability to recognize the value of new information, assimilate it, and apply it to commercial ends which . . . collec-tively constitute a firm's "absorptive capacity." (Levinthal, chapter 10, this volume)

Moreover, as emphasized in Cohen and Levinthal (1989, 1990), such absorp-tive capacity is path-dependent, given its cumulative nature and its coevolu-tion with expectation formation (see also Dosi, 1988a). From an evolutionary point of view, the development of specific problem-solving competence is a necessary condition for survival, but such competences are inevitably "lo-cal," reinforced by past history but not necessarily relevant today.[4] Indeed, our general conjecture is that it is precisely these features of knowledge that tend to produce many of the biases discussed above. For example, cumula-tive and idiosyncratic knowledge may easily imply an "inside view" of fu-ture outcomes. Previously successful problem-solving routines can be ex-pected to lead to overconfidence on their future applicability. And the Schumpeterian perception of the permanent existence of unexploited oppor-tunities of innovation are likely to result in "destrategizing" of behaviors – actions whose outcomes also depend on interacting firms are seen on the contrary, as part of a "game against nature" (Dosi & Marengo, 1993). Putting it more vividly, as a senior officer of Intel told one of us when asked about their strategies, ". . . strategies might be a concern for our competitors; we are just better than the others and our, only goal is to remain that way. . . ."

In summary, we suggest that decision biases are to a large extent the downside of competence building, Schumpeterian processes of discovery, and the implementation of cognitive frames and routines, which are used to make sense of and control imperfectly understood environments.

Knowledge bases, entry and post-entry performances

A "knowledge-centered" view of organizational behaviors also makes a nice contrast to "information-centered" or "incentive-centered" ones with respect to entry decisions. Drastically simplifying, an "incentive story" on the entry process would start with the identification of proxies for expected profitabilities, then make some assumptions based on the information to which would-be entrants have access (rational expectation being the most extreme one), and then make predictions on entry dynamics microfounded on rational and unbiased decision processes.[5] A similar modeling strategy can obviously be applied to, for example, the propensity to innovate of incumbents versus entrants (cf. Arrow; 1962, Reinganum, 1983, and the critical discussion in Henderson, 1993). The major point, in any case, is that some hypothesis of an unbiased rationality and a fine perception of the "objective" incentive structure allows the theorist to work, so to speak, "backward" from future outcomes to past entry decisions. Conversely, the "knowledge-centered" (or "evolutionary") story only needs to assume, on the incentive side, what elsewhere we have called *weak incentive compatibility* (Dosi & Marengo, 1993), that is, put very roughly, the perception (no matter how biased, self-condescending, etc.) that ". . . there are some unexploited opportunities out there and if I'm good I can derive some economic benefit from them. . . ."[6] Rather, the core of the story relates expected behaviors to some specific characteristics of the knowledge bases on which agents are likely to draw and to some internal characteristics of the agents themselves, including, of course, their problem-solving competences. In this perspective, the predictions of the theory rest on exercises of "mapping" between a) modal learning processes approximately shared by the entire relevant population of agents or some subsets of them; b) the institutional arrangements under which agents interact; and, c) their revealed performances.

A good deal of work has already been done along these lines, at both empirical and theoretical levels. In terms of empirical investigation, and related "appreciative theorizing," as Nelson and Winter would call it, one finds, for example, Pavitt's taxonomy of the sectoral patterns of generation and use of innovation (Pavitt, 1984). The basic exercise there is to identify the fundamental sources and procedures of innovative activities specific to each sector. For example does innovative knowledge draw heavily on scientific advances? Or is it much more informal and, for example, rely on tacit design skills? Is innovation mainly related to the introduction of new products or to the adoption and efficient use of inputs produced by someone else? etc. Next, it derives propositions on the characteristics of the innovating firms (whether they will be typically big or small; single-product firms or diversified ones; etc.).[7] Another exercise in a similar spirit is that by Dosi, Teece, and Winter (1992) and Teece et al. (1994) who derive predictions on the boundaries of the firm – conditional on their principal activities – from the nature of the competences which their principal activities imply.

From a dynamic point of view, several studies have analyzed the typical patterns of evolution of industries following the emergence and establishment of a "technological paradigm" (for example, Dosi, 1984) or "dominant designs" (for example, Utterback & Suarez, 1993), often identifying some invariant features along a "technological life cycle" (Gort & Klepper, 1982, Klepper, 1992). Moreover, continuities or breaks in the process of knowledge accumulation – yielding "competence-enhancing" or "competence-destroying" technical progress – have been found to be robust predictors of the relative performance of incumbents versus new entrants (Henderson & Clark, 1990, Henderson, 1993).

At the level of more formal theory, diverse *regimes of learning and market selection* – have been used to explain different patterns of evolution of industrial structures, including changes in industrial concentration, size distributions, turbulence in market shares, growth and death probabilities conditional on size and age (Winter, 1984, Dosi & Salvatore, 1992, Dosi et al. 1994). Basically, the exercise involves some stylized representation of the learning regime (formally captured by a particular stochastic process driving the access to new firm-specific technologies), the analysis of the collective outcomes of competitive interactions, and their comparison under different regimes.[8]

Our general conjecture – which unfortunately we are still unable to substantiate in this preliminary report – is that the characteristics of learning regimes are also major predictors of (i) the rates of entry into an industry, (ii) the relative frequencies of different types of entrants (new started versus diversifiers), and (iii) post-entry performances.

Among the discriminating features of each regime the evolutionary literature has identified 1) the richness of innovative opportunities, 2) the degrees of codifiability of knowledge (versus its "tacitness"), 3) its serendipity versus specificity to a particular activity; 4) the levels of "cumulativeness" of technological and organizational learning. We predict these factors to be discriminating also in terms of patterns of entry and performances. So, for example, one may derive propositions like the following. a) Other things being equal, the higher the perceived technological opportunities, the higher will be entry rates, irrespective of post-entry performances. b) Knowledge serendipity positively affects entry rates but not necessarily survival probabilities. c) The rates of failures of de novo entrants are a positive function of the cumulativeness of technological learning. (And indeed, there is a much longer list of empirically testable propositions that can be derived with respect to corporate entry and mortality from evolutionary theories of learning and market selection.)

The way these theories link up with the evidence discussed earlier on decision biases is that they fully acknowledge them and in a sense try to predict their importance and impact on the grounds of some generalizations regarding the patterns of knowledge accumulation, the sources of competitive advantage, and the modes of market interaction. So, for example, evolutionary ("knowledge-centered") theories of industrial dynamics are perfectly at ease with the finding that entrants – and, most likely, also incumbents – tend to take an "inside view" in their strategic choices; having recognized it, they will try to predict under what circumstances the outcomes will turn out to be, with a reasonable probability, brave self-fulfilling prophecies, or, conversely, miserable delusions. Not only that, decisions that turn out to be biased from the point of view of individual forecasting rationality might have, collectively, a positive evolutionary value.

Heroes and martyrs in the dynamics of collective exploration

Entry dynamics are most often analyzed in terms of their effects on competition (which are generally rather modest), the waste of resources associated with the frequent failures (which appear to be significant), or long-term impact of successful entrants on industrial efficiency (again, quite important). On the first two points, cf. Geroski (1991) and on the latter, Baldwin (1994).

Here, however, we want to look at entry from a complementary point of view, namely the collective effect of *both successes and failures* upon industrial learning. A suggestive way to put the question is, following March (1991), in terms of the fundamental dichotomy in evolutionary environments between "exploitation" and "exploration." Briefly, "exploitation" concerns adaptation to a given environment and efficiency (improvements made in reaction to a given set of perceived opportunities). Conversely, "exploration" implies the discovery of novelties; for example, in the domains of products, processes, or organizational forms.[9] It is straightforward that in a "knowledge-centered," evolutionary view such a dichotomy might easily emerge. First, the knowledge bases required for "exploitation" might be quite different from those most conducive to "exploration." Second, we have mentioned earlier that learning generally entails path-dependency and locks in phenomena into particular regions of a high-dimensional, and quite ill-defined, search space. For both reasons, the search for novelty – and in particular, those forms of novelty that are not contemplated by the competences embodied into incumbent organizations – requires "deviant" behaviors often associated with new start-ups.[10] As argued at greater length in Dosi (1990), the distribution of mutations might be heavily biased in favor of mistakes; hence, search efforts are likely to turn out to be, on average, disappointing economic failures for the individual actors who undertake them. Nonetheless, collectively, they might be a crucial ingredient of change. In this sense, *the biases* reviewed in sections II to IV – especially overconfidence, inside view thinking, and illusions of control – are essential to sustain exploration, even when the latter is not individually rewarding.[11]

There is another, related, way in which individual mistakes are an essential part of collective learning. This occurs whenever "mistakes" also contribute to increased collective knowledge. In that case they represent a sort of externality for the whole system.

These propositions are finding increasing corroboration in the evolutionary literature in the domains of both natural and social systems. The general requirement of variety generation is, indeed, a quite established proposition (in economics, see Metcalfe, 1991 and Saviotti, 1992).[12] And it is also well established that, apart from the most restrictive cases, it is hard to identify – for the theorist and a fortiori for the empirical agents – any equilibrium distribution of "exploratory" versus "exploitative" behaviors. More technically, only under highly demanding assumptions on the nature of the environment, it is theoretically fruitful to interpret such dynamics in terms of (mixed) evolutionary stable strategies (ESS). This is so for different reasons. First, innovation, almost by definition, involves uniqueness and surprise. As a consequence, it is misleading to assume that the strategic pattern learned in the past will necessarily be the optimal one for the future. Second, successful exploration inevitably adds to the menu of available strategies and thus deforms the shape of the "fitness landscape" in ways that may well be unpredictable to individual agents.[13]

An illustration of the collective role of "Schumpeterian sacrificial lambs" is presented in Silverberg, Dosi, and Orsenigo (1988). There, the diffusion of a new technology under the assumption that learning-by-using is partly appropriated by individual adopters and partly leaks out as an externality was studied. Under some parametrizations of the learning process, they showed that unequivocally superior innovations might diffuse *only* if there were overoptimistic entrepreneurs who pay the price of the initial exploration: their failure opens the way to the takeoff of the industry. Somewhat similarly, one of the properties of the model in Chiaromonte and Dosi (1992) is that a necessary condition for sustained aggregate growth is some degree of diversity of macroeconomic behaviors (related to, for example, the propensity to innovate and imitate).

This theoretical argument easily relates also with the empirical evidence on the multiple contributions of a growing number of actors (quite a few firms, but also public agencies, universities, etc.) to the rise of new technologies and new industries. At one level, the process can be described in some technology space in terms of emergence and establishment of "technological paradigms," "dominant designs," etc. However, at a more behavioral level, the dynamics are driven by a network of diverse agents who, via trial and error, increasingly develop a commonly shared knowledge base, recognizable modes of interactions, collective institutions, etc.[14] The construction of a socially distributed knowledge base inevitably rests also upon a multitude of failed entrepreneurial efforts, in addition to a few impressive jackpots hit by the most ingenious or the luckiest.[15] In spite of that, we suggest that the stubborn pursuits of unlikely courses of search, together with the other biases, might well be a wasteful, imperfect, but crucial ingredient.

VII. Some conclusions

We have emphasized from the start the preliminary nature of this work. Still, if our interpretation is correct, it promises to provide closer and more coherent links among four domains of empirical investigation that so far have proceeded along quite separate paths, namely:

1. the nature of cognitive and decision biases of individuals and organizations;

2. the regularities and patterns in the processes of innovation and diffusion (associated with the emergence of "technological paradigms" and "dominant technological trajectories");
3. the (related) social dynamics underlying the development of technological systems by communities of firms, technical societies, universities, etc.;
4. the patterns of corporate entry, exit, and industrial dynamics.[16]

In a nutshell, our argument is that various forms of cognitive and decision biases are likely to be *intrinsic ingredients* of technological development and corporate strategies, including those concerning start-ups of new firms and diversification.[17]

This view easily links up with several other contributions to this volume. For example, it is certainly consistent with Langlois' "cognitive" analysis of corporate competences and behaviors (chapter 5). Indeed, the "inside view" – with associated biases of "illusion of control," etc., discussed above – might be considered as essential corollary of cumulative and local learning, as analyzed by Levinthal (chapter 10). And it is also consistent with the *systematic* errors of oversight of potentially rich opportunities, stubborn pursuit of past commitments, or, conversely, overconfidence in novelty and change considered in chapter 3 by Garud, Nayyar and Shapira. Having recognized this sort of inevitability of errors – grounded in the very nature of individual and collective learning, and in the decision procedures of single humans and aggregates of them – there is little scope, in our view, to develop any sort of positive (or normative) theory able to accurately predict (or correct) these biases. However, we have suggested – largely in the form of a research agenda – that it might be possible to undertake taxonomic exercises mapping particular types of behavior into particular characteristics of the knowledge bases upon which agents draw. We have outlined an example, linked to research in progress, and concerning entry decisions. Of course, the first task is to show that entry patterns – as observed both cross-sectionally and longitudinally – are systematically affected by persistent decision biases. Second, we conjecture that the biases themselves (and, relatedly, post-entry performances) can be partly understood on the grounds of the *learning regimes* characteristic of specific industries and of their degrees of development (for example, whether a dominant technological paradigm has emerged or not). In a somewhat similar spirit, Bercovitz, Figuercido, and Teece, (chapter 13, this volume) attempt to map corporate strategies onto characteristics of the decision problems facing the firms and the competences that they embody.

In any case, are decision biases necessarily "bad"? At first glance, an affirmative answer is based on the intuition that biases tend to degrade the future performances of the decision-maker, compared – as economists would easily do – with an agent endowed with "rational expectations" and unbiased decision algorithms. However, in the final part of this work we have argued that what might hold for the individual agent (or organization) might not hold for the whole population of them, even for each of them over longer time spans.

In the evolutionary interpretation we proposed, mistakes – *and biases that make these mistakes more frequent* – are likely to be a necessary ingredient of the exploration of technological and organizational novelties. Paraphrasing David (1992), collective change might generally require heroes, herds and a lot of failures. And hence, biases and mistakes might be considered as a sort of powerful externality through which society learns. We want to emphasize that there is no teleological connotation in that statement (biases exist because they are collectively useful). Rather, this is primarily a conjecture on the collective dynamics of a particular form of social organization – call it "capitalism" – which, for reasons well beyond the scope of investigation of this paper, have been able to steadily generate these forms of "animal spirits." Indeed it might even be that, in one form or another,., the strongest individual biases survive both heightened incentives and organizational processes across different cultures because they might have to do with some basic features of human cognition. This is clearly the view of the evolutionary biologist Lionel Tiger, who discusses the evolutionaly useful role optimism likely played in our ancestors' ability to proceed with the hunt and find new territory in spite of numerous dangers. He argues that

Thinking rosy futures is as biological as sexual fantasy. Optimistically calculating the odds is as basic a human action as seeking food when hungry or craving fresh air in dump. Making deals with uncertainty marks us as plainly as bipedalism. This has very practical outcomes. It is relatively easy to cater to and exploit this "psychological sweet tooth." I believe that optimism, not religion, is the opiate of the people. Religion is only one expression of the optimistic impulse. As well, exploitation based on optimism occurs in a wealth of places, not only religious ones; it occurs as much in betting shops as cathedrals and stock exchanges as confessionals." (Tiger, 1979, p. 35)

However, irrespective of whether one entirely subscribes to this general anthropological view, and sticking nearer home, major implications follow from the foregoing argument, in terms of both theory and normative prescriptions.

To end provocatively on the latter: are we sure that we want to teach any sort of "rational" decision making in business schools? How can one avoid the risk that less-biased assessment of any one decision environment yields more conservatism and slower collective change? Should one not emphasize the heuristics of knowledge accumulation capable of increasing the probability that biased gambles turn out to be self-fulfilling prophecies, rather than improving the "quality" of decisions as such?

Acknowledgments

Support to this research, at different stages, by the Center for Research in Management, U.C. Berkeley; the Italian National Research Council (CNR); the Italian Ministry of Universities and Research ("MURST 40%"), International Institute of Applied System Analysis (IIASA), Laxenburg, Austria;

and the Huntsman and Jones Centers at the Wharton School, University of Pennsylvania is gratefully acknowledged. This version benefited from the comments of the participants and organizers of the conference on "Technological Oversights and Foresights," L. N. Stern School of Business, New York University, March 1994, in particular, Raghn Garud, Praaven Nayyar, Zur Shapira, and Jim Utterback. This work is partly based on ongoing research with John Baldwin, Analytical Studies, Statistics Canada.

Notes

1   On all these properties, see Dunne, Roberts, and Samuelson (1988), Baldwin and Gorecki (1990, 1991), Cable and Schwalbach (1991), Bianco and Sestito (1992), Aldrich and Auster (1986), Acs and Audretsch (1990, 1991), Phillips and Kirchoff (1989), Audretsch and Mahmood (1991), Mahmood (1992), Geroski and Schwalbach (1991), Baldwin (1994), Baldwin and Rafiquzzaman (1994).

2   Holland (1975), Holland et al. (1986), Dosi and Egidi (1991), Schrader, Riggs, and Smith (1993), March (1988), Dosi and Marengo (1993), Marengo (1992), Levinthal (1994), among others.

3   On the notion of ambiguity as distinct from uncertainty, see Einhorn and Hogarth (1985), March (1988), Marengo (1992), Schrader, Riggs and Smith (1993).

4   On the notion of organizational competence and its characteristics, see Dosi, Teece, and Winter (1992), Teece et al. (1994), Dosi and Marengo (1993), Teece, Pisano, and Schuen (1992).

5   More sophisticated variants of this same story would also allow for incomplete information on one's own ability relative to the other competititors, as in Jovanovic (1982).

6   Of course there are cases in which not even such weak incentive requirements are fulfilled. Think, for example, of many features of the past Soviet innovation system, or think of circumstances with zero appropriability of innovation, such as long-time, seed-related agricultural innovations. (See Dosi (1988a) for more on appropriability issues.

7   For further evidence on this point, see Malerba and Orsenigo (1995a,b,c).

8   A discussion of diverse corporate behaviors under different technological regimes in evolutionary models of industrial change is in Malerba and Orsenigo (1995b,c).

9   The trade-offs and dichotomies between "exploration" and "exploitation" also carry over to a more aggregate level, in terms of average or modal behaviors of the population of firms embedded in particular national institutions, collective competencies, perceived opportunities, and constraints. For discussions at this broader level of notions like "dynamic" or "Schumpeterian" efficiency as opposed to "static" or "allocative" efficiency, cf. Klein (1977) and Dosi (1988b).

10 It is a matter of debate to what degrees incumbents are able to internalize search for radical novelties and endogenize, in a biological metaphor, the generation of "mutations." It has been suggested, for example, that the institutional organization of markets influences such an ability. In particular, it is claimed that "market-based" financial systems, such as those of most Anglo-Saxon countries, induce strong pressures towards short-termism and "exploitation," thus relying much more on new firms for exploratory activities. Conversely, "bank-based"

systems – such as Japan or Germany – might confer on incumbents much greater room for time-consuming and uncertain attempts to search for new trajectories of learning. For discussions, cf. Zysman (1994), Dosi (1990), Aoki and Dosi (1991).

11 Note that this argument is quite distinct from the hypothesis that "explorers" are rational and risk-loving. Our point is that, irrespective of whether they are risk-lovers, they certainly have also to be biased in their decision making in order to do what they do. Or, putting it in another way, given their risk preference, if they were endowed with "rational expectations" about the future, they would do otherwise.

12 See also Allen (1988) and Allen and McGlade (1988) for a suggestive model of the dynamics of fishery driven by the interaction between "Cartesian" fishermen ("exploiters") and "stochasts" ("explorers").

13 Interrelatedness of the contribution to "fitness" by different traits, coevolutionary effects and nonlinearities are clearly sufficient to induce unpredictability. (See Levinthal (1993, 1994) and Dosi and Metcalfe (1991).

14 For analyses from different angles see Rip (1992), Rip, Misa, and Schot (1994), Metcalfe and Boden (1991), Garud and Rappa (1994), Garud and Van De Ven (1989), Callon (1993), Nelson (1994), Appod, Harrison, and Kelley (1993), Miller and Blais (1992). In general, the view presented here is highly complementary with the idea of coevolution between cognitive traits, artifacts, and routines outlined in Garud and Rappa (1994) and Garud and Ahlstrom (1995).

15 This statement is in principle consistent with formal investigation of "distributed learning models" (cf., for example, Huberman and Hogg, 1988, Huberman and Glance, 1992) as well as with the experimental evidence on cooperative learning in new problem-solving activities (some suggestive results are in Egidi, 1993).

16 The diversity between these fields and their relatively low degrees of communication with each other also motivates the choice of providing a rather extensive bibliography at the end of this chapter, which might help the reader in unfamiliar territories.

17 Throughout the text, as a first approximation, we took a rather naive and anthropomorphic view of "organizational decisions" (and related biases). In fact, our approach does not have any difficulty in accommodating a more complex view whereby organizational behavior is also the outcome of processes of political negotiation within the organization itself, grounded in the specific pieces of knowledge embodied in various "experts" (e.g. the "engineer," the marketing person, etc.) (see Lane et al., 1995). Also "experts," our argument would go, are likely to display the biases discussed above. In fact, insofar as these experts share the knowledge of broader communities (software specialists, copyright lawyers, chemical engineers, etc.) they might partly curb the "inside view" associated with each individual firm, but at the expense of bringing in the "inside view" dominant in the expert community to which they belong.

References and bibliography

Acs, Z. J. and Audretsch, D. B. (1990). *Innovation and the Small Firm.* Cambridge, MA: MIT Press.

Acs, Z. J. and Audretsch, D. B. (1991). New-firm startups, technology and macroeconomic fluctuations. Discussion Paper, FS IV 91–17, Wissenschaftszentrum, Berlin.

Aldrich, H. and Auster, E. (1986). Even giants started as dwarves. *Research in Organizational Behaviour*, 8.

Aldrich, H. and Fiol, C. M. (1992). Fools rush in? The institutional context of industrial creation. Working paper.

Allen, P. M. (1988). Evolution, innovation and economics. In Dosi et al. (eds.), *Technical Change and Economic Theory*. London: Pinter, and New York: Columbia University Press.

Allen, P. M. (1991). Modeling evolution and creativity in complex systems. *World Futures*, 34, 105–123.

Allen, P. M. and McGlade, J. M. (1988). Dynamics of discovery and exploitation: The case of the Scotian Shelf groundfish fisheries. *Canadian Journal of Fishery and Aquatic Sciences*.

Aoki, M. and Dosi, G. (1991). Corporate organization, finance and innovation. In V. Zamagni (ed.), *Finance and the Entreprise*. San Diego: Academic Press.

Appod, S. J., Harrison, B. and Kelley, M. R. (1993). Spacially distributed and proximate inter-organizational networks, agglomeration and technological performance in U.S. manufacturing. Paper delivered to the annual meeting of the Association of American Geographers, Atlanta, April.

Argote, L., Seabright, M. A. and Dyer, L. (1986) Individual versus group: Use of base-rate and individuating information. *Organizational Behavior and Individual Decision Processes*, 38, 65–75.

Arnold, J. III, (1986). Assessing capital risk: You can't be too conservative. *Harvard Business Review*, 113–121.

Arrow, K. J. (1962). Economic welfare and the allocation of resources for inventions. In R. Nelson (ed.), *The Rate and Direction of Inventive Activity: Economic and Social Factors*. Princeton, NJ: Princeton University Press.

Audretsch, D. B. and Mahmood, T. (1991). The rate of hazard confronting new firms and plants in U.S. manufacturing. Discussion Paper, FS IV 91–7, Wissenschaftszentrum, Berlin.

Baldwin, J. R. (1994). *The Dynamic of Industrial Competition, A North American Perspective*. New York: Cambridge University Press.

Baldwin, J. R. and Goreki, P. K. (1990). *Structural Change and the Adjustment Process*. A study prepared for Statistics Canada and the Economic Council of Canada, 1990.

Baldwin, J. R. and Goreki, P. K. (1991). Firms entry and exit in the Canadian Manufacturing Sector. *Canadian Journal of Economics*, 24, 300–323.

Baldwin, J. R. and Rafiquzzaman, M. (1994). Selection versus learning as determinants of post-entry performance. Ottawa: Statistics Canada, Working Paper.

Bateman, T. and Zietham, C. (1989). The psychological context of strategic decisions: A test of relevance to practitioners. *Strategic Management Journal*, 10, 587–92.

Bazerman, M. H., Giuliano, T. and Appleman, A. (1984). Escalation in individual and goup decision making. *Organizational Behavior and Human Decision Processes*, 33, 141–152.

Bianco, M. and Sestito, P. (1992). Entry, growth and market structure. A preliminary analysis of the Italian case. Presented at the International Conference on "Birth and Start-up of Small Firms," Milano.

Brüderl, J., Preisendorfer, P. and Ziegler, R. (1992). Survival changes of newly found-ed business organizations. *American Sociological Review*, 57, 227–242.

Cable, J. and Schwalbach, J. (1991). International comparison of entry and exit. In P. Geroski and J. Schwalbach (eds.), *Entry and Market Contestability: An International Comparison*. Basil Oxford: Blackwell, pp. 257–281.

Callon, M. (1993). Variety and irreversibility in network of technique conception and adoption. In D. Foray and C. Freeman (eds.), *Technology and the Wealth of Nations*. London: Pinter.

Carroll, G. R. and Swaminathan, A. (1992). The organizational ecology of strategic groups in the american brewing industry from 1975 to 1990. *ICC*, 1, 65–97.

Chiaromonte, F. and Dosi, G. (1992). The microfoundations of competitiveness and their macroeconomic implications. In D. Foray and C. Freeman (eds.), *Technology and the Wealth of Nations*, London: Pinter.

Cohen, W. and Levinthal, D. (1989). Innovation and learning: The two faces of R&D. *Economic Journal*, 99, 657–674.

Cohen, W. and Levinthal, D. (1990). Absorptive capacity: A new perspective on learning and innovation. *Administrative Science Quarterly*, 35, 128–152.

David, P. (1992). Heroes, herds and hysteresis in technological history. Thomas Edison and the battle of the systems reconsidered. *Industrial and Corporate Change*, I.

Dosi, G., (1984). *Technical Change and Industrial Transformation, The Theory and an Application to the Semiconductor Industry*. London: Macmillan.

Dosi, G., (1988a). Sources, procedures and microeconomic effect of innovation. *Journal of Economic Literature*, 26, 1120–1171.

Dosi, G., (1988b). Institutions and markets in a dynamic world. *The Manchester School*.

Dosi, G., (1990). Finance, innovation and industrial change. *Journal of Economic Behavior and Organization*.

Dosi, G. and Egidi, M. (1991). Substantive and procedural uncertainty. An exploration of economic behaviors in complex and changing environment. *Journal of Evolutionary Economics*, 1, pp. 145–168.

Dosi, G., Freeman, C., Nelson, R., Silverberg, G., Soete, L. (eds.) (1988). *Technical Change and Economic Theory*, London: Pinter, and New York, Columbia University Press.

Dosi, G. and Malerba, F. (eds.) (1995). *Organization and Strategy in the Evolution of the Entreprise*. London: Macmillan.

Dosi, G. and Marengo, L. (1993). Some elements of an evolutionary theory of organizational competences. In W. England (ed.), *Evolutionary Concepts in Contemporary Economics*. Ann Arbor: University Michigan Press.

Dosi, G., Marengo, L., Bassanini, A., and Valente, M. (1994). *Norms as Emergent Properties of Adaptive Learning The Case of Economic Routines*. Laxemburg, Austria: IIASA. Working Paper.

Dosi, G., Marsili, O., Orsenigo, L. and Salvatore, R. (1995). Learning, Market Selection and the Evolution of Industrial Structures. *Small Business Economics*, 7, 1–26.

Dosi, G. and S. Metcalfe (1991). On some notions of irreversibility in economics. In P. P. Saviotti and S. Metcalfe (eds.), *Evolutionary Economics*. London: Harwood Academic Press.

Dosi, G. and Salvatore, R. (1992). The structure of industrial production and the boundaries between organization and markets. In A. Scott and M. Stolper (eds.), *Pathways to Regional Development*. Boulder, CO: Westview Press.

Dosi, G., Teece, D. J. and Winter, S. (1992). Towards a theory of corporate coherence: Preliminary remarks. In G. Dosi, R. Giannetti, and P. A. Toninelli (eds.), *Technology and Enterprises in a Historical Perspective*. New York: Oxford University Press.

Dunne, T., Roberts, M. J. and Samuelson, L. (1988). Patterns of firm entry and exit in U.S. manufacturing Industries. *Rand Journal of Economics*, 19, 495–515.

Egidi, M. (1993). Routines, hierarchies of problems, procedural behaviours: Some evidence from experiments. Laxemburg, Austria, IIASA, Working Paper.

Einhorn, H. J. and Hogarth, R. M. (1985). Ambiguity and Uncertainty in Probabilistic Inference. *Psychological Review*, 86, 433–461.

Foray, D. and Freeman, C. (eds.). (1993). *Technology and the Wealth of Nations*. London: Pinter.

Fox, F. V. and Staw, B. (1979). The trapped administrator: Effects of job insecurity and policy resistance upon commitment to a course of action. *Administrative Science Quarterly*, 40.

Freeman, C. (1982). *The Economics of Industrial Innovation*. London: Pinter,.

Garud, R. and Ahlstrom, D. (1995). Technology assessment: A socio-cognitive perspective. New York: New York University, L. N. Stern School of Business, Working Paper.

Garud, R. and Nayyar, P. R. (1994). Transformative capacity: Continual structuring by intertemporal technology transfer. *Strategic Management Journal*, 15, 365–385.

Garud, R. and Rappa, M. (1994). A socio-cognitive model of technology evolution: The case of cochlear implants. *Organization Science*, 5, 344–362.

Garud, R. and Van de Ven, A. H. (1989). Development of the cochlear implant program at 3M Corporation. *Strategic Management Research* Center, University of Minnesota, Minneapolis.

Garud, R. and Van de Ven, A. H. (1992). An empirical evaluation of the internal corporate venturing process. *Stategic Management Journal*, 13, 93–109.

Geroski P., (1991). Innovation and the Sectoral Sources of UK Productivity Growth. *Economic Journal*, 101, 1438–1451.

Geroski, P. and Schwalbach, J. (eds.). (1991). *Entry and Market Contestability: An International Comparison*. Oxford: Basil Blackwell.

Gort, M. and Klepper, S. (1982). Time paths in the diffusion of product innovation. *The Economic Journal*.

Hannan, M. T. and Carroll, G. R. (1991). *Dynamics of Organizational Populations: Density, Competition and Legitimation*. New York: Oxford University Press.

Hannan, M. T. and Freeman, J. (1989). *Organizational Ecology*. Cambridge, MA: Harvard University Press.

Heiner, R. (1983). On the origin of predictable behavior. *American Economic Review*.

Heiner, R. (1988). "Imperfect decisions, routinized behavior and inertial change. In Dosi et al. (1988).

Henderson, R. M. (1988). The failure of established firms in the face of technical change: A study of photolothographic alignment equipment. Dept. of Business Economics, Harvard University, Cambridge, MA.

Henderson, R. M. (1993). Underinvestment and incompetence as responses to radical innovation: Evidence from the photolithographics alignment equipment industry. *Rand Journal of Economics*, 24, 2.

Henderson, R. M. and Clarck, K. B. (1990). Architectural innovation: The reconfiguration of existing product technologies and the failure of established firms. *Administrative Science Quarterly*, 35, 9–30.

Holland, (1975). *Adaptation in Natural and Artificial Systems*. Ann Arbor: University of Michigan Press.

Holland, K. Holyook, R. Nesbatt and Thagard, P. (1986). *Induction: Processes of Inference, Learning and Discovery*. Cambridge, MA: MIT Press.

Huberman, B. A. and Glance, N. S. (1992). Diversity and collective action. Palo Alto: Xerox Palo Alto Research Center, Working Paper.

Huberman, B. A. and Hogg, T. (1988). The behavior of computational ecologies. Palo Alto: Xerox Palo Alto Research Center, Working Paper.

Janis, I. L., (1982). *Groupthink*. 2nd Edition. Boston: Houghton Mifflin.

Jovanovic, B. (1982). Selection and evolution of industry. *Econometrica*, 50, 649–670.

Kahneman, D. and Lovallo, D. (1993). Timid choice and bold forecast: A cognitive perspective on risk taking. *Management Science*, 39, 1.

Kahneman, D. and Tversky, A. (1973). On the psychology of prediction. *Psychological Review*, 80, 237–251.

Kahneman, D. and Tversky, A. (1979). Intuitive prediction: Biases and corrective procedures. *TIMS Studies in Management Sciences*, 12, 313–327.

Kahneman, D. and Tversky, A. (1986). Rational choice and the framing of decisions. *Journal of Business*, 59, S251–S278.

Klein, B. (1977). *Dynamic Competition*. Cambridge, MA: Harvard University Press.

Klepper, S. (1992). Entry, exit and innovation over the product life cycle: The dynamics of first mover advantages, declining product innovation and market failure. Paper presented at the International J. A. Schumpeter Society, Kyoto, August.

Klepper, S. and Miller, J. H. (1994). Entry, exit and shakeouts in the United States in new manufactured products. Carnegie-Mellon University, Working Paper.

Lane, S. J. (1989). *Entry and Industry Evolution in the ATM Manufacturers Market*. Stanford University, UMI.

Lane, D., Malerba, F. and Maxwell, R. (1995). Choice and action. *Journal of Evolutionary Economics*. forthcoming.

Levinthal, D. (1992). Surviving Schumpeterian environments: An evolutionary perspective. *Industrial and Corporate Change*, 1, 427–443.

Levinthal, D. A. (1993). Learning and Schumpeterian Dynamics. Philadelphia: The Warton School, Working Paper.

Levinthel, D.A. and March, J. G. (1994). The myopia of learning. *Strategic Management Journal*.

Lovallo, D. (1996a). From Individual Biases to Organizational Errors. In G. Dosi and F. Malerba (eds.), *Organization and Strategy in the Evolution of the Enterprise*. London: Macmillan.

Lovallo, D. (1996b). *Entry Decision: A Psychological Perspective*. Unpublished doctoral dissertation, University of California at Berkeley.

Mahmood, T. (1992). Does the hazard rate of new plants vary between low and high-tech industries? *Small Business Economics*, 4, 201–209.

Malerba, F. (1985). *The Semiconductor Business*. London: Pinter .

Malerba, F. and Orsenigo, L. (1993). Technological regimes and firm behaviour. *Industrial and Corporate Change*, 2(1), 74–89.

Malerba, F. and Orsenigo, L. (1995a). On new innovators and ex-innovators. Laxemburg, Austria, IIASA, working paper.

Malerba, F. and Orsenigo, L. (1995b). Schumpeterian patterns of innovation. *Cambridge Journal of Economics*.

Malerba, F. and Orsenigo, L. (1995c). Schumpeterian patterns of innovation are technology-specific. *Research Policy*.

March, J. (1988). *Decision and Organizations*. Oxford: Blackwell.

March, J. (1991). Exploration and exploitation in organizational learning. *Organization Science*, 2, 71–87.

March, J. and Olsen, J. P. (1976). Organizational learning and the ambiguity of the past. In J. G. March and J. P. Olsen (eds.), *Ambiguity and Choice in Organizations*. Bergen: Universitetsforlaget.

March, J. and Shapira, Z. (1987). Managerial perspectives on risk and risk taking. *Management Science*, 33, 1404–1418.

Marengo, L. (1992). Structure, competence and learning in an adaptive model of the firm. *Papers on Economic and Evolution*, edited by the European Study Group for Evolutionary Economics, Freiburg, no. 9203.

Merrow, E. et al. (1981). *Understanding Cost Growth and Performance Shortfalls in Pioneer Plants*. Santa Barbara, CA: Rand Corporation.

Metcalfe, S. (1991). *Variety, structure and change: An economic perspective on the competitive process*. Manchester: University of Manchester, Discussion Paper.

Metcalfe, S. and Bodem, M. (1991). Innovation strategy and the epistemic connection: An essay on the growth of technological knowledge. *Journal of Scientific & Industrial Research*, 50, 707–717.

Miller, R. and Blais, R. A. (1992). Configuration of innovation: Predictable and maverick modes. *Technology Analysis & Strategic Management*, 4, 4, 363–386.

Mitchell, W. (1989). Whether and when? Probably and timing of incumbents entry into emerging industrial subfields. *Administrative Science Quarterly*, 34, 208–230.

Mitchell, W. (1991). Dual clocks: Entry order influences on incumbent and newcomer market share and survival when socialized assets retain their value. *Strategic Management Journal*, 12, 85–100.

Mitchell, W. (1993). Invasion of the subfield snatchers: Newcomer and incumbent entry and success in new technical subfields of the medical diagnostic imaging equipment industry. Working Paper: University of Michigan.

Nelson, R. R. (1994). The co-evolution of technology, industrial structure and supporting institutions. *Industrial and Corporate Change*, 3, 1.

Nelson, R. R. and Winter, S. G. (1982). *An Evolutionary Theory of Economic Change*, Cambridge MA: The Belknap Press of Harvard University Press.

Pavitt, K. (1984). Sectoral patterns of innovation: Towards a taxonomy and a theory. *Research Policy*, 13, 343–373.

Pelkey, J. (1993). *Economic Growth and Technological Innovation: The Computer Communications Market Structure 1968–1988*. Santa Fe: SFI.

Philips, B. D. and Kirchoff, B. A. (1989). Formation, growth and survival: Small firm dynamic in the U.S. economy. *Small Business Economics*, 1, 65–74.

Reid, G. C. (1991). Staying in business. *International Journal of Industrial Organization*, 9.

Reinganum, J. F. (1983). Uncertain innovation and the persistence of monopoly. *AER*, 73, 741–748.

Reinganum, J. F. (1984). Uncertain innovation and the persistence of monopoly: re-play. *AER*, 74, 243–245.

Rip, A., (1992). *Cognitive Approaches to Technology Policy*. University of Twente, The Netherlands.

Rip, A., Misa, T. and Schot, J. (1994). *Managing Technology in Society. New Forms for the Control of Technology*. University of Twente, The Netherlands.

Ross, J. and Staw, B. (1986). EXPO 86: An escalation prototype. *Administrative Science Quarterly*, 31 p. 274—297.

Saviotti, P. P. (1992). Variety, economic and technological development. Presented at the 1992 Conference of the International Schumpeter Society.

Saviotti, P. P. and Metcalfe, S. (eds.). (1991). *Evolutionary Economics*. London: Harwood Academic Press.

Schoemaker, P. J. H. and Marais, M. L. (1995). Technological innovation and firm inertia. In G. Dosi and F. Malerba (eds.), *Organization and Strategy in the Evolution of the Enterprise*. London: Macmillan.

Schrader, S., Riggs, W. and Smith, R. P. (1993). Choice over uncertainty and ambiguity in technical problem solving. *Journal of Engineering and Technology Management*, 10, 73–99.

Shafir, E. and Tversky, A. (1992). Thinking through uncertainty: Non-consequential reasoning and choice. *Cognitive Psychology*, 24, 449–474.

Silvelberg, G., Dosi, G., and Orsenigo, L. (1988). Innovation, diversity and diffusion. A self-organization model. *The Economic Journal*, 98, 1032–1054.

Simon, H. A. (1982). *Models of Bounded Rationality*, vols. 1 and 2. Cambridge, MA: MIT Press.

Sterman, J. D. (1989). Modeling managerial behavior: Misperceptions of feedback in a dynamic decision making experiment. *Management Science*, 35, 321–338.

Teece, D. J., Pisano, G. and Schuen, A. (1992). Dynamic capabilities and strategic management. Center for Research in Management, University of California at Berkeley, CCC Working Paper.

Teece, D. J., Rumelt, R., Dosi, G., and Winter, S. (1994). Understanding corporate coherence: Theory and evidence. *Journal of Economic Behavior and Organization*.

Thaler, R. H. (1992). *The Winner's Curse: Paradoxes and Anomalies of Economic Life*. New York: The Free Press.

Tiger, L. (1979). *Optimism: The Biology of Hope*. New York: Simon and Schuster.

Utterback, J. M. (1994). *Mastering the Dynamics of Innovation*. Cambridge, MA: Harvard Business School Press.

Utterbark, J. and Suarez, F. (1993). Innovation, competition and market structure. *Research Policy*.

Winter, S. G. (1984). Schumpeterian competition in alternative technological regimes. *Journal of Economic Behavior and Organization*, 5, 287–320.

Zysman, J. (1994). How institutions create historically rooted trakectories of growth. *Industrial and Corporate Change*, 3, 1.

Section III
Tailoring fits

5   Cognition and capabilities: Opportunities seized and missed in the history of the computer industry

Richard N. Langlois

1. Introduction

That organizations, broadly defined,[1] are cognitive structures is an observation at once trivial and profoundly complex. It is trivial because, at some level, it is a commonplace that organizations can (or at least should) learn, in something quite analogous to the sense in which people learn. That organizations "process information" is a staple of organizational-behavior theory.[2] When examined in detail, however, the identification of organizations with cognitive structures raises more questions than it answers. In exactly what sense does an organization learn or perceive? This chapter will not attempt to resolve all these complexities; ultimately, it may not even stray far from the trivial. But it will attempt to frame the issue of organizational cognition in a general way and to apply that idea to the problem of "organizational perception," that is, to the problem of why organizations seize, or fail to seize, profitable opportunities.

The chapter proceeds as follows. Relying on some perhaps idiosyncratic sources in cybernetics, the theory of information, and cognitive theory, Section 2 sets forth a general – indeed, rather abstract – picture of knowledge, information, and learning. Section 3 applies that picture to the issue of organizational perception: Why are some organizations, again broadly defined, able to notice and seize opportunities for profitable innovation while other organizations are not? Drawing on the evolutionary theory of economic capabilities, that section goes on to work up a typology of the causes of innovative success and failure. Section 4 canvasses the history of the computer industry for examples to fit the typology. And Section 5 attempts to apply what went before to the much-discussed issue of (in Alfred Chandler's terms) personal capitalism versus managerial capitalism as engines of innovation.

2. Knowledge and structure

It is conventional to see the distinction between knowledge and information as a distinction between a stock and a flow. This is certainly unobjectionable, and maybe even useful, as long as we don't take the metaphor too seriously. Knowledge is not a stock in the same sense that oil in a tank is a stock, something modified in a purely quantitatively way by the inflow or outflow of info-fluid[3] (Langlois 1983, pp. 586–387). Knowledge is about structure. As the late Kenneth Boulding put it

We cannot regard knowledge as simply the accumulation of information in a stock-pile, even though all messages that are received by the brain may leave some sort of deposit there. Knowledge must itself be regarded as a structure, a very complex and frequently quite loose pattern, . . . with its parts connected in various ways by ties of varying degrees of strength. Messages are continually shot into this structure; some of them pass right through its interstices . . . without effecting any perceptible change in it. Sometimes messages "stick" to the structure and become part of it. . . . Occasionally, however, a message which is inconsistent with the basic pattern of the mental structure, but which is of a nature that it cannot be disbelieved hits the structure, which is then forced to undergo a complete reorganization. (Boulding 1955, pp. 103–104, quoted in Machlup, 1983, p. 643n)

In order for a message to "stick" to the structure – or, more importantly, for the message to modify the structure in a useful way – that message must be meaningful to the receiving system. The message must somehow "fit." As Kenneth Arrow (1974, chapter 2) notes, individuals and organizations have information structures that are in the nature of message decoders. To understand messages in Chinese, for example, one needs to have learned Chinese. Choosing an information structure, like learning a language, thus involves an investment that is typically costly in both money and time. To put it another way, information structures develop or evolve slowly and cannot be recreated or "reengineered" quickly or costlessly.

The association of knowledge with structure is intuitively appealing, if still rather vague. What makes a structure "knowledge"? At some level, a structure constitutes knowledge if that structure is ordered in a way that produces results.[4] Think of genetics. We can say that DNA is a knowledge structure because it is an orderly arrangement that "knows how" to do something, namely how, in conjunction with an existing organism, to generate a new organism. That new organism in turn is also an ordered structure that does something, namely survive the evolutionary process. Thus knowledge is a pudding whose proof is in the eating, even if modern philosophers of science don't agree about how much the eating proves.

Donald MacKay thinks of a system's structure as defining "conditional states of readiness" on which a signal operates. It is the overall configuration that determines the meaning – and the meaningfulness – of a message. "It isn't until we consider the range of other states of readiness, that *might have been considered but weren't*, that the notion of meaning comes into its own. A change in meaning implies a different selection from the range of states of readiness. A meaningless message is one that makes no selection from the range. An ambiguous message is one that could make more than one selection" (MacKay, 1969, p. 24, emphasis original). MacKay offers the metaphor of a railroad switching yard in which the configuration of tracks and switches stands ready to direct the trains passing through it. By sending the right electronic signal (or, in older yards, by inserting the correct key in a switch-box) one can rearrange the configuration of tracks. The meaning-fulness of a message thus depends on its form – on the shape of the key. And that meaning consists in the change the message effects in the arrange-ment of the yard, the selection it makes from the set of all possible configu-rations.

But where does the structure of knowledge – the railroad switching yard – come from? How does it form, and how is it modified by experience? In a work only now being appreciated by cognitive psychologists[5] (Weimer, 1982; Edelman, 1987), F. A. Hayek (1952) put forward a rich and sophisticat-ed theory of mind as structure. In this theory, "that which we call knowl-edge is primarily a system of rules of action assisted and modified by rules indicating equivalences or differences of various combinations of stimuli" (Hayek, 1978, p. 41).

To survive, an organism must respond appropriately to the stimuli – the information – provided by its environment. Both phylogenetically and on-togenetically, organisms, in Hayek's view, use the pattern of stimuli to which they are subjected to create complex interpretive or classificatory sys-tems that help them take appropriate action in response to future stimuli. The neural system of the brain (and, more generally, the nervous system as a whole) creates, with experience, a semipermanent structure or "map" that guides action – not only in response to new stimuli but also through processes of internal reclassification and recombination that lead to innova-tion.

Consider, with Hayek, an organism as *tabula rasa*.[6] As the organism re-ceives stimuli, it sorts those stimuli into classes, and thus begins to form a structure for interpreting future stimuli. Initially, each stimulus has a large effect on the categories the organism forms and on the actions it takes. With increasing stimuli, however, interconnections or "linkages" begin to form among the categories.[7] As stimuli build up, the accumulation of stimuli from the past will come to dominate new stimuli.

It is a corollary of this steadily increasing influence of the preexisting excitory state that the main significance of any new stimulus will be that it will alter the general disposition for responding in particular ways to further stimuli, and that less and less of its effect will consist in producing a specific response. In other words, a greater and greater part of the effects of impulses set up by any new stimuli will go to create a "set" controlling future responses, and a smaller part directly to influenc-ing current responses. As we reach higher levels, the classification of the impulses becomes thus less specific to a particular function, and more general in the sense that it will help to *create a disposition to a certain range of responses to an ever-growing variety of stimuli.* (Hayek, 1952, p. 113, emphasis added)

Thus new messages do not merely make selections among existing conditional states of readiness: They also help create and slowly modify those states.

The linkages in this "apparatus of orientation" (Hayek, 1952, p. 113) arrange themselves in hierarchical fashion so that higher-level centers classify stimuli sent from lower levels.

We should have to think of the whole system of connexions as consisting of many vertically superimposed sub-systems which in some respects may operate independently of each other. Every sub-system of this kind will constitute a partial map of the environment, and the maps formed at the lower levels will serve for the guidance of merely a limited range of responses, and at the same time act as filters or preselectors for the impulses sent to the higher centres, for which, in turn, the maps of the lower levels constitute a part of the environment. (p. 111)

What this suggests is that conceptual thought is not fundamentally different from thought processes at "preconscious" or "unconscious" levels. Abstract thought is also a matter of classification and reclassification of experience.

The map is in effect a complex modular construction set that allows the organism to generate novelty through recombination.

It will, as a result of its own operations, continuously change its structure and alter the range of operation of which it is capable. It will scarcely ever respond twice in exactly the same manner to the same external conditions. And it will as a result of "experience" acquire the capacity of performing entirely new actions. Its actions will appear self-adaptive and purposive, and it will in general be "active" in the sense that what at any given moment will determine the character of its operation will be the pre-exisitng state of its internal processes as much as the external influences acting upon it. (p. 122)

At the same time, however, the dependence of the cognitive map on past experience and the categories created from it implies limitations on the organism's ability to anticipate and respond appropriately to entirely new stimuli.

Perception is thus always an interpretation, the placing of something into one or several classes of objects. An event of an entirely new kind which has never occurred before, and which sets up impulses which arrive in the brain for the first time, could not be perceived at all. All we can perceive of external events are therefore only such properties of these events as they possess as members of classes which have formed past "linkages." The qualities which we attribute to the experienced objects are strictly speaking not properties of that object at all, but a set of relations by which our nervous system classifies them or, to put it differently, *all* we know about the world is of the nature of theories and all "experience" can do is change these theories. (p. 142, emphasis original)

This suggests that a kind of cognitive blindness is inevitable at some level.

Although "animals initiate true learning only when an element of novelty, surprise, or violation of expectation is present" (Edelman, 1987, p. 262),[8] it is nonetheless the case that information too novel or too surprising is not expected at all and therefore completely fails to register.

3. Organization and cognition

In the case of organizations, this characterization of knowledge as a structure that leads to results is particularly congenial. It fits with much of the recent trend toward the evolutionary theory of the firm (Nelson & Winter, 1982) and the dynamic-capabilities view of strategy (Teece & Pisano, 1994). In those approaches, one is concerned with the useful knowledge organizations possess for undertaking various productive tasks. To Nelson and Winter, individuals and organizations follow routines – persistent patterns of behavior – that, like the DNA of organisms, shape the phenotype upon which a selection mechanism operates. These routines embody knowledge that is (perhaps even mostly) tacit in the manner of Michael Polanyi (1958): that is to say, they embody, in Gilbert Ryle's (1949) famous terms, "knowledge how" rather than "knowledge that." For Nelson and Winter, organizations "remember by doing" (p. 99).

Thus knowledge in an organization is not something that resides in the heads of managers; rather, the organization's knowledge is nothing other than its complex of routines, including routines for coordinating among routines and routines for changing or creating routines. This repertoire of routines is what defines the conditional states of readiness on which messages from the environment operate. To put it another way, the complex of routines that make up an organization not only determines what that organization can do well but also conditions how the organization will interpret messages: how information from the environment will alter the organization's existing repertoire of routines. That is to say, the organization's routines are in a broad sense its cognitive apparatus, its "map." They determine what information the organization recognizes as meaningful, and they strongly influence how the organization learns and how it perceives opportunities.

The dynamic capabilities approach, in most of its versions, builds on the Nelson–Winter framework (Langlois & Robertson, 1995; Teece & Pisano, 1994). Organizations possess certain capabilities or *competences*, which consist of various tangible and intangible assets useful for production. In Nelson–Winter's terms, however, we can think of competences as the skills the organization possesses by virtue of its complex of routines. The value of these competences is that they are not product specific, and may be a source of rent in a variety of applications. *Core competences* are those that are crucial to an organization's survival. Good management, in this theory, must identify, nurture, and develop core competences, and must constantly sample the market to identify goods and services to produce with them. The meaning of the term *capabilities* is ambiguous in the literature, often seeming synonymous with competence but sometimes also seeming to refer to higher-level routines, that is, to the organization's ability to apply its existing competences and create new ones (Teece & Pisano, 1994).

It is clear even from this brief account of the theory that the strategic task of management is fundamentally a cognitive one. This has not gone entirely unnoticed in the literature, of course. For example, Cohen and Levinthal (1990) argue that research and development activity benefits an organization not only by generating new knowledge but also, and perhaps more importantly, by providing the organization with the "absorptive capacity" to take advantage of ideas developed elsewhere. In effect, the organization's own R&D creates a receptor apparatus – a complex of routines – that can recognize and make use of messages from the environment. What I want to stress here, however, is that absorptive capacity is not a property of the organization's higher-level subsystems only (like an R&D lab or even "management" itself); it is, rather, a property of the entire complex of routines within the organization.

The dynamic-capabilities approach suggests that, to be successful in a world of change, an organization must have perceptual ability in two broad areas: (1) the ability to see ways of gaining and improving core competences and (2) the ability to recognize opportunities for applying those competences in a way that generates value. At the risk of oversimplifying a bit, let's call these areas *operational perception* and *market perception*. We can think of "operational" here as having mostly to do with issues of technology, including both product and process aspects, and "market" as having broadly to do with commercialization.

Success or failure in noticing profitable opportunities can thus result from either operational misperception or market misperception. But in the view of perception just outlined, misperception is not simply a matter of failing to notice. Misperception is always *miscategorization*, putting stimuli in the wrong interpretive box;[9] and only in the limit does misperception involve the complete failure of stimuli to trip any cognitive switches at all. Moreover, since misperception is miscategorization rather than simply blindness, it involves errors of inclusion as well as errors of exclusion. Although such miscategorization is fundamentally a qualitative matter, we can in the end see all perceptual errors as either Type I errors (thinking that an opportunity exists when, by ex post standards, one doesn't) and Type II errors (failing to perceive as profitable an opportunity that turns out profitable ex post).[10] This gives us a matrix of four possibilities, as depicted in Table 5.1. One could imagine "operational" Type I errors and Type II errors: on the one hand, erroneously changing routines in ways that fail to build useful competences and, on the other hand, failing to notice ways to change organizational routines in ways that do build useful competences. And one could also imagine "market' Type I errors and Type II errors: On the one hand, erroneously committing organizational resources in ways that do not

Table 5.1. *Types of misperceptions.*

	Type I errors	Type II errors
Operational opportunities	Changing operational routines in ways that do not enhance or effectively utilize (core) competences	Failing to notice opportunities to improve or utilize operational competences
Market opportunities	Applying operational competences in ways that do not create value	Failing to notice opportunities to apply existing operational competences to create value

create value and, on the other hand, failing to recognize opportunities to apply competences in ways that do create value. We will see examples of all these types of misperceptions in the next section.

In many, if not most, cases, of course, these types of misperception are linked. Brian Loasby (1976, pp. 85–86) offers the example of an attempt by Briggs manufacturing, a maker of car bodies, to diversify into bathtubs (Miller, 1963). Briggs used steel-press technology to stamp out parts for car bodies. When a dropoff in car sales left them with excess capacity, they sought an alternative product to absorb some of the overhead of the presses. As the company had experience with stamping steel sinks for a mail-order house, they decided to diversify into bathtubs. It turned out, however, that the firm's capabilities in marketing to auto makers – or even to mail-order plumbing-supply houses – turned out to be largely inapplicable to marketing plumbing supplies to plumbing contractors, who were the primary market for bathtubs. Thus, this appears to be a case of marketing misperception, one located in the lower left of Table 5.1. As Loasby notes, however, the most interesting aspect of this experience was that the diversification turned out to be an operational misperception as well, at least in the sense that the firm's stamping and related technology turned out to be less than effective in producing bathtubs, which posed special problems not only in materials and ceramic coating but also in stamping itself. This case illustrates another relevant point as well. Ultimately, the diversification was successful, but it didn't solve the original problem of excess capacity that had motivated it. The firm was forced to acquire three entirely new presses and had to enter into a joint venture with a steel company to develop new materials. This may have added to the firm's core competences, but only as an unintended consequence of misperception rather than as a conscious strategic decision.

What determines the ability of an organization correctly to perceive opportunities? It is my contention here that perceptual ability is a matter of the "fit" between the environment and the organization as cognitive apparatus. Putting aside unintended consequences, if an organization is to be able to classify information in the right (the most useful) categories, it must possess a structure of categories that is somehow "like" those of the outside world, or at least that small piece of the outside world most relevant to it. As Hayek would insist, the world does not exist ontologically in categories; categories are always creations of the mind. But we can say loosely that the economic and technological environment does possess a certain structure. For example, the literature is full of the idea that there are natural structures to technological change and innovation. Like scientific knowledge, technological development may have an inchoate or "preparadigmatic" structure before coalescing eventually around a "paradigm" (Dosi 1982) or "dominant design" (Utterback & Suarez, 1993). That paradigm may then be supplanted or attacked by alternative structures. One can argue that learning on the market side by firms or, more interestingly, by consumers – may also have a similar structure, even if demand-side learning is comparatively neglected in the literature. The upshot is this: When operational or market conditions are inchoate, they may call for an organization with a cognitive structure able to receive and respond to a diverse set of messages[11] (Nelson & Winter, 1977). By contrast, when the operational or market environment is highly focused, those organizations do best whose cognitive apparatus allows them to perceive the finer details and to solve the smaller but important puzzles of "normal science."[12]

One final point deserves mention before turning to the case studies. I have talked about success as if it were a matter of perception alone. An organization is successful if it correctly perceives – which means correctly categorizes – information from the world around it. But isn't there a difference between perception and action? Cannot someone (or some organization) *perceive* what needs to be done but yet be unable to *get it done*? The cases in the next section may shed some light on this issue, and I win return to it more directly in the final section. For the moment, however, let me suggest that the cognitive approach I have outlined tends to blur rather than sharpen the distinction between perception and action. In a cybernetic theory of knowledge, what an organism (or organization) knows is in fact its entire structure. Although a subsystem of the organism can obviously perceive what needs to be done without the whole system being able to respond, can we say that the whole system – the whole organization – has perceived what needs to be done if it cannot respond effectively to what the subsystem knows?

4. Perception and misperception in the computer industry

Episode 1: The rise of IBM

The story of IBM's rise to dominance of the worldwide computer industry during the 1950s and 1960s is a much-told tale (Katz & Phillips, 1982; Fisher,

McKie, & Mancke, 1983; Flamm, 1988), which, like most much-told tales, is subject to considerable interpretation and reinterpretation. The commercial computer emerged from government-sponsored work during World War II. Those who get the most credit are J. Presper Eckert and John W. Mauchly of the Moore School at the University of Pennsylvania, who, in November 1945, produced the ENIAC, the first all-electronic digital computer, under contract with the Army. The machine took up 1,800 square feet, boasted 18,000 tubes, and consumed 174 kilowatts. Collaboration with the mathematician John von Neumann led a couple of years later to the idea of a stored-program – that is, a programmable rather than a special-purpose – computer, an approach called the von Neumann architecture and used almost universally today in computers of all sizes.[13] By 1951, Eckert and Mauchly had joined Remington Rand, where they produced the UNIVAC, whose first model went to the Census Bureau. Perhaps the principal commercial competitor to Remington Rand (and its Eckert–Mauchly division) was Engineering Research Associates (ERA), a St. Paul, Minnesota firm comprising mostly veterans of the Office of Naval Research's wartime computer efforts. ERA produced the Atlas computer (later called the 1101), which was delivered to its first customer a few months before the first UNIVAC arrived at Census. In 1952, Remington-Rand absorbed ERA as well, making it for a brief moment the dominant producer of computers in the world (Norberg, 1993; Fisher, McKie, & Mancke, 1983, pp. 4–10; Flamm, 1988, pp. 43–51).

IBM's early efforts at computers also had military roots. During World War II, the company became involved in the Harvard Mark I project and, after a dispute with Harvard, began developing a similar machine called the Selective Sequence Electronic Calculator (Flamm, 1988, pp. 61–65; Fisher, McKie, & Mancke, 1983, p. 11). Both of these were electromechanical machines rather than genuine electronic computers. It was, in fact, the Korean War, along with the sponsorship of Thomas Watson, Jr., son of reigning Thomas Watson, Sr., that spurred IBM's development of electronic computers. The company set up a small lab and factory in Poughkeepsie, New York – separate from the company's main lab and factory in Endicott, New York – to focus on government needs. And there they developed the IBM defense calculator, which led to the IBM 700 series of electronic computers.

Significantly, IBM's commercial successes came more from the work of the Endicott facility, seat of the company's older electromechanical capabilities, even if what the company learned at Poughkeepsie was not irrelevant to its success. Endicott produced the low-priced 650, of which 1800 units were sold (Fisher, McKie, & Mancke, 1983, p. 17), and later the 1401, of which some 12,000 units were sold (Flamm, 1988, p. 65). Whereas the high-end 700–series machines were perceived as "IBM UNIVACs," the 650, often called the Model T of computing, thrust IBM into industry leadership (Katz & Phillips, 1982, p. 178; Flamm, 1988, p. 83). Table 5.2 summarizes IBM's success as of 1963.

Table 5.2. *EDP revenues, 1963 ($ millions).*

Firm	1963 EDP Revenues
IBM 1	$1,244
Sperry Rand	$145
AT&T	$97+
Control Data	$84
Philco	$74
Burroughs	$42
GE	$39
NCR	$31
Honeywell	$27
RCA	N/A

Source: Fisher, McKie, and Mancke 1983, p. 65.

Why did IBM become the industry leader in the 1950s? Why did Remington Rand (later Sperry Rand), with its head start and government-developed expertise, not outpace the others? Why did electronics giants GE and RCA, with greater size and resources than IBM, not become the leaders? There are a couple of closely related explanations, both of which are broadly within the capabilities framework.

One explanation is very much in the spirit of the work of Alfred Chandler (1990). In this view, IBM in the fifties and early sixties made – while others failed to make – the "three-pronged investments" in marketing, high-throughput manufacturing, and managerial capabilities necessary to competitive advantage. When Thomas Watson, Jr. took over leadership in the mid 1950s, he poured money into R&D and committed the company to electronic computing; he hired new personnel, including the head of the Office of Naval Research's computer operations; and he continued the strong marketing thrust that had been his father's hallmark (Fisher, McKie, & Mancke, 1983, pp. 94–98). Thus IBM succeeded because it fostered both its operational and its market capabilities. All of this is no doubt true. The problem is that, from the perspective of this essay (and perhaps others as well), this explanation begs many of the central questions. *Why* was IBM able to make these investments while others weren't? How did IBM *know* what to do?

A second, if related, explanation focuses more narrowly (and, for present purposes, more usefully) on IBM's preexisting capabilities. The company started off in 1911 as the Computer-Tabulating-Recording Company, a maker of punch-card tabulating machines springing from the pioneering work of Herman Hollerith. In 1914, Thomas J. Watson, Sr., gained control of the company, changed its name to International Business Machines Corporation, and developed its capabilities in mechanical information devices. For example, IBM introduced the electric typewriter in the 1930s, a period during which it prospered by selling equipment to a growing federal bureaucracy. It was this mechanical experience that made the difference in IBM's move into electronic computers. In the view of Kenneth Flamm

IBM built on its position as the dominant manufacturer of punched card business equipment. Its traditional skills and experience in manufacturing electromechanical machinery were the base on which an outstanding record of research and development in high-speed peripherals – input–output devices – was built. The card readers and punches used with early computers, even those not built by IBM, were often IBM products. An ambitious development program for printers, magnetic tape drives, and magnetic drums and disks added new strengths to traditional expertise. The availability of quality peripheral equipment for IBM computers was crucial to its phenomenal growth. (Flamm, 1988, p. 83)

This explanation has some of the flavor of Teece (1986): IBM succeeded because it already possessed complementary capabilities cospecialized to the innovation of the electronic computer. Again, this is largely true. But suggesting that the peripheral tail wagged the computer dog underplays IBM's development of competences in electronic computing (Norberg, 1993). Moreover, if IBM was driven by its capabilities in electromechanical equipment, its move into electronics seems all the more surprising, since that move would surely have threatened to cannibalize the company's existing electromechanical sales. In this reading, indeed, IBM's move into electronics appears as a bold perceptual leap – of the sort one might expect from reading Chandler or Lazonick (1991) – that is inexplicable in terms of the company that existed before computers.

Recently, however, Steven Usselman (1993) has added some subtlety to the conventional explanations in a way that accords well with the themes of this essay. For one thing, although it is true that IBM's electromechanical capabilities gave it an advantage in peripherals, it is also true that the form those capabilities took made the company much more receptive to the innovation of electronics than one might think a priori. At the operational level, IBM had long pursued what Henderson and Clark (1990) call architectural innovation, and they did so in a context that might be described as flexible production.

The production facility in Endicott operated as a mechanical job shop, responding to requests from the field for solutions to particular problems. It constantly took gears, ratchets, and relays obtained from outside suppliers from which it produced novel machines, and it devised numerous ways of joining counters, printers, and other machines in complex installations. Naturally, the mechanics at Endicott routinely looked for opportunities to reduce the variations and build in volume. Sales statistics and education programs helped the company strike a balance between novelty, which generated revenue, and standardization, which produced economy. The production facility also worked in close collaboration with engineers who installed and maintained the equipment in the field. (Usselman, 1993, pp. 7–8)

This approach carried over into the making of electronic equipment. Both Poughkeepsie and Endicott "took basic components and arranged them in complex machines that were leased to customers and maintained by IBM in the field" (p. 8).

The leasing strategy and the emphasis on maintenance were, of course, another part of IBM's early capabilities that carried over into computers. But there was more to the firm's marketing competences. For example, salesmen were given the incentive to increase their "installed base" of leased equipment, but they could do that "by persuading existing customers to use novel arrangements of IBM equipment to perform new tasks" (p. 7). Cannibalization was not in fact much of a problem, as IBM could appropriate the rents from re-leasing obsolete machines, often outside the United States.

Thus, we might argue that IBM's success in this era flowed from a cognitive structure that enabled it to perceive learning opportunities in both the operational and market spheres. Although we should not entirely forget the role of Thomas Watson, Jr. – a point to which I will return in Section 5 – IBM's ability to seize the opportunity of the electronic computer was a matter of the structure it already possessed. And that structure was a flexible and open one permeable to both operational and market messages from outside.

Episode 2: System 360

Although Watson poured resources into research and development, the fundamental structure of IBM did not change through the mid 1960s. The company remained an assembler of machines (rather than also a producer of components) devoted to solving a wide range of problems. Usselman (1993, p. 13) sees it as part of IBM's success that it participated in all four major market segments in the decade of the fifties.[14] By the mid 1960s, however, the openness and diversity of IBM's approach had become in certain respects a liability rather than a benefit. First of all, the company was riding herd on a multiplicity of physically incompatible systems – the various 700 series computers and the 1400 series, among others – each aimed at a different use. Relatedly, and more significantly, software was becoming a serious bottleneck. By one estimate, the contribution of software to the value of a computer system had grown from 8% in the early days to something like 40% by the 1960s (Ferguson & Morris, 1993, p. 7). And writing software for so many incompatible systems greatly compounded the problem.

IBM's response, of course, was the System 360 series. The name meant to refer all the points of the compass, for the strategy behind the 360 was to replace the diverse and incompatible systems with a single modular family of computers. Instead of having one computer (like the 701) aimed at scientific applications, a second (like the 702) aimed at accounting applications, etc., the company would have one machine for all uses. This was not to be a homogeneous or undifferentiated product; but it was to provide a modular framework in which product differentiation could take place while retaining compatibility.[15] In effect, IBM attempted to resolve the bottleneck by switching from a structure of architectural innovation to a structure of modular innovation. The 360 was a modular system (Langlois and Robertson 1992), albeit one that remained mostly closed and proprietary despite the efforts of the "plug compatible" industry to pick away at parts of the system.

As Brian Loasby (1976, p. 83) notes, an organization's response to one "reverse salient"[16] often becomes the trigger to effect other changes. There is no doubt a similarity here to cognitive processes of recombination. A major reevaluation of one piece of our knowledge may often lead to reevaluations in other areas. In the case of IBM, the change to the standardized 360 series brought with it a change in vertical integration. Whereas IBM had been principally an assembler and system integrator in both the mechanical and the electronic eras, IBM after the 360 would become a major internal manufacturer of components. In part, this reflected the shift from vacuum tubes to solid-state components, a change that was competence destroying[17] to suppliers and to some extent to IBM itself. There were, of course, plenty of suppliers of solid-state components around, many of whom, like Texas Instruments, could supply at a cost substantially less than IBM internal production (Pugh, Johnson, & Palmer, 1991). But IBM's decision to create, virtually from scratch, internal capabilities in semiconductors and many other components was apparently based on a conscious perception of economies of scope between component design and computer design. In an era before genuine integrated circuits, processing speed depended on the integration of component and system, and IBM wished to preserve the ability to adjust both component and system simultaneously instead of responding to autonomous changes in components fabricated – even at low cost – by outside suppliers. Moreover, in a world of centralized mainframe computers, reliability is crucial, and IBM wished to control directly as many determinants of quality as possible.

Obviously, the cognitive aspects of such a radical change are of considerable interest, and I will touch on them below. But my principal concern here is with the subsequent effects of the System-360 changes on IBM as cognitive structure. Despite the radical changes, IBM did preserve many of its previous core competences, especially in the market dimension. IBM marketing retained its direct lineage to the days of Thomas Watson, Sr. And the company continued to work with customers to meet specific needs. The company also continued its tradition of looking out for future technologies and opportunities. Nonetheless, this search function was constrained by – or, rather, undertaken by – a cognitive structure significantly different from that of the 1950s. On the one hand, marketing choices were necessarily shunted into categories of compatibility: Where once the problem alone constrained designers, now the need to remain compatible with the 360 architecture also loomed large, at least for the company's biggest and most profitable machines. And, whereas operational choices were once open to the range of components available on the outside, those choices were now limited by procurement regulations giving internal divisions privileged access to resources.

Episode 3: The RISC architecture

This new structure was, of course, phenomenally effective, and was copied with little success by the Europeans and with somewhat more success by the Japanese. With the extent of the market growing rapidly, and with IBM possessing a commanding position in that market, it made perfect sense to reduce redundancy and variety in order to concentrate on improvements within the paradigm. Equally predictably, however, this "normal science" reinforced existing routines and deepened existing categories of interpretation.

A case in point is the development of the reduced instruction set computing (RISC) architecture (Ferguson & Morris, 1993, pp. 37–50). One of the innovations of the 360, copied in almost all computers today, is that the basic library of logical steps the computer follows – the so-called instruction set – was hard-wired into the central processing unit. As computers became faster and more sophisticated, the instruction set became more complicated. In the 1960s, John Cocke, a scientist at IBM's Yorktown Heights Research Center, came up with a way to simplify and fine-tune the instruction set so that each instruction is executed within a single cycle of the computer's clock. In this way one can speed up computer operations without changes in hardware or software.

Despite this early discovery, it was not IBM but two start-up firms, Sun and MIPS, who first commercialized RISC technology and who dominated the RISC workstation market in the early 1980s. These firms based their architectures on (apparently) independent work by government-sponsored academics at Berkeley and Stanford. IBM did not disclose its own RISC technology until 1982, and the company's first commercial use of the technology was in an unsuccessful workstation in 1986.

Ferguson and Morris portray the saga of RISC at IBM as a story of how a promising technology, one that later formed a core competence of smaller firms who came to dominate the industry, was "buried" by a stultifying bureaucracy.[18] On close reading, however, we can see that what was at work was not simply generic "bureaucracy" but the particular cognitive structure that the 360 had imposed.

Of course, one cognitive factor at work in this era was both significant and exogenous: The costly antitrust suit that the U.S. Department of Justice waged against IBM for more than a dozen years (Fisher, McGowan, & Greenwood, 1983). Apart from wasting perhaps a billion dollars of resources and diverting scarce managerial attention, this suit also arguably muted IBM's aggressive attitude toward new markets. Nonetheless, there were other cognitive factors at work that may have been of even greater significance. Ferguson and Morris, for example, give great weight to the failed

F/S (Future Systems) Project. In the early 1970s, IBM received an important message from the environment: A task force reported that, because of the falling costs of computer power, IBM would begin to lose revenue in the future if they continued along the architectural path of the 360 (which by then had been supplanted by the compatible 370). The F/S project was an attempt to leapfrog a generation into a new development path. It was thus a project modeled very much on the 360 experiment: a bold leap requiring the internal creation of new capabilities along many margins. Unlike the 360, however, F/S was not the solution to the problem of its era; but it absorbed resources, and then, once it had failed, it colored the company's attitude toward a number of otherwise promising technologies.

The legacy of the 360 was also apparent at a more microscopic level. Almost all the company's attempts to develop a RISC machine were either scotched or killed by the requirements of 360/370 compatibility. And the IBM internal-procurement approach proved a hindrance when the Burlington semiconductor facility, accustomed to memory-chip production, was unable to produce the a RISC microprocessor of the quality outside suppliers could have yielded.

The IBM 360 was an extremely successful solution to the problems posed for the computer industry by the growing extent of the market in the early 1960s. By the late 1970s and early 1980s, however, that market had grown even further, and the costs of computer power had fallen dramatically. This called for a solution quite different from the 360, a solution involving new – and open – modular architectures. In the view of Ferguson and Morris, IBM missed the chance in this era to reorient the company toward a new architecture based around the RISC design. And one might add that it was in many ways the very success of the 360 – and the structure it imposed – that made it difficult for IBM to perceive that possibility.

By contrast, the most successful vendor of RISC machines, Sun Microsystems, has taken full – even extreme – advantage of modularity and system openness (Garud & Kumaraswamy, 1993). Like IBM with the 360, Sun took the path of modular innovation rather than architectural innovation. But unlike IBM, Sun opened the system to others. Indeed, Sun invested resources to "sponsor" public standards, including the UNIX operating system. Moreover, unlike IBM, Sun relies on outside suppliers for key components, including its SPARC microprocessor, and licenses its technology to others in an effort to widen the influence of the standard. This is a quite different kind of cognitive structure, one indeed for which the relevant "organization" may not be a single firm but rather the "market" as a whole. I will explore these issues further in a related context – that of the personal computer.

Episode 4: The personal computer

The personal computer became possible with Intel's invention of the Microprocessor in the early 1970s.[19] Originally, of course, these machines were hobbyist toys that interested existing electronics firms not at all. When Stephen Wozniak, soon to cofound Apple Computer, approached his then-employer Hewlett Packard (HP) with the idea of a personal computer, he was turned away. "HP doesn't want to be in that kind of a market," Wozniak was told (Moritz, 1984, p. 126). His partner Steven Jobs had a similar experience at Atari. One of the implications of these humble beginnings is that the personal computer started out on a technological trajectory of open modular standards – simply because none of the early makers of microcomputers had the wherewithal to offer a proprietary system. Each maker had to rely on the capabilities of the market for those parts of the system it could not itself provide.

An avid reader of Alfred Chandler might have predicted at this point (say, 1980) that a large vertically integrated firm would arise (either from within the ranks or from related fields of electronics) to become a dominant first mover and to take the microcomputer industry along a trajectory similar to that of IBM and the 360. Of course, quite the opposite happened.

In the wake of the failed F/S System, and as a partial response to antitrust paranoia, IBM began decentralizing product development in the 1970s. For the most part, however, this decentralization was reigned in by a centralized command-and-control system (Ferguson & Morris, 1993, p. 36). One exception was the development of the original IBM PC, which broke the 360 mold completely. In a sense, in fact, the original PC was a success because IBM created it outside its own structure. The company commissioned a team of engineers in Boca Raton, Florida to produce a machine under strict deadline, exempting them in the process from all internal quality-control and procurement requirements (Chposky & Leonsis, 1988). The resulting PC was made almost entirely from off-the-shelf parts (including the Intel microprocessor and the Microsoft operating system), and it was sold through mass-marketing channels outside the IBM sales system. It was also modular like the hobbyist machines it closely imitated, and for much the same reason: The IBM team knew that they could not produce the complementary components themselves in time to meet the deadline.

The original IBM PC set the standard and was a phenomenal success – for a time, anyway. Was this an instance of equally phenomenal perceptual ability by IBM? On the whole, I would argue, the PC, despite its success, was mostly an exercise in misperception. It is certainly true that the IBM Central Management Committee (CMC) was perceptive on the day in July, 1980, when they commissioned William Lowe to get IBM into the market for desktop computers. "The only way we can get into the personal computer business," Lowe told the CMC, "is to go out and buy part of a computer company, or buy both the CPU and software from people like Apple or Atari – because we can't do this within the culture of IBM" (Chposky & Leonsis, 1988, p. 9). The Committee was perceptive enough to agree with him and to give him free reign at Boca Raton. On the other hand, the cognitive category to which both Lowe and his superiors assigned the PC was not "the future of computing" but "marginal product to fill out our line." Few people inside or outside IBM foresaw the sweeping changes the PC would make in computer markets. It is also significant that, unlike the 360, the PC initially threatened no existing IBM products, and the PC development team made conscious decisions (like choosing the 8088 chip over the more powerful 8086) in order not to intrude on turf elsewhere in the company (Chposky & Leonsis, 1988, p. 24).

More significantly, as I have argued, organizational perception is a matter not of an isolated subsystem (like the CMC in 1980) but of the organization as a whole. And it is evident that, very quickly, IBM's traditional perceptual categories began to reassert themselves. By 1984, the PC division was combined with the office systems group, thus losing much of its autonomy. And by 1987, IBM was clearly placing the PC back in the "proprietary" category. The PS/2 line, which emerged that year, used a proprietary graphics standard; a new "bus" (or central architecture) called the MicroChannel that was incompatible with the old PC and its clones; and a mandatory 3.5-inch disk drive in a world where most people still used 5.25-inch disks. Moreover, the basic PS/2 used the obsolescent 80286 chip at a time when rival Compaq, accurately perceiving the power dynamic of the microcomputer, pushed ahead with the 80386 chip. That is, IBM still categorized the PC as a marginal product not requiring much speed; anything faster would have fallen into the category "minicomputer." IBM built the PS/2, and waited for everyone to rush to its doors to buy machines and ask for cloning rights. They built it, but nobody came (Carroll, 1993). Within months, IBM was offering a non-MicroChannel version of the PS/2 model 30, and soon it abandoned the standard altogether.

Some (including an eminent industrial-organization economist in private conversation with the author) would argue that IBM failed not because it tried to take the PC proprietary but because it neglected to appropriate the original standard. Had IBM not built an "off-the-shelf" machine and, especially, licensed the operating system to Microsoft, the company could have dominated microcomputers the way it dominated mainframes. As I have argued here and elsewhere (Langlois, 1992), this is not so. One piece of evidence is the fact that the companies most closely placed to IBM tried exactly that and failed. The lessons of Digital Equipment Corporation's (DEC) early foray into microcomputers illustrates both this point and the cognitive theme of this essay.

The second-largest computer maker in the world, DEC's success revolved around its VAX line of time-sharing minicomputers. Indeed, the VAX (and its predecessor, the PDP series) played for DEC the kind of formative role that the 360 played for IBM. DEC saw itself as a minicomputer maker; more than that, it saw itself as a company that provides total system solutions to solve particular problems using the proprietary modularity of the VAX system. Initially, Ken Olsen, DEC's founder and chairman, did not want to enter the PC market because he saw no way to do that within the minicomputer framework (Rifkin & Harrar, 1988, p. 199). Even when he relented, he retained a low opinion of IBM's machine and its strategy. "If you ever built me something like this," he told an underling after the first PC arrived at DEC's headquarters, "you wouldn't be here anymore." DEC's own entry into the fray was to be the Professional series, which began development about the same time as the IBM PC. It would have a proprietary operating system based on that of the PDP-11 minicomputer, bit-mapped graphics, and multitasking capabilities. But, despite winning design awards, the computer was a commercial flop. All told, the company lost about $900 million on its development of desktop machines.

Why? A technical perfectionist, Olsen believed that DEC could be successful by creating a superior product. This had worked in minicomputers: put together a machine that would solve a particular problem for a particular application. The PC is not, however, a machine for a particular application; it is a machine adaptable to many applications – including some its users hadn't imagined when they bought their machines. Moreover, Olsen underrated the value of software. In minicomputers, DEC could generate adequate software inhouse, and users, who are highly skilled technically, could write their own applications. But this was not the case in the wide-open microcomputer market. And, unlike IBM, DEC chose to ignore existing third-party capabilities. Except for the hard disk and the line cord, DEC designed and built every piece of the Professional. The company tooled the sheet metal and plastics, manufactured the floppy drive, and even developed the microprocessor. There is no reason to think that IBM, arguably a less flexible company than DEC, would have been able to pull off the proprietary strategy any better. A more telling piece of evidence, however, is provided by Sun's success in the workstation market. Sun's aggressive open-system strategy is a model for what IBM might have done with the PC if its cognitive structure had been different.[20]

5. Cognition and "personal capitalism"

The notion that one can think of organizations as cognitive structures is an idea that obviously will continue to require definition and elaboration. One especially needs to look carefully at the nature of an organization's structure. Can we make any generalizations about the perceptual abilities of various kinds of structures?

At a very general level, I have argued that an organization's ability to seize opportunities is not so much a matter of its structure a priori as of the "fit" between its cognitive structure and the economic structure of the opportunity. IBM's early structure as an architecturally innovative job shop with strong links between sales and design helped it seize the opportunity of the electronic computer. IBM's structure as a modular innovator with large captive capabilities in component production contributed to missing the opportunity of the RISC architecture and even to a large extent the personal computer.

Yet this notion of structure is still vague. And I do not want to claim too much for it. One should be wary of organizational determinism. At the same time, however, one can also explain in cognitive terms instances in which the overall structure of the organization does not seem to determine its perceptual abilities. Perhaps IBM's seizing of the opportunity inherent in the 360 series, which required a creative self-destruction of some capabilities and their replacement by others, is an example. The wild card here is the hierarchical nature of perceptual subsystems. I have argued against the idea that perception always takes place in a special subsystem or "brain" set aside for cognitive functions and is then implemented by the noncephalic parts of the organization. In organizations that follow routines and remember by doing, all of the organization is its cognitive apparatus. But this does not mean that certain subsystems do not in some cases have special importance. The issue here is in some ways an organizational variant of a longstanding debate in the social sciences more broadly: When do ideas matter? One answer is that ideas can matter when there is a focal individual or "big player" (Koppl & Langlois, 1994) whose personal knowledge, beliefs, and preferences swing the balance.

Under "personal" capitalism, a significant fraction of what the organization knows and perceives is, for better or worse, in the "subsystem" of a dominant manager or owner. Perhaps Thomas Watson, Jr. was such an individual.[21] If so, the secret of IBM's ability to conceive and execute the 360 program may lie in the fact that the IBM of 1965 was a family firm, whereas the IBM of 1982 was a Chandlerian managerial hierarchy.

This idea cuts both ways, of course. Dominant figures as cognitive subsystems are as likely to make errors as are more decentralized cognitive structures. DEC's misperceptions about the microcomputer were as much Ken Olsen's misperceptions as they were the company's. And consider Apple Computer's failures with the Apple III, the Lisa, and the early Macintosh under the sway of founder Steve Jobs. The original Apple II, the key to the company's phenomenal early success, was in important respects a compromise between Jobs and Wozniak. Jobs saw the machine as a limited toy, and he was concerned primarily with its appearance and its marketing. Wozniak, the hobbyist, saw the machine as an open system, and insisted on modularity and the sharing of technical specifications with outsiders – ideas Jobs opposed. I have argued (Langlois, 1992) that it was Woznlak's victory over – or at least stalemate with – Jobs that, by making the Apple II a modular system, led to its success. In the development of newer machines, however, Wozniak soon found himself on the outside, and eventually left the company.

This left Jobs free to create machines in his own image. The essence of his view lay not so much in the proprietary character of the machine as in the basic nature of the machine. Jobs saw himself as designing not open-ended modular systems but "closed geographical systems" (Butcher, 1988, p. 142). This was evident perhaps even more in the Lisa and early Macintosh computers, which bore Jobs's personal stamp. As Jef Raskin, the original Mac project director, put it, "Apple II is a system. Macintosh is an appliance" (Moritz, 1984, p. 130). Upon the Mac's introduction in 1984, Apple decided it should be known as "the second desk appliance after the telephone" (Moritz, 1984, p. 326). In large part, the nonsystemic character of the later machines was simply a reflection of the fact that they were bounded in conception by a single mind: Jobs's. His approach was visionary, personal, and aesthetic. He wanted to design the ideal machine he would himself like to own. Alan Kay, a computer innovator who is now an Apple Fellow, describes Jobs and the Macintosh this way. "Take a look at the Mac. If you look at it from the front, it's fantastic. If you look at it from the back, it stinks. Steve doesn't think systems at all. Different kind of mentality. . . . Looking at the original Mac, you can see Steve. It's like Steve's head in a sense because it has the good parts of Steve and the bad parts. It has this super quality control and the parts where his brain didn't function" (Sculley, 1987, p. 238).

Having said this, of course, it remains true that the cognitive structures of "personal capitalism" are arguably likely to make different kinds of errors from those of "managerial capitalism." We would expect powerful figures to be brilliantly right like Watson and the 360 or brilliantly wrong like Jobs and the Apple III. But we would nonetheless also expect personal capitalists to be more alert to, and more able seize, opportunities of a radical or extra-paradigmatic nature. By contrast, the elaborated cognitive structures of managerial capitalism may be more alert to both operational and market opportunities of a paradigmatic sort.

Acknowledgments

The author would like to thank Cliff Jones, Roger Koppl, Scott Moss, Praveen Nayyar, Zur Shapira, and Sid Winter for helpful comments.

Notes

1 Indeed, the term "organization" is misleading, in that I mean it here to include even markets (properly understood) and the various kinds of networks intermediate between firm and market. A better term might be "business institutions." See, generally, Langlois and Robertson (1995) and Langlois (1995).
2 For one of the best examples of this, see Stinchcombe (1990).
3 On this point cf. also Hayek (1952, p. 105) on the "storage" theory of memory.
4 Indeed, cybernetic information theory has tended to think of knowledge and information in behaviorist terms. A stimulus is information to the extent that it elicits some response from the structure it stimulates. As MacKay (1969) notes, however, such a Skinnerian conception is as naive in this as it is in other matters. A signal may change a knowledge structure in a way that is meaningful – i.e., it may modify the future or potential behavior of the system – without that

change resulting in any directly observable response. In fact, as Machlup points out, "[a]ny kind of experience – accidental impressions, observations, and even 'inner experience' not induced by stimuli received from the environment – may initiate cognitive processes leading to changes in a person's knowledge. Thus, *new knowledge can be acquired without new information being received*" (Machlup, 1983, p. 644, emphasis original).

5   And by economists. See Butos and Koppl (1993).

6   Hayek well understands that organisms are not clean slates at birth. But whatever "map" they come programmed with is itself the result of learning by previous generations. The split between nature and nurture is not crucial to the theory.

7   In a work very much consistent with Hayek's framework, Edelman (1987) discusses these linkages in terms of evolutionary competition among nodes of receptors in what is effectively a distributed processing system with redundancy.

8   And cf., of course, Popper (1965).

9   "Wrong" in this case means wrong not with respect to "objective" reality but rather simply ineffective for successful action. As I will suggest, stimuli that seem miscategorized by ex post intellectual standards may still lead to successful action as an unintended consequence. Like people, organizations can be right for the wrong reasons.

10 These two kinds of mistakes are defined this way: "We make a Type I error when we reject a true hypothesis; we make a Type II error when we retain a false hypothesis" (Hinkle, Wiersma, & Jurs, 1982, p. 175). In classical statistics, however, the hypothesis accepted or rejected is always some kind of null hypothesis. In this case I assume the null hypothesis is that the project is not innovative, in the sense that it is actually "drawn" from a population with a "normal" rate of return. To reject the null hypothesis, then, is to believe that the project is innovative, in the sense that it is actually "drawn" from a population of innovative projects whose mean rate of return is higher than normal. This strikes me as somewhat counterintuitive, but it is apparently in keeping with general usage. See, for example, chapter 3 by Garud, Nayyar, and Shapira in this volume.

11 Keep in mind that an "organization," for present purposes, may mean not just a firm but also such structures as networks or even markets.

12 The reference to paradigms and "normal science" is, of course, from Kuhn (1970).

13 The stored-program idea was also contained in the work of Turing in England, and the first functioning storable-program computer was run for the first time on June 21, 1948 at the University of Manchester.

14 As identified by Flamm (1988, p. 105).

15 Much as Dan Raff (1991) has argued was the case with General Motors's innovation of the annual model change in automobiles.

16 To use the terminology of Thomas Hughes (1992).

17 In the terminology of Tushman and Anderson (1986).

18 On which see also Carroll (1993).

19 For a longer discussion of the history of the microcomputer that also develops many of the themes of this essay in greater detail, see Langlois (1992).

20 To use the language of the evolutionary theory of games (Maynard Smith, 1982), the success of Sun and the PC clones suggests that in world of high de-

mand, network externalities, and low economies of scale and scope in assembly
– the world of both the PC and the workstation – a proprietary strategy is not
"evolutionarily stable." That is, it can be driven out by an aggressive open-sys-
tems strategy.

21 This was arguably Watson's own view. In the late 1950s, for example, he de-
creed unilaterally that IBM stop all development of vacuum-tube machine to
concentrate on transistors. "Years later, he enjoyed citing his 'visceral decision'
forbidding further development of vacuum tube machines to illustrate that authoritarian management is sometimes required to move an organization rapidly." (Bashe et al., 1986, p. 387.)

References

Arrow, K. J. (1974). *The Limits of Organization*. New York: W. W. Norton.

Bashe, C. J., Johnson, L. R., Palmer, J. H., and Pugh, E. W. (1986). *IBM's Early Computers*. Cambridge, MA: MIT Press.

Boulding, K. E. (1955). Notes on the information concept. *Explorations* [Toronto] 6,
103–112.

Butcher, L. (1988). *Accidental Millionaire: The Rise and Fall of Steve Jobs at Apple Computer*. New York: Paragon House.

Butos, W. N. and Koppl, R. G. (1993). Hayekian expectations: Theory and empirical
applications. *Constitutional Political Economy*, 4(3), 303–329.

Carroll, P. B. (1993). *Big Blues: The Unmaking of IBM*. New York: Crown Publishers.

Chandler, A. D., Jr. (1990). *Scale and Scope: The Dynamics of Industry Capitalism*. Cambridge, MA: The Belknap Press of Harvard University Press.

Chposky, J. and Leonsis, T. (1988). *Blue Magic: The People, Power and Politics Behind the
IBM Personal Computer*. New York: Facts on File.

Cohen, W. M., and Levinthal, D. A. (1990). Absorptive capacity: A new perspective
on learning and innovation. *Administrative Science Quarterly*, 35, 128–152.

Dosi, G. (1982). Technological Paradigms and Technological Trajectories. *Research
Policy*, 11, 147–162.

Edelman, G. M. (1987). *Neural Darwinism: the Theory of Neuronal Group Selection*. New
York: Basic Books.

Ferguson, C. H., and Morris, C. R. (1993). *Computer Wars: How the West Can Win in a
Post-IBM World*. New York: Times Books.

Fisher, F. M., McGowan, J. J., and Greenwood, J. E. (1983). *Folded, Spindled, and Muti-
lated: Economic Analysis and U.S. v. IBM*. Cambridge, MA: MIT Press.

Fisher, F. M., McKie, J. W., and Mancke, R. B. (1983). *IBM and The U.S. Data Processing
Industry*. New York: Praeger.

Flamm, K. (1988). *Creating the Computer*. Washington: Brookings Institution.

Garud, R. and Kumaraswamy, A. (1993). Changing competitive dynamics in network industries: An exploration of Sun Microsystems' open systems strategy.
Strategic Management Journal, 14: 351–369.

Hayek, F. A. (1952). *The Sensory Order: An Inquiry into the Foundations of Theoretical
Psychology*. Chicago: The University of Chicago Press.

Hayek, F. A. (1978). *New Studies in Philosophy, Politics, Economics, and the History of
Ideas*. Chicago: The University of Chicago Press.

Henderson, R. M, and Clark, K. B. (1990). Architectural innovation: The reconfiguration of existing product technologies and the failure of established firms. *Administrative Science Quarterly*, 35, 9–30.

Hinkle, D. E., Wiersma, W., and Jurs, S. G. (1982). *Basic Behavioral Statistics*. Boston: Houghton-Mifflin.

Hughes, T. P. (1992). The dynamics of technological change: Salients, critical problems, and industrial revolutions. In G. Dosi, R. Giannetti, and P. A. Toninelli (eds.), *Technology and Enterprise in a Historical Perspective*. Oxford: Clarendon Press, pp. 97–118.

Katz, B. and Phillips, A. (1982). The computer industry. In R. R. Nelson (ed.), *Government and Technical Progress: A Cross-Industry Analysis*. New York: Pergamon Press.

Koppl, R. G. and Langlois, R. N. (1994). When do ideas matter? A study in the natural selection of social games. *Advances in Austrian Economics*, 1, 81–104.

Kuhn, T. S. (1970). *The Structure of Scientific Revolutions*, second edition. Chicago: The University of Chicago Press.

Langlois, R. N. (1983). Systems theory, knowledge, and the social sciences. In F. Machlup and U. Mansfield (eds.), *The Study of Information: Interdisciplinary Messages*. New York: Wiley, pp. 581–600.

Langlois, R. N. (1992). External economies and economic progress: The case of the microcomputer industry. *Business History Review*, 66(1), 1–52.

Langlois, R. N. (1995). Capabilities and coherence in firms and markets. In C. A. Montgomery (ed.), *Resource-based and Evolutionary Theories of the Firm: Toward Synthesis*. Dordrecht: Kluwer Academic Publishers.

Langlois, R. N. and Robertson, P. L. (1992). Networks and innovation in a modular system: Lessons from the microcomputer and stereo component industries. *Research Policy*, 21(4), 297–313.

Langlois, R. N. and Robertson, P. L. (1995). *Firms, Markets, and Economic Change: A Dynamic Theory of Business Institutions*. London: Routledge.

Lazonick, W. (1991). *Business Organization and the Myth of the Market Economy*. New York: Cambridge University Press.

Loasby, B. J. (1976). *Choice, Complexity, and Ignorance*. Cambridge, U.K.: Cambridge University Press.

MacKay, D. M. (1969). *Information, Mechanism, and Meaning*. Cambridge, MA: MIT Press.

Machlup, F. (1983). Semantic quirks in studies of information. In F. Machlup and U. Mansfield (eds.), *The Study of Information: Interdisciplinary Messages*. New York: Wiley, pp. 641–671.

Maynard Smith, J. (1982). *Evolution and the Theory of Games*. Cambridge, U.K.: Cambridge University Press.

Miller, S. S. (1963). *The Management Problems of Diversification*. New York: Wiley.

Moritz, M. (1984). *The Little Kingdom: The Private Story of Apple Computer*. New York: William Morrow.

Nelson, R. R. and Winter, S. G. (1977). In search of more useful theory of innovation. *Research Policy*, 5, 36–76.

Nelson, R. R. and Winter, S. G. (1982). *An Evolutionary Theory of Economic Change*. Cambridge, MA: Harvard University Press.

Norberg, A. L. (1993). New engineering companies and the evolution of the United States computer industry. *Business and Economic History*, 22(1), 181–193.

Polanyi, M. (1958). *Personal Knowledge*. Chicago: University of Chicago Press.

Popper, K. R. (1965). Science: Conjectures and refutations. In *Conjectures and Refutations: The Growth of Scientific Knowledge*. New York: Harper.

Pugh, E. W., Johnson, L. R., and Palmer, J. H. (1991). *IBM's 360 and Early 370 Systems*. Cambridge, MA: MIT Press.

Raff, D. (1991). Making cars and making money in the interwar automobile industry: Economies of scale and scope and the manufacturing behind the marketing. *Business History Review*, 65(4), 721–53.

Rifkin, G. and Harrar, G. (1988). *The Ultimate Entrepreneur. The Story of Ken Olsen and Digital Equipment Corporation*. Chicago: Contemporary Books.

Ryle, G. (1949). Knowing how and knowing that. In idem, *The Concept of Mind*. London: Hutchison's Universal Library.

Sculley, J. with Byrne, J. A. (1987). *Odyssey: Pepsi to Apple . . . the Journey of a Marketing Impresario*. New York: Harper and Row.

Stinchcombe, A. L. (1990). *Information and Organizations*. Berkeley: University of California Press.

Teece, D. J. (1986). Profiting from technological innovation: Implications for integration, collaboration, licensing, and public policy. *Research Policy*, 15, 285–305.

Teece, D. J. and Pisano, G. (1994). The dynamic capabilities of firms: an introduction. *Industrial and Corporate Change*, 3(3), 537–556.

Tushman, M. L. and Anderson, P. (1986). Technological discontinuities and organizational environments. *Administrative Science Quarterly*, 31, 439–65.

Usselman, S. W. (1993). IBM and its imitators: Organizational capabilities and the emergence of the international computer industry. *Business and Economic History*, 22(2), 1–35.

Utterback, J. and Suarez, F. (1993). Innovation, competition, and market structure. *Research Policy*, 22(1), 1–2 1.

Weimer, W. B. (1982). Hayek's approach to the problems of complex phenomena: An introduction to the psychology of the sensory order. In W. B. Weimer and D. Palermo (eds.), *Cognition and the Symbolic Processes*. Volume II. Hillsdale: Lawrence Erlbaum.

6 Changing the game of corporate research: Learning to thrive in the fog of reality

John Seely Brown

Introduction: Setting my sights

In the context of corporate research, questions of foresight and oversight are always present. But there are different ways to address them. From a theoretical point of view, many of the issues are clear. From a practical point of view, however, attempts to discern unfolding technological and social trajectories are always clouded by what I call "the fog of reality." What I'd like to do in this chapter is take the practical rather than theoretical road and address the topic of foresight and oversight from my practical experience of life in the fog.

In particular, I'd like to talk about ways in which the fog is getting thicker. This is because the game of corporate research is itself changing even as we play it. (One of the changes, as I hope to make clear, is that we in the labs can no longer afford to regard the rest of the corporation as the opposing team!) Rapid and continuous changes are making it inevitable that we not only learn to live with the fog of reality, but that we learn to thrive on it – and I'll try to suggest some ways we're trying to do that.

From my own experience, however, I don't think oversight and foresight can be discussed without first introducing another "sight" and that is "hindsight." Corporate research is a ripe field for Monday morning quarterbacks telling the players what they should have seen and done. So a good deal of what I want to talk about is not just the difference between foresight and oversight, but also between foresight and hindsight, between looking through the fog and looking back when the fog has cleared.

Working in the fog

Inevitably, one of the problems of coming from the Xerox Corporation's Palo Alto Research Center (PARC) is that hindsight has already declared our biggest oversight. The Monday morning quarterbacks already know what we fumbled and when. We invented the personal computer and didn't know it.

Rather than try to duck this accusation, let me take it as a useful place to start. Looking again at this well-known story as more of the fog is lifting, we can perhaps begin to see not so much a different story (I don't want to be accused of trying to rewrite history) but some intriguing issues different from those that made headlines and book titles. These issues, in turn, raise some interesting questions about foresight and oversight and, in particular, about when oversight becomes foresight.

The first thing that needs to be said (and this is not just corporate false modesty) is that Xerox did not invent the personal computer. Others did that, and they deserve the credit for doing so. What Xerox did, and it does deserve credit for, is invent distributed computing. In one way, you could say Apple was heading for one goal while Xerox was heading for quite another. Both, unfortunately, were judged by the same standard.

The confusion between the two is understandable. About the time Apple's Lisa first appeared, Xerox introduced the first version of the Star, which in many ways was the precursor of both the Lisa and the Mac. Apart from similarities in the technology, both introductions also had in common that they were minor disasters. With radical innovation, that's not surprising. But what is instructive is the different ways the two corporations responded to their failures. Apple looked at their flawed machine, then went through several iterations until they emerged with a successful Macintosh, with which they went on to make history. Xerox looked at their flawed machine, then went through several managers, and in the process made a very different sort of history.

But to understand the story twelve years later, you have to separate the two very different technologies each corporation was looking at. Or perhaps it would be better to say you need to separate the two very different ways each corporation looked at what appeared to be very similar technologies.

Apple looked at its neat little box and its individual user and through several iterations tried to make the two increasingly compatible. Xerox, meanwhile, struggled on with its notion of distributed computing. We were focused on environments that would enable people not simply to work alone, but, though alone, to also be able to work collaboratively. We didn't aim to have individuals isolated in cubicles and offices working on "his" or "her" computer, but to have them – even though they might be isolated in a cubicle or on the other side of the world for that matter – working both individually and collectively on a distributed network. Now, some dozen years later, our original views of client–server and networking architectures are allowing that to happen.

The technological demands of these architectures were an incredible challenge. But it was not the only challenge. A major part of the problem was that while we could at least see the technological challenge, for a long time we couldn't see the other challenge that kept these technologies from the market. Apple, in a way, cleared the fog to expose our oversight – but our oversight was not what people think it was. What we had failed to see was not the personal computer revolution, but the fact that the innovative products we were creating challenged conventional practices, in particular, conventional buying practices.

Changing practice

Now that, I think, is so wild a claim that I need to spend a little time justifying it. And for that I'm going to take a relatively long detour back to where (for Xerox) it all began, with Chester Carlson and the invention of xerography.

For a long time it looked as if that technology also wasn't going to get out the door. Even though it was extremely powerful, no one could really see a huge market for it. The story is fairly well known now, told as another example of corporate oversight on the part of some big corporations – RCA, IBM, A.B. Dick, and Kodak – who were offered and turned down the photocopier patent. Given the market analysis, their rejection is actually understandable. What's almost inconceivable now is the market analysis. Put together by Arthur D. Little, it could see little value in the photocopier in that the authors decided there wasn't a market for more than a few thousand machines. Reading the report today is simply shocking. How could they have been so befogged?

We need to understand, though, that if we have trouble seeing back into Arthur D. Little's world view to understand their monumental oversight, they had far more trouble seeing forward to our world view – a world view that takes for granted the inescapable usefulness of copiers in every office and on almost every street corner. We know the value of the copier. We copy résumés, agendas, minutes, portfolios, theses, tax forms, letters, checks, and on and on. Why couldn't they see that? Hadn't there always been copies?

Well, copying goes back for millennia – classical literature wouldn't exist today with out it. But all the studies of the copier were, you might say, filtered through carbon paper. That's what copiers hoped to replace. Moreover, where people simply typed and copied simultaneously with carbon, the new machine would expect them first to type and then to copy. That didn't seem like a step forward.

What no one saw – how could they? – was that the copy machine wouldn't just be used for making a copy of an original. It would be used for making copies of copies and copies of copies of copies and so on. If people had continued to make copies of originals, market growth for Carlson's machine would have been a simple linear progression (some coefficient times the number of originals being generated). What Arthur D. Little and the various potential manufacturers couldn't see was that if, on the other hand, people started to make copies of copies, the progression would be exponential. The number of copies and the copier market would explode. And that's what happened. People started to see the power of copying for supporting collaborative group work, and this process – in effect a process of midcasting – has changed the way people work together around documents. Since it couldn't happen with carbons, no one could see it coming. The Xerox copier, in effect, was invented for an office that didn't yet exist, an office that the machine itself would have to bootstrap.

And here, rather circuitously, I've come around to the question of buying patterns. People don't buy machines for practices that don't exist. They can't be expected to. They will respond to recognized needs, and even to unrecognized ones, but not to needs that don't exist. So Carlson's copier in fact had to rely on not one, but two profound innovations. One was the copier itself, a technological innovation. The other was how it was put into circulation, a marketing innovation quite as profound.

Haloid, who bought the patent (and later renamed themselves Xerox), elected to take their return from use fees instead of trying to sell into a reluctant market. Each time a copier was used, they made money. And, as we now know, copiers were widely used. But before that was known, this marketing innovation allowed people "in the fog" to take a chance on the machine at minimal cost. It didn't take a leap of faith, unreasonable foresight, or monumental risk. So the machines were able to make it into offices and from there into both technological and marketing history.

Both stories are frequently told. But one is usually told in a technological arena, and the other in a marketing one. It seems to me crucially important to have the two together. It was the synergy of technological and marketing foresight that made Xerox possible. Foresight is not the purview of research labs, it is a coproduction of the research arm and the marketing arm together.

From units to systems

To return from this long digression to the point I was making, distributed computing met similar barriers. To buy a system for a practice that at the time did not yet exist took a monumental act of faith and an investment of a quarter of a million dollars to get the first few workstations plus file server plus print server plus a local area network (LAN) to connect them all. Back in 1982, there were very few people prepared for that kind of experiment. In contrast, with a couple of thousand dollars, you could get a Mac up and running. Now, a dozen years later, all the costs have fallen dramatically. No one would think about buying a computer system that was not basically networked. Once again, a change in technology has helped people to change the way they work.

So, I want to suggest, foresight and oversight begin to blend in subtle and interesting ways. Distributed computing was a foresight whose value is only now becoming understood. The oversight part of that foresight was in-compatibility in buying patterns, something "Mac in a box" circumvented.

Where we go from here

The essence of these stories is that business is always conducted in this "fog of reality." You're forever aiming at targets you can't see, or you don't un-derstand, or that change as a result of things you do. Even in this fog, how-ever, two things stand out as centrally important issues. I will try to develop them in the rest of this chapter.

The first is that living productively in the fog, developing foresight when you can't see ahead, is a collective, collaborative, "coevolutionary" process. It involves collaboration within the corporation. Research isn't going to do it alone. And it involves collaboration beyond the corporation – with suppli-ers and customers and all the people whose changing practices are the fun-damental grist to Xerox's research mill. This, as I'll explain in the next sec-tion, requires an understanding of the complex interplay of formal and in-formal processes and a great deal of listening from researchers – people who are often more inclined to gather an audience than to join one.

The second point is that the challenge of research is dramatically increas-ing because the reality we are trying to navigate now is subject to an ever-accelerating pace of change. Consider, only as an illustration, that when the Lisa and the Star were being developed, information was being processed at more or less 1 Mips. By 1994 the rate was 100 Mips, and within the next two years we may well see 1,000 Mips processing. The corporation and corpo-rate research have to keep pace. So the "great challenge," which I take up in the penultimate section, involves corporate research in changing and rein-venting the corporation and itself.

From "across the transom" to crossing the transom

There's an old, well-known model of the relation of corporate research to the corporation. Essentially, it says, researchers develop a new technology, preferably in a well-funded lab, then chuck it across the transom with a note that says, in effect, "The ball's in your court now – and here's the bill."

For researchers this is a pretty comfortable position. If anything goes wrong, it's blamed on the corporation. Perhaps that's why the story that Xe-rox invented the personal computer but failed to market it has lasted so long. As my account of the development of the copier shows, although I am a researcher, this isn't a position I subscribe to. Anything chucked across the transom should be chucked right back with the original note attached.

Within this model, which we all know enough to ridicule as brain dead, is a serious core that persists despite the ridicule. That is the belief that re-search's relations with the corporation are mediated through explicit, for-mal exchanges either in the form of requests from the corporation or the technological "push" from researchers. These are also passed across the transom, but people are not.

At Xerox, for example, such formal exchanges took place in annual "gap closure" meetings, when the two sides got together and contemplated the distance between them before returning to their separate spheres. Because these meetings were always struggles over power and turf conducted with varying amounts of passive–aggressive behavior, the gaps were almost impossible to close. The result was that very little technology came out, and the serious money seemed to go to those who wrote books about our failure to make money from our own technology.

As a first step in improving relations between research and the rest of the corporation, we learned to cross the transom regularly ourselves. A Technology Decision-Making Board, made up of the presidents of the business divisions and members of the research and technology centers, now meets once a month. This board – chaired by Mark Myers, Senior Vice President of Corporate Research and Technology and a member of the Corporate Office – provides a context for formal discussions having to do with portfolio balancing, how to decide what technology platforms to build, how to allocate resources, and so on. This attempt to straddle the transom has been an important change, but it has only addressed the formal aspects of interaction between the labs and the business divisions. It was necessary, but not sufficient for real change. (For an account of the formal structures, see Myers and Rosenbloom, in press.)

At the heart of the new relationship is the understanding that, for real exchange back and forth, we need mechanisms to bring out the informal, too. When the informal insights, understandings, and world-views of each side are allowed to emerge, you can really start something going.

To understand this, see Table 6.1, designed by Susan Stucky of the Institute for Research on Learning to illustrate our sense of what knowing or understanding really involves. As the table suggests, knowledge has both ex-

Table 6.1. *Distributed intelligence*

Knowledge	Individual	Group
Explicit	Concepts Procedure Rules of thumb	"Best practices" War stories Business processes
Tacit	Intuition Know-how/expertise Common sense Good judgment	Work practices Core competencies Communities of practice*

*Communities of practice refers to the social fabric that emerges from sharing a task over a period of time.

plicit and implicit components Equally, intelligence has both individual and group characteristics. One of the problems with much of the education system of the past hundred years is that it has put most of its money on the top left quadrant, individual, explicit knowledge. Thus it has focused almost exclusively on concepts and procedures. Similarly, instruction and workplace learning has looked at explicit rules and the like.

That's starting to change. People are beginning to notice the role of the group or social mind. They are starting to see how intelligence is distributed throughout a work team, for instance. As a consequence, explicit group characteristics such as "best practices," or "war stories," and business processes are gaining more and more attention. That's progress.

But there's further to go. We need also to start to take into account the tacit and informal nature of knowledge. In individuals this goes by names like "intuition," "know-how," or "good judgment," and collectively it's found in work practices, core competencies, and the collective, communal center of these, which I call the "community of practice" using a powerful notion developed by learning researchers over the last few years (Lave & Wenger, 1991). It's a term for the social network, often quite unnoticed, that binds together a work group, whose members gradually come to develop an implicit, informal, but shared and coordinated sense of what it is they do.

Where we believe we have started to break some new ground is in realizing that for any formal structure to work, it has to be complemented by informal structures shared in groups like this. Indeed, the formal and informal are not really separate but part of a reciprocating cycle in which people continually make some work practices explicit while they implicitly reinterpret some "war stories" and the like. In other words, Table 6.1 represents a dynamic process, not a static state.

From this view of active knowing rather than static knowledge, we've come to see that technology transfer has much more to do with how to get a constellation of interlocking communities of practice – communities of practice of researchers, communities of practice of developers, and communities of practice of end users – to develop shared understanding of each others' emerging insights. For this, they need to attend to the implicit assumptions behind each other's informal practices, which are revealed in ongoing conversations rather than formal pronouncements.

Attending to conversations

How does this fit with innovative research? Well, we believe that, given the accelerating pace of change, every market is an emerging market. There are no fixed markets to be mapped, only emerging markets that are continually being shaped by coevolving emerging technologies. Our job is to be there as those markets evolve, to learn to recognize them even before they recognize themselves because we can't afford to wait for the clarity of hindsight as we construct linkages between emerging markets and emerging technologies.

We allow technologies to shape the markets and the markets to shape the technologies.

Attending to the informal is, thus, particularly important. Getting a sense of the informal allows us to understand changing practice as it emerges long before it has been codified and made formal and explicit. So one of our goals has been to develop ways of doing this.

One way, we've discovered, is to engender ongoing informal conversations between research and the business divisions. You can do this, for instance, by focusing on practices around "boundary objects" – objects shared by two communities. Conversations about these reveal both shared and distinct attitudes. And you can do it by trying to elicit the critical questions about the emerging markets and the emerging technologies. What are the sustainable competitive edges? What are the market feedback mechanisms? What are the forms of coevolution? How would a certain technological insight enable us to see aspects of the emerging market? How do certain things in the emerging market help us reevaluate certain things being done in technology?

For this sort of research, we bring to the table a profoundly diverse body of people. At PARC, we run the gamut, we like to say, from atoms to culture, from people developing new materials to people developing new cultural understandings. So, as well as computer scientists, we have physicists, mathematicians, logicians, linguists, historians, sociologists, and anthropologists.

With this array, of course, we've already got some fairly profound, multidimensional conversations going on within PARC. These form around a problem space rather than an abstract desire to collaborate. The problem rather than the collaboration being the issue, this tends to bootstrap the participants beyond the methodological barriers that impede interdisciplinary collaboration on many campuses. At PARC, the increasing spirit of interested and willing interdisciplinary cooperation is probably one of the most striking and productive changes of the last decade.

A second real asset of this diversity is that the very culture we work in is itself an emergent one, not a dominant one. In a lot of corporations that have turned their attention to "culture," what you actually have is a demand for conformity. That's what Kunda's research (1992), for example, showed. These corporations don't really open themselves up to emergent cultural practices, to the formation of new communities of practice. What they do, instead, is expect everyone to join the dominant culture. This quashes radical departures rather than sparks them.

Quality listening

Perhaps a surprising motor for turning researchers into sophisticated listeners of emergent conversations was the movement for total quality management (TQM). At Xerox we had a company-wide program called "Leadership Through Quality" – widely known as LTQ (though one version of the culture insisted we weren't supposed to abbreviate it). I know of little that is less popular than trying to impose "quality" on researchers. We tend to feel that we know what quality is and to resent anyone trying to tell us how to achieve it.

But if you go to the essence of what the quality movement is really about, you get an interesting meeting between quality and research. For the corporation in general, Leadership Through Quality was profoundly valuable because it taught it to listen to its customers. After a while we researchers also found we, too, could gain invaluable insights by listening to our customers – both in and out of the corporation. What they had to say taught us a lot and kept us grounded in the real world. Indeed, our customers are often sources of innovations quite as insightful as anything we do on our own. Moreover, their innovations tend to be practical and useful. What emerged was a transposition from LTQ to QTL[4]:

> Quality through
> Linking to the world
> Listening through that linkage
> Learning through that linkage, and then
> Leading.

We couldn't offer to lead without first being prepared to listen, and so it became increasingly important to develop ways to listen. We approached this through something we call "listening through participation."

Listening through participation

We have developed several approaches to this. One has been through anthropology, which has as one of its primary methods participant observation. Several of our researchers have undertaken this sort of study and have developed rich and productive understandings of what our customers do and how we can support them.

Another is interaction analysis, a method we are developing in which a diverse group of researchers come together to try to make sense out of interactions and practices captured on video. This is an interestingly reciprocal method. A 30-second video fragment of a user–computer interaction is a powerful tool for bringing diverse points into productive friction, sparking genuine collaboration and coevolution among the body of researchers. And, out of the coevolving ideas, a rich insight into the practice captured on the video can emerge.

But there are other ways to listen. A third, particularly interesting, way exploits some of the increased computer power that we have on our platforms today. Instead of just adding feature, after feature, after feature, we try to build truly scalable and flexible platforms.

Practice is always versatile. If the technology supporting practice is equally adaptable, it's possible to develop incremental and reciprocal changes in both practice and technology that spiral upwards in exciting ways. You start by honoring the existing practice with the scalable technology. This technology allows practice to change in both expected and unexpected ways thus establishing a new practice. The new practice in turn requires new technological support, which a truly scalable platform should be capable of providing.

What you really have here is three spirals, as I've tried to show in Figure 6.1. Both work practice and the technology platform are being constantly modified in situ.

Emerging technology platforms linked to emerging work practices together enact something fundamentally new. And, as the right-hand side of Figure 6.1 suggests, this is where we believe value is really created. From this coevolutionary perspective, the researcher's challenge becomes not the invention of the future from outside, but its enactment from within.

Such a view of the development of technology and work practice can change conventional practices in many ways and calls for innovative responses. Let me just take one as an example. Consider the conventional contracts that govern relations between employers and employees or businesses and suppliers. They are usually written in a carefully prescriptive language specifying exactly what is expected at exactly what point in time. But this has two problems. In the first place, a contract is a "boundary object," which will have slightly different interpretations in each of the communities it concerns. It is thus almost impossible to be precise, for what may be precision in one community may not be in another. In the second place, if you look at Figure 6.1 again, you can see that what was specified when the contract was written is probably no longer exactly suitable at the time when the contract is executed, by which time the whole relationship will have advanced one turn along the spiral.

As I noted earlier, the challenge for research, and for the corporation in general, given the accelerating pace of change, is not simply to change technology or to change work practices or contractual arrangements, but to change ourselves. This is what I call The "great challenge."

The "great challenge"

Technology transfer for radical innovations turns, I believe, on the ability to change our preconceptions, to revise our mental models, to reframe the world. The corporation has to be able to do this, and so do its employees, from top to bottom. Let me talk first about changing the employees, individually, then I'll talk about the challenge to change presented by the group mindset.

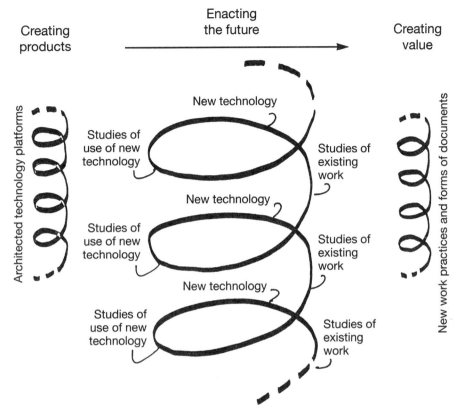

Figure 6.1. Enacting the future.

Changing mental models

From a cognitive-science point of view, changing mental models is a very real challenge. Your mental model determines how you perceive the world. In so doing, it excludes alternatives and tends to make new concepts conform to the old rather than adapting the old to the new.

Before talking about how to change, though, let me first give an example of why it needs to be done. As I noted, Xerox's prosperity was founded not on the number of machines sold, but basically on the number of pieces of paper that cycled through the machines. In that way, we are like razor-blade companies, producing razors, but making money on the blades. We do something similar with paper, toner, and service, and we're very good at it. Consequently, that's how we see the market – in terms of keeping paper moving through machines.

This view of the world has also helped us to focus on the "high end" of the market, because that's where people move high volumes of paper. Many

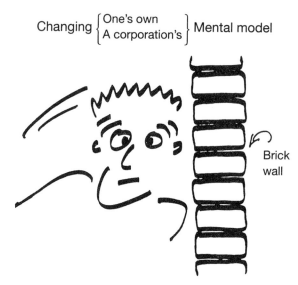

Changing $\left\{\begin{array}{l}\text{One's own} \\ \text{A corporation's}\end{array}\right\}$ Mental model

Brick
wall

Figure 6.2. The great challenge.

people don't even know we make laser printers. Yet probably more pages are printed per year by Xerox laser printers than by Hewlett Packard and Canon laser printers combined. It's not widely known because most printers we build wouldn't fit through most doors. Our printers are big, production-grade printers, printing at over a hundred pages a minute. This is good for us because the more pages printed, the more money we make – on printing supplies.

This way of thinking about our market is profound. It determines the machines we build, the way we service them, the toner and paper we provide, the business units we develop, the research we do, and on and on.

What happens, though, if the market and the technology change but we don't see it? This is likely to happen because between the fog on the one hand and our mental models on the other, we don't have the distinctions to even describe the change.

Consider changes in technology. When we come up with a new kind of copier, the questions we know to ask are: "How many pages per minute and what's the copy quality?" So these are the questions we ask about digital copiers regardless of whether they are the crucial questions.

Now consider our customers. They, like everyone else, are drowning in paper. The extreme examples are well known. The manuals for airplanes weigh several tons and those on aircraft carriers actually make a significant difference to the ship's displacement. But even in more down-to-earth circumstances, people want to get out from under the paper burden. They want only the information they need, not all the information they get. Essentially they're looking to have the phone book *without* having to take all the pages they'll never need. Intuitively, they recognize that paper makes a great interface, but a burdensome storage medium.

In this context, the digital copier could become a very powerful new platform. With light-lens copiers, you copy first, then distribute. But digital copiers change that. The first step is to scan. With scanned, digital text you can distribute over a network before copying – or what now becomes, in effect, printing. You can store in digital form rather than on paper and you need only print to read. For a scan–distribute–store–print process, it no longer makes sense to think of customer needs solely in terms of image quality and number of pages printed.

That's just one difference. Once you've got digital copy from scanning, there are many other things you can do with it. In particular, a range of powerful new computational as well as distributing and printing services can be added. For example, software is now becoming available that will allow you to summarize a pile of scanned articles, articles you once would have just copied. That's a wonderful way to deal with the flood of paper. But it no longer submits the copier to the old paradigms. Using summarizing software, for every 25 pages you put in, you may come out with only one. If you end up with only four percent of the paper you would otherwise have had to read and file, you will probably be very happy. But if we at Xerox continue to ask "How many pages at what kind of quality?" we shall be very unhappy. The digital copier requires us to rethink our conception of our market and how we provide value to the customer.

Now you would think that would be an easy idea to get across, but it is in fact a profound ontological shift and very difficult to see from the how-many-pages-and-what-kind-of-quality mindset. Changing these mental models is very hard. Indeed, over the past few years I've come to feel that organizational learning is relatively trivial. The real challenge is organizational forgetting. Moving a corporation built on light-lens copiers into the era of digital copying requires a lot of forgetting.

So it is becoming increasingly clear (despite the fog) that an important part of our job in research is to help change mental models, to envision what new work practices will be, and to determine where new markets will be emerging. And we have to do this quickly, because the markets are already changing.

Fostering organizational forgetting

One strategy for fostering organizational forgetting is something we call the "open ended video document." Here we ask four or five scientists who have developed a radical new technology to act out a new work practice enabled by that technology and we videotape their "skit." On the same video, the same group then discusses what they have done. What was key to the new work practice? How did the technology enable it? And similar questions. This process is then repeated several more times in which yet more new work practices are envisioned and reflected on.

The idea is to use this video document as an intuition pump to help both push and pull people into the mental model behind the new technology. For example, we took it to one of the most senior executive vice presidents of the company and asked him to watch the tape and then to create a scenario of how he personally would use the technology – essentially to add his own skit to complement the three on the video. The document was to pump his intuition to help him produce his own ideas in his own way. And then we did the same thing singly and in groups with others in the company. What we wanted was to help each participant enact new practices, to envisage what working with this technology would be like. And we hoped to reach beyond intellectual analysis to draw out instinctive responses based on personal practice and intuitions.

As an example of another strategy, we tried to get members of the corporation to think not only of the notion of trends but also of the notion of discontinuities. Here we asked business division presidents what "destabilizing events" they intended to introduce over the course of the year. They were also asked to predict what destabilizing events they were likely to encounter. With both these examples, our intent was to break the standard framework, to ask people to think in fundamentally new ways, and to provoke insights into new practices. We felt that new distinctions could allow latent insights to emerge, rather as the seeding of a solution causes crystals to precipitate.

Fostering changes in the group mindset

These strategies were aimed primarily at changing individuals and their mental models. When we began to work on the corporate organizational architecture, however, we discovered that we needed to focus attention beyond the individual. Here we were interested in perhaps the least understood quadrant of Table 1, the bottom segment of column two, which represents the tacit knowledge and expertise of the group. This knowledge and expertise is informal in the extreme. It is also, I contend, a crucial contributor to the creation of value. I suspect the reason that so many attempts at corporate reengineering fail is that they focus almost exclusively on the formal, on the explicit, and fail to grasp the group mindset at its implicit level.

The methods I have described are in themselves relatively slight and I am not trying to maintain that either individually or collectively they have irretrievably altered all mental models or the corporation's mindset. The "great challenge," getting the corporation to understand a radical innovation, is still a challenge. What I hope I have suggested is the nature of the challenge and the sorts of ways we have tried to meet it. More importantly, I hope I have indicated that it must increasingly become part of the research effort to meet this challenge – both by helping others to change their conceptual lenses, and by allowing them to change ours. It may well be that in times of constant change we need to focus our research effort on how to foster organizational change and forgetting as well as on providing technological innovation. For, in the face of constant change, we need to change constantly, and for this we need to develop a multiplicity of methods to help bend and break old frames built for old conditions.

Conclusion: Becoming "reflective practitioners"

In our case, the frame we need to break is the "document company" as a company for (re)producing (conventional) documents. Instead, we need to see documents themselves as technology around which work happens and value gets produced and begin from there the seamless merging of the paper and digital worlds. This will involve moving from just delivering hardware artifacts to also supporting social artifacts.

Undergoing this transformation involves changing one's conceptual eyeglasses to move from the left-hand column to the right-hand column of Figure 6.3. Making this change has involved a new expansion of our research activity into "soft" issues. It has also involved being prepared to change ourselves. Not long ago, Chris Argyris wrote a paper called "Too Smart to Learn" (1991). Without reading beyond the title it helped me understand both our assets and our limitations. It also reminded me that we, as researchers, need to become what Don Schön (1983), Argyris's colleague, calls

Learning	→	Learning and *un*learning
Thinking ‖ doing	→	Thinking ⌢doing
Individual learning	→	Collective learning
Strategic plans	→	Strategic intent and core competency
Making products	→	Making sense
Communicating	→	Listening

Learning to see learning

Figure 6.3. Changing our eyeglasses.

"reflective practitioners" – able continually to reflect and change our own practice as well as that of others. Promoting radical change is part of our agenda, but so is co-evolution, which cannot happen if we are not willing to evolve ourselves. Without using our insights to help others break their framing assumptions, the corporation isn't going to be in business. Without opening ourselves to have our own frames broken, corporate research is not going to be in business. As I tried to suggest with the story of the first copier, the two form a symbiotic relationship, and real foresight – insights and innovations that come to have real consequences – is a coproduction. We're all working in the fog, we've all got to keep our feet upon the ground. By putting them on different bits of the ground while supporting each other, we should get maximum collective traction.

In closing, I'd like to quote John Ruskin (1856–1960), art and architecture critic and early champion of many painters, including Turner, when few had the foresight to see more than fog in his paintings. It captures, I think, the essence of what it's like living in the "fog of reality," and gets to the core idea of insight that emerges between the oversight of some and the foresight of others.

On Seeing Clearly

The greatest thing a human soul does in this world is to see something and to tell what it saw in a plain way. Hundreds of people can talk for one who can think, but thousands can think for one who can see. To see clearly is poetry, prophecy, and religion – all in one. (Vol. 111)

References

Argyris, C. (1991). Teaching smart people how to learn. *Harvard Business Review*, 69(3), 99–109.

Kunda, G. (1992). *Engineering Culture: Control and Commitment in a High-tech Corporation*. Philadelphia: Temple University Press.

Lave, J. and Wenger, E. (1991). *Situated Learning: Legitimate Peripheral Participation*. New York: Cambridge University Press.

Myers, M. B. and Rosenbloom, R. S. (1999). Rethinking industrial research. In R. S. Rosenbloom and W. J. Spencer (eds.), *Engines of Innovation: U.S. Industrial Research at the End of an Era*. Boston: Harvard Business School Press.

Ruskin, John. (1856–1860). *Modern Painters*. 5 vols. London: Smith & Elder.

Sabel, Charles F. 1994. Learning by monitoring: The institutions of economic development. In N.J. Smelser and R. Swedberg (eds.), *The Handbook of Economic Sociology*. New York: Russell Sage Foundation.

Schön, Donald. (1983). *The Reflective Practitioner*. New York: Basic Books.

7 Environmental determinants of work motivation, creativity, and innovation: The case of R&D downsizing

Teresa M. Amabile and Regina Conti

Innovation, even technological innovation, has a distinctly human face. It is a serious technological oversight to ignore the human side of innovation – the motivation driving those who create new technologies. In particular, it is important to consider the impact of the work environment surrounding these individuals, an environment that emerges from management attitudes toward technological progress and risk-taking. Such attitudes are likely to be significantly affected by major organizational change. In this chapter we consider the effects of the work environment on innovation and, in particular, the effects of organizational downsizing on the work environment for innovation. What happens to entrepreneurial, risk-taking activity among scientists and technicians during periods of turbulence? If there is an impact on such behaviors, it is likely that technological innovation itself will be affected as well.

In chapter 3 in this volume, Garud, Nayyar, and Shapira treat technological oversights and foresights as consequences of choices by firms to invest or withhold investment in a particular technology. The focus is on risk-taking behavior by key managers in the firm. At a more microscopic level, however, the creation and development of new ideas for technological innovations depends on appropriate risk-oriented thinking among the inventors themselves. Garud, Nayyar, and Shapira briefly suggest that such behavior depends, at least in part, on the organizational environment that top management has established in the firm. This is the central thesis that we present here.

Definitions

In our research, creativity is defined as the production of novel and appropriate ideas or products by individuals or small teams of individuals working closely together. In other words, in order to be considered creative, something must be different from what has been done before, but it cannot be merely bizarre. It must, in some way, be useful, valuable, correct, meaningful, or otherwise appropriate to a specific problem or goal. We define innovation as the successful implementation of creative ideas by an organization. Thus, creativity is a necessary but not sufficient condition for innovation. Most of our early work – starting about 18 years ago – focused on verbal, artistic, and problem-solving creativity in individuals. In recent years, we have turned our attention more toward team creativity in business organizations, and (in a preliminary way) to overall organizational innovation.

A model of organizational innovation

Over the past several years, we have been developing an organizational innovation model (cf. Amabile, 1988) that is based on our model of individual creativity (Amabile, 1983a,b) and our empirical research within organizations. In addition, the model draws upon concepts presented in the empirical and theoretical work of other innovation scholars, especially Van de Ven (1986), Andrews and his colleagues (Andrews & Farris, 1967; Pelz & Andrews, 1966), Cummings and his colleagues (Ashford & Cummings, 1965; Cummings, 1985), Kanter (1983), and Bailyn (1985). The model attempts to incorporate all aspects of organizations that influence innovation. Because the model has been described at length elsewhere (Amabile, 1988; Conti & Amabile, in press), we will focus only on those segments of the model that are important for our present discussion.

Individual creativity

According to the model, the process of individual (or small-group) creativity figures prominently in the overall process of organizational innovation, as a necessary (but not sufficient) condition. Individual creativity depends on three components, which combine in a roughly multiplicative fashion. If any is absent, creativity will be absent; that is, ideas will be appropriate but mundane, or ideas will be novel but inappropriate, or no ideas will be generated. Moreover, in general, the higher the level of each of the three components, the higher the final level of creativity produced.

Skills in the task domain include everything the individual knows and can do in the domain of endeavor. *Skills in creative thinking* include a cognitive style favorable to taking new perspectives on problems, an application of heuristics for the exploration of new cognitive pathways, and a working style that is conducive to the persistent, energetic pursuit of one's work. These two skill components determine what the individual is capable of doing, with skills in creative thinking largely determining the novelty of the idea and skills in the task domain largely determining its appropriateness.

However, it is the third component, the motivational component, that determines what the individual *will* do. With no motivation, no responses will be generated. The type of response is influenced by the type of motivation. *Intrinsic motivation to do the task* is motivation arising from interest, enjoyment, deep task involvement, or a sense of personal challenge in the work. By contrast, extrinsic motivation arises from goals that are extrinsic to the task itself, such as attaining a promised reward, or winning a competition. Several theorists and researchers over the past two decades have argued that intrinsic and extrinsic motivation interact in complex ways and that, often, extrinsic motivation will undermine intrinsic motivation (for example, Deci, 1971, 1975; Deci & Ryan, 1985; Lepper, Greene, & Nisbett, 1973; Shapira, 1989).

In a number of experimental studies, we have found that creativity can be undermined by a variety of extrinsic motivators: Expected evaluation (Amabile, 1979; Amabile, Conti, & Coon, 1994; Amabile, Goldfarb, & Brackfield, 1990), surveillance (Amabile, Goldfarb, & Brackfield, 1990), contracted-for reward (Amabile, Hennessey, & Grossman, 1986), competition (Amabile, 1982, 1987), restricted choice (Amabile & Gitomer, 1984), and a general cognitive focus on extrinsic motivation (Amabile, 1985). Moreover, in these experimental studies and in other, nonexperimental studies, we generally find positive correlations between creativity on a task and intrinsic motivation toward the task (Amabile, et al., 1994).

We have summarized these findings in *the intrinsic motivation principle of creativity*: Intrinsic motivation is conducive to creativity, but extrinsic motivation is detrimental. In other words, people will be most creative when they feel motivated primarily by the interest, enjoyment, satisfaction, and challenge of the work itself – and not by external pressures. People who are primarily extrinsically motivated may produce technically proficient work, but it will be less creative.

Organizational innovation

The three components of organizational innovation represent the within-organization factors that can impact upon the innovation process. Most importantly for our present discussion, part of that impact derives from the influence of these factors on the creativity of individuals and teams. In other words, these organizational components constitute the work environment for creativity and innovation – the environment that can directly affect the generation of creative ideas by individuals and teams as well as the implementation of those creative ideas by the organization.

Like the three components of individual creativity, the three components of organizational innovation are assumed to combine in a roughly multiplicative fashion. All must be present to some degree, and the higher the level of each, in general, the higher the level of ultimate organizational innovation. We have derived these components from our own research on the effect of social factors on individual creativity, from the research of other innovation scholars and from an interview study with R&D personnel that we conducted several years ago (Amabile & Gryskiewicz, 1987). In that study, scientists and technicians were asked to describe both a high-creativity and a low-creativity event from their work experience. Analysis of the responses was performed through a detailed content analysis of verbatim transcriptions of the interviews. This analysis revealed several work-environment factors that appeared repeatedly in the high-creativity events, which we termed "environmental stimulants to creativity," as well as several work environment factors that appeared repeatedly in the low-creativity events, which we termed "environmental obstacles to creativity."

Motivation to innovate. This component of organizational innovation comprises the basic orientation of the organization toward innovation. Although it stems from the highest managerial levels, it is evident in many aspects of the organizational culture, including: management that is participative and collaborative; an absence of political problems and "turf wars" within the organization; a spirit of cooperation and collaboration; frequent, constructive, and supportive feedback on work efforts; and equitable recognition of creative efforts as well as creative successes.

Other key aspects of the organizational motivation to innovate are illustrated by quotes from the R&D interview study. The first of these is one of the most crucial: An encouragement and acceptance of risk taking. As one interviewee noted in describing his high-creativity event, "What helped here was people feeling secure – having an environment where they could say anything and not feel dumb." Another important aspect was the presence of open communication systems for top-down, bottom-up, and lateral communication. The absence of such systems was notable in several of the low-creativity events, for example:

The opportunity to share information was hindered by the fact that everything had to go up and then come down. The people in management would determine what information was shared and what was not.

Finally, the motivation to innovate is marked by an enthusiasm for innovative undertakings and a willingness to depart from the status quo.

From the beginning, the concept really lacked any innovative thought. It was a defensive strategy. Instead of looking for a concept that would be one step beyond what was currently available, we settled for coming out with something that was a "me too" product. (Low-creativity event)

The company made a commitment. There was an environment in this company that prized creative solutions to problems, and wonderful things happened. (High-creativity event)

The contrast between these two examples suggests that companies that lack what we term the motivation to innovate are more likely to engage in "exploitation" behavior, while companies that have the motivation to innovate are more likely to engage in "exploration" behavior (cf. Garud, Nayyar, & Shapira, chapter 3, this volume; Levinthal, chapter 10, this volume).

Resources in the task domain. This component includes everything the organization has available to aid work in the target domain, including a sufficient number of expert personnel, marketing resources that can effectively gauge market needs, testing equipment, physical facilities, materials, information, software, adequate budgets, and sufficient time for the technical work that must be done.

Something very important was the support provided. There was an allocation of people and capabilities across the organization. It was possible to get lots of diverse information. (High-creativity event)

There was pressure to get the product produced quickly. It was a long-range product, but this is a short-range company. (Low-creativity event)

He was insulated from day-to-day fire fighting, so he was able to step back and think of the process and develop it over several months. (High-creativity event)

Skills in innovation management. This wide-reaching component includes a number of elements relevant to management at all levels, from top management to project supervision. Each of these elements can directly influence individuals' intrinsic motivation for their work. Management skills and styles that are conducive to individual creativity and other aspects of the organizational innovation process include open communication between project teams and their supervisors, and managers who are models of professionalism. These and several other skills of innovation management appeared with high frequency in the high-creativity events described by interviewees in our R&D study. Among the most important, as revealed by our subsequent research, is the appropriate match of project assignments to employees' skills and interests, so as to capitalize on their sense of intrinsic motivation and, especially, their sense of positive challenge in the work.

There was no defined reward; people were working for the challenge and the potential that a business would be established that they could benefit from. (High-creativity event)

Another important aspect of innovation management appears to be an appropriate balance between freedom and constraint:

As the manager of this product, I gave the people involved a clear idea of what the end product was going to be. I attempted to get each person involved in those aspects that were in their expertise, and I asked them how they would go about doing it. I let people set their own goals and manage their own business. (High-creativity event)

Finally, the R&D interview study (as well as our subsequent research) highlighted the importance of forming work groups that are diversely skilled, cooperative, constructively challenging, and enthusiastic about the task at hand:

There were a number of good things about the group. We had similar abilities, but different backgrounds – different ways of looking at the problem. Also, we had mutual respect for each other's abilities and a willingness to listen but not hang on someone's idea – to say, "Well, that's a good idea, but here are some problems. . . ." (High-creativity event)

These three components of organizational innovation – the motivation to innovate, resources in the task domain, and skills in innovation management – constitute the climate in which technological advances are born. Not only does the model predict that these work-environment factors will relate to creativity, but it also suggests that, when organizations change radically, these aspects of the work environment will be likely to change.

Relationship between work environment, creativity, and innovation

The R&D interview study helped to establish the theoretical base that has guided our subsequent investigations in organizations, and it was also instrumental in the development of the principal tool we have used in those investigations – KEYS: Assessing the Climate for Creativity [formerly known as the Work Environment Inventory (WEI)] (Amabile, 1995; Amabile & Gryskiewicz, 1989). We then set out to use that tool to address a fundamental question that grows out of the theoretical model: Is there clear evidence of a relationship between work environment and actual product creativity, beyond the perceptions of creativity as viewed by the scientists involved in the work? We predicted that there would be. To this end, we carried out a three-phase study at a large firm that we call High-Tech Electronics International, a Fortune 500 United States company of over 30,000 employees that provides diversified electronics products to international markets (Amabile et al., in press).

Although it relied on quantitative data obtained from KEYS, this study's methodology was conceptually similar to that of the R&D interview study. We asked individual scientists and engineers to consider the most creative and least creative projects with which they had been recently associated in the company, and to use KEYS to describe the work environments surrounding those projects. We expected that, as we found in the interview study, the work environments of the high-creativity projects would be markedly different from those of the low-creativity projects. In addition to the initial project nominations and descriptions provided by these nominators, however, we attempted to provide validation in two ways. We set out to validate the creativity nominations by asking experts to assess the creativity of each of the nominated projects. And we set out to validate the environment descriptions by obtaining such descriptions from all members of the nominated project teams.

In Phase 1 of this study, each of 161 individuals across four divisions of the company nominated two projects: The highest-creativity project and the lowest-creativity project, chosen from the company projects over the last three years with which they were closely familiar. These nominators also completed KEYS to describe the work environment surrounding each of their nominated projects. In Phase 2, approximately 40 experts within the company (high-level managers and high-level technical staff) independently rated the nominated projects on creativity, with creativity being defined as "the production of novel and useful ideas." These experts were unaware of which projects had been nominated as high creativity and which had been nominated as low creativity. For Phase 3, a subset of 23 projects from Phase 1 (12 high and 11 low creativity) were subjected to further data collection. Each member of each of those project teams was asked to independently complete KEYS to describe the work environment of that particular project; these individuals were asked to describe only the one work environment, and they were unaware that the project was being studied for its creativity status.

As expected, compared to the low-creativity projects, the high-creativity projects had work environments that were higher on perceived positive challenge in the work; freedom; organization-wide encouragement of risk taking and innovative thinking; diversely skilled, cooperative work teams; project supervisor support and encouragement; and sufficient resources. Moreover, high-creativity projects had work environments that were lower on organizational rigidity and political problems, and somewhat lower on workload pressures. Most of these differences were obtained in both Phase 1 (project nominators' environment descriptions) and Phase 3 (other project-team members' environment descriptions). However, there was a considerable range of effect sizes. The high- and low-creativity projects were most different on the dimensions of challenging work, organizational encouragement, and work-group supports, and least different on the dimensions of sufficient resources and workload pressure. As expected, the high- and low-creativity projects were significantly different on both KEYS performance criterion scales, creativity/innovation and productivity, but in both Phase 1 and Phase 3, the effect size for the creativity/innovation scale was considerably stronger.

Finally, both the creativity nominations and the work-environment descriptions of the Phase 1 nominators were validated. The Phase 2 experts rated the previously nominated high-creativity projects significantly higher on creativity than the previously nominated low-creativity projects. The Phase 3 project team members showed considerable agreement with each other and with the original Phase 1 nominators in their descriptions of the project work environments.

The case of R&D downsizing: Impact on the work environment for creativity and innovation

Our study of high- and low-creativity projects at High-Tech Electronics International clearly established the relationship between each of the three organizational innovation components – the work environment factors – and creativity and innovation. The study provided evidence that projects differing on creativity also differ on the motivation to innovate, on resources in the task domain, and on skills in innovation management. The study also suggests that perhaps these components are differentially weighted in their impact on creativity and innovation, with the resources component being less crucial.

However, the work environment is rarely stable. For us, the next important question concerned possible changes in the work environment for creativity and innovation during times of turbulent organizational change. The downsizing that often accompanies corporate restructuring provides a currently prominent focus for this question. Answering the question will not only contribute significantly to our theoretical conceptualization of the innovation process; it will also have important implications for the management of innovation.

To this end, we recently conducted a second study at High-Tech Electronics International (Amabile & Conti, 1994). The stage for this study was set by a series of events that, from our point of view, was quite serendipitous. When we conducted our high–low project–creativity study, the company also requested that we distribute KEYS to a sampling of employees throughout the company, in order to simply assess the current work environment. We did so, collecting data from nearly 500 individuals. Approximately 4 months after this data collection, the company announced a major downsizing (as part of a restructuring); at least 15%, and up to 30%, of the work-force was to be eliminated through a program of early retirement packages, voluntary severance packages, and involuntary layoffs.

The company-wide KEYS administration that we conducted during the previous study provided us with an ideal predownsizing baseline of the work environment, creativity, and innovation. The design of the downsizing study was a simple one. At each of three points in time, we collected a cross-sectional sampling (with different individuals each time) of KEYS; this provided quantitative measures of the work environment, creativity, and innovation. The KEYS was accompanied by a questionnaire that assessed, in some detail, the degree of downsizing and other changes that the individual had experienced since the previous data collection (such as changes in one's work team, workload, level of authority, and physical workspace). The company has many different divisions and physical locations, and the rate and type of change varied considerably. In addition, we conducted interviews with a subset of the individuals who completed the questionnaires.

Wave 1 of data collection was conducted when the downsizing was approximately 70% toward its initially stated target. Wave 2 was conducted just as the downsizing was ending (100% of target). Wave 3 was conducted 5 months after completion of the downsizing. We also obtained two more objective measures of creativity and innovation covering part of the time span of the study – invention disclosures and patent applications.

We predicted the following patterns: work environment, as assessed by KEYS, would significantly change from Baseline to Wave 1; there should also be changes between Wave 1 and Wave 2, as well as Wave 2 and Wave 3, because the downsizing was coming to an end at Wave 2; work environment perceptions would correlate with the degree of downsizing and work-team disruption that individuals experienced; feelings about one's work and about the organization would correlate with the work-environment perceptions and the degree of downsizing; and creativity/innovation, as assessed by both KEYS and by the more objective measures, would show changes that parallel the downsizing and the work-environment perceptions, although one of the objective measures, patent applications, was expected to be a lagging indicator.

The quantitative data reveal that most indicators of the work environment, creativity, and productivity show a significant decline from the pre-downsizing Baseline to Wave 1. Specifically, the work-environment stimulants to creativity (as assessed on KEYS) declined, and the work-environment obstacles to creativity (also from KEYS) increased. However, the Wave 2 data indicate a modest rebound effect, and the Wave 3 data suggest that the work environment continued to improve for some time after the end of the downsizing. On some (but not all) dimensions, the work environment several months after the downsizing appeared to have improved back to baseline levels.

Notably, employees' ratings of the creativity of the work being done declined significantly during the downsizing, and had not returned to baseline level even five months after the downsizing had ended. The two objective measures of innovation – invention disclosures and patent applications – provide some additional insights into actual creative productivity. The number of employees decreased by 15% from the year during which the downsizing started through the year during which it ended, and the number of patent applications declined to about the same degree (12%). However, because of the long process required to submit patent applications, this indicator would be expected to show effects considerably later in time. By contrast, the number of invention disclosures submitted during a particular period of time is a more immediate indicator of current technological invention. Importantly, invention-disclosure submissions declined by a disproportionate 24% during the same period. These data suggest that, indeed, declines in creativity and innovation accompanied the negative changes in the work environment during the downsizing.

Mechanisms of psychological impact during downsizing

Even more interesting – and somewhat more surprising – than the work-environment changes over time are the correlates of downsizing changes throughout the course of the study, and the comments made by our interviewees. Both provide some insight into possible mechanisms by which the work environment, and the actual creativity of work being done, change during the course of downsizing. As expected, the stimulants to creativity, and creativity itself, negatively correlate with the degree of downsizing and other changes experienced, and the obstacles to creativity positively correlate. Moreover, feelings about one's work and about the organization correlate, in the expected directions, with downsizing and the other changes. (The more downsizing in one's department, and the greater the number of negative changes experienced, the less positive the feelings.)

Surprisingly, however, examination of quantitative data on employees' experiences, perceptions, and reactions reveals that relatively few of the observed declines in the perceived work environment can be directly attributed to the simple magnitude of the downsizing (reduction in force) already experienced by a particular individual within his or her department. Rather, another change appeared to be much more important: the instability of one's own work group. This measure, which assessed the percentage of one's current coworkers who were new (since the last data collection) and the percent of one's former coworkers who were no longer coworkers, correlated significantly with a large number of work-environment perceptions, feelings about the work and the organization, and reported work behaviors. Perhaps most importantly, reports of entrepreneurial, risk-oriented behavior correlated negatively and strongly with experienced instability of the work group. Combining across the waves of data collection, similar strong correlations were found for measures of anticipated future downsizing of one's department, the degree of uncertainty currently being experienced, and the efficiency of communication within the organization.

Interviews conducted with employees at Waves 1, 2, and 3 provide some detail concerning the mechanisms by which these effects might be operating during downsizing. The interviews focused primarily on questions about employees' initial reactions to the downsizing, the impact of downsizing on their team, and the impact on them personally. Content analysis of the interviews suggests that three major categories of changes are occurring, as perceived by these employees.

Structural changes. These changes concern the size, structure, and expertise of work groups, work assignments, and procedures within the organization. Quotes from several interviewees reveal that, often, lack of clarity and coordination in the changing work environment can lead to a focus on exploiting established paradigms, rather than exploring for something new:

I was concerned, and I wondered, How small can we get? What will the workload be – 50 hours? 60 hours? At first I was favorable: Maybe this time they'll do it right. But they didn't. They're firing all the people who do the work, and you can't get anything done. They're leaving all the managers (like me).

The red tape is much worse; the bureaucracy is much worse. The other departments have been trying to foist people on us, to give them something to do.

I'm not even sure what group or "team" I'm part of.

The work is more standard, less creative than before. Also, there's a significant decline in quality. The technical-support people have no time to meet your needs, so little thought goes into the work. What used to take 15 minutes now can take weeks, because the networks are gone. You don't know who to call for a piece of equipment or some information. You call the person who used to do it, and they're laid off with no replacement. It's unclear who (if anybody) is doing the job. No one knows who the players are.

We have a lot more time pressure – trying to do the work of two or three people. But there are other people out there doing nothing.

I'm bored to death, and so are many others. We're just maintaining pieces of what was, and bridging gaps, rather than doing something new.

Social changes. Many of our interviewees reported that the downsizing resulted in social changes, primarily having to do with the nature and quality of interactions between individuals and groups. Communication, cooperation, and trust were negatively affected.

There was competition for new placements, and the new teams were forced – not natural.

The "yes men" – the people who were not creative, who didn't speak their mind – they have advanced.

The impact has been negative, in all respects. Communication is not as open and honest. Cooperation is politically based, not oriented toward the customer's benefit. Trust within the group has deteriorated, because people are worried about their jobs. They don't take risks; they're very careful. As for the blend of skills within the group, downsizing has resulted in retention of the people who are liked by those in power – not necessarily the people who are needed. Finally, openness to new ideas has suffered tremendously. Technical managers, at the director level especially, say that you try something new at your own peril.

The newer employees especially are insecure, and are grappling to be seen and noticed. There's rivalry among some people.

Communication, cooperation – all that's gone down the toilet. There's no trust, because we were thrust together from lots of different organizations within the company. There are a tremendous number of power plays, and they're very visible. People have a sense of fear about the company. They think, "How can I trust you? You've let me down already." The common theme is that people just want to find a way out.

There's a lot more tension, leading to a lack of trust. Those about to leave are treated as outcasts. There's no eye contact, no chit-chatting; people avoid you like the plague.

The impact on creativity and innovation has been very negative. There's now a preconceived notion that there's *one way* to be creative – which, of course, is antithetical to creativity. We're all being constrained into the methods used by the organization we've been put into; it's stifling and directive. They're not capitalizing on the diversity they now have.

It's like the nuclear holocaust has happened, and you're the survivors, and no one knows each other.

Motivational and attitudinal changes. Perhaps the most interesting (though nebulous) category of changes reported by our interviewees has to do with alterations in employees' motivations, attitudes, and feeling states. These often appear to arise from sources no more specific than the simple fact of the downsizing/restructuring and the manner in which it was implemented.

I was ambivalent, and felt lots of anxiety, because the change would be so massive.

At first, I was very much aligned with it, because it seemed to signal a change in the way top management viewed things. But my feelings changed after we were a few months into it. It was clear that they'd screwed up, that politics were in control. Cost and improvement were not the issues; power was the issue.

Morale was very low; people experienced a great deal of anger, hostility, and anxiety.

The quality of our work dropped, because the sense of pride declined. We were no longer really a team. Instead, everyone was trying to protect their job – to justify themselves by looking good. They're *not* focused on the work itself.

The impact on me has been very negative. I don't so much care what happens to me, because I own my own business on the side. But I do want to do good, creative work, and I don't want to be BS'd. I want to work for the *real* goal – the creation of great new products – achieving something real, and helping others achieve. But it seems impossible now.

I'm very stressed and angry. My ulcer started acting up again recently, after 13 years. I thrive on good stress, but it's all bad now.

Everything's being stifled. There's no feeling of pride or ownership; people are frightened.

I've never seen worse morale anywhere. There's no trust; everything's in pencil. I spend 10% of my time worrying about whether I'll get laid off, and 90% wondering how I can get out. We lost great people because they can't stand the stress.

Avoiding or reversing the negative effects of downsizing

It appears, from our very preliminary analyses of these downsizing data, that the passage of time may be effective in reversing some of the negative effects of downsizing – as long as the downsizing has indeed been halted. However, it may be possible to take a more proactive approach to avoiding these effects, by altering the way in which downsizing is undertaken and implemented. The suggestions that our interviewees made focus primarily on social factors having to do with the behavior of top management, top-level decision-making, and communication.

Leadership is very important, particularly regarding the timeliness and flow of crucial information. People look outward for hope and guidance. The leadership wasn't there.

Have integrity. Say what you mean and mean what you say. Do what you say you'll do. If you say teams will decide how to do the restructuring, then follow what they recommend.

If they had gotten their act together long ago, with good, clear vision, maybe this could have been avoided.

Our CEO had the right idea, but he had to believe in his management to carry it out. And that was the problem – the old dinosaurs, the Good Ole Boy Club.

There should be a sense of fairness in treatment, and a sense of open communication. Share as much information as possible, on issues that affect people. A lot of our technical managers are from the "old guard" hierarchical management school. When times get tough, as they are now, they revert to the old ways. This should be guarded against.

Offer more long-term security. Say that you're *done* laying off, and will now concentrate on cultivating the people we have. Start investing in us.

Summary

We know, from our experimental research, that social/environmental factors can indeed have a significant impact on both work motivation and creativity. We know from the High-Tech Electronics study of high- and low-creativity projects that work environment is clearly related to creativity and technological innovation. The changes occurring throughout the course of downsizing, in our most recent study, begin to suggest a causal link between significant change in the organizational environment, work motivation, creativity and innovation.

Many intriguing questions remain, and new ones have been suggested by our results. Will the distinction between structural, social, and motivational/attitudinal aspects of the work environment be a generally useful one? Might the KEYS items and scales be categorized along these dimensions? Upon closer examination, will we find differential effects of events like downsizing on these different aspects? Will they, in turn, have differential effects on work motivation, creativity, and innovation? Are the three major organizational components, as presented in our innovation model, differentially important in their effects?

In addition to these specific questions about the work environment and its effects, we are still left with the broader questions. Can we confidently establish causal links in the relation between particular events, work environment, creativity, and innovation? Can we obtain strong evidence in organizational settings that intrinsic/extrinsic work motivation is indeed a potent mechanism through which these effects occur? Will it be possible to track changes in individuals' work motivation over time, as a function of work environment changes and as a function of project life cycle?

And, finally, considerable work must be done to uncover management techniques for alleviating the negative effects of downsizing on technological innovation, or, ideally, avoiding them altogether. Our interviewees made suggestions about the behavior of top management, top-level decision making, and communication. In addition, the quantitative analyses of our downsizing data suggest that it may be wise to maintain intact work groups and to complete the downsizing as quickly as possible. Finally, it will be useful to investigate other means by which organizations can cushion innovation against such "environmental jolts" – means such as those suggested by the research of Murmann and Tushman (chapter 14, this volume).

In addressing these issues, and many others having to do with motivation and the work environment, we begin to remove the veil from the human face of technological innovation. And, in doing so, we may avoid yet another form of technological oversight.

References

Amabile, T. M. (1979). Effects of external evaluation on artistic creativity. *Journal of Personality and Social Psychology*, 37, 221–233.

Amabile, T. M. (1982). Children's artistic creativity: Detrimental effects of competition in a field setting. *Personality and Social Psychology Bulletin*, 8, 573–578.

Amabile, T. M. (1983a). Social psychology of creativity: A componential conceptualization. *Journal of Personality and Social Psychology*, 45, 357–377.

Amabile, T. M. (1983b). *The Social Psychology of Creativity*. New York: Springer-Verlag.

Amabile, T. M. (1985). Motivation and creativity: Effects of motivational orientation on creative writers. *Journal of Personality and Social Psychology*, 48, 393–399.

Amabile, T. M. (1988). A model of creativity and innovation in organizations. In B. M. Staw & L. L. Cummings (eds.), *Research in Organizational Behavior*, Vol. 10. Greenwich, CT: JAI Press.

Amabile, T. M. (1990). *The Work Environment Inventory*, Unpublished instrument, Center for Creative Leadership, Greensboro, NC.

Amabile, T. M. (1995). *KEYS: Assessing the Climate for Creativity*. Greensboro, NC: Center for Creative Leadership.

Amabile, T. M. and Conti, R. (1994). *Changes in the Work Environment for Creativity and Innovation during Organizational Downsizing*. Unpublished manuscript, Brandeis University, Watham, MA.

Amabile, T. M., Conti, R., and Coon, H. M. (1994). *Effects of Intrinsic Motivational Orientation and Expected Evaluation on Task Persistence and Artistic Creativity*. Unpublished manuscript, Brandeis University, Waltham, MA.

Amabile, T. M., Conti, R., Coon, H., Lazenby, J., & Herron, M. (in press). Assessing the work environment for creativity. *Academy of Management Journal*.

Amabile, T. M. and Gitomer, J. (1984). Children's artistic creativity: Effects of choice in task materials. *Personality and Social Psychology Bulletin*, 10, 209–215.

Amabile, T. M., Goldfarb, P., and Brackfield, S. C. (1990). Social influences on creativity: Evaluation, coaction, and surveillance. *Creativity Research Journal*, 3, 6–21.

Amabile, T. M. and Gryskiewicz, N. (1989). The Creative Environment Scales: The Work Environment Inventory. *Creativity Research Journal*, 2, 231–254.

Amabile, T. M. and Gryskiewicz, S. S. (1987). *Creativity in the R&D Laboratory*. Technical Report Number 30. Greensboro, NC: Center for Creative Leadership.

Amabile, T. M., Gryskiewicz, N., Burnside, R., and Koester, N. (1990). *Creative Environment Scales: Work Environment Inventory. A Guide to its Development and Use.* Unpublished technical manual, Center for Creative Leadership, Greensboro, NC.

Amabile, T. M., Hennessey, B. A., and Grossman, B. S. (1986). Social influences on creativity: The effects of contracted-for reward. *Journal of Personality and Social Psychology*, 50, 14–23.

Amabile, T. M., Hill, K. G., Hennessey, B. A., and Tighe, E. (1994). The Work Preference Inventory: Assessing intrinsic and extrinsic motivational orientations. *Journal of Personality and Social Psychology*, 66, 950–967.

Andrews, F. M. and Farris, G. F. (1967). Supervisory practices and innovation in scientific teams. *Personnel Psychology*, 20, 495–575

Ashford, S. J. and Cummings, L. L. (1985). Proactive feedback seeking: The instrumental use of the information environment. *Journal of Occupational Psychology*, 58, 67–80.

Bailyn, L. (1985). Autonomy in the industrial R&D laboratory. *Human Resource Management*, 24, 129–146.

Conti, R. and Amabile, T. M. (in press). The impact of downsizing on organizational creativity and innovation. Chapter to appear in A. Montuori (ed.), *Social Creativity*

Cummings, L. L. (1965). Organizational climates for creativity. *Journal of the Academy of Management*, 8, 220–227.

Deci, E. L. (1971). Effects of externally-mediated rewards on intrinsic motivation. *Journal of Personality and Social Psychology*, 18, 105–115.

Deci, E. L. (1975). *Intrinsic Motivation.* New York: Plenum.

Deci, E. L. and Ryan, R. M. (1985). *Intrinsic Motivation and Self-Determination in Human Behavior.* New York: Plenum.

Kanter, R. M. (1983). *The Change Masters.* New York: Simon and Schuster.

Lepper, M. R., Greene, D., and Nisbett, R. E. (1973). Undermining children's intrinsic interest with extrinsic reward: A test of the "overjustification" hypothesis. *Journal of Personality and Social Psychology*, 28, 129–137.

Pelz, D. C. and Andrews, F. M. (1966). *Scientists in Organizations.* New York: Wiley.

Shapira, Z. (1989). Task choice and assigned goals as determinants of task motivation and performance. *Organizational Behavior and Human Decision Processes*, 44, 141–165.

Van de Ven, A. H. (1986). Central problems in the management of Human Decision Processes, innovation. *Management Science*, 32, 590–607.

Section IV
Remembering to forget

8　Local rationality, global blunders, and the boundaries of technological choice: Lessons from IBM and DOS

Joseph F. Porac

There is no business in the world which can hope to move forward if it does not keep abreast of the times, look into the future and study the probable demands of the future.

Thomas J. Watson, Sr., 1968

Introduction

An everyday observation about technological innovation is that some firms seem to make better technological choices than others. Common sense tells us that innovators have great technological reach, that they possess an uncanny capacity for divining the marketplace and offering timely and exciting products or services. It is difficult not to attribute these differential rates of success to the technological "foresight" of first movers and/or to the technological "oversights" of laggards. First movers are visionaries with a knack for making the right choice among highly uncertain technological options. Laggards, on the other hand, miss opportunities by being wedded to the past, and thus forego future gains. These dispositional attributions frame foresight and oversight as issues of cognitive competence – some firms have technological vision, while others don't. Moreover, to the extent that cognitive competence can be measured and manipulated, dispositionalizing means that the propensity for foresights and oversights can be engineered. Technologists, consultants, and managers can create organizing routines that promote creativity, enhance the innovativeness of design, and generally incite firms to be recipe-makers rather than recipe-takers.

As obvious as these observations might be, however, the concepts of technological foresight and oversight rest on two *non-obvious* assumptions about the way the managerial mind interacts with technological environments. First, any claim to foresight or oversight assumes that technological environments exist independent of the decisions and actions of firms, that there is an external technological imperative at work that can and should act as an ex ante guidepost for technological choices. Without an ex ante criterion for "good" technological judgment, decision foresight and oversight reduce to statistical abstractions, since we would expect that, by chance alone, some choices pay off while others fail. Enacting the laws of chance is hardly grounds for claiming technological prescience when a firm succeeds, and is equally suspect as grounds for claiming technological ignorance when a firm fails. Ex ante guideposts are a prerequisite for evaluating the cognitive competence underlying technological judgment.

Second, the concepts of foresight and oversight require that firms differ in their access to, and understanding of, these external technological contingencies. It must be assumed that some firms are locked into a myopic and short-term decision perspective in which the concrete details of what is already known hold sway, while other firms can scan the technological environment in panoramic fashion and suspend their reliance on present certainties in favor of future ill-defined breakthroughs. Foresight and oversight are meaningful only if interfirm differences in technological awareness exist.

What makes the guidepost and awareness assumptions nonobvious is the fact that technological knowledge is both socially constructed and enacted over long periods of time. With respect to the former, the socially constructed nature of technology means that technical change occurs within communities of practitioners who share standards of evaluation, technological recipes, and skills (Bijker, Hughes, & Pinch, 1987). It is these shared cognitive structures that provide the epistemic justification for any single technological choice by members of the community. The rationality of a technical decision is dependent upon and embedded within the community's collective frame of reference. Two or more communities often see the world very differently. The quality of judgment is thus relative to the frame of reference being used to evaluate it. What one technical community views as prescience, another may view as stupidity. Technological foresight and oversight thus depend on whose point of view dominates, not on who has a greater awareness of some underlying set of universal technological contingencies.

With respect to enactment, the construction of technological knowledge over time means that technical innovations shape market realities as much as they respond to them (Garud & Rappa, 1994). Innovation is open-ended and indefinite. Technological paradigms are built "on the fly." Over time, thoughts, artifacts, and standards of evaluation get intertwined and accepted as objective truths, but this apparent "closure" is a result of, rather than a cause of, technological progress (Bijker, Hughes, & Pinch, 1987). The open-endedness of technological trajectories undermines any straightforward evaluation of technological right and wrong. Because breakthroughs often take years to fully understand and appreciate, ex ante evaluations of technological choices, especially those that are radical departures from existing paradigms, are difficult at best.

In this chapter, I want to examine the implications of these construction-ist arguments for determining whether the technological judgment of a firm is good or bad. Constructionism as a general approach to managerial think-ing breaks down the oppositional relationship between managers and their business environments by viewing knowledge and environment as recipro-cally determined. Simultaneously, constructionism embeds this reciprocal relationship within a community of actors whose collective beliefs and practices provide the grist for determining what is useful and what is not. Constructionism does not mean that "anything goes" with respect to judg-ment, that it is impossible to evaluate the merits of a choice. It does, howev-er, localize decisions within particular frames of reference believed at partic-ular points in time by particular people. This localization encourages a sen-sitivity to the construals of managers at the point of a technological choice. Moreover, it suggests that technological trajectories are constituted by chains of locally rationalized decisions, each being made by actors for rea-sons that make sense to them at the time of their choice. Over time, these lo-cal decisions may jointly create conditions that make some local choices seem more prescient than others, even though all choices were reasonable when they were made. The more uncertain and less closed the technological environment, the more likely these displacements will occur. When they do occur, and with the benefit of hindsight, there are strong pressures to cele-brate the winners and chide the losers. These accolades and criticisms, how-ever, are post hoc attributions that should not be confused with the cogni-tive competence underlying the local choices themselves. This difference be-tween the local rationality of technological choice and the global effects of, and attributions about, these choices complicates the concepts of foresight and oversight substantially. These complications are the subject I wish to pursue in this chapter.

My vehicle for exploring a constructionist treatment of technological foresight and oversight will be what many experts view as the costliest commercial blunder of all time: IBM's loss of market leadership in the per-sonal computer (PC) business. The story is well known and has been ana-lyzed extensively by both journalists (for example, Carroll, 1993; Manes & Andrews, 1993; Ferguson & Morris, 1993; Chposky & Leonis, 1988) and aca-demics (e.g., Steffins, 1994). Moreover, few companies have been written about as much as IBM and a great deal of information about the company's history and culture are available in the published literature (for example, Rodgers, 1986; Sobel, 1981; Foy, 1974; Rodgers, 1969; DeLamarter, 1986). These accounts provide fine-grained detail for understanding the context of IBM's choices regarding the personal computer business.

For space considerations, I limit my analysis to one aspect of IBM's choice set: Its dealings with Microsoft Corporation over the DOS operating system for the first personal computer. This is a reasonable simplification, since most treatments of the PC industry single out the IBM–Microsoft DOS transaction as a defining moment in computing history. By untangling some of the social and cognitive aspects of this transaction, I wish to show how a constructionist treatment of technological choice complicates simple attributions of technological foresight and oversight. In the pages that follow, I will first introduce the context of IBM's DOS transactions, and then suggest four propositions that together provide a constructionist interpretation of the choices of IBM and Microsoft in agreeing on DOS as the PC's operating system. I then address the question of whether a cognitive claim of oversight can be leveled against IBM, and foresight in the case of Microsoft. I conclude with a general discussion of whether technological foresight and oversight are theoretically useful concepts.

IBM's global "blunders"

For over 30 years, IBM dominated the computer industry with blue-chip products and a stellar reputation for crisp marketing and incredible skill in exploiting its strong position in the industry. When the company first commercialized its version of a personal computer in the early 1980's, the IBM PC quickly captured 80% of the market for desktop computing and became the industry standard. IBM's PC business rapidly grew into a multibillion dollar enterprise. This domination was short-lived, however, as IBM's market share began to erode steadily from 1984 to the present. By 1993, IBM was selling only 15% of all personal computers, and the company was struggling to keep pace with a host of smaller firms that had wrested technological leadership from "Big Blue" sometime in the late 1980's.

Along the way, IBM made a series of fateful business and technological decisions that sealed the fate of its PC division. The company

1. Purchased the DOS operating system for its original PC from Microsoft Corporation with a contract that prevented IBM from controlling the source code yet permitted Microsoft to sell DOS openly to other computer manufacturers for a per-copy royalty. Software written for IBM PC's was thus compatible with any non-IBM machine running DOS, and the per-copy royalty motivated Microsoft to supply DOS to any manufacturer who requested it.

2. Outsourced production of its microprocessors to Intel Corporation, buying 20% of Intel to insure a stable supplier. IBM sold its stake in Intel (and refused an additional 10% of the company), only to see Intel stock skyrocket as its microprocessors became established as the standard in the industry. By some estimates, IBM lost more than $5 billion in potential cumulative returns by dumping Intel stock prematurely. More importantly, the company lost control of its microprocessor technology as Intel proceeded to sell 80286, 386, and 486 chips on the open market.

3. Refused exclusive marketing rights to Lotus' 1-2-3 spreadsheet software in 1982, foregoing billions of dollars of future profits and missing an opportunity to control the one software application that became the reason why many customers actually purchased personal computers.
4. Attempted to protect its market share by introducing the PS/2 line of personal computers that were differentiated from AT clones on the basis of their internal bus technology. Customers neither understood nor valued this difference. Competitors immediately exploited this uncertainty by forming an anti-IBM coalition that destroyed any chance that IBM had to solidify its dominant position in the PC industry.
5. Failed to agree with Microsoft on an appropriate division of labor for developing a graphical user interface for OS/2, IBM's second generation PC operating system. Microsoft eventually marketed "Windows" software on its own and established the current PC standard with a Windows plus DOS operating system.

Cumulatively, these decisions cost IBM billions of dollars in unfruitful development costs and lost profits. More importantly, they triggered a new paradigm of computer technology and distribution that not only made it difficult for IBM to capture long-term monopolistic profits in the PC business, but also undermined IBM's dominant position in it's historical stronghold, mainframe computing.

The sheer magnitude of these consequences has attracted enormous attention. Volumes of material have been written about the transformation of the computer industry since the introduction of the IBM Personal Computer. Still more has been written about how and why IBM lost money in this transformation. The prevailing view emphasizes IBM's skewed and narrow technological vision. Regis McKenna (1989), in his book *Who's Afraid of Big Blue*, states the case succinctly:

> Because of its size and its myopic view of the computer world, IBM was very slow to see that new technology was fragmenting its markets. As a result, IBM missed the opportunity to adapt its technology to the new markets, and to develop new distribution channels that could move the technology to untapped markets.

A complimentary explanation often found in the press attributes farsightedness and technological vision to the clear winners of the computer wars – Bill Gates and Microsoft are technological wizards, Andrew Grove and Intel are shrewd masters of the microprocessor game. These are technological oversights and foresights in their rawest forms.

Or are they? I suggest a different explanation. Simple accounts of technological oversight and foresight mask the complexities of the competing technologies and the enormous uncertainties involved in the shift from mainframe to distributed computing. None of the key actors in this transformation anticipated the direction and magnitude of the paradigm shift that would eventually occur. Just as one example, Burgelman (1994) noted that in the early 1980's Intel listed the top 50 uses for its microprocessors and personal computing didn't even make the list! It is unreasonable to claim that any single person or company had a more (or less) accurate understanding of the paradigm shift. Each actor was pursuing narrow and locally defined interests, interests that were themselves shaped by unique decision histories and past experiences. Each actor was thus acting rationally *within the unique decision situations these histories created*. It was the long-term *interaction* of these local decisions that changed the computing world, not the foresights or oversights of the actors involved. Supporting evidence for this argument is no clearer than in the case of the IBM–Microsoft DOS transaction.

The DOS deal: Four propositions about local rationality

For IBM in 1980, personal computers were strictly a secondary product category in an industry where profitability and prestige stemmed from mainframe innovation. Nearly a decade earlier, a summer task force at the company had warned that the cost of computing power would fall precipitously, and that it would be increasingly difficult for IBM to squeeze profits out of its current technological trajectory. In response, IBM launched its F/S (or Future Systems) project in the mid-1970's to redefine computing technology and leapfrog a generation or two in mainframe computing power. The project was, by all accounts, a failure, draining financial and human resources away from other more-promising technologies, and setting IBM back in producing succeeding generations of its bread-and-butter machine, the IBM 360. F/S was killed in 1976, and for the rest of the decade, the formative years of the personal computer industry, IBM's top management was preoccupied with reclaiming lost ground in its core business. Ferguson and Morris (1993) labeled the F/S project IBM's "own Vietnam," and suggested that it singlehandedly destroyed the confidence of company executives – most notably Frank Cary, IBM's CEO – in centralized projects and massive technological directives. In doing so, it set in motion political forces that fractured the company into divisional fiefdoms, and made it difficult for IBM to achieve any semblance of coordinated product planning.

This fractionated administrative culture was the backdrop for IBM's foray into personal computers. By 1980, over 35 companies were manufacturing microcomputers, annual sales had topped 200,000 units, over 3000 application programs were available, and Apple Corporation had become the darling of the business press (Steffins, 1994). IBM itself had experimented with small low-end computers for years, and during the late 70's the company's business units in Atlanta and Boca Raton had researched many of the pioneering hobbyist computers such as the MITS, IMSAI, and Commodore machines. But it wasn't until IBM executive Bill Lowe convinced

CEO Cary that it was time for IBM to make a concerted effort to build a personal computer that the company entered the market with a low-end machine of its own in August of 1981. According to published accounts, Lowe argued that the machine could be designed, built, and marketed in one year. To make this a reality, Lowe, and his successor Donald Estridge, broke the IBM internal sourcing mold by seeking outside suppliers for most of the machine's parts, presumably well aware of the "open systems" implications of this strategy.

One such supplier was Microsoft Corporation, at the time a software developer specializing in adapting computer languages to the many models of microcomputers that had proliferated in the early years of the industry. Microsoft was originally asked to provide a version of BASIC for the IBM machine, but when IBM executives failed to connect with the developer of the dominant operating system of the time, CP/M's Digital Research, Microsoft was asked to provide an operating system for the machine as well. For a small fee, Microsoft purchased a system from a small Seattle software house, and sold it to IBM as the now famous DOS. The terms of the deal were that Microsoft received an advance of $400,000 for DOS plus per-copy royalties somewhere between $1 and $15 (Manes & Andrews, 1993). Most significantly, IBM was prevented from licensing the DOS source code to any other company for a period of seven years. The contract was nonexclusive, however, and gave Microsoft the right to provide DOS to any other computer manufacturer it chose to supply. In the years following the introduction of the IBM PC, Microsoft exercised this right repeatedly, in the process leveraging its critical supplier position into domination of the entire PC software business. In doing so, Microsoft fed a growing stream of IBM "clone" machines that eventually overtook the personal computer segment from IBM itself.

Because the IBM–Microsoft DOS deal was so pivotal to the growth of the personal computer industry, and because the two companies' fortunes took dramatically different turns after the deal was consummated, it offers important lessons concerning the ability of managers to understand the implications of their technological choices. Given its tremendous financial and intellectual resources, how could IBM mortgage its future by becoming so dependent upon tiny Microsoft and an operating system that most experts viewed as second-rate? Was it technological blindness? Market naiveté? Arrogance? And what about Microsoft? Was Bill Gates so familiar with the personal computer industry that he was able to divine its underlying trends to pull off the deal of the century? Published accounts of the transaction suggest a very different scenario. I offer four propositions to explain the case.

Proposition 1: IBM managers interpreted the DOS transaction using logics and analogies imprinted by the capabilities and past history of the company. They saw what their history allowed them to see.

Evolutionary (for example, Nelson & Winter, 1982) and resource-based views of innovation (for example, Teece, 1988) suggest that technological decisions depend upon a natural trajectory that is embodied in a firm's knowledge base and past experiences. This creates a path dependence in technological decision-making, as past resource commitments, existing organizational routines, and salient managerial talents define what is a reasonable choice by influencing the costs involved in any course of action. Proposition 1 is consistent with this argument, and reflects the fact that IBM managers were constrained in what they could accomplish with the PC and were acting quite rationally within these constraints. IBM managers brought a particular mindset to the negotiations with Microsoft, a mindset illustrated in the right side of Figure 8.1.

Several major historical influences were operating to shape IBM's local decision perspective. First, IBM had a terrible track record in producing operating systems for its computers. By some estimates, for example, the operating system for IBM's System 360 mainframe eventually required $500 million in development spending and was still bug-ridden and late. In his published memoirs, Thomas Watson, Jr., the CEO of IBM during the 360's rollout, looked back on the development of the machine's operating system as

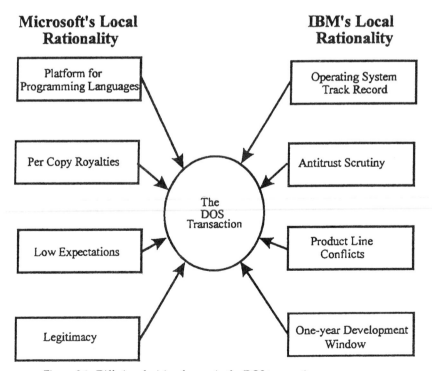

Figure 8.1. Differing decision frames in the DOS transaction.

one of the bleakest times in the company's history (Watson & Petre, 1990). Moreover, some of the executives involved in the development of the PC, particularly Donald Estridge, had experienced similar problems in developing operating systems in the past, and were reluctant to try their hand again. Contracting an operating system from a software house specializing in microcomputers was a viable way to avoid operating-system embarrassments yet another time.

Second, IBM had for many years been preoccupied with antitrust laws and government charges of anticompetitive practices. Thomas Watson, Sr. was convicted of antitrust violations while still a young executive working for National Cash Register in the early part of this century. Throughout its history, IBM had been consistently targeted by government antitrust lawyers. In fact, the company was involved in a government antitrust investigation that extended from 1969 through 1980, eventually being closed just before the personal computer was brought to market. According to accounts by company insiders, antitrust sensitivity pervaded almost all of IBM's operations and decisions. Secrecy (the government collected millions of documents from IBM over the course of its last major investigation), the heightened involvement of lawyers in market decisions, a minimal competitive strategy (lawyers refused to allow IBM executives to discuss market-share statistics and to collect competitive intelligence), and a reluctance to overcontrol small companies that could become potential competitors were all offshoots of the company's antitrust phobia. Signing a nonexclusive contract with Microsoft that was clearly to Microsoft's benefit was one way of avoiding any future claim that IBM was dominating the personal computer market.

Third, IBM traditionally protected its existing product lines when developing new products. Rather than offer potentially competing machines, IBM's strategic recipe was to fragment markets and develop hardware for well-defined niches. The goal was to dominate each small market through close customer support. At the time of the PC's development, IBM had a stable of profitable mainframe and minicomputer systems. Protecting these profitable cash flows (particularly minicomputers) from any encroachment of the PC was a salient concern. No plans were made to make the PC very powerful, so a sophisticated operating system was not really necessary. Moreover, the PC business had to compete with other product groups for access to corporate resources. Subcontracting the operating system to a small company like Microsoft was a way of getting the work done more cheaply than if IBM produced the system itself.

Finally, top management's approval of the PC project hinged substantially on Bill Lowe's original claim that it could be sent to market in one year. According to Ferguson and Morris (1993), in 1980 CEO Cary was still smarting from the failure of the F/S project and was not inclined to approve another multiyear commitment of company resources on a product whose potential was still unclear. Lowe's one-year commitment was a clever appeal to overcome this resistance, but placed the PC development team in the position of having to build the machine using off-the-shelf components from non-IBM manufacturers. The internal development of an operating system within a one year time frame, especially given IBM's software development problems, was simply out of the question.

Proposition 2: Because Microsoft did not share IBM's organizational history, it's own trajectory was quite different, and thus the context of its actions in the DOS deal were different as well. There was no universal technological environment imposing itself on both firms. Each firm responded to an environment that its past created for it.

IBM's decision context created a reasonable rationale for the company to strike a deal for DOS. This was true for Microsoft's decision frame as well, but for very different reasons. This is illustrated in the left side of Figure 1. First, Bill Gates and Paul Allen, the company's founders, started out writing programming languages rather than operating systems. Gates and Allen were early enthusiasts of personal computers. The company was formed around a version of the BASIC programming language that Gates and Allen wrote for the Altair computer. Early in its history, Microsoft's revenues came from writing high-level programming languages for the several different varieties of personal computers that had begun to emerge in the hobbyist market. For Microsoft, writing an operating system was not a primary objective. Indeed, the company never fully wrote DOS for IBM. For Microsoft, one major objective of the IBM agreement was to sell an operating system that would be just another platform for its programming languages.

Second, Gates and Allen had learned quickly that one-time fees for software were not profitable. Personal computer vendors were typically small and undercapitalized, and were reluctant to absorb high up-front advances for software. This meant that there was a low ceiling for Microsoft's profit margins on software development and distribution. To adapt, Gates and Allen initiated the practice of charging small royalties on each copy of their software. In this way, the upfront costs to the vendor were kept low, while Microsoft's revenues expanded as more personal computers were sold. Microsoft brought this pricing recipe to the table in their dealings with IBM.

Third, Gates, in published recollections, claims to have had very low expectations for the success of IBM's PC's (Manes & Andrews, 1993). Most industry insiders at the time were not forecasting large PC sales, nor explosive sales growth. Moreover, IBM had failed in two earlier attempts to build a small computer. For this reason, Gates sought to maximize his gains by pushing for a nonexclusive marketing contract for DOS that permitted Microsoft to sell the software to other PC vendors. In Microsoft's view, this was simply a rational, profit-maximizing move.

Finally, in 1980 Microsoft Corporation, although one of the most successful vendors of personal-computer software at the time, was still small and concerned with legitimating its place in the business. Producing an operating system for IBM, historically a company closed to outsiders, was viewed in the industry as a prestigious and lucrative contract. Because of the IBM deal, Microsoft gained instant credibility.

It is clear from the above that the decision frame of Microsoft was very different from IBM's. For IBM, the DOS transaction was a way of quickly getting an operating-system written for a computer that was being introduced as a small segment of the company's total business. Past experience had convinced IBM executives that operating-system development was complex, time consuming, and expensive. At the same time, keeping an arm's-length relationship with Microsoft, and offering Microsoft latitude in the sale of DOS to other computer manufacturers, was an important signal to federal antitrust watchdogs that IBM was not attempting to use its size to manipulate the nascent market for small desktop computers. For Microsoft, on the other hand, the deal was an opportunity to legitimate itself in the computer industry, as well as a chance to gain a foothold in a new operating system that could be leveraged to support the company's main line of business – high-level languages ported to the machines of different PC vendors. Selling DOS to other vendors was Microsoft's way of protecting its development costs against the real possibility that IBM's PC would be a flop.

Clearly, then, although subsequent events have proven the DOS transaction to be one of the most critical events in the history of personal computing, both IBM and Microsoft entered the negotiations with remarkably local and parochial business concerns: expediency, legal propriety, risk management, and profit maximization. Each of the two companies constructed excellent justifications for consummating the deal, and from the point of view of rational business management, the transaction made an enormous amount of sense for each company, albeit for totally different reasons. In the end, both companies got what they bargained for. Indeed, they got much more, since they changed the way the world views computers.

Proposition 3: The technological path of the personal computer industry after the DOS transaction was shaped by many different firms using local decision rationales to make market choices. There was no underlying technological imperative independent of these local decisions.

The parochial nature of IBM's and Microsoft's decision making regarding DOS makes it clear that no powerful technological imperative was shaping the choices of either party. There was apparently very little awareness that a new paradigm of computing would emerge from an IBM–Microsoft partnership. And yet, that is precisely what happened. This discrepancy, between the scope of the respective decisions and the scope of their consequences, is perhaps the most interesting aspect of the DOS deal – at least as it pertains to the issue of technological foresight and oversight. Both IBM and Microsoft showed reasoned foresight in articulating their local objectives and making them happen. Simultaneously, both were unaware of the enormous global impact that their partnership would have on the two companies and on the industry as a whole.

This apparent paradox is the key to understanding why competence-based accounts of technological foresight and oversight are incomplete. When the quality of technological judgment is framed as a cognitive problem, one must establish a benchmark of rational and informed choice against which to evaluate the quality of a firm's decisions. Otherwise, there is no basis for claiming that a choice is good or bad, rational or irrational. But what are the appropriate standards to use to evaluate the decisions of IBM and Microsoft? Should we use the local criteria that were salient at the time of the transaction? If so, both companies come out foresightful winners because both companies achieved their implicit objectives. In doing so, however, do we not miss the forest for the trees? Does not the question of technological foresight imply something much broader, much more important, than whether a group of managers achieves what it sets out to achieve? Isn't there the question of whether managers understand the underlying technological trajectory that is controlling the fate of their firms? Using this global criterion, however, Microsoft and IBM were both terribly narrow-minded and ignorant, even though the technological trajectory quickly shifted in favor of Microsoft and against IBM.

The question here is whether a technological trajectory, unfolding over an extended period of time, can and should be used as an standard to judge the quality of managerial thinking. At least in the IBM–Microsoft case, it would be very inappropriate to do so. Not only were managers from these two companies unaware of the paradigmatic importance of their transaction, the very paradigm shift that was induced by this transaction was dependent upon their ignorance. If both parties to the DOS contract had been aware of the criticality of the deal for the future of their companies and the computer industry, the perceived stakes would have been so high, especially for IBM that it is unlikely that the contract would ever have been signed. The paradigm shift was *created by* the DOS contract, the DOS contract was not consummated *because of* it. The intelligence operating in the DOS deal was not the intelligence of individual minds attuned to underlying technological forces. It was the collective intelligence of a market system making the most out of a locally rationalized business transaction.

Steffins' (1994) detailed account of the PC industry during the period 1981 through 1990 reinforces this argument by illustrating the tremendous upheavals that were occurring in this new technological niche. Massively complex interactions, unfolding over time, drove the dynamics of the industry in a way that would have been difficult for any one player to foresee. These interactions were created by individual firms making local decisions about their own best interests. Within the year spanning June 1991 through June 1992, no less than 11 of the major electronics companies, including NEC, Xerox, IBM, DEC, Sanyo, and Toshiba, entered the market with their own version of a small computer. The early success of IBM's machine, according to Steffins, was due in part to Big Blue's powerful brand image, its cadre of sales personnel who effectively marketed the PC to the company's corporate customers, and its creative advertising campaign.

Just as importantly, however, Lotus Corporation ported its increasingly popular 1-2-3 spreadsheet program to the DOS platform, creating real value-added to executives who quickly saw that the labor savings from automatic spreadsheets were more than sufficient to offset the PC's $4,000 price tag. The demand for the IBM machine was so great that a host of smaller companies entered the market to fill the gap in IBM's own supply as the legitimating effect of IBM's success freed venture capital for entrepreneurial startups. One such company was Compaq, which copied a recipe pioneered by the Osborne I and developed a DOS-based portable PC. These early dynamics gave way to a period between 1984 and 1991 of increased demand for processing speed and RAM to take advantage of the new software that had begun flooding into the market, of the growing popularity and acceptance of the Apple Macintosh's graphical user interface, and of market experimentation around the DOS standard as PC-compatible vendors continually differentiated themselves in their quest for competitive advantage. Aside from generic forces such as increasingly favorable price/performance ratios in processing power, software functionality, and peripheral capabilities – forces that most players were well aware of at the time – the PC industry was a confluence of opportunistic moves by individual firms battling for position in a very turbulent organizational field.

These complex interactions are a good example of the displacement effects of technological innovation. Schumpeter's (1942) well-known concept of "creative destruction" applies quite well to this case. As Schumpeter argued, capitalist industries are continuously renewing themselves as a process of opportunistic innovation creates ongoing industrial mutations that vie for dominance with the existing status quo. Yet this process of creative destruction is unpredictable and unknowable until after the fact. In Schumpeter's words, "there is no point in appraising the performance of that process ex visu of a given point in time" (p. 83). A similar point was made by Dosi (1988) when he noted that "the technical (and, even more so, the commercial) outcomes of innovative efforts can hardly be known ex ante" (p. 222). Moreover, since this unpredictability is systemic rather than localized, any particular firm's role in the process is inconclusive until the whole has been analyzed. As Schumpeter put it, "Every piece of business strategy acquires its true significance only against the background of that process and within the situation created by it. It must be seen in its role in the perennial gale of creative destruction; it cannot be understood irrespective of it or, in fact, on the hypothesis that there is a perennial lull" (pp. 83–84).

Proposition 4: Any claims to foresight and oversight in the DOS transaction are post hoc *attributions of a judging community rather than intrinsic aspects of the transaction itself. They are social constructions rather than cognitive characteristics.*

The implication of these arguments is that the lack of global foresight by both IBM and Microsoft is not only to be appreciated, it is to be expected, given the complex sequence of events that unfolded in the industry after 1981. The dynamism created in the market by many firms demonstrating the possibilities of inexpensive computing technology was surely beyond the perspective of any single actor. The IBM brand name did have a legitimating effect on PC sales, but it was the usefulness of spreadsheet software from a little-known developer in Cambridge, Massachusetts that provided much of the justification for buying the machines. Compaq leveraged its position as a supplier of portables into segment domination, but it was the innovativeness of the short-lived Osborne 1 that demonstrated that bundling mobile functionality into a single machine was attractive to a large group of customers. It is tempting to claim that the process was certainly not random, that there was an underlying logic developing to lock-in some technological choices and exclude others. But as Arthur (1988) argued, technological lock-in around a dominant design does not have to follow some underlying necessity, that small events accumulating over time can, by chance alone, create the economic and technological conditions for lock-in to occur. How can any single actor anticipate the complex interactions unfolding over time as small and large players alike capitalize on the opportunities being created "on the fly" by thousands of localized choices?

One important aspect of technological trajectories is that they are lived front to back, but are interpreted back to front. The ex ante uncertainty and unpredictability of path creation within the PC industry contrasts sharply with the certainty of post hoc evaluations of IBM's and Microsoft's cognitive competence. With its fortunes quickly turning downward, IBM has been particularly susceptible to negative attacks. Nobody has summarized the plight of the company more succinctly than Paul Carroll (1993) in his recent book, *Big Blue*:

In many people's eyes, IBM wasn't so much a company as an institution. Yet the things that made the company so widely admired are what now make it vilified. People once referred to IBM's passion for being right, its rigorous processes, its thorough training of employees, its focus on customers' desires, its guarantee of lifetime employment. . . . So, referring to the same values IBM has always had, people talk about IBM's fear of risk, its civil service mentality, its brainwashing of employees, its failure to make innovative products that anticipate customers' desires, its inability to adapt its work force quickly enough to react to shifts in the industry (p. 7).

In short, the same organizational routines that were being touted even into the late 1980's to explain IBM's domination of the computing world are now being used as explanations for its loss of market leadership. The sheer magnitude and rapidity of this explanatory transformation is evidence enough that something other than the imperatives of the market are working to control attributions about technological foresight and oversight. If foresight and oversight are such ambiguous terms in highly uncertain technological environments, why do so many people feel comfortable scorning IBM for the characteristics that, until quite recently, were used to explain its success?

Much research by social psychologists has revealed that people have a basic distaste for complex explanations of social events (for example, Ross & Anderson, 1982). Although most events are overdetermined by webs of many overlapping causes, people usually shun complexity and explain the behavior of systems very simply. Matrices of causal interactions are replaced by one or two commonsense causal attributions. The telescoping power of hindsight creates the illusion that complex chains of locally rational choices, interacting in essentially unpredictable ways, were perfectly inevitable. This "creeping determinism," as Fischoff (1982, p. 342) once called it, brings order out of chaos, and creates the conditions for singling out champions and goats.

Thus, far from being matters of cognitive or organizational competence, the technological foresight of Microsoft in the DOS deal, and the oversight of IBM, are causal attributions made after the fact. The technological circumstances of the paradigm shift from mainframe to distributed computing were far too complex and ambiguous, far too historically overdetermined, to be useful in commonsense explanations for profits and losses. The institutionalized environments in which these firms conduct business employ simple criteria for evaluating success and failure, and equally simple causal models for explaining performance relative to these criteria. These models are short-term rather than long-term, cross-sectional rather than historical. Too much depends upon a firm's performance to waste time ruminating about why some of its technologies have succeeded and others failed. Managers get paid for results, not to be right, so notions of technological right and wrong don't have to be very complex, or very complete. Attributions about the prescience or ignorance of a company's technologists are useful proxies for the complexities inherent in evaluating uncertain technologies and bringing to market innovative new products. Never mind that IBM was severely constrained from years of scrutiny by government lawyers and by successful products that existing customers depended on. IBM simply lost sight of where the industry was going. Never mind that Microsoft was simply maximizing its short-run profits by selling DOS to all who wanted it. Bill Gates was a market visionary. These attributions are quite understandable, and are very amenable to empirical investigation. However, they should not be taken so far as to be believed as they stand. They are attributions about the managerial mind, not the managerial mind itself

Conclusions and implications

The DOS transaction is only one case of technological decision-making. It is important not to overgeneralize from this single instance. Yet because of their impact on society, the activities and decisions during the development of the PC hold special relevance for theories and models of technological choice. The converging interactions among multiple players that created the conditions for IBM's misfortune and Microsoft's rise to prominence show just how difficult it is to map the causal chain underlying critical technological innovations. It is even more difficult to ferret out the factors that have controlled the commercial performance of IBM and Microsoft over the course of the 15 years since the PC was first conceived. Several explanations for the different outcomes experienced by the two companies are plausible. IBM was a monopolist whose market share and reputation had no where to go but down. Increased competition from imitators riding IBM's commercial coattails was an inevitable result of visible success in a free market. Add to this the institutional encrustation that accumulated from years of antitrust burdens and it is not clear that something as simple as technological oversight adds anything to the explanatory mix. Similarly, Microsoft was a clear beneficiary of IBM's market reputation, exemplifying what Arthur (1988) would argue was a case of technological lock-in around PC-compatibility. Technological foresight seems a surface description of this lock-in, not an explanation of it.

Are foresight and oversight, then, simply redundant descriptions of more fundamental social and economic processes. Are they merely epiphenomena that get used as lay explanations for commercial success and failure because they capture attention in the press? Much of what I have argued above would be consistent with this view. As Vincenti (1990) has argued, technological innovation always involves a certain degree of "blindness," of happenstance. If this were not the case, the resulting technology would, by definition, lack novelty and innovativeness. New knowledge would never be created. By assuming that ex ante criteria can be imposed on technological choices, such that technological right and wrong can be ascertained, the concepts of foresight and oversight seem to imply that the stochastic quality of innovation can be eradicated, or at least managed. Clearly, this implication is questionable, and any forceful claims about foresight and oversight are likely to have a strong dose of post hoc attributions embedded within them.

But taken to its extreme, an attributional explanation of foresight and oversight suggests that it is *never* possible to evaluate the quality of a firm's technological judgment. This seems equally questionable. The stochastic aspects of innovation are partial, not complete. Technological judgment occurs within the context of established "givens" that often provide a reasonable set of standards for technological right and wrong. One set of givens has to do with a firm's inherent capabilities. Innovation occurs along paths that are dependent upon a firm's skills and competencies (Teece, 1988). Technological choices must remain consistent with these competencies or the firm risks overextension or dilettantism. For example, IBM's continuing, and expensive, efforts to develop OS/2 as a replacement for DOS is inconsistent with the company's poor track record in operating-system design and implementation. Despite its publicly acknowledged merits, one could argue that OS/2 has been an expensive technological blunder. A second set of givens has to do with a firm's market environment. To the extent that the preferences and tendencies of a firm's competitors and customers are well known – there is widespread knowledge about how customer's respond to particular product characteristics – it is reasonable to use these preferences as ex ante standards in technological judgment. This would be the case, for example, with incremental innovations in a broader architectural platform. Thus, one could justifiably claim poor judgment in the case of IBM's failed attempt to recapture the nascent PC market with a microchannel bus, since there were clear market signals present at the time that bus technology was unimportant to most customers and made little difference in the performance of popular application programs (Ferguson & Morris, 1993).

In short, an attributional approach to technological choice does not rule out evaluating a firm's technical savvy. The epistemic grounds for any evaluation, however, rest on the degree to which consensual standards exist within the relevant technological and market domains. When such standards do exist, they can be employed as ex ante judgmental benchmarks, and thus foresight and oversight become plausible cognitive claims prior to the implementation of a choice. In the end, though, admitting this qualification suggests an important paradox in the relationship between the ex ante evaluation of a choice and post hoc attributions about it. Ex ante evaluations are possible when consensus exists, but when consensus exists it is unlikely that the technological choice involves a paradigm-breaking alternative. Hence, there is not much to explain that is not already known, and the pressure to attribute cognitive competence or incompetence after the fact will not be great. It is when radical dislocations of technology change the rules of the game, and make some firms dramatic winners and others losers, that attributional pressures will be strongest and explanations involving foresight and oversight will be most attractive. But it is radical change that brings with it the complex interactions and unpredictability that make global decision criteria so difficult to use and foresight and oversight implausible generic explanations for success and failure. It is thus a peculiar characteristic of technological choice that when conditions exist to rule out strong claims to foresight and oversight, such claims are most likely to be made.

References

Arthur, W. B. (1988). Competing technologies: An overview. In G. Dosi, C. Freeman, R. Nelson, G. Silverberg, and L. Soete (eds.), *Technical Change and Economic Theory*. London: Pinter.

Bijker, W., Hughes, T. P., and Pinch, T. (1987). *The Social Construction of Technological Systems*. Cambridge, NM: MIT Press.

Burgelman, Robert A. (1994). Fading memories: A process theory of strategic business exit in dynamic environments. *Administrative Science Quarterly*, 39, 24–56.

Carroll, P. (1993). *Big blues: The Unmaking of IBM*. New York: Crown.

Chposky, J. and Leonis, T. (1988). *Blue Magic*. New York: Facts on File.

DeLamarter, R. T. (1986). *Big Blue*. New York: Dodd, Mead.

Dosi, G. (1988). The nature of the innovative process. In G. Dosi, C. Freeman, R. Nelson, G. Silverberg, and L. Soete (eds.), *Technical Change and Economic Theory*. London: Pinter.

Ferguson, C. H. and Morris, C. R. (1993). *Computer Wars*. New York: Random House

Fischoff, B. (1982). For those condemned to study the past: Heuristics and biases in hindsight. In D. Kahneman, P. Slovic, and A. Tversky (eds.), *Judgment under Uncertainty: Heuristics and Biases*. New York: Cambridge University Press.

Foy, N. (1975). *The Sun Never Sets on IBM*. New York: William Morrow.

Garud, R. and Rappa, M. (1994). A sociocognitive model of technological evolution. *Organizational Science*, 5, (August), 344–362.

Manes, S. and Andrews, P. (1993). *Gates*. New York: Simon and Schuster.

McKenna, R. (1989). *Who's Afraid of Big Blue?* Reading, MA: Addison-Wesley.

Nelson, R- R. and Winter, S. (1982). *An Evolutionary Theory of Economic Change*. Cambridge, MA: Harvard University Press.

Rodgers, B. (1986). *The IBM Way*. New York: Harper and Row.

Rogers, W. (1969). *Think*. New York: Stein and Day.

Ross, L. and Anderson, C. A. (1982). Shortcomings in the attribution process: On the origins and maintenance of erroneous social assessments. In D. Kahneman, P. Slovic, and A. Tversky (eds.), *Judgment under Uncertainty: Heuristics and Biases*. New York: Cambridge University Press

Schumpeter, J. A. (1942). *Capitalism, Socialism, and Democracy*. New York: Harper & Row.

Sobel, R. (1981). *IBM*. New York: Times Books.

Steffins, J. (1994). *Newgames: Strategic competition in the PC revolution*. Oxford: Pergamon Press.

Teece, D. (1988). Technological change and the nature of the firm. In G. Dosi, C. Freeman, R. Nelson, G. Silverberg, and L. Soete (eds.), *Technical Change and Economic Theory*. London: Pinter.

Vincenti, W. G. (1990). *What Engineers Know and How They Know It*. Baltimore: Johns Hopkins University Press.

Watson, T. J. and Petre, P. (1990). *Father, Son and Company*. New York: Bantam Books.

9 On the dynamics of forecasting in technologically complex environments: The unexpectedly long old age of optical lithography

Rebecca Henderson

1. Introduction

Accurate technological forecasting is extraordinarily important. It can allow managers to shape technology strategy, to prevent continued investment in technologies that are long past their prime, and to guard against premature commitment to untried technologies whose long-term potential is limited. Unfortunately, accurate technological forecasting is notoriously difficult (see some of the other chapters in this volume).

In this chapter, I hope to contribute to the practice of technological forecasting through a detailed analysis of the usefulness of one tool that has been widely advanced as a guide to technological foresight: the technology life cycle (Van Wyk, 1985). I use the history of optical photolithographic alignment technology to suggest that the uncritical application of the life cycle as a forecasting tool may have quite dangerous implications. The life cycle is a useful ex post descriptive device: appropriate *proscriptive* use of it requires a detailed understanding of the underlying technological, economic, and social dynamics on which it rests, in combination with a critical awareness of the ways in which industry acceptance of the life cycle as a descriptive tool can obscure these dynamics, making it very difficult to use it with any accuracy.

Industry pundits have been confidently using the technological life cycle to predict the death of optical photolithography since 1977, yet it remains the tool of choice in leading-edge semiconductor production (Figure 9.1). The factors that lie behind this singularly unsuccessful forecasting effort throw considerable light on the limits of the technological life cycle as a forecasting tool.

The history of optical photolithography suggests that the life cycle may be more useful as a summary of current assumptions about the structure of the industry's dominant design than as a statement about the absolute

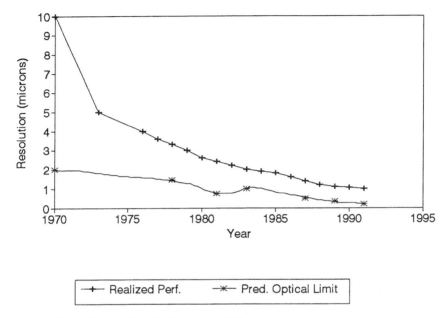

Figure 9.1. Predicted limits of optical lithography versus realized performance.

physical limits to a technology. For any given technology, it suggests that projections of its limits based on the technology life cycle are likely to be accurate only if the structure of the dominant design remains constant, if the capabilities of crucial complementary technologies remain unchanged, and if user capabilities do not evolve. If the dominant design mutates such that the available set of component technologies changes, if complementary technologies improve unexpectedly, or if user capabilities change in unexpected ways, a technology may reach levels of performance that far outstrip those that can be predicted from a naive interpretation of the life-cycle model.

Unfortunately the history of optical lithography also suggests that this complexity may be effectively invisible to industry participants, since aggressive incremental exploitation of the prevailing dominant design leads knowledge about component performance, user capabilities, and complementary technologies to develop an embedded, tacit, "taken-for-granted" quality that can result in current design structures, complementary technology performance, and user capabilities being mistaken for absolute limits. As a result arguments framed in terms of underlying technological dynamics may have a seductive clarity that can blind observers to the real nature of the constraints that limit the technology.

Thus the chapter suggests that the life cycle may be more useful as a description of the embedded knowledge of industry participants and hence as a tool for predicting patterns of investment than as a means of predicting absolute physical limits. Any use of the life cycle as an aid to forecasting must be predicated upon careful exploration of the possibility of change in the dominant design, in complementary technologies, and in user needs, if it is be a useful source of technological foresight.

The chapter opens with a brief discussion of the technological life cycle and its use in technology forecasting as a background to the discussion of optical photolithography. Section 3 outlines a brief description of the history of optical photolithographic aligners. I show that the technology life cycle provides a plausible ex post description of the technology's history but that predictions of the limits to the technology's performance derived from it have been consistently proved wrong. Section 4 explores the evolution of the limits to optical lithographic limits in detail to show that they are a function of the structure of the dominant design, of user capabilities and of the evolution of complementary technologies, and explores the tacit assumptions that led industry experts to predict the limits of the technology with such spurious accuracy. The chapter closes with a discussion of the implications of these results for the use of the technology life cycle as a predictive tool.

1. Technological life cycles and the dominant design

Many technologies move from a period of "infancy," through the adoption of a dominant design to a period of maturity and eventual "exhaustion" of the dominant design (Abernathy & Utterback, 1978; Anderson & Tushman, 1990; Tushman & Rosenkopf, 1992). In the case of technologies whose evolution follows this pattern, the adoption of a dominant design facilitates a transition to a focus on incremental product development and aggressive investment in process technology. However the adoption of a dominant design simultaneously limits the technology's ultimate performance.

As the limits of a dominant design are reached, returns to investment in the technology eventually fall dramatically, setting the stage for a move to another generation of technology and a repetition of the cycle (Dosi, 1982; Foster, 1986; Gardiner, 1984, Sahal, 1985) (Figure 9.2).

For example in his book *Innovation, The Attackers Advantage*, Foster (1986) suggested that no matter how much the design of sailing ships is refined, fundamental limits in the efficiency with which sails can translate the power of the wind to motion constrains the speed at which sailing ships will ever be able to sail. Similarly Sahal (1985) hypothesized that the elaboration of a dominant design usually takes place through changes in scale or increases in complexity, and suggested that beyond a certain point this process causes designs to collapse "under their own weight." A technology ultimately becomes too small, too large, or impossibly complex. A similar idea is advanced in the work of Gardiner (1984) who drew a distinction between "robust" and "lean" designs. He suggested that when a dominant design is first adopted it is usually "robust" in that it can be extended or

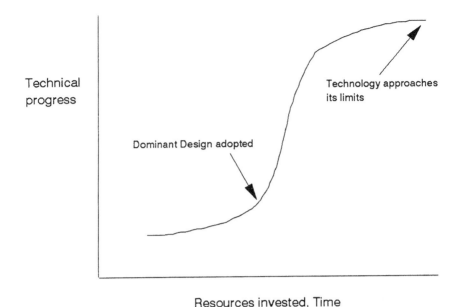

Technical
progress

Technology approaches
its limits

Dominant Design adopted

Resources invested, Time

Figure 9.2. Schematic of the life cycle.

"stretched" in a variety of ways. Over time, as the possibilities inherent in the technology are exhausted, designs become increasingly "lean" and must ultimately be replaced.

The technology life cycle has been shown to be a useful ex post descriptive device in industries as diverse as automobiles, cement, sailing ships, heart implants, disk drives, tubro jets, and computers (Abernathy & Utterback, 1978; Constant, 1980; Foster, 1986; Anderson & Tushman, 1990; Christensen, 1993), and it has been widely recommended as a forecasting tool (Van Wyk, 1985).

However, its usefulness has been recently challenged by evidence suggesting that technologies sometimes substantially exceed their "natural" limits. For example, Utterback and Kim (1985) describe the dramatic improvements in the performance of home iceboxes that occurred when the industry was confronted with competition from home electric refrigerators; some of the major innovations in steam-locomotive technology that occurred when diesel technology was introduced, and improvements in the quality and efficiency of gas illumination that "nearly bankrupted the fledgling Edison Electric Company." Similarly, Christensen (1993) suggested that the life cycle provided little guidance to firms seeking to understand the limits of disk-drive component technology, and demostrated that individual components often showed dramatic and unexpected improvements in performance. He suggested that the technology was simply "too complex" to forecast accurately, and the predictions of limits within particular firms tend to become self-fulfilling since they lead to resources being allocated to competing technologies. In the remainder of the chapter, I build on these ideas to explore the limitations of the technology life cycle as a forecasting tool.

II. Technological forecasting in optical lithography

Photolithographic aligners are complex pieces of capital equipment used in the manufacture of solid-state semiconductor devices. They are designed to transfer small, intricate patterns to the surface of a wafer of semiconductor material such as silicon.[1] During the photolithographic process the surface of a wafer is coated with a light-sensitive chemical, or "resist," while the pattern that is to be transferred to the wafer is drawn onto a template, or "mask." The image of the mask is then projected down onto the surface of the resist, so that only those portions of the resist defined by the mask are exposed to light. The exposed resist is stripped away, and the pattern that remains is used as the basis for further processing (Figure 9.3). This process may be repeated as many as twenty times during the manufacture of a semiconductor device, and each layer must be located precisely with respect to the previous layer (Watts & Einspruch, 1987). Photolithographic aligners are used to position the mask accurately with respect to the wafer and to project the image of the mask onto the wafer surface.

There are many different kinds of alignment technology. In general they are distinguished by the nature of the radiation that they use to expose the resist, since the use of different types of radiation requires quite different masks, resists, and alignment mechanisms. Optical photolithographic aligners use visible light to expose the resist, whereas electron-beam ("e-beam") aligners use electrons and X-ray aligners use X-rays. Since it is considerably easier to manipulate visible light than either X-rays or e-beams, all other things equal optical photolithographic aligners are much cheaper to build and to operate than either electron beam or X-ray aligners, and optical photolithographic equipment has dominated commercial production of semiconductor devices since its first introduction in the early sixties.

An aligner's performance is defined principally by its *minimum-feature-size capability,* or by the size of the smallest pattern element that it can successfully transfer to the surface of a wafer.[2] Since smaller circuits run both faster and cooler than larger ones, progress in the manufacture of solid-state semiconductor devices has come largely through continued reductions in circuit size, and progress in photolithography has taken the form of continuous, dramatic, reductions in minimum feature size. The optical aligners of the late sixties cost a few thousand dollars and produced images that were about 10–15 microns (μm) in size, whereas a modern optical production aligner sells for two to three million dollars and can produce lines considerably less than a micron in width.[3]

Figure 9.4 shows this evolution as a function of time and of the cumula-

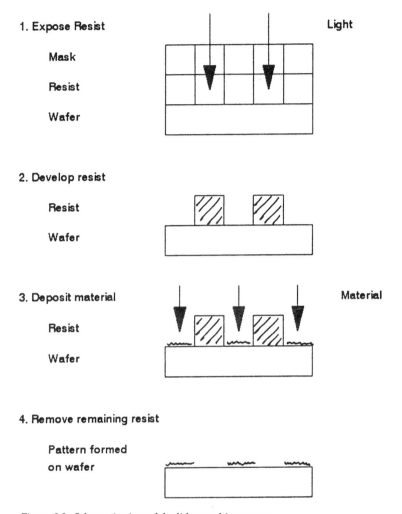

1. Expose Resist   Light

   Mask

   Resist

   Wafer

2. Develop resist

   Resist

   Wafer

3. Deposit material   Material

   Resist

   Wafer

4. Remove remaining resist

   Pattern formed
   on wafer

Figure 9.3. Schematic view of the lithographic process.

tive resources invested in product development, respectively. At first glance these curves appear to be strikingly consistent with the classical theory of the technology life cycle.

As Abernathy and Utterback (1978) and Anderson and Tushman (1990) have suggested, the transition to a regime of rapidly increasing technological capability occurred simultaneously with the introduction of a product embodying a "dominant design," in this case Kulicke and Soffa's 686 model in 1966. And as Sahal (1985) and Foster (1986) suggest, progress in optical technology has become increasingly expensive as its "limits" have been approached. Early rapid advances in performance have been succeeded by much slower progress more recently, and industry experts now suggest that

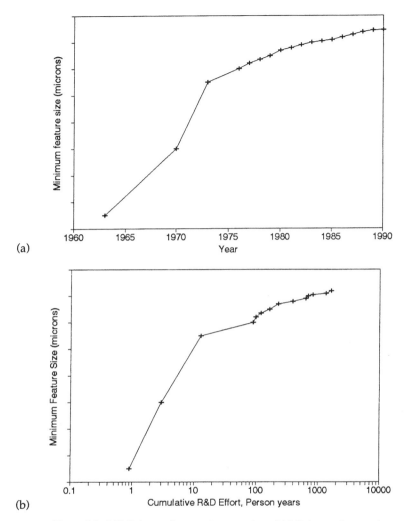

(a)

(b)

Figure 9.4. (a) Minimum feature size over time. (b) Minimum feature size versus effort.

the wavelength of visible light constrains the performance of optical lithographic aligners to a minimum feature size of around 0.20 μm. At current rates of progress in semiconductor processing, this implies that optical lithography will be replaced in leading-edge applications within the next three to four years.

A more detailed exploration of the industry's history, however, highlights the dangers inherent in using the life cycle as a predictive device. In the first place, the belief that technologies are ultimately limited by physical constraints inherent in their basic design has been widely used to predict the obsolescence of optical photolithographic aligners since at least 1977.

Figure 9.1 graphed predictions of the "limits" to optical lithographic performance over time. Industry experts have been confidently predicting the obsolescence of optical lithography for the last 15 years. The first investments in e-beam and X-ray lithographic technology were made before 1970, and e-beam aligners were in (limited) use as a production tool in at least one company by 1977. IBM alone has invested over a billion dollars in X-ray lithography.

But despite the continued publication of articles with titles like "Electron Beam – Now a Practical LSI Production Tool" (*Solid State Technology*, 1977), "X-Ray Lithography: Optical's Heir" (*Semiconductor International*, 1982), and "X-Ray Lithography, Wave of the Future?" (*Electronic Business*, 1989), optical photolithography continues to dominate industrial production.

Understanding the unexpectedly long old age of optical lithography – and hence of the difficulties inherent in predicting technological limits – offers considerable insight into the dangers of using the life cycle as a predictive device. It suggests that forecasting the limits to a technology requires an appreciation of two core issues: on the one hand, a recognition of the degree to which the limits to a technology's performance are shaped by unexpected evolution in the structure of the dominant design, in user capabilities, and in the potential of complementary technologies and, on the other hand, a recognition of the ways in which deeply embedded tacit knowledge, developed during extended periods of incremental development, obscures the possibility of changes in these dimensions so that industry debate can be plausibly framed in terms of inherent physical constraints.

III. Defining the limits of optical lithographic performance

The first challenge to optical photolithography was the electron beam based photolithographic aligner, which uses a fine beam of electrons rather than visible light to expose the resist on a mask. So called "e-beam" aligners were first used in the mid-1970s and quickly showed themselves capable of generating minimum feature sizes far smaller than those of the most advanced optical photolithographic aligners. However e-beam aligners were (and continue to be) both very slow and very expensive, and given equivalent performance, the vast majority of semiconductor manufacturers preferred to use optical aligners.

X-ray aligners, which use X-ray radiation to expose the resist, emerged to challenge optical aligners a few years later. But like e-beam aligners, for equivalent performance they have remained consistently significantly more expensive than optical machines. Thus all other things equal, semiconductor manufacturers have had strong incentives to use optical photolithographic aligners as long as they possibly could: that is, as long as they could produce minimum feature sizes on the wafer small enough to sustain the current generation of semiconductor designs,

In 1977, it seemed as though optical aligners could not meet this requirement much beyond 1985 or 1986. The fact that optical radiation is of a much longer wavelength than either X-rays or electron beams seemed to pose an insuperable barrier.

The structure of the debate

The experts who first forecast the death of optical lithography based their predictions on the fact that X-rays and e-beams have much smaller wavelengths than optical light. The most important determinant of the minimum-feature-size capability of an aligner is its resolution, or the size of the smallest image that it can focus successfully at the wafer surface.

Aligner resolution is given by the Rayleigh criterion, or by the expression:

$$\text{Resolution} = k_1 \times \frac{\text{wavelength}}{\text{numerical aperture}} \tag{1}$$

where wavelength is the wavelength of the exposing source, numerical aperture is a measure of the size of the aligner's lens, and k_1 is a constant determined by a variety of factors including the optical characteristics of the aligner lens and the chemical composition of the resist.

From the Rayleigh criterion it is immediately clear that there are three routes to improving the minimum-feature size of an aligner, or reducing its resolution: reducing the wavelength of the exposing source, increasing the size of the aligner lens or reducing the value of k_1.[4] In 1977, when the inherent limits of optical lithography were first confidently predicted, aligner lenses were believed to be limited to a numerical aperture of about 0.167 and k_1 was believed to have a value of around 1.0. Given these values, it was straightforward to use the Rayleigh criterion to predict the limits of optical lithography.

The optical aligners of the late seventies used "g-line" sources – optical sources with a wavelength of about 436 manometers, or 0.436 μm,[5] and thus were limited to the production of devices whose smallest feature size was around 2.61 μm. Stretching the dominant design by moving to smaller and smaller wavelengths would improve aligner resolution, but industry experts believed that it would be difficult to use optical wavelengths shorter than the "i-line," around 240 nm, or 0.2401 μm. This implied that the limits to optical photolithography were around 1.44 μm.

Dramatic increases in numerical aperture, or lens size, were considered unlikely, since industry experts believed that optics was a relatively mature, well-understood science. Moreover, increases in numerical aperture were rejected as a route to improved resolution because of their effect on the aligner's *depth of focus*. Depth of focus is the distance above and below the wafer plane in which the image is accurately projected, and hence is a measure of the margin of error available to an aligner's user (see Figure 9.5). Too

Light projected through mask

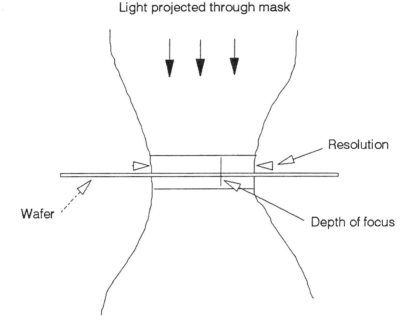

Figure 9.5. Depth of focus and resolution.

small a depth of focus makes it impossible to focus the aligner on the wafer, so that improved resolution buys the user no benefit in terms of smaller feature size. Depth of focus is given by the expression

$$\text{depth of focus} = \frac{\text{wavelength}}{2 \times \text{numerical aperture}^2} \qquad (2)$$

Thus increasing numerical aperture as a road to smaller resolution carries a much greater penalty in the form of reduced depth of focus than does simply reducing wavelength, since although resolution falls as the inverse of numerical aperture, depth of focus falls as the *square* of numerical aperture. Figure 9.6 shows depth of focus as a function of resolution for the two strategies of reducing wavelength and increasing numerical aperture. Increasing numerical aperture greatly reduces the ratio between depth of focus and resolution, and hence the "margin of error" available to the semiconductor manufacturer.

In general, high-volume production of semiconductors requires depth of focus to be significantly greater than resolution, or

$$\text{depth of focus} \geq k_2 \times \text{resolution} \qquad (3)$$

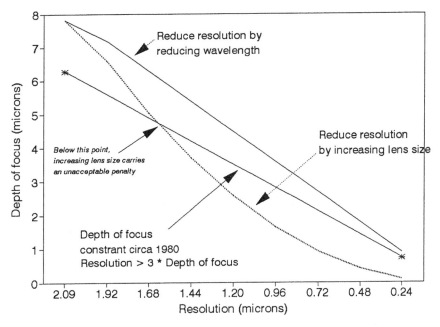

Figure 9.6. The depth of focus to resolution constraint, circa 1980.

In the early eighties semiconductor manufacturers required a depth of focus that was about three times that of an aligner's resolution, imposing a value of k_2 of around 3.

Substituting equations (1) and (2) into equation (3) gives the size of the largest lens that can be used effectively:

$$\frac{\text{wavelength}}{2 \times \text{numerical aperture}^2} \geq k_2 k_1 \frac{\text{wavelength}}{\text{numerical aperture}}$$

or:

$$\text{numerical aperture} \geq \frac{1}{2 k_1 k_2}$$

With k_1 equal to 1 and k_2 equal to 3, the maximum feasible numerical aperture is thus around 0.170. (This constraint is shown graphically in Figure 9.6.) Thus as long as semiconductor manufacturers continued to require a depth of focus three times that of their target resolution, or $k_2 = 3$, and k_1 had a value of about 1.0, reductions in the wavelength of the exposing sources seemed to be the only practical means of improving minimum-feature size, and industry expects could confidently predict that the limit to optical lithographic performance was around 1.4l μm. Thus in 1978 either X-ray or e-beam aligners were expected to replace optical lithography before the end of the 1980s (Figure 9.7).

Notice that if X-ray or e-beam aligners *had* replaced optical lithography "on schedule," ex-post analysis might well have framed the technological trajectory of optical lithography in terms of ever-decreasing wavelength with the exhaustion of the dominant design predictable from a knowledge of the Rayleigh criterion.

Understanding why this prediction, and the series of predictions made over the course of the next 10 years proved to be incorrect highlights both the role of unexpected changes in customer needs and capabilities, in component technologies and in complementary technologies in defining the limits to a technology, and the role of tacit or taken-for-granted assumptions about the sources of technological change in technological forecasting.

Understanding the sources of forecast error

The Rayleigh criterion does indeed describe the minimum achievable resolution of an aligner, given acceptable depth of focus, and it was referred to extensively in discussions of the industry's future. However a majority of industry experts not only took the Rayleigh criterion as a statement about

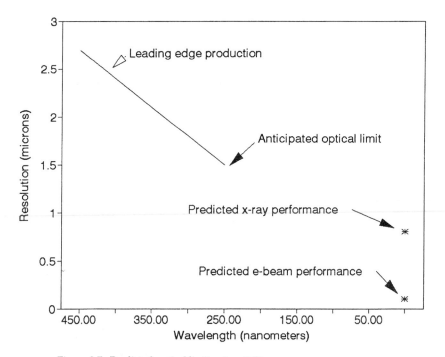

Figure 9.7. Predicted optical limits, circa 1978.

physical limits, but also assumed that k_1 and k_2 were fixed physical parameters. In the event it became clear that neither parameter was, in fact, fixed. The value of k_2 turned out to reflect the capabilities of the aligner's users, and the value of k_1 turned out to be a function of the complementary technologies on which the aligner was dependent. Moreover unexpected advances in refractive optics – unexpected both because they were thought scientifically impossible and because the assumption that k_1 and k_2 were fixed had meant that increased lens size had been discounted as a route to improved resolution – made it possible to design lenses with significantly higher numerical apertures.

Between 1980 and 1990 advances in lens design and production techniques pushed numerical apertures to previously inconceivable sizes, rapid advances in semiconductor processing technology and a concomitant increase in photolithographic user sophistication relaxed the constraint that depth of focus had to be three times aligner resolution, and a combination of increasing user sophistication and the development of new resists pushed the value of k, from 1.0 to 0.8 in production and less than 0.5 in research settings. In combination, these advances have pushed the limits of optical lithography to within 0.2 μm.

User needs and capabilities

As the discussion above suggests, given adequate resolution, the performance of an optical aligner is limited by its depth of focus. As long as semiconductor manufacturers required a depth of focus to resolution ratio of 3: 1, or as long as k_2 remained equal to 3, a strategy of improving numerical aperture in order to improve resolution was indeed inherently limited and the adoption of technologies with shorter wavelengths appeared to be the most plausible route to improved resolution. Unexpected changes in semiconductor-manufacturer requirements broke this constraint.

As optical aligners nudged their "limits," semiconductor manufacturers devoted increasing amounts of time to managing the depth of focus constraint. Current leading-edge manufacturing practice requires a resolution to depth of focus ratio of only around 1:1, or a value of k_2 of around 1, such that increasing lens size, or numerical aperture, became a viable route to improving resolution (Figure 9.8).

Taking component performance for granted

Of course, this potential could only be exploited if it proved possible to use lenses with larger numerical apertures, and thus the second challenge to the wavelength of light as an insuperable barrier to smaller feature sizes came from the successful introduction of ever larger lenses (Figure 9.9). Breakthroughs in optical design and in manufacturing techniques coupled with the use of new materials enabled the construction of lenses with numerical

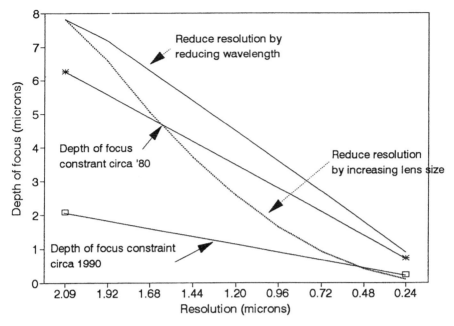

Figure 9.8. Changes in the depth of focus to resolution constraint.

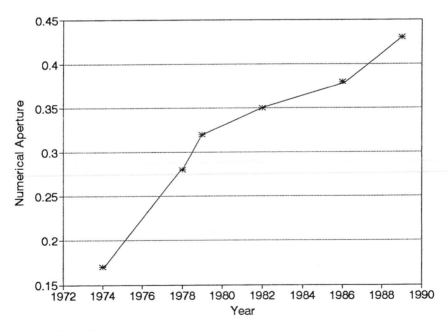

Figure 9.9. Increasing lens size over time.

apertures that were unthinkable by the standards of five years before and pushed the "limits" of optical lithography – even with the use of the old "g-line" sources – to around 0.9 μm.

To the degree that these larger lenses could be optimized to work with the shorter-wavelength "i-line" sources – as, by the end of the decade they increasingly were – they extended the limits of the technology to around 0.5 μm, all other things equal (Figure 9.10).

An exploration of why it was that 0.167 came to be accepted as a *physical* limit for numerical aperture hints at the complexity of the construction of technical "limits." The belief that 0.167 was a realistic limit rested on three core assumptions: on the extrapolation of the then current product architecture, on the belief that refractive lens technology was essentially mature and unlikely to improve significantly, and on the belief that the need to maintain a ratio of 3:1 between depth of focus and resolution was a binding constraint. As we have seen, this last assumption was rendered obsolete by advances in user capability, while the first fell foul of architectural changes in product architecture (Henderson & Clark, 1990), and the second to unanticipated advances in the design and manufacture of large-scale refractive lenses.

Between 1974 and 1980 optical photolithography was dominated by

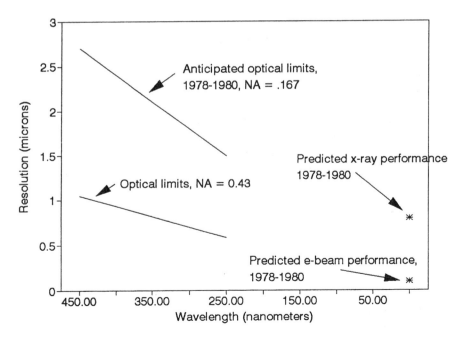

Figure 9.10. Impact of improved numerical aperture (NA) on optical photolithographic resolution.

scanning projection alignment technology. Scanning projection aligners use reflective lenses to scan the image of the mask across the wafer surface. Whereas reflective lenses can be easily modified to take advantage of lower wavelengths, it is very difficult to increase their numerical aperture beyond 0.167. Photolithographic aligners that use the refractive lenses that can be built with larger numerical apertures were not introduced until 1978, and it was not until 1980 that it became clear that they would be widely accepted.[6] Pre-1980 projections of the limits to optical lithography were thus contingent on a particular product architecture – that of the scanning projection aligner – rather than projections of absolute physical limits.

Projections of the difficulties implicit in improving numerical aperture were also confounded by unexpected developments in refractive lens technology. Two large Japanese conglomerates with extensive experience in optics, Nikon and Canon, entered the industry in the early 1980s and between them made a series of breakthroughs in lens design that took some years to diffuse to their Western rivals.

Complementary technologies

The limits of optical lithography were also relaxed by unanticipated developments in component technologies, notably in masks and resists. Early discussion of the limits to optical lithography assumed that in a production setting k_1 was approximately 1.0. Subsequent developments showed that any assumption about the value of k_1 summarized an enormous amount of tacit and only poorly understood information about the performance of a particular semiconductor-manufacturing process. Progress in production-control techniques, better resist systems, and finer control of alignment technology – nearly all of them initiated by users, rather than by the producers of alignment equipment – have since reduced the commonly accepted value of k_1 to around 0.8 in production settings and to as low as 0.5 in more controlled conditions. This advance has further shifted the limits of optical lithographic performance (Figure 9.11).

Unanticipated developments in the evolution of complementary technologies have also been important in determining the performance of X-ray and e-beam aligners. Improvements in the performance of optical lithography have put increasing pressure on alternative lithographic techniques. For example, the first X-ray aligners were designed to have minimum feature size capability in the 1–1.5 μm range. To replace optical aligners now, they must demonstrate performance into within 0.1 μm. Without accurate masks and reliable resists an aligner's ability to resolve the smallest imaginable image onto a wafer surface is quite useless, and it has proved to be surprisingly difficult to develop robust X-ray masks that can deliver this level of performance. Sufficiently powerful X-ray sources have also proved to be almost prohibitively expensive.

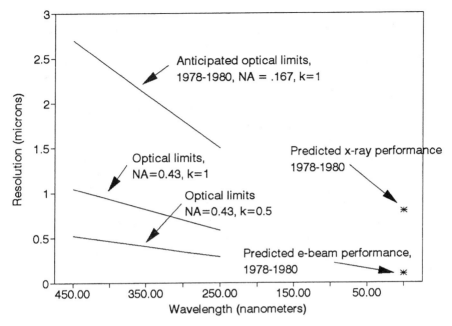

Figure 9.11. Impact of improved values of k_1 on optical photolithographic resolution.

Conclusions

The unexpectedly long old age of optical lithography suggests that the belief that the limits of a technology are determined by the internal structure of the technology may be fundamentally misleading. In the case of optical photolithography, the "natural" or "physical" limits of the technology were relaxed by unanticipated progress on three fronts: by significant changes in the needs and capabilities of users, by advances in the performance of component technologies – particularly lenses – stemming from architectural development of the dominant design, and by unexpected developments in the performance of complementary technologies. These advances were unanticipated both because they were driven by forces beyond the immediate control of the photolithographic manufacturers who dominated production in the late 1970s and early 1980s and because a reliance on the Rayleigh criterion as a means to predict the limits of optical photolithographic technology led to knowledge about the capabilities of users and complementary technologies becoming deeply embedded as physical "constants" that were not actively challenged.

Thus two quite distinct conclusions can be drawn from these data with respect to the use of the technological life cycle as a forecasting tool. The first is relatively straightforward. The history of optical photolithographic technology suggests that the use of the life cycle as a tool to predict the limits of a technology must be tempered by the recognition that a statement of the problem in terms of inherent technical limits rests on a series of assumptions about the probable evolution of user needs and capabilities and the potential of component and complementary technologies that may or may not be accurate.

The second is more subtle. These results suggest that a simple awareness that factors beyond the industry may shape technological progress is not a sufficient basis for accurate technological forecasting. It may also be necessary to actively challenge commonly held assumptions about the nature of the constraints imposed by forces beyond industry control: in effect, to ask "what drives the value of (a parameter such as) k_1, what drives the value of k_2?" A thorough analysis should thus combine careful analysis of the technology's scientific or physical potential with a willingness to question the common wisdom that provides the stable context for incremental development. The case of optical lithography suggests that this is not an easy or straightforward exercise.

Acknowledgments

This chapter draws heavily on material presented in my "Of Life Cycles Real and Imaginary: The Unexpectedly Long Old Age of Optical Lithography," published in *Research Policy*, Spring 1995. I am grateful to the publishers for permission to reprint parts of that article here.

This research was partially supported by the Division of Research, Harvard Business School, and by the Leaders for Manufacturing Program, a partnership between eleven major manufacturing firms and MIT. Their support is gratefully acknowledged. I would also like to thank Dataquest and VLSI Research Inc., the staffs of Canon, GCA, Nikon, Perkin Elmer, and Ultratech, and all of those individuals involved with photolithographic alignment technology who gave generously of their time to this research. This chapter has greatly benefited from conversations with Raghu Garud, Lori Rosenkopf, Stephan Schrader, Eric Von Hippel, and Jim Utterback, and from the helpful comments of two anonymous referees. Any errors or omissions remain entirely the author's responsibility.

Notes

1   Here and in the discussion that follows I draw upon a detailed qualitative and quantitative database collected over the course of 18 months field work in the photolithographic industry. A description of the data and of the study's methodology is given in the Appendix.
2   Other important dimensions of aligner performance include throughput and yield. During the period covered by this chapter, however, both X-ray and e-beam aligners were notably slower than optical aligners, and were not characterized by significantly higher yields.

3 One micron (1 μ) = one-thousandth of a millimeter.
4 Notice that improving the performance of an aligner means *reducing* resolution. Smaller resolution implies finer lines on the wafer.
5 Before the introduction of excimer laser sources into production settings around 1989, optical aligners used in production settings used ultraviolet sources. These sources emit light at a range of frequencies. A "g-line" source emits most of its energy at around 436 nm, but also emits some energy at adjacent frequencies.
6 Reflective lenses focus light by reflection, refractive lenses focus light by refracting it through the body of the lens.

Appendix

Data and methodology

The data were collected during a two-year, field-based study of the photolithographic alignment equipment industry (full details can be found in Henderson, 1988). The core of the data is a panel data set consisting of research and development costs and sales revenue by product for every product development project conducted between 1962, when work on the first commercial product began, and 1986. This data is supplemented by a detailed managerial and technical history of each project. The data were collected through research in both primary and secondary sources. The secondary sources, including trade journals, scientific journals, and consulting reports, were used to identify the companies that had been active in the industry and the products that they had introduced and to build up a preliminary picture of the industry's technical history.

Data were then collected about each product-development project by contacting directly at least one of the members of the product-development team and requesting an interview. Interviews were conducted over a fourteen month period, from March 1987 to May 1988. During the course of the research, over a hundred people were interviewed. As far as possible, the interviewees included the senior design engineer for each project and a senior marketing executive from each firm. Other industry observers and participants, including chief executives, university scientists, skilled design engineers and service managers were also interviewed. Interview data was supplemented whenever possible through the use of internal firm records. The majority of the interviews were semistructured and lasted about two hours. Respondents were asked to describe the technical, commercial and managerial history of the product development projects with which they were familiar, and to discuss the technical and commercial success of the products that grew out of them.

In order to validate the data that were collected during this process, a brief history of product development for each equipment vendor was circulated to all the individuals that had been interviewed and to others who knew a firm's history well, and the accuracy of this account was discussed over the telephone in supplementary interviews. The same validation procedure was followed in the construction of the technical history of the industry. A technical history was constructed using interview data, published product literature, and the scientific press. This history was circulated to key individuals who had a detailed knowledge of the technical history of the industry who corrected it as appropriate.

References

Abernathy, W. J. and Utterback, J. (1978). Patterns of industrial innovation. *Technology Review*, June–July, 40–47.

Anderson, P. and Tushman, M. (1990). Technological discontinuities and dominant designs: A cyclical model of technological change. *Administrative Science Quarterly*, December.

Christensen, C. M. (1992). Exploring the limits of the technology S-curve. Part I: Component technologies; Part II: Architectural technologies. *Production and Operations Management*, 1, 4.

Constant, E. W. (1980). *The Origins of the Turbojet Revolution*. Baltimore: The Johns Hopkins University Press.

Dosi, G. (1982). Technological paradigms and technological trajectories. *Research Policy*, 11, 147–162.

Foster, R. (1986). *Innovation, The Attacker's Advantage*. New York: Summit Books.

Gardiner, J. P. (1984). Robust and lean designs with state of the art automotive and aircraft examples. In C. Freeman (ed.), *Design, Innovation and Long Cycles in Economic Development*. London: Design Research Publications.

Henderson, R. (1988). The failure of established firms in the face of technological change: A study of the product development in the photolithographic alignment equipment industry. Ph.D. Dissertation, Harvard University.

Henderson, R. M. and Clark, K. (1990). Architectural innovation: The reconfiguration of existing product technologies and the failure of established firms. *Administrative Science Quarterly*, 35, March, 9–30.

Sahal, D. (1985). Technological guideposts and innovation avenues. *Research Policy*, 61–82.

Tushman, M. L. and Rosenkopf, L. (1992). On the organizational determinants of technological evolution: Towards a sociology of technology. *Research in Organizational Behavior*, 14, 311–347.

Utterback, J. and Kim, L. (1985). Invasion of a stable business by radical innovation. In P. Kliendorfer (ed.), *The Management of Productivity and Technology in Manufacturing*. New York: Plenum.

Van Wyk, R. J. (1985). The notion of technological limits: An aid to technological forecasting. *Futures*, June, 214–223.

Watts, R. K. and Einspruch, N. G. (eds.). (1987). *Lithography for VLSI, VLSI Electronics – Microstructure Science*. New York: Academic Press.

10 Three faces of organizational learning: Wisdom, inertia, and discovery

Daniel Levinthal

Are technological oversights and foresights the realization of some random process, or are there systematic forces influencing the predisposition to one outcome or another? Clearly, there is a wealth of management literature that suggests that there are some systematic forces at work – a literature that strives to highlight the levers available to managers to direct those forces. If there is to be some intelligence to the process of decision making regarding technological opportunities, then it must be the case that some existing knowledge is being applied to inform judgments about these new opportunities. Absent divine inspiration, this existing knowledge, or wisdom is presumably the result of past experiences. The organizational challenge, the paradox that must be confronted, is that this knowledge based on prior experiences may not be an appropriate guide to the new circumstances the organization faces. However, if the organization is not leveraging its past knowledge, how is it to have a competitive advantage in confronting the future? To address this paradox, one must address the multifaceted nature of organizational learning.

Organizational learning has many virtues. One of the most commonly articulated virtues is the tendency for organizations to become more proficient at their current activities with experience (Alchian, 1959). A different virtue, often cited (Senge, 1990), is that learning processes facilitate an organization's adaptation to changing circumstances in its competitive environment. These two facets of learning, the codifying of past experiences and responding to novel contexts, are, in important respects, at odds. This inherent conflict poses another facet of learning. In stable worlds, we tend to view the codification of past experiences as wisdom. In changing environments, we tend to view this same phenomenon less favorably and term it inertia. This essay explores these three "faces" of learning processes and speculates on some of the ways in which they interrelate.

Learning as wisdom

The most familiar representation of learning as wisdom is the notion of the learning or experience curve (Alchian, 1959; Yelle, 1977). In many settings, the level of past production activity is associated with a systematic reduction in production costs. However, despite this well known mapping of past activity to cost reduction, there is little understanding of whether, or what sort of, knowledge accumulation is occurring (for exceptions see Cohen & Bacdayan, 1994, and Epple, Argote, & Devadas, 1991). For the most part, studies of learning curves are largely disconnected from processes of learning and fit rather comfortably in the "black box" tradition of microeconomic analyses of production functions.

Indeed, learning need not be associated with an enhancement of performance. For instance, March and Olsen (1976) identify the phenomenon of superstitious learning. Beliefs may develop – be learnt – that do not reflect the actual environment in which the actor resides. Some false beliefs may be self-sustaining because the beliefs guide actions in such a manner that contrary information is not generated. Major retailers held a belief that a discount store was not viable in a city of less than 30,000 until Wal-Mart proved to the contrary (Ghemawat, 1986). A considerable literature within psychology suggests that individuals are reluctant to change their beliefs, even when confronted with contrary evidence (Nisbett & Ross, 1980). Indeed, the catharsis associated with confronting the falsehood of previously held beliefs has been noted by philosophers of science (Kuhn, 1970) as well as organizational theorists (Argyis & Schon, 1978).

Nonetheless, across a wide variety of cultures there is a tendency to associate wisdom with age and, underlying this relationship, an association between wisdom and experience. Wisdom accrues whether it be in the form of organizational routines (March & Simon, 1958; Nelson & Winter, 1982) or individual heuristics (Simon, 1979).

Wisdom and discovery

Technical skills

Not only may past experiences be a source of wisdom, but the wisdom derived from such understanding of the past can facilitate the discovery of new insights and knowledge. Nelson and Winter (1982) suggest two possible means by which this may occur. They note that well understood routines, that is, routines for which there is a large experiential basis, form an effective building block for innovative activity. Innovative activity may consist of novel combinations of existing activities. Holland (1975) makes a similar argument in his work on complex systems. Effective innovation, that is, changes that hold a reasonable promise of being superior to the current set of actions, are likely to be based on a recombination of existing blocks of actions. In contrast, more random mutations have an exceedingly small likelihood of enhancing the fitness of the system.

Indeed, notions of technological trajectories (Nelson & Winter, 1977; Dosi, 1982) imply that innovative activity is cumulative. Absent a strong footing on the current state of the art, one is going to be unable to advance the frontier of technical capabilities.

Similar in spirit to this line of reasoning is Cohen and Levinthal's (1989 & 1990) argument that past learning provides a firm with the "absorptive capacity" to acquire new knowledge. Thus, firms with a strong technical base in a given domain will find it relatively easy to follow and exploit subsequent research, whether produced by competitors, equipment manufacturers, or university or government laboratories. Firms, or individuals, typically learn by building upon what has been learned previously. A pharmaceutical firm, for example, requires expertise in molecular biochemistry before it can understand the latest advances in genetic engineering, let alone derive novel application of these new techniques. In addition, the possession of related expertise will permit a firm to better interpret intermediate technological advances that provide signals as to the eventual merit of a new technological advance (Cohen & Levinthal, 1994).

Administrative capabilities

A second fine of argument provided by Nelson and Winter (1982) points out that innovative activity itself can benefit from the codification and refinement of past experience. They note that although the results of innovative activity may remain highly uncertain, organizations may develop considerable insight and expertise with regard to the innovation process itself. This learning may be in the form of heuristics regarding the appropriate allocation of resources to research and development, such as a fixed percentage of sales revenue allocated to R&D, or goals regarding the fraction of sales associated with new products. Such heuristics do not speak directly to technological innovation, but to the broader context in which such innovation might occur.

Other administrative wisdom may develop with regard to appropriate structures for facilitating innovative activity. This administrative wisdom may be with regard to effective organizational forms for encouraging corporate innovative activity, whether it be a business development group, skunk works, or the use of strategic alliances.

The firm's structural position may also facilitate current innovative activity. Rosenkopf and Tushman (1994) argue that the emergence of dominant designs and product standards is, in important respects, the outcome of political as well as economic forces. Thus, a firm's position within a political network may allow it to promote its own technological solutions and, by influencing the direction of technological change, effectively enhance its technological "foresight."

A firm's position in a network may also guide and facilitate the development of its technological capabilities. Powell (1991) makes an argument of this form in the case of biotechnology. The set of ties a biotechnology firm has with leading university and government scientists and other firms is a critical resource and an important determinant of its ability to be technologically progressive. Von Hippel's (1987) work on knowledge sharing offers similar implications. Even between direct competitors, scientists are willing to exchange important technical information, but the "ticket" of entry to this exchange is a past history of exchange and the prospect of future reciprocity.

False learning and inertia

The codification and institutionalization of past experiences, i.e., learning, is generally considered to enhance one's ability to take intelligent future action. Put more simply, learning is typically thought of as a source of wisdom. Indeed, central to Nelson and Winter's (1982) notion of organizational capabilities is the codification of past experiences in the form of organizational routines. Hannan and Freeman (1984) argue that this process importantly contributes to the enhanced reliability of organizations as they age.

There are at least two respects in which the codification of past experiential learning may not be a source of wisdom. First, learning processes should be viewed in a positive rather than normative manner. False beliefs may be learnt as well as correct ones. Complex environments in which actions and outcomes are only loosely coupled are ripe settings for the development of superstitious learning (March & Olson, 1976).

More germane to the issue of technological oversights is that old truths may become new falsehoods. Environments change. Not only may current beliefs about the attractiveness of a class of technologies, the threat posed by a substitute industry, or the importance of new set of potential customers be outdated, but these beliefs may impede future learning and adaptation. Shifting paradigms is notoriously difficult, whether those who face the need for such a shift are scientists (Kuhn, 1970) or managers (Argyris & Schon, 1978). Indeed, Leonard-Barton (1992) argues that a firm's core capabilities may act as core rigidities in that past practice and skills may impede the adaption to new circumstances.

Unlearning and discovery

For these reasons, several authors have argued for the need for various forms of "unlearning" (Hedbert, Nystrom, & Starbuck, 1976; Hedberg, 1981; March, 1988). March (1988) advocates the relaxation of the rules of rational choice, for a technology of foolishness, in order to facilitate the discovery of alternative goals and rules of behavior. In a similar spirit, Hedberg (1981) argues that unlearning is necessary for organizations to adapt to changing circumstances. As a mechanism of unlearning, Hedberg, Nystrom, and Starbuck (1976) suggest that organizations do not hold tightly to standard tenets of rational choice such as consistency of action. Similarly, March (1988) suggests that playfulness or experimentation may be facilitated by reducing the extent to which past experiences constrain future actions. It is likely that most manifestations of foolishness or unlearning will not lead to desirable outcomes. However, some initiatives carried out under this relaxation of the standard rules of rational action may constitute a promising basis for future action. This unlearning of the past facilitates discovery in the present.

Trading-off wisdom and discovery

A classic statement of this tension between learning as the intelligence derived from past experience and learning as a discovery process leading to novel insights is the tradeoff between exploiting current wisdom and exploring for alternative bases of wisdom (Holland, 1975; March, 1991). A canonical representation of this tradeoff is the n-armed bandit problem.

The n-armed bandit problem is a decision problem under uncertainty. The decision maker must choose which of n "arms" to pull. There are two distinct outcomes as a result of the decision maker's choice. One is an immediate payoff, and the other is information regarding the attractiveness of the arm that was pulled. If the decision maker is aware, through past experience and prior beliefs, that a particular arm tends to yield favorable outcomes, then there is clear reward to exploiting this wisdom gained from experience and using this same arm in the future. However, by using the same arm, the decision maker deprives himself of learning about the attractiveness of alternative arms.

An important feature of the n-armed bandit problem is that the decision maker is restricted to a single choice of an arm to pull each period. One might view the organizational problem as less constrained. Shouldn't a large organization be able to sustain multiple choices within the same time period? However, even if the organization can choose multiple "arms" within the same period, it still faces a trade-off on the margin as to whether a given initiative should exploit its current understanding of the environment (i.e., its choice set), or should it experiment with less familiar alternatives? Furthermore, as discussed below, there are strong organizational forces that reduce the amount of experimentation and variation within the organization.

Dominance of wisdom over discovery

Although there are clear occasions on which organizations need to stimulate exploitation and restrain exploration, the more common situation is one in which exploitation tends to drive out exploration. Learning processes are driven by experience. Exploitation generates clearer, earlier, and closer feedback than does exploration. As a result, the primary challenge to sustaining an optimal mix of exploration and exploitation is the tendency of rapid learners and successful organizations to reduce the resources allocated to exploration. In this sense, learning in the form of wisdom tends to lead to inertia.

Competency traps[1]

Inevitably an organization develops better skills in some parts of the organization, in some markets, in some technologies, and in some strategies than in others. The mechanism is one of mutual positive feedback between experience and competence. Organizations engage in activities at which they are more competent with greater frequency than they engage in activities at which they are less competent. The differences in the frequency with which different activities are pursued translates into differences in the amount of experience at the various potential activities, which in turn translates into differences in competence. These distinctive competencies invite utilization, which furthers their additional development. The self-reinforcing nature of learning makes it attractive for an individual or organization to sustain current focus. The result is that distinctive competence is accentuated. The learner develops increasing competence at current activities, but at the same time becomes increasingly removed from other bases of experience and knowledge. Thus, the degree to which firrns or individuals learn about alternative opportunities is a function of their level of involvement in them (Cohen & Levinthal, 1994), and knowledge of old competencies inhibits efforts to change capabilities.

Opportunity costs

The cost of experimentation is an opportunity cost – the foregone opportunity to exploit alternatives that are known to be attractive. This opportunity cost of experimentation can, in part, explain the reluctance of successful enterprises to explore alternative bases of action. This opportunity cost explanation of inertia lies in contrast to explanations within the economics literature that revolve around issues of cannibalization of product markets (Reinganum, 1989). The focus on cannibalization within the economics literature reflects the broader tendency, noted by Nelson and Winter (1982), to focus on product *choices* rather than production *capabilities*. Thus, inertia may emerge as the result of firm strategizing with regard to product market competition. As suggested here, however, there is a simpler economic justification for inertia relying on the more basic construct of opportunity cost. Furthermore, the opportunity cost should be interpreted broadly to reflect not just the best return to the firm's physical resources and operating capabilities, but also the firm's knowledge about its external environment, including its understanding of how to compete in a given market.

Political structures

Past learning not only gets institutionalized in the form of standard operating rules (Cyert & March, 1963; Nelson & Winter, 1982) and cognitive frameworks (Weick, 1979), but power within the organization may also reflect past demands of the environment. Pfeffer and Salancik (1978) in their work on resource dependency argue that power within the organization will tend to accrue to those individuals and groups that control critical resources. However, power derived from the control of critical resources in a prior epoch will not be readily relinquished when circumstances change and the set of critical skills and resources change. As partial evidence of this, Boeker (1989) finds that the legacy of founding executive teams is markedly persistent on the internal political structure of firms.

Collective learning

Collective wisdom

Intelligence resides within individuals as well within collectives. One of the important insights of Nelson and Winter's work (I 982) is that organizations may possess capabilities that do not reside in any individual member of the organization, but are a property of a collective – the set of routines that emerge, the patterns of interaction, and so on.

Collective wisdom is a central component of Brown and Duguid's (1991) notion of communities-of-practice. In their view, learning occurs in the context of work and the sharing of narratives of work experiences. The idea of communities-of-practice is quite compatible with Nelson and Winter's view of organizational capabilities and provides some insight as to the mechanisms by which tacit knowledge is transmitted. However, Brown and Duguid's communities-of-practice are not tightly delineated and certainly need not lie within organizational boundaries. Indeed, communities-of-practice are emergent structures rather than the outcome of intentional design.

There are many other forms of collective wisdom. Economists have long been intrigued by the public good nature of knowledge. One manifestation of this interest has been a concern with knowledge spillovers across firms and the associated incentive problems that such spillovers imply. Although Cohen and Levinthal (1988 and 1990) note that economists may have exaggerated the public nature of such knowledge, there is clearly an important sense in which knowledge develops at the community level.

Recent work on economic development focuses on the importance of knowledge, as well as other resources, at the community level. The return to investing in knowledge, or other resources, is argued to be an increasing function of the level of these resources in the firm's environment (Romer,1986). Thus, there exist significant increasing returns or positive feedback effects (Arthur, 1990) permitting some communities to flourish in a virtuous cycle of ever-increasing investment and knowledge infrastructure and other communities to persist in a low-level equilibrium trap, in which the absence of resources at the community level diminishes the incentive of individual actors to make investments that would contribute to this public good.

Institutional theorists (DiMaggio & Powell, 1983) provide another basis by which learning occurs at the community level. Organizations may engage in mimetic learning, by which they learn by adopting the practices of what are construed by their organizational community as exemplar or high status organizations. Mimetic learning in fact has become highly popularized in the form of benchmarking and the incessant search for "best practice."

Collective inertia

Just as organizational learning can be a source of inertia, so can learning at the collective level. One powerful driver of collective inertia is the emergence of standard designs (Utterback & Abernathy, 1975; Farrell & Saloner, 1985). The emergence of a dominant design is an important milestone in the development of collective wisdom in that it facilitates the cumulation of knowledge at the community level. Organizations are no longer segmented by distinct approaches to product and production technology. Specialized providers of supporting goods and services are also likely to emerge, further facilitating the sharing of a common pool of expertise.

With the emergence of a dominant design, the returns to refinement of that "design" tend to greatly exceed the returns to experimenting with alternative approaches. This "lock-in" (Arthur, 1989) is an extraordinarily powerful inertial force. It is perhaps this internal, within-industry focus, that follows from a dominant design that results in the fact (cf. Sherer, 1980) that many radical innovations have their origins in organizations outside the existing industry's boundaries.

From an evolutionary point of view, the emergence of a dominant design radically diminishes the variation that exists within the industry population. A natural implication of this is that the industry population will not be robust to changes in its niche and may be subject to the rapid, successful invasion by a new organizational form. Indeed, this is precisely the Schumpeterian dynamics that Tushman and Anderson (1986) and others have characterized.

Collective discovery

Discovery may occur at the collective level through the birth of new entities, and the possible death of existing ones. This argument is clear with respect to organizational birth and death and is a primary driver of wealth creation in a capitalist economy (Schumpeter, 1934). However, a similar argument can also be made at the organizational level.

Brown and Duguid (1991) make the interesting observation that if an organization is viewed as a collection of communities-of-practice, then, contrary to the standard view, large complex organizations should be quite effective in fostering innovative activity. The diversity among the communities provides an important degree of robustness for the organization as a whole.

However, these distinct communities must be legitimate in two important respects. First, their relative autonomy must be accepted. Absent such autonomy, the various communities will be subject to pressures to conform to the dominant beliefs and actions of the organization. In addition, these communities must be legitimate in the sense that initiatives and new conceptions of business practice that emerge within a given community be considered by the broader organization and have the potential to influence the existing dominant set of practices and beliefs.

Oldtimers retire, newcomers arrive. Some existing communities-of-practice wither away and others flourish. A few internal venture efforts take on a life of their own and others are still-born. In an organization in which newcomers are not rapidly socialized into existing codes of beliefs (March, 1991), in which emerging communities-of-practice are allowed to take on their own distinctive identity, and in which internal venture efforts can effectively segregate themselves from the organizational core (Burgelman, 1983), these internal dynamics bode well for organizational learning in the form of discovery and for organizational viability in the face of changing environments.

Levels of aggregation and technological foresight and oversight

Learning and discovery take place within communities of organizations and among individuals within an organization. It is argued here that exploiting these processes at different levels of aggregation is critical to managing the paradox of organizational learning.

As a manager of an organization, one is concerned with the effective functioning of the overall organizational system and, only indirectly, with the particular subsystems comprising the organization. Similarly, as a social planner, one is focused on the functioning of the overall population of organizations and, to a lesser extent, the well-being of an individual organization.

How do these different levels of aggregation affect processes of technological oversight and foresight? First, the potential for technological innovation is importantly tied to the degree of variation generated. This in turn raises the question as to the degree of variation that can be sustained within an organization in contrast to the variation present in a population of organizations. Even apart from considerations of resource availability, whether financial or technical, there seems to be a marked difference in the degree of variation supported by the two sorts of collectives.

Organizations have difficulty sustaining a variety of perspectives regarding a given technological opportunity (Levinthal, 1996). In part, this may stem from the greater intensity of socialization processes within an organization than across organizational boundaries. More central, though, is the tendency for resources to be allocated by a singular authority structure within the organization. Thus, although a large organization may have sufficient resources to make multiple "bets," those individuals who control resource allocation decisions are unlikely to be of multiple minds. Although there may well be considerable diversity of opinion within the organization, there is typically a dominant political coalition (Cyert & March, 1963; Tushman & Romanelli, 1985), and the perspective of this ruling group will drive the resource allocation decisions.

Contrast this setting with a population of organizations. Even if an individual organization is making a singular "bet" with regard to a given technological opportunity, there may be tremendous diversity across the population of organizations. While there may be some pressure to conform to the perspective of other, respected, organizations, individual organizations receive highly differentiated feedback from their environment (Adner & Levinthal, 1995), and this distinct feedback may lead them to different views of the same technological opportunity.

For instance, Christensen and Bower (1994) find that computer disk manufacturers were highly responsive in pursuing technological opportunities that yielded benefits to their existing set of customers. However, by the same token, these firms ignored other opportunities that were not critical to the immediate needs of these current customers. In particular, the leading manufacturers of 5 ¼" disk drives were well aware of the possibilities associated with the development of smaller drives with lower requirements for electric power. However, their current customers were producing desk top machines and, as a result, were not particularly concerned with size and power requirements. Thus, depending on the set of manufacturers to which a disk drive developer was most closely tied, the organization developed a different set of beliefs regarding technological opportunities. Indeed, the motivation of entrepreneurs to leave their prior organization seems as much driven by their inability to convince their prior firm to pursue an opportunity that they feel has tremendous promise as it is associated with an incentive to appropriate for themselves the returns associated with the pursuit of the opportunity (Tilton, 1971).

Positive feedback cascades: Organization and populations

Insight and foresight are properties of individuals (Simon, 1991). The managerial question is how these individual insights effect the broader system. Systems that are subject to positive feedback (Arthur, 1990) may engender radical changes in the face of modest initial impetus.

Consider this phenomenon at the population level. Much has been written in recent years regarding the impact of dramatic, so-called Schumpeterian changes in the technological landscape. However, if one examines such episodes closely, it is often the case that rapid change occurs not as the result of a singular dramatic discovery, but that an initial breakthrough causes a wave of resources to be channeled to support the pursuit of the newly identified technological opportunity. For instance, the initial breakthrough of Boyer and Cohen was a powerful signal that there was tremendous opportunity in the field of biotechnology, however, in and of itself, the initial work was quite preliminary and surely posed no immediate threat to the technological base of the established pharmaceutical firms. Their "signal," however, unleashed a torrent of venture capital that facilitated the start-up of a large set of new biotechnology companies and, over time, caused the established firms to devote tremendous amounts of their own resources in pursuit of these new technological opportunities.

Such positive feedback processes can also operate within an organization to lead to a cascade of changes whereby initially minor efforts are reinforced and ultimately may fundamentally change the organization's business. Burgelman's (1991) account of Intel's shift from the memory business is illustrative of such a phenomenon. Intel had an articulated strategy that its primary products were memory devices and that the production of memory devices was a prime driver of the firm's process technology capabilities. The firm's research funds were allocated on the basis of this perspective of upper management. However, other functions within Intel, particularly its manufacturing operations, were driven not by the strategy of the firm, but by the relative margins that Intel's products received in the market. As a result, the firm gradually was pulled by market feedback away from the memory business. Thus, while the shift in strategy was dramatic and, at the time painful for the firm, the shift in behavior was fairly gradual.

Conclusion

The vision of technological foresight would certainly be wonderful to have, but such insight is likely to be rare and certainly unpredictable ex-ante. Lacking such vision, organizations must exploit their current wisdom about the world *and* engage in on-going experiments as to future possibilities. The firm should attempt to experiment in a wide variety of settings to enhance the diversity of feedback that it receives (Adner & Levinthal, 1995). Reliance on what is believed to be a leading edge customer merely substitutes the organization's own biases and beliefs for those of another. The successful balancing of the processes of exploration and exploitation require understanding the power of aggregation and parallelism in organizational learning. Experimentation at the level of an aggregate entity is extremely risky, whether the aggregate entity is a government betting on a particular energy source or a firm banking on a new product offering. Experimentation should occur at the level of subsystems, whereas the aggregate entity should exploit the chance discoveries of its subsystems.

Such a view places a premium on the presence of diversity at the subsystem level. The notion of balancing exploitation and exploration becomes recast as a balance of incentives for diversity and the intelligent selection and culling of this diversity. Organizations do not lack for diversity within themselves. Tremendous diversity emerges as a by-product of an organizations ongoing operations. The challenge is to allow this diversity at a subsystem level to provide the basis for a "cascade" of actions influencing resource flows and strategy that have the potential to change the direction of the overall organization.

Acknowledgment

Support for this research was provided by the Sol C. Snider Entrepreneurial Center at the Wharton School, University of Pennsylvania.

Note

1   This subsection draws from Levinthal and March (1993).

References and bibliography

Adner, R. and Levinthal, D. A. (1995). Organizational renewal: Variated feedback and technological change. Unpublished working paper, Wharton School, University of Pennsylvania.

Alchain, A. (1959). Cost and output. In M. Abramovitz et al., eds. The Allocation of Economic Resources: Essays in Honor of B. F. Haley. Stanford, CA: Stanford University Press.

Argyris, C. and Schon, D. (1978). Organizational Learning: A Theory of Action Perspective. Reading, MA: Addison-Wesley

Arthur, B. (1989). Competing technologies, increasing returns, and lock-in by historical events: The dynamics of allocation under increasing returns. Economic Journal, 99, 116–131.

Arthur, B. (1990). Positive feedbacks in the economy. Scientific American, 262:92–99.

Boeker, W. (1989). The development and institutionalization of subunit power in organizations. Administrative Science Quarterly, 34, 388–410.

Brown, J. S. and Duguid, P. (1991). Organizational learning and communities-of-practice: Toward a unified view of working, learning, and innovation. *Organizational Science*, 2, 40–57.

Burgelman, R. A. (1991). Intraorganizational ecology of strategy making and organizational adaptation: Theory and field research. *Organizational Science*, 2, 239–262.

Cohen, M. and Bacdayan, P. (1994). Organizational routines are stored as procedural memory: Evidence from a laboratory study. *Organization Science*, 5, 554–568.

Cohen, W. M. and Levinthal, D. A. (1989). Innovation and learning: The two faces of R&D. *Economic Journal*, 99, 569–590.

Cohen, W. M. and Levinthal, D. A. (1990). Absorptive capacity: A new perspective on learning and innovation. *Administrative Science Quarterly*, 35, 128–152.

Cohen, W. M. and Levinthal, D. A. (1994). Fortune favors the prepared firm. *Management Science*, 40, 227–251.

Cyert, R. M. and March, J. G. (1963). *Behavioral Theory of the Firm*. Engelwood, NJ: Prentice-Hall.

DiMaggio, P. and Power, W. (1983). The iron cage revisited: Institutional isomorphism and collective rationality in organizational fields. *American Sociological Review*, 48, 147–160.

Dosi, G. (1977). Technological paradigms and technological trajectories: A suggested interpretation of the determinants and direction of technical change. *Research Policy*, 11, 147–162.

Epple, D., Argote, L., and Devadas, R. (1991). Organizational learning curves: A method for investigating intra-plant transfer of knowledge acquired through learning by doing. *Organizational Science*, 2, 58–70.

Ghemawat, P. (1986). Wal-Mart Stores' Discount Operations. Intercollegiate Case Clearinghouse No. 9-387-018.

Hannan, M. T. and Freeman, J. (1984). Structural inertia and organizational change. *American Sociological Review*, 49, 149–164.

Hedberg, B. L. T., Nystrom, P. C., and Starbuck, W. H. (1976). Camping on seesaws: Prescriptions for a self-designing organization. *Administrative Science Quarterly*, 21, 41–65.

Holland, J. H. (1975). *Adaptation in Natural and Artificial Systems*. Ann Arbor, MI: University of Michigan Press.

Kuhn, T. S. (1970). *The Structure of Scientific Revolutions*. Chicago: University of Chicago Press.

Leonard-Barton, D. (1992). Core capabilities and core rigidities: A paradox in managing new product development. *Strategic Management Journal*, 13, 111–125.

Levinthal, D. A. (1996). Organizational capabilities: The role of decompositions and units of selection. Unpublished working paper, University of Pennsylvania.

Levinthal, D. A. and March, J. G. (1993). The myopia of learning. *Strategic Management Journal*, 14:95–112.

March, J. G. (1978). Bounded rationality, ambiguity, and the engineering of choice. *Bell Journal of economics*, 9, 587–608.

March, J. G. (1991). Exploration and exploitation in organizational learning. *Organizational Science*, 2, 71–87.

March, J. G. and Olsen, J. P. (1976). *Ambiguity and Choice in Organizations*. Bergen, Norway: Universitetsforlaget.

March, J. G. (1988). *Decisions and Organizations*. Oxford, United Kingdom: Basil Blackwell.

Nelson, R. and Winter, S. (1977). In search of an useful theory of innovation. *Research Policy*, 6, 36–77.

Nelson, R. and Winter, S. (1982). *An Evolutionary Theory of Economic Change*. Cambridge, MA: Harvard University Press.

Nisbett, R. and Ross, L. (1980). *Human Inference: Strategies and Shortcomings of Social Judgment*. Englewood Cliffs, NJ: Prentice-Hall.

Pfeffer, J. and Salancik, G. (1978). *The External Control of Organizations*. New York, NY: Harper & Row.

Powell, W. W. and Brantley, P. (1991). Competitive cooperation in biotechnology: Learning through networks. In N. Nohria and R. Eccles (eds.) *Networks and Organizations*. Cambridge, MA: Harvard Business School Press.

Reinganum, J. J. (1989). The timing of innovation: Research, development, and diffusion. In R. Schmalensee and R. D. Willig (eds.), *Handbook of Industrial Organization*. New York: North-Holland, pp. 849–908.

Romer, P. M. (1986). Increasing returns and long-run growth. *Journal of Political Economy*, 94:1002–1036.

Rosenkopf, L. and M. L. Tushman. (1994). The coevolution of technology and organization. In J. Baum and J. Singh (eds.) *Evolutionary Dynamics of Organizations*. New York: Oxford University Press.

Scherer, F. M. (1980). *Industrial Market Structure and Economic Performance*. Chicago, IL: Rand McNally.

Schumpeter, J. A. (1934). *The Theory of Economic Development*. Cambridge, MA: Harvard University Press.

Senge, P. M. (1990). *The Fifth Discipline: The Art and Practice of the Learning Organization*. New York: Doubleday.

Simon, H. A. (1979). *Models of Thought*. New Haven, CT: Yale University Press.

Simon, H. A. (1991). Bounded rationality and organizational learning. *Organizational Science*, 2, 125–134.

Tilton, J. E. (1971). *International Diffusion of Technology: The Case of Semiconductors*. Washington, DC: Brookings Institute.

Tushman, M. L. and Anderson, P. (1986). Technological discontinuities and organizational environments. *Administrative Science Quarterly*, 31, 439–465.

Tushman, M. L. and Romanelli, E. (1985). Organizational evolution: A metamorphosis model of convergence and reorientation, In L. Cummings and B. Staw (eds). *Research in Organizational Behavior*, Greenwich, CT: JAI Press.

Utterback, J. M. and Abernathy, W. J. (1975). A dynamic model of process and product innovation. *Omega*, 3, 639–656.

Von Hippel, E. (1987). Cooperation between rivals: Informal know-how trading. *Research Policy*, 16, 291–302.

Weick, K. (1979). *The Social Psychology of Organizing*. Reading, MA: Addison-Wesley.

Yelle, L. E. (1979). The learning curve: Historical review and comprehensive survey. *Decision Sciences*, 10, 302–328.

11 Organizational entrepreneurship in mature-industry firms: Foresight, oversight, and invisibility

Mariann Jelinek

When rapid environmental change is endemic, old methods fail

Many accounts of innovation, entrepreneurship, change, and growth have focused on the successful efforts of "high tech" firms pioneering changes the rest of industry eventually had to adapt to. The "low tech" or "mature" firms seeking to adapt have often been characterized as change-resistant organizations whose sluggish, inept managerial modes fail to accomplish effective response. Fair or not, the popular impression is that high tech firms are innovative, entrepreneurial, and flexible, whereas mature firms are not.

Successful major innovations in mature-industry firms are all the more impressive because they must overcome a variety of innovation dilemma that were identified long ago (e.g., Quinn 1979; Miller & Friesen 1980). Slow response to external change can be followed by frantic, ineffectual efforts to catch up. Scarce R&D dollars may be devoted to poorly understood projects, particularly where little research or product development has taken place for years, and radical change can derail firms already near the edge. New developments may be starved in vain hopes of preserving once-dominant products, on the reasoning that successful products should not be cannibalized. Or new efforts may simply fail.

In short, for mature businesses especially, innovation is often risky, poorly understood, and poorly executed. All these responses disclose a common failure to respond entrepreneurially to the changing competitive environment. Examples will illustrate their relevance today.

Slow response and catch-up

The majority of economic activity takes place in industries that are by definition "mature." Only firms and industries having twice the national average of research expenditures or research employees are considered "high technology," so all others are "mature." Yet the efficiency and productivity of such firms and their capability for self-renewal through innovation profoundly affect global economic well-being, if for no other reason than that such firms make up so great a fraction of all economic activity. We argue that such firms increasingly require entrepreneurial focus to survive.

Many so-called mature-industry firms are increasingly technological. Moreover, mature industries too have been revolutionized in recent decades, as computers invade both administrative tasks, production, and products as well. Many mature-industry firms face the intensifying global competitive pressures, no less than high tech firms. So, like high technology firms, mature firms too need to innovate.

Older technology can be supplanted quickly in mature industries. The advent of radial tire technology obsoleted in-place bias capacity swiftly, even though radials entered the U.S. market at more than twice the price of bias tires. The shift was exacerbated by exchange rates during the 1980s that favored imports at a time when U.S. tire makers had limited radial capacity. Worldwide, the tire industry has experienced a technology-driven consolidation visible in the U.S.: Employment in the industry dropped about in half between 1977 and 1987, and some 37 U.S. plants were closed in the same era. To stay in the game, Goodyear planned to invest well over $1 billion in the early 1990s in an effort to bolster its position; not coincidentally, the firm was also fighting off takeover efforts.

Wasted dollars

Investment per se is no panacea. General Motors, from a dominant share in the U.S. domestic automobile market of nearly 50% and worldwide leadership, has seen its position erode both at home and abroad over the past 15 years – despite $67.2 billion dollars of investment in plant and R&D beyond depreciation. Indeed, GM's expenditures were well in excess of what would have been required simply to purchase outright the equity of rivals Toyota, Honda, and Ford (see Jensen, 1993 for a financial assessment of GM's poor record of R&D productivity). GM's record early 1980s profits have been succeeded by record losses, even after all the dollars for new technology; only recently has GM returned to profits, which Ford achieved for far less cost. GM has continued to trail the domestic automobile industry's recovery.

By most accounts, GM has truly accomplished researchers and technical specialists. Yet the many dollars expended somehow failed to address the underlying problems, perhaps because the fundamental attitude of investment seemed to be "more of the same," just at a time when the technical possibilities demanded quite a different perspective on how to run the business. So-called "lean manufacturing" methods pioneered by Toyota and Honda were only belatedly adopted by GM, well after W. Edwards Demming had begun his efforts at Ford (Womack, Jones, & Roos, 1990; Petersen & Hillkirk, 1991). Clearly, hardware alone is insufficient, and management of technology must go well beyond mere investment to achieve the potential of new technical systems.

Starving technology

Market leaders in mature industries often find it difficult to invest in new technology that may subvert existing products, plant or even their human skills (Foster, 1986; Rogers, 1983). Examples abound, leading many to suggest that only crisis can lead to change, or only outsiders can transform an industry. One obvious indicator is the general level of R&D investment for American industry. Although significant debate rages among finance specialists and economists about whether U.S. investment has or has not produced adequate productivity growth (for two opposing views, see Baumol, Blackman & Wolff, 1989; Peterson, 1993), a consistent note of concern about the level of investment has echoed for the past several decades. Hayes and Wheelwright (1984) noted a decade ago that major trading partners consistently out-invested U.S. industries, a complaint repeated by Reich (Reich, 1983; Reich, 1991) and Peterson (1993), among others.

What keeps mature industries from innovating?

Explanations of why mature-industry firms are so slow to innovate often rely on technological, economic, or strategic explanations. The key issues may instead be cognitive, however. Keisler & Sproull suggest that one "crucial component of managerial behavior in rapidly changing environments is problem sensing, the cognitive processes of noticing and constructing meaning about environmental change so that organizations can take action" (Keisler & Sproull, 1982, p. 548). Others suggest that environmental change must evoke changes in managers' "cognitive maps," the interpretive schemes by which they make sense of the world, if managers and their organizations are to produce organizational change (Barr, Stimpert, & Huff, 1992; Bartunek, 1984; Huff & Schwenk, 1990). These recognitions are central to change and innovation, yet they are especially problematic in mature-industry firms because their "maps" so often stress stability.

Studies of declining organizations (e.g., Barr et al., 1992; Whetten, 1980; and Cameron, Sutton, & Whetten, 1988) suggest that failure to adapt cognitive patterns may be more difficult because strategic change is so frequently externally driven and concern factors not hitherto important, which may initially go unnoticed because they are outside the firm's normal purview of attention. Then when attention is given to something new, managers are confronted with what Kuhn (1972) referred to as "an anomaly" and without a framework within which to interpret it, managers may well discount such anomalies until the cumulative weight of problems becomes overwhelming.

This may be especially crucial when technological change is involved, for it often requires reallocation of assets and activities away from long-established activities. Thus it carries unpleasant implications of fault, decline, and failure (Whetten, 1980). As a result, response can be unduly delayed, which makes change all the more difficult. In a declining industry, especially one of intensive capital investment, rivals will resist exit to fight, so more stringent competition will narrow the window of opportunity to respond (Porter 1980; Porter 1985; Oster 1994). Restricted profits may reduce available resources, pressure may produce a "siege mentality" fixated on cost-cutting, rather than innovation, and perceptions of threat may reduce willingness to accept the risk inherent in any innovation. All the while, if the limited available resources are allocated to shoring up old activities, still less is available for redeployment to new activities.

Delay can be costly, both because resources that might have supported the change can erode, and because other eager competitors – particularly those who happen to be ahead on the technology – can seize the potential advantage to be gained by adopting newer, more advantageous technology. The industrial economics of such technological advances is clear: Newer, lower-cost, and more up-to-date plant will displace the less efficient capacity (Porter, 1980; Porter, 1985).

However, recognizing that change is necessary can be difficult, and new technology may not be the answer at all. As Table 11.1 illustrates, Toyota's 20-year-old plant bested its more up-to-date rivals in 1984; rivals had many explanations – like tariffs barriers, the Ministry of International Trade and Industry (MITI) support, and allegations of unfairly low labor costs – that also seemed to fit the data. Managerial and organizational arrangements, and not technology per se, may be the key factors in the automobile industry's technological struggle (Ettlie, 1988; Petersen & Hillkirk, 1991; Womack et al., 1990). Technology will not bring about superior economic improvement if the organization and management of work is inappropriate. In short, management dictates whether technology will provide its promised benefits; "management" may be especially hard to perceive from the outside.

Required management changes can affect the entire array of mature-industry firms' activities – including product design, materials, process layout and control, information processing and order entry, performance assessment, marketing, and distribution, among others. Firms that seize opportunities to build pioneering capabilities into their business can develop completely new approaches to old businesses that mystify competitors because they overthrow fundamental assumptions about the industry (Goldhar & Jelinek, 1983). Yet such vision is rare. Mature-industry firms have stressed stability in the past, whereas the requirements for technological innovation require entrepreneurship.

Large-firm dilemmas

Innovation difficulties are compounded for large, established firms – the focus of this chapter – the survivors in late stages of the life cycle characteris-

TABLE 11.1. Efficient old technology performance

	1984 Manufacturing Comparisons		
	Toyota No. 9 Engine	Chrysler Trenton	Ford Dearborn
Products	2.4 L 4-cylinder 2.0 L 4-cylinder	2.2 L 4-cylinder Including turbo	1.6 L 4-cylinder HO; turbo; EFI
Plant size	310,000 ft^2	2.2 million ft^2	2.2 million ft^2
Hourly workers: Employees	180	2250	1360
Production rate	1500/day	3200/day	1960/day
Manhours/engine	0.96 hrs./engine	5.6 hrs./engine	5.55 hrs./engine
Shifts	2		1 assembly, 2 machining
Inventory (average)	4–5 hrs	2.5–5 days	9.3 days
Absenteeism	5% (scheduled)	3% (AWOL)	N.A.
Wages	$11.35/hr, excluding fringes	*	*
Robots	None	5	N.A.

*U.S. auto industry average is $12.50/hr excluding fringes.
Note: Chart is adapted from "Quality Goes In," Automotive Industries (Nov. 1984), pp. 51–52. Toyota's Number 9 plant used 20-year-old equipment at the time of this comparison. The U.S. factories were more modern, as well as employing more shifts, more workers, more space, and more inventory to produce their output.

tic of mature industries (Chandler, 1990). Again, a cognitive approach offers insight into why such firms have difficulties. Established, mature firms succeeded in the past with practices they have institutionalized in elaborate work specification and performance assessment systems. Yet when situations change, these long-successful efforts to insure stability undercut effective response. Standardized behavior encourages "mindlessness," the very antithesis of the alert awareness to anomalies that signal the need for change (Langer, 1988; Langer & Piper, 1987).

Mature firms are often characterized by what seems an institutionalized inability to comprehend the need for change. Their formal systems are commonly inhospitable to the exploratory, developmental activities of innovation, because they emphasize efficiency instead. Such a perspective is often reinforced by accounting measures and practices that no longer reflect the underlying nature of their businesses (Johnson, 1992; Johnson & Kaplan, 1987). These, too, cue organization members to continue old behavior and avoid deviation.

Both standard accounting systems and organization cultural norms typically favor predictability and replication of past practices. These go along with exhaustive controls aimed at cutting slack resources, the very resources most necessary for market research, fresh planning, or strategic reconsideration. Slack resources, and thus capability to innovate, come under particularly stringent review in downturns. But this makes sense if and only if the period of stringency can be expected to end "soon," and conditions return to their former state.

Operational procedures also favor stability. Firms in mature industries are very likely to have long-established technologies, distribution networks, and customer bases, coordinated by stable procedures and technologies. Customers' technologies are often tightly intertwined, where mature industries serve original equipment manufacturers (OEMs) or industrial customers. To institute change, mature-industry firms may have to convince customers to innovate, or even worse, convince customers' end users.

The literature of institutional environments and evolution offers little assistance to understanding how and why organizations might change, or might resist change. A central difficulty: much of the discussion is framed at a high level of abstraction and with much reification, addressing whole organizations' capabilities (often, as if they were monolithic, thinking and acting entities), if not at the level of industries or nations (see, for example, Nelson 1993). Yet innovation in fact occurs as the outcome of individual actors' decisions, as persons and as group members in concert with one another (or, often, in conflict): people innovate, not organizations, even though people must access organizational resources and must ultimately convince others to cooperate so that "the organization" is moved (Silverman, 1971).

The innovation literature is virtually silent on people's interactions or their cognitive processes, typically focusing instead on the organizational level. We know very little indeed about how people experience innovation, although we do know it is typically a complex, ambiguous, and messy process somehow carried out by people in groups, interacting with one another. We know that innovation is a shared, social process, not an "only, lonely inventor" unilaterally creating change (Jelinek & Schoonhoven, 1994). Human interaction and human understanding are at the heart of the process: a cognitive approach is required.

This brief review of the problems of innovation in mature industries identifies a core of basic issues: failure to properly perceive conditions that require change; failure to understand the nature of problems; and thus reluctance to take action that would undercut older solutions or might fail to provide adequate levels of investment, because of assumptions that old stabilities will endure. Although many causes contribute, these breakdowns all involve recognition of anomalies, understanding complex, poorly defined problems, and interpretation of unclear data and events – all cognitive processes. This chapter is guided by the premise that the study of individuals' shared cognitions can offer valuable insight into innovation and entrepreneurship, or the lack thereof, in mature-industry firms.

The many roots of cognitive theory

Organizations can be described as information-processing systems (Galbraith, 1982; Daft & Weick, 1984), as sets of shared cognitions (e.g., Georgiou, 1973; Brown, 1978; Clark, 1985; Lincoln, 1985; Zey, 1992), and self organizing systems. Yet these systems are not mere abstractions capable of independent action: it is people within organizations that perceive, interpret, decide, and act (Silverman, 1971): typically abstract information-processing perspectives must be substantially amended to include people. Necessarily people act or decide on the basis of shared meanings that they create (Berger & Luckman, 1966; Van Maanen, 1979; Louis, 1980, 1983; Pfeffer, 1981). Organization members share information among themselves to create the necessary basis for action (Bartunek, 1984; Lenz, 1981; Keisler & Sproull, 1982; Weick, 1979; Weick & Bougon, 1986), and share as well the underlying assumptions about interpreting data that enable them to coordinate their activities, and innovate, just as they share the potent inhibitors to change described above.

Organizational entrepreneurship and new technology both demand that people within the organization develop new ways of acquiring information and creating new interpretations. Organizational learning is an important factor, but again a shifted perspective is essential. Much past organizational learning is captured in procedures, norms, rules, forms, and paradigms (March 1958, 1990; Jelinek, 1979; Weber, 1947), which in their turn shape members' thinking. This context is a cognitive frame against which efforts to innovate occur. Thus particularly within established firms in mature industries, innovation must often revise, contradict, or overthrow "what everyone in the organization knows," creating organizational "unlearning" (Hedberg 1981).

"Unlearning" a past strategic paradigm is especially difficult, for strategy must necessarily evolve through successive and interrelated sequences of sense-making, decisions, and actions (Ansoff 1987). Burgelman (1988) described shifts in strategy as resting upon "social learning," the outcome of "autonomous behavior" to reinterpret new or ambiguous data by operational, mid-level and corporate level actors within the organization. Dougherty (1994) refers to innovation efforts as "organizationally illegitimate," within traditional, rational, stability-seeking organizations; whereas Meyerson (1991) noted that organization cultures "legitimate" or "delegitimate" paradigms, explanations, and perceptual data more broadly, including the acknowledgment of ambiguity so essential to successful innovation. These varied insights are central to comprehending innovation and entrepreneurship from a cognitive perspective.

Cognitive schema select, deselect, and interpret information

Technological change and entrepreneurship, which necessarily involve attempting the new and hitherto unfamiliar, poses special challenges illuminated by a cognitive perspective. Within organizations, reality is a social construct (Berger & Luckman, 1966): that is, the organizational context and social interaction provide a framework for the creation of shared of meaning. Because only people within organizations act or decide, and, further, because they act upon what they perceive and believe to be the case, whether or not their beliefs are objectively "true" (Silverman, 1971), any serious effort to understand technological entrepreneurship – replete as it is with ambiguous data – must incorporate much beyond the simplistic dictates of pure rational choice models. People within a shared social construct interpret new or ambiguous data in terms of what they expect, and their expectations are likely to be tailored by organizational norms, procedures, and assumptions. Individuals interpret ambiguity in terms of preexisting frames or schema (Bruner & Postman 1949–1950; Langer, 1988; Dearborn & Simon, 1958), and evidence suggests that groups do, too (e.g., Janis, 1972).

Individuals' efforts to make sense, particularly in circumstances of ambiguity or uncertainty, will be constrained by the older social construct embodied in rules, procedures, and norms – which may be inadequate or obsolete in light of changing competitive environment, technology shifts, and the like. Put more simply, as individuals and as organizational members, people see what they expect to see, and their organizational context of shared meaning tells them what to expect. The more outdated the organization's view, embodied in the daily constraints and assumptions of rules, procedures, and stated strategy, the more difficult innovators will find it to perceive what is new as relevant, to interpret it properly, or to craft new shared meaning from which to enact innovation.

Especially in instances of strategic change, the codified insights of the past can be actively dysfunctional in several ways. First, procedures or accepted interpretations contain unexamined assumptions about the reality they are intended to describe, which may be misleading when the environment changes. Thus assumptions about the necessity to trade off between volume and quality, for instance, can encourage assumptions that better performance is "impossible."

Next, the old mental maps may dominate new data, compelling individuals to distort or deny what they cannot fit into their expectations. Individuals' propensity to utilize old schemata in ambiguous situations, or indeed even in situations where a new schemata is clearly called for, are well documented (Argyris & Schon, 1978; Barr et al., 1992; Bruner & Postman, 1949; Dearborn & Simon, 1958; Langer, 1988; Kiesler & Sproull, 1982). Such depictions are highly suggestive when applied to repeated insistence by auto industry executives that the Japanese "couldn't" be producing compact cars of superb quality at competitive prices – or semiconductor executives' disbelief about Japanese yield rates. Because competitors' costs and yields did not fit existing expectations about what was possible, the new information was rejected. Outdated strategies endure (Barr et al., 1982; Dutton, Walton,

& Abrahamson, 1988; Dutton & Duncan, 1987; Harrigan, 1980; Kearnes & Nadler, 1992), affecting members' ability to make sense of change. Technological entrepreneurship is a special challenge for mature-industry firms because they will have successfully learned and retained so much that is attuned to an embedded old technology. As a result, expectations and corroborating data from the past will tend to confirm the "correct" view of incoming data, including new or ambiguous data that do not fit the old paradigm. These distortions, rooted in old insights frequently reaffirmed in the past, can seriously constrain organization members' capability of perceiving that data are new: underlying assumptions favor continuance of the past. As one example, U.S. machine tool firms' propensity to utilize automated technology as if it were simply a more expensive version of older technology, documented by Jaikumar (1986), suggests that many simply didn't comprehend new technological capabilities.

This brief look at innovation and entrepreneurship from a cognitive perspective suggests important factors for investigators to have in mind when studying organizations. Some central concerns: How can innovators develop readiness to examine, rather than dismiss, anomalous data that doesn't fit into extant organizational descriptions of how the business operates, what is important, or what works? How can innovators overcome contextual stability assumptions to recognize when change is desirable? Next, how can they craft a coherent sense of what the changed circumstances mean, what is important, and how to make sense of the new data? And finally, how can innovators bring their insights into good organizational currency, despite many organizational barriers to the new view? Put in other words, innovators must first understand that something different is afoot. Then they must overcome a presumption of illegitimacy their perspective carries (Dougherty, 1994). Finally, they must induce others to participate in a new reality. All of these preliminary tasks, so often unrecognized, are part and parcel of the innovation process, deeply intertwined in the sense-making that formulates or executes any major change. They are the focus of the present chapter.

Technological entrepreneurship efforts in mature-industry firms: Three accounts

Data gathering and preparation

Drawing on earlier work in high technology firms' innovation as well as on a substantial literature of cognitive processes, the Mature Industries Innovation Study addresses the question of how innovators in mature-industry firms experience their efforts to execute innovation strategies. The perspective of the innovators is the central focus of this research, to illuminate the functional interaction of organizational contexts and innovation efforts at the point of action, where the actors make sense of their efforts.

The accounts presented here are drawn from a larger study of 21 innovation episodes. Sixteen mostly Fortune 500 firms agreed to participate in this study, with anonymity a condition of their initial participation; thus they will not be named here. Twenty-one innovation episodes were identified by company senior managers in personal interviews as "of strategic interest." That is, these innovation efforts were sufficiently important to be known directly to top management, and identified by them as having major potential impact on the future of the firm. Three of these episodes provide the raw material of the present study.

The innovation episodes were investigated by means of semi-structured interviews conducted with the persons directly responsible for their execution. Responsible managers and senior functional specialists involved in the projects, some 175 persons in all for the larger study, were interviewed. Interviews were conducted on site in private offices and with assurances of anonymity as to any specific datum. The taped interviews were transcribed into electronic form and corrected against the original audio tapes to insure accuracy, eliminate spelling errors, and the like. These transcriptions constitute the primary research data of the present study.

The University of Minnesota's Innovation Research Project (MIRP) offers an excellent starting place. MIRP followed numerous innovation efforts with multidisciplinary research projects undertaken by scholars building upon a common baseline research agenda. The research was structured to permit both reasonable comparability across projects (Van de Ven & Angle, 1989), using a simple framework of five basic concepts:

From a managerial perspective, the process of innovation consists of motivating and coordinating people to develop and implement new ideas by engaging in transactions (or relationships) with others and making the adaptations needed to achieve desired outcomes within changing institutional and organizational contexts.

MIRP researchers uncovered several important contradictions among assumptions implicit in the innovation literature, and their projects' data. These it anomalies, summarized in the right column of Table 11.2, highlight the complexity and dynamism of innovation endeavors. Table 11.2 also reports summary findings of the Mature Industries Study (from which the present chapter is drawn).

Mature Industry innovators inhabit an innovation universe far more like MIRP's portrayal than like the simplified theoretical models assumed in past innovation research literature. As Table 11.2 suggests, innovators in mature-industry firms often find their organizational context, which typically favors continuance of established practice, set routines (often instituted to insure control and facilitate audit practices), less than hospitable to innovation efforts. A cognitive process perspective suggests how and why such organizational realities inhibit innovation. Three different innovation episodes, focused at different levels of organization, will summarize the Mature Industries study and highlight key findings.

Table 11.2. Comparison of conventional wisdom with MIRP observations and mature-industry innovation

	Conventional wisdom	Mature-industry innovations	MIRP findings
Ideas	Incremental improvements or unitary product inventions, operationalized	Redefinition, ressurection, reimplementation, and revision, as well as termination	Reinvention, proliferation, reimplementation, discarding, and termination
People	An entrepreneur, in charge of a fixed, fulltime team	An entrepreneur who "borrows," influences, cajoles, and trades people over time	Many entrepreneurs, distracted, fluidly engaging and disengaging over time in a variety of organizational roles
Transactions	A fixed network of firms and people, consistently interacting on a single idea	Fluid network of people/firms working out elements of a changing idea from diverse perspectives	Expanding and contracting network of partisan stakeholders diverging and converging on ideas
Context	A single, relatively well-defined environment provides opportunities or constraints for innovation	Environmental constraints on the innovation process include many normal procedures, whereas reinterpretation of context makes innovation possible	Innovation process constrained by and creates multiple enacted environments
Outcomes	Clear, simple, outcomes: success or failure, with a stable new order the final result	Final results may be ambiguous or indeterminate; multiple criteria for success/failure at different levels and over time; "failures" can be retrieved and recycled for information	Final results may be indeterminate; multiple in-process assessments and spin-offs; integration of new orders with old
Process	Simple, cumulative stages or phases, predictable in advance	Rarely simple, often complex, "illogical" and serendipitous, with competing parallel tracks, significant "abnormal" use of organizational rules	From simple to multiple progressions of divergent, parallel, and convergent paths, some of which are related and cumulative, others not.

Source: Compiled by the author from project data and information drawn from Van de Ven and Angle, 1989, p. 11.

Fundamental market shift

Executives at the "Denby Company"[1] noticed declines in the major U.S. steel makers with growing concern during the 1970s. Steel, a primary customer industry of Denby's, was experiencing very hard times. From a peak of 600,000 employees in 1957, domestic big steel came under increasing pressure as its prices rose relative to imports. In the mid-1970s, the decline accelerated: Fully 20% of U.S. steel-making capacity disappeared between 1975 and 1986, victim to slow growth in demand for steel; an overvalued dollar that favored imports; older, inefficient production facilities, particularly in comparison with Japan's; and changing technology.

The integrated mills that were Denby's customers, were worst hit, losing a third of their capacity and millions of dollars. Between 1976 and 1985, integrated firms' stock prices dropped an average of over 45% (for comparison, the average New York Stock Exchange (NYSE) closing prices increased by almost 81% during the period). Minimills, smaller and much more efficient producers that melt scrap in electric furnaces (and thus avoid the costs for metallurgical coal as well as ores), have prospered mightily during the same era, doubling their U.S. output in the teeth of a global downturn (Barnett & Crandall, 1986).

But minimills didn't use Denby's product; their customers were traditional, integrated, big steel producers suffering most. LTV, McLouth, Kaiser and Wheeling-Pittsburgh among integrated mills disappeared or sought bankruptcy protection; others diversified away from steel. Integrated mills' difficulties translated directly into major hazards for Denby.

In response, Denby's managers first diversified into energy, seeking independence from faltering steel industry customers. One joint venture in coal successfully moved to long-term contracts with electricity generators. A second opportunistically pursued spot-market contracts and a short-term increase in demand for metallurgical coals – to bring the company once again into closer union with faltering steel. A third diversification effort, into oil-field service, fared no better. Denby's acquired joint venture grew over a three-year period from 190 rigs to over 400 well rigs, with a hundred million dollars more on order, only to see its business dwindle to nothing in the mid-1980s oil-patch recession. This final venture, "Well Service" (also a pseudonym) eventually went bankrupt, when its banks refused to renegotiate loan covenants, another victim of the domestic oil business downturn that cut domestic drilling by more than two-thirds, with no sign of recovery during four long years.

Long-standing Denby philosophies about how to finance risky endeavors and how to structure liabilities prevented total disaster: Denby was responsible for little of the joint venture's contingent liabilities, and not by chance:

The whole history of [Denby] from [the 1950's] had been, no matter what you're in, don't pick up these contingent liabilities. Don't pick up all this debt, because if things do turn sour at some point in time, [then] the leverage isn't going to kill you.

These abortive efforts at diversification are important in understanding the mindset of Denby managers as the 1980s wore on. Having tried for nearly a decade to diversify without success, Denby senior management saw increasing evidence that their major customer industry's downturn reflected structural change, not just another business cycle. One indicator was the world spot market price for their commodity. Although long-term U.S. contracts at higher, older rates protected Denby in the short run, prices on the world market began to drop precipitously in the 1980s, as Denby learned from its European sales efforts, suggesting very much worse times in the longer term:

We were into a situation where the price in the States was not going down, and the price in Europe was going down very rapidly. At the worst time, to give you a sense of what we were talking about, the U.S. price was $50 a [unit], and the world price was maybe $24, $25 a [unit]. So the gap was 50 percent.

Nor was even this the worst of it.

The market at this same time started to contract so . . . not only were you going to lose money, it became . . . even more grave . . . you can't sell it at all – you can't [even] give it away.

Stringent efforts to restructure and close capacity followed, at Denby and throughout both steel and supplier industries, in hopes of riding out the downturn, but to little avail: demand simply disappeared as big steel's troubles increased. Contracts or no contracts, the market was gone: "There was one period, I guess it was in late 1982 where, we didn't have a plant running; . . . none of the [commodity] producers did."

Acknowledgment of just how serious conditions were was a while coming. From the perspective of 1988, however, one large fact was clear:

[Integrated steel mill customers] had no need for you. They didn't want you, and frankly never will again in this country, or at least – I shouldn't say "never" – in my lifetime, because the industry today, the steel industry, hasn't just restructured to get through a cyclical thing. It's had a basic restructuring as far as the capacity and ability to make hot metal. And these steel plants that you heard about going down, they're not coming back.

Why fundamental change is so difficult

What is so clear in retrospect was much harder to discern in the midst of action, as the response of many others in embattled mature industries suggests. The tire industry, another mature industry hammered by change, illustrates how difficult it is to press to logical conclusions, even amid widespread recognition of industry problems. Testimony by GenCorp Chairman and CEO A. William Reynolds before a Congressional hearing in 1988 is revealing:

The tire business was the largest piece of GenCorp, both in terms of annual revenues and its asset base. Yet General Tire was not GenCorp's strongest performer. Its relatively poor earnings performance was due in part to conditions affecting all of the tire industry. . . . In 1985 worldwide tire manufacturing, capacity substantially exceeded demand. At the same time, due to a series of technological improvements in the design of tires and the materials used to make them, the product life of tires had lengthened significantly. General Tire, and its competitors, faced an increasing imbalance between supply and demand. The economic pressure on our tire business was substantial. Because our unit volume was far below others in the industry, we had less competitive flexibility. . . .

Despite General Tire's weak position, Reynolds and his executives elected to invest more money in the declining tire business, only reluctantly withdrawing older capacity they acknowledged was obsolete and noncompetitive:

We increased our involvement in the high performance and light truck tire categories, two market segments which offered faster growth opportunities. We developed new tire products for those segments and invested heavily in an aggressive marketing program designed to enhance our presence in both markets. We made the difficult decision to reduce our overall manufacturing capacity by closing one of our older, less modern plants. . . . (Cited in Jensen, 1993)

Decisions are difficult because, once having recognized new realities, those who see must persuade others, to move the organization. At Denby, convincing senior managers to move in the midst of the ambiguous data was difficult. One senior officer, responsible for European sales, struggled to convince the others that the downturn was more than merely another cyclical shift to be weathered. The struggle was doubly difficult because it was highly emotional:

He came in my office and he was damn near in tears, [insisting] that I had to convince [the board of directors] to close down [a plant]. Had to convince them. I said "Bill, I'm on your side." He was, I mean, just emotional about it. He knew it was going to be disaster.

Acknowledging impending disaster was particularly difficult for those who had been directly involved in building the business in earlier times:

But you know, there's one thing that is just so terribly evident. You cannot ask the fellows who are intimately involved in most cases, you can't ask the fellows that are intimately involved in building up something to tear it down. I mean, it's a tough mentality gap to get over. And I mean, to be honest about it, [Denby's then-CEO] didn't want to hear about this crap.

Eventually, the CEO did listen, and, to his credit, took decisive action, as we shall see. But convincing other senior managers took several years:

Bill had started preaching the gospel in late 1970s, and we made our first moves in '82. . . . Well, I would say probably three or four years between the time that we started worrying about it and [when we] really bit the bullet. During those times we thought we were going to solve a lot of this by diversifying in energy.

Those who began to understand the coming problems had not only to convince senior management and Denby's board of directors, but to negotiate with a host of other companies in the industry, with whom Denby had joint ventures, alliances, and co-ownership of capacity that was, increasingly, unneeded. The steel industry's conventional wisdom was, in psychological terms, simply denial:

The disaster was complicated by the fact that in the early 1970s the steel companies' projections were for ten, twenty years [out], [for] world demand for steel were, as history will tell you, just tremendously inflated. [Expletive], we're not even back to where we were in some of the good years. . . . Everybody, if you recall, everybody was planning to build a new steel mill.

Despite all the difficulties, perhaps even because of them, it was extraordinarily difficult and painful to contemplate the obvious, leaving the industry.

The exit option

The decision to exit stands as one of the most extreme "innovations," a wholesale shift in basic strategy, corporate identity, core competence, and fundamental technology as well. Cognitive factors play an obvious role in interpreting the ambiguous data of such massive change, in recognizing the exit option. Personal involvement, denial, deep emotional attachment to the scenes of past success, personal conviction that a deep enough understanding might turn the tide – all are visible.

Senior managers at Denby initially recognized desirability to diversify, to reduce reliance on a cyclical customer industry, but recognizing that the change they faced was a "disaster" requiring exit was more difficult. They clearly had no intention to exit, at first. Their abortive diversification efforts took time and resources, and foreclosed what had seemed a promising alternative route. But whereas failed diversification substantially raised the urgency of their situation as the downturn continued, the data were still not conclusive. One individual, Bill, brought the desperate news into discussion, only to discover that others resisted it. Some, who agreed with Bill, still found the new view incomprehensible or threatening, and important senior managers "didn't want to hear this crap." As conditions worsened, however, the message began to come through, and senior executives at last determined to move Denby to a new industry.

These difficulties testify to a cognitive environment characterized by a (highly understandable) initial unwillingness to look clearly at new data or reexamine fundamental assumptions: it is little wonder that convincing management took several years. Shared cognitive schema here are embodied in a common view of the industry – one that fits anomalous data into past expectations, distorts, or denies it – and thus profoundly affect organizational capacity for effective response. The denial visible in widespread industry plans "to build a new steel mill" reinforces others' older views, and is quite parallel to tire executives' reluctance to acknowledge that their industry's overcapacity includes them. Denial, resistance, distortion, and emotional turmoil are all cognitive constraints directly relevant to innovation, at Denby to the decision to exit one industry in favor of another.

When finally executed, the decision required enormous change. Denby repositioned itself by selling off some assets and acquiring small firms in a new target industry (with a completely different technology). The sole similarity was that the new activity also involved industrial customers. As a result, management concluded that acquired management would have to run the new subsidiaries; that corporate "value added" was in coordination, financial assistance, and facilitating exchange of "best practices." The corporation was restructured (from a centralized, functional structure to decentralized, autonomous divisions), and old corporate management, to its credit, stepped aside in favor of new executives hired for their autonomous division management experience.

Heresy within: Changing basic production technology

"Harrison Corporation" (another pseudonym) had fought off the competition, including rivals from Japan, for decades. Harrison possessed an almost evangelistic fervor in its devotion to cost-cutting, highly efficient production operations, and genuine technical mastery. Harrison was the source for in-depth technical knowledge about the century-old, thoroughly mature underlying technology of its main product lines. For a time, its products benefited from a weak U.S. dollar that sustained exports and discouraged imports. In more difficult and competitive markets, Harrison used its technological expertise to lower its customers' costs, an enduring advantage for sales. Attention to cost reduction was a pervasive commitment within the company as well, but it became increasingly difficult to achieve. Competitors manufacturing in China or Thailand incurred labor costs at only a fifth of U.S. rates or less. Recognizing the company's needs, Harrison's CEO initiated two important technological innovation projects.

Were Harrison manufacturing workers resistant to change? According to an engineer responsible for one project,

No. If it's a lower cost [to] manufacture, without compromising quality, then no. It's everyone kind of grasps it as an opportunity to reduce our costs. And then normally we feed that right through to our customer so we end up with the lowest manufacture cost to our customer which is our goal. That's why our sales force has such a good time selling our products.

Harrison had two technology change projects under way in the late 1980s. The first and more limited effort was to increase integration in manufacture of an important component (already manufactured in semiautomated fashion). The proposed change would enable much more rapid manufacture of the component – within a day – at much lower cost. Thus Harrison would do all its own prototyping internally, speeding and improving design. The new equipment's flexibility and speed would also significantly reduce the need for component inventory and with it the dangers of inventory obsolescence, while improving the company's response capability for dealing with new customer needs, problems, or technical developments. This project, which will be referred to as "The A component line," affected much of Harrison's core product line.

A second line of industrial product, also mature and highly efficient, like the first, had also prospered despite fierce competition. As was typical of the industry, Harrison's product offering in the secondary line was based on a 20-year-old design, manufactured in a traditional, albeit highly efficient, factory. There was little room for further improvements, so competitors in much lower labor-cost settings would drive Harrison out. Only a substantial improvement – through expensive and dramatic simultaneous change in technology, design, new materials, and new manufacturing methods – would overcome labor cost differentials. The second project was a highly automated manufacturing operation for the secondary product line, which will be referred to as "The B line."

From a strategic perspective, both projects would fail if they merely met Harrison's traditional cost-reduction criterion. Both were intended to capture strategic and technical benefits not accessible through older methods, and thus to change the rules of competition. The A line would support much more sophisticated components, at a fraction of the time and cost required to make simpler current components. The B line would enable Harrison to make a product that was cheaper to manufacture than the lowest-cost contemporary product – but one so redesigned that its operating cost and reliability would be vastly superior to existing offerings.

Harrison had been alert to evolving production technologies, moving into new electronic discharge methods for metal cutting as well as some computer-controlled equipment. Electronics were being adapted for use on Harrison's industrial products. However, rigorous standards for justifying investment had driven discussions thus far, and new equipment was expected to achieve payback within two years. The decision to investigate automated production in both projects constituted a major shift for three reasons. First, in the projects' initial steps, project leaders were told not to employ the standard payback calculations.

Second, both projects involved simultaneous change in a product and its production processes. Indeed, the redesigned B line product could not be manufactured by traditional manual methods – a significant source of its strategic advantage. The B line project was intended to provide performance, initial cost and life-cycle operating cost benefits well in excess of traditional designs, manufactured by traditional manual methods, so that rivals using cheap foreign labor could not produce genuinely competitive products. The A line project supported substantially more complex components than before, while demanding closer interface between engineers and the component processing operation, especially for prototyping.

Finally, the new technologies, particularly the B line, were vastly more complex than anyone appreciated beforehand. Despite Harrison's enormous manufacturing sophistication, the B line project was an attempt to pioneer well beyond current industry capabilities. Some problems were commercial: Vendors delivered equipment late, for instance, despite contractual agreements. Other problems were purely technical: equipment arrived improperly wired.

At the conceptual level then, there was some recognition of strategic criteria, other than just cost reduction, that could arise and be used to evaluate these projects. However, events were not so clear or simple for those carrying out the projects on a day-to-day basis. Against a backdrop of long-established efficiency criteria, close and detailed attention to reducing cost, and emphasis on individual efficiency, all corroborated by the company's overall success when so many mature-industry firms were failing, both projects carried the whiff of heresy.

Problems began, in part, because of general agreement that the projects were "strategic":

We went out and evaluated various processes throughout the country and then wrote a specification list of what we thought we needed to manufacture the [components] the way we wanted to manufacture them. We basically set up our own specifications. We weren't given any guidelines, just that, "Boy wouldn't it be neat to have a more automated [production process]?"

This initial enthusiasm was quickly tempered as the old cost reduction criteria emerged to call into question the projects' justification:

So we went out and we evaluated it. We determined that our normal cost reduction program is a one-year payback. This project is not a one-year payback. Depending on what numbers you read, it's between two and seven. And if it's seven, that means there's a good chance using net present value that it's "never."

The new projects had no possibility of fitting with the older framework because the locus of benefit – in time reduction in the design cycle and in increased flexibility with consequent reductions in inventory – simply cannot be adequately addressed by standard cost-reduction criteria and cost comparisons with existing equipment:

We . . . actually did net present values on all the investments and the tax consequences and depreciation and everything else trying to justify it any way we could, and basically we found that it could not be justified in our normal realm of concepts.

Both of Harrison's projects were clearly justified on grounds of technical benefits, strategic advantages, and the entry barriers they put in position to protect the company. However, despite initial exemption from cost-reduction justification and payback evaluation, project evaluation was affected by cost-reduction and payback criteria at every step of the way. In essence, the old paradigm for evaluation swamped strategic benefits that could not be fitted readily into existing metrics for evaluation (Leonard-Barton 1992). This difficulty is a significant barrier to technological entrepreneurship (e.g., Goldhar & Jelinek, 1983; Jelinek, 1987; Jelinek & Goldhar, 1983; Johnson, 1992; Johnson & Kaplan, 1987), principally because it misdirects attention to inappropriate criteria.

Laying aide these long-standing and obviously valuable criteria of cost reduction was difficult; they continually reappeared in varying forms and explicitness. From a cognitive perspective, we can observe an in-place paradigm and its criterion in action – despite early efforts to shelter these clearly different, strategically valuable projects from payback constraints: Without anyone clearly identifying cost-reduction as a constraint or an appropriate criterion, nevertheless cost-reduction arose to slow progress on these two important projects. The CEO finally intervened to insure the projects' continuance, through pointed discussions with critical middle managers and equally explicit praise and merit bonuses for project teams.

Harrison's past success left the company unprepared for the manifest intricacy of change they faced. Beyond technical difficulties, problems were rooted in the complexities and interconnected consistency of Harrison's internal cognitive processes. A long-corroborated paradigm of cost-cutting, efficiency, and hard work was insufficient basis for appreciating the nature of the change required or the benefits offered by the new technologies of the two projects. Recognizing the internal barriers to change was a lengthy process of social negotiation, requiring the careful delegitimating of long-established criteria, expectations, and norms in favor of experimentation, new realities, and pervasive technological change. In short, change required cognitive, as well as technological, entrepreneurship.

Innovation revived

"Draco" (another pseudonym) was also the leader in its industry. Its product offerings so far exceeded those of rivals that for years the company effortlessly maintained premium pricing and profits without new products or much innovation. Market share began to slip only when rivals began to equal Draco's best, at half the price, after Draco's manufacturing had stagnated in an aged, inefficient plant. After decades of experience during which Draco products commanded a premium price, workers found incomprehensible management's urgent efforts to cut costs, looming layoffs, and threats of plant closure, so labor relations were increasingly tense. Draco's difficulties led to the firm's take over by new management determined to cut costs and sell or shut down unprofitable operations.

Against this context, an engineer with background in physics and a bent for tool geometry came up with an improved tool – Draco's first new product in more than a decade – with some help from a metallurgist. According to the engineer:

Our metallurgist was playing around – he always played around with new materials that are coming out – and he ran across this one that he thought was really good. We talked about doing something [with it]: What does it do? Why is it good? Why do you think it's good? And he says, "It does this." And then my answer was, "Well, if it does that, then we can do this with the geometry."

The engineer characterized such interchange as normal and frequent, for her and for her metallurgist:

Even to this day, Jan will walk up and down the hall and he'll stop in and I'll say, "Well, what have you got, Jan?" And we'll kibitz. Now Jan is part of our marketing crew, so he puts a ball in play. And he'll say, "I've got this," and I'd say, "Well, what do you do with this?" We just kibitz a lot.

The new product was a departure both for Draco, and also for its industry:

The theory behind [the new product] is that it is a totally unique tool. There is virtually no competition for where it goes and what it does. [This is] easy to say, hard to do.

The new product – rooted in metallurgical qualities of a newly-available alloy plus a sophisticated tool design – proved very interesting indeed to some customers. But getting a few key customers interested proved the least of the difficulties facing the engineer, who was now product manager for the new device. First, the metal from which the product was made became scarce. When disputed ownership tied up the alloy in the courts, the engineer bought up the entire available supply as a temporary fix. The engineer and the metallurgist began searching for a substitute for their dwindling but superior original material.

Meanwhile, Draco's sales force found it difficult to sell the superior tool. Its performance was so good that customers dismissed the sales presentation as pure hype, refusing even to try the tool because its performance characteristics were such a departure from the expected, so far beyond industry norms. The first product launch failed, despite a genuinely superior product. Customers' expectations and what they thought they "knew" killed the effort.

Detours and revivals

The remaining inventory of special material became a problem as Draco's new management struggled to cut costs. The engineer found a key customer who was convinced to try the new product, and embraced it enthusiastically. This one customer's demand was enough, over a period of months, to use the inventory of material. Metallurgical development finally produced an acceptable substitute for the unavailable alloy, while further process development, and still more effort on the geometry of the tool resulted in the second version of the new product. During the almost three years since the failed introduction, new Draco management had first offered to sell off many activities in the core product lines, next opened a new, nonunion plant after bitter labor disputes, and finally, when these efforts had not revived Draco's fortunes, departed, to be replaced by second new management team.

Recommitment to traditional Draco business lines followed, as the new CEO described it:

. . . So when [the first new CEO] departed we said, "Well, we've been trying to sell these things for a number of years. We're not going to realize any value out of them, so let's stop kidding ourselves and let's say we are what we are. And let's get back to the basics and become the best that we can be in these businesses."

That recommitment to the core of Draco's business brought a new atmosphere, one much more receptive to new ideas, into which the engineer rebid her new product idea – redeveloped, and complete with a new plan for selling a product she enthusiastically proclaimed as unique. She presented her idea in operational review meetings with senior management, stressing the unique, proprietary nature of the new product, and noting that manufacture as well as geometry and material were departures from industry practices.

This juxtaposition of product, process, and materials advances echoed far back to traditions in Draco history. But these traditions had fallen by the wayside in the downturn of Draco's industry – which lost almost half its U.S. companies and sales volume to foreign competitors, bankruptcy, or buy-out by the mid 1980s. Draco, like Denby, was closely associated with the decline of the steel industry and U.S. manufacturing more generally as part of the same industrial context. As the CEO described Draco's original source of competitive advantage, formerly,

. . . Draco Company was very active in developing products, and particularly materials. They acquired, I think, their preeminent position many years ago as a result of some of the development efforts that they had with some of the steel companies in developing specially high [performance materials]. And over the course of the years, they lost, if you will, the proprietary advantage that had evolved or grown out of that kind of a relationship, so that they . . . no longer had anything unique [except] some . . . processing practices that are perceived by our people to give them an advantage, and also a mind set commitment and a set of quality standards that just through the culling process makes certain that only the very best [tools] get out. It's a very expensive process, but historically, in recent years, that's how they've been able to maintain their advantage in the marketplace.

Without steel industry support, such development was far more difficult, but by the mid-1980s, steel industry interest had waned:

. . . Back in the 1950s and '60s, many steel companies were very interested in doing development work [with high performance materials]. And I think that as we moved into the late '60's and the '70s, and certainly the '80s, there was a general lessening of interest, and looking in other areas for the steel companies.

Observations like these are forcibly reminders of the integral, intricate nature of an industrial environment for innovation (e.g., Porter 1990; Reich 1991), a far more complex arena than is typically envisioned for product innovation.

Despite these difficulties, under new Draco management the engineer did find the necessary response. At her own level first, she found "kibitzing partners" who helped to develop the idea initially, then redevelop it later:

You only kibitz with someone that you feel, first off, that's going to listen. And secondly, if you think it's a dynamite idea and they shoot it down right away, you're not going to kibitz with them again. And if you think it's a great idea and they think it's a great idea, then you'll support each other to do something about the great idea. So there's listen[ing], positive [response], implementation. Or not implementation, even for the research, because it may be a great idea this far, but if you're going to take it – [farther], you need help.

She also found others on the shop floor willing to bootleg pilot quantities of tools for her as a personal favor. Later, as head of production for her new tool, she found many others willing to learn new methods and undertake new procedures to assist.

How did such a receptiveness emerge? Both the engineer and her kibitzing colleagues were longtime Draco employees, who remembered the old days and saw development as an opportunity. But shifts in the company environment were also clearly important. The CEO's comments about how he saw strategic recommitment seem most apropos: ". . . We've said that we're committed to our . . . businesses that we now have. All the talk about selling things off, all it does is get people agitated, and they lose focus of what they're really about."

This emphasis on what Draco was "really all about" proved fertile ground for the engineer's rebid of the new product, in the CEO's view:

Well, Diana is always a cheerleader, enthusiastic sort of person, so I don't know that her approach changed dramatically from the first point in time [the initial product launch] to the second point in time. But I think the environment in which she found herself had changed, and the environment, I think, was certainly more supportive and constructive and enthusiastic.

An aggressive new marketing plan and Diana's personal expertise both played roles in enlisting senior management. Without the more supportive environment that recommitted senior management created, Diana would not have succeeded: Discussion of the failed first effort centered on what was being done differently in the relaunch, not on past problems. Management was enthusiastic despite the earlier failure, and the relaunch proceeded.

The champion's role

Draco senior management was most appreciative of Diana's efforts. Both the CEO and the division president each commented that the new product was "her baby," and that without her, it would not have seen the light of day. Her varied roles ranged from hands-on design expertise that developed the geometry of the product, to hands-on demonstration before a major customer:

She's an engineer by training. . . . We've had some people in from . . . [a major customer company] the other day. And they were going to demonstrate this product, and so we had Diana in a white coat and she went down on the floor. She took this [new product] and actually operated the machine herself to demonstrate it. She really addressed the [task] with aggressiveness. She [did more with the tool] probably, than what these people had ever expected or had seen, you know?

Diana's contributions went farther still: she personally developed a sales kit that displayed the new product attractively, a kit "cute" enough that every sales rep wanted one. She also demonstrated the product and provided with convincing performance facts and figures, in a stimulating sales meeting that excited field sales people who had had nothing to cheer about in years. She brainstormed ways to overcome customer cynicism and resistance: getting sales people to demonstrate the new product on customers' machines – working for them, on their problems.

Next, she set up a contest to have sales people collect customer testimonials, which were then printed up and shared with the rest of the sales force in a sales support notebook. Winning sales reps had their customers' quotes featured, and won both prizes and recognition, so a friendly rivalry developed between reps to see who could get the best testimonials and the most. Diana also talked the company into buying a highly visible full page ad in the leading trade journal for their industry, further increasing market awareness of the new product – something Draco had not done in years. Diana generated a new way to sell that supported the unique new product. She made it easy for field sales people to succeed in a market that had been all too difficult for all too long, both with a genuinely superior product and with a winning sales method.

Draco was enormously fortunate in a past history of entrepreneurship recent enough for revival, and a senior management willing to embrace Diana's bootleg process, when they found out about it. Despite tough times, Diana and her colleagues were able to muster enough resources – supplies of an interesting new material; machine time on the production floor to run samples and trials – to investigate in the first place, often by virtue of personal requests and favors, and personal risk-taking. Yet every step of the way, from kibitzing metallurgists to cooperative factory personnel to receptive senior managers to field sales people willing to be convinced into enthusiasm, Diana's efforts intersected with people across Draco whose cooperation was essential to the new product's success. Clearly the new product was the result of many peoples' joint efforts – sparked as they were by Diana's enthusiasm and creativity.

The fit between an entrepreneurial individual's paradigm and the entrenched paradigm of the rest of the organization can crucially affect success or failure of technological entrepreneurship efforts. To successfully champion change, Diana had to enlist many others to address technical problems, overcome production difficulties and create new procedures, marshal marketing attention, and surmount many other potential barriers. While she resurrected older Draco values, overcoming defeatist attitudes and customers' reluctance to revive a view of Draco as a technology leader, she did not do so alone. Project success appears to correlate with broad reconvergence around a consistent, or at least not inconsistent, shared paradigm. The innovator, even in this instance, is not an "only, lonely inventor."

Building technological entrepreneurship into organizations

What can be learned from these diverse accounts of innovation episodes in large, mature-industry firms? More particularly, since accounts of innovation are by no means rare, what can be learned that is new? Above all, these episodes suggest that rather than emphasizing a single individual as the entrepreneur, research on innovation should shift attention to the shared cognitive reality experienced by organizational members. The organization's cognitive context is an important framework within which innovations take place, consistent with Murman and Tushman (Chapter 14, this volume).

Innovation is a collective activity that occurs over time, within the continuing revision of the shared cognitive framework of participants. Whether the innovation is major strategic reconfiguration, as at Denby; significant product-process redesign, as at Harrison; or new product development and launch, as at Draco, mature industry innovation appears an irreducibly joint activity centered on understanding necessary change. As a result, our attention will turn to a series of questions about shared cognitions within an organization, and how they evolve. What does it mean that a shared reality is favorable to technological entrepreneurship? How can a fertile context be provided so that creative efforts can flourish? How do these supportive efforts fail, and what can be done about it?

A major entrepreneurial effort occurs over time, during which its progress may be buffeted by unpredictable events. In-place strategy constitutes a powerful schemata that guides management thinking, and can constrain capability to recognize anomalous data and properly interpret it, particularly during the important early days of change, before the ambiguous message is fully understood.

Denby managers agonized for three long years before concluding that they should exit their company's historic home industry. During this time, ambiguous data included both signals that change was unavoidable – and signals that led many steel industry experts to expect business to return to normal. Sorting this data is an enormously difficult cognitive task that cannot be accomplished either by strictly calculative methods, nor by means of older paradigms: both may prove dysfunctional. The crux of the matter is that "more of the same" is an erroneous expectation, industry-wide denial notwithstanding.

Moreover, interpreting the data to define a new shared reality is a quintessentially social task. Structure – both organization structure and industry structure – are powerful schemata that must shift before the social cues for interpreting data will readily be read in a new paradigm. For an organization to change, many members must embrace a new direction, a new view, and the emotional impact of change; the inertial tug of old paradigms as well as ambiguous data are played out among people.

Each of the implementation accounts highlights this interplay. Harrison could readily embrace cost-reduction changes, which fit nicely into the old model of its competence (Leonard-Barton 1992). Harrison's old paradigm – "cut manufacturing costs, minimize prices, and we'll prosper" – identified cost-cutting as a core competence, and alerted members to technological changes that supported cost reduction, which they welcomed. This context had kept Harrison technologically up to date and cost-competitive for decades. It was useless for assessing strategic projects that did not center on cost reduction, however. Past success can encourage inertia in the form of "competency traps," to use one researcher's evocative phrase (see Levinthal, Chapter 10 in this volume).

Even while major change is underway in some areas, other aspects of the firm's philosophy, culture, and practices carry over to the new situation. Denby's managers did not abandon their company philosophy with the decision to shift to a new industry. Their diversification efforts were guided by conservative financial philosophies of the past. These philosophies provided a baseline for some security, yet the difficulty of interpreting ambiguous data, especially ultimately negative data, is all too apparent. Different managers bring different habits of mind to the discussion; their contention, in enacting differing roles supportive or critical of change, can compel discussion into more sophisticated channels. (See Van de Ven and Grazman, Chap-. ter 15, this volume, for a focused discussion of such roles.)

At Draco too, older core values and perspectives gave shape and energy, at last, to successful change efforts. Harrison's traditions of "can do" initiative fueled innovation efforts – even as its cost-efficiency norms slowed evolution of a new paradigm for interpreting them. The conflicted interplay of these older values and new visions can hinder change as well as assist it, and conflict per se can raise the emotional ante, with real costs to participants. Particularly in circumstances of threat of organizational decline (Whetten 1980; Cameron, Sutton et al. 1988; Barr, Stimpert et al. 1992), emotional costs make innovation more difficult.

Recognizing the need for change in the midst of anticipated stability. A major area for further investigation by strategy and cognitive theory researchers must be to examine how managers and their organizations can recognize such dramatically changed circumstances, interpret them correctly, and manage the process of exit or reconfiguration as gracefully as possible (Bartunek 1984; Huff 1990; Huff & Schwenk 1990; Barr, Stimpert et al. 1992). The general assumption that a company will forever continue in the industry of its founding has come into increasing question in recent decades, the victim of globalized markets and rapid technological change. What is needed is better management of the evolution of shared cognitions effectively amid turbulently changing circumstances (Keisler & Sproull 1982).

Recognizing how accounting and information systems practices screen what is "really" happening in an industry is another important insight. Where tax codes and accounting procedures drive business activities that make little economic sense, not only shareholders, but managers and employees and society as a whole bear the ultimate cost, one large fraction of which is delayed response to substantial environmental change. Although this insight is not unique – see, for example (Hayes & Abernathy, 1980; Johnson, 1992; Johnson & Kaplan, 1987), the view from inside Denby suggests that another whole line of attack on the problem revolves around how we teach managers to interpret the data of their systems and environment.

At best, managers will need far better tools for recognizing the need for substantial technological change within an industry. Had Denby's earlier diversification efforts succeeded, much of its struggle might have been avoided. Yet it is difficult to envision how changes of the magnitude that racked the U.S. steel industry and its customer and supplier industries, and the oil industry afterward, could have been foreseen: they were epochal. Another topic for serious consideration must be how we shall, as a society, recycle people, assets, and capital from defunct industries with least cost (in both personal and social terms). Whereas some advocate wholesale shutdown of "excess" capacity (e.g., Jensen, 1993) and others advocate continued investment in R&D (e.g., Reich, 1983, 1991; Peterson 1993), future developments in a global technology marketplace will remain unpredictable.

Firm culture: Cognitions of support and subversion for innovation

All firms studied here also illustrate the enduring power of a strong culture – for good or ill. More importantly still is the pervasive power of an ingrained paradigm's criteria (cf. Kuhn, 1972). Criteria consistent with a paradigm – at Harrison, the cost-reduction paradigm and the concomitant need to justify every investment for its cost-reduction potential, for instance – will reemerge to dominate managers' decision processes, even after initial acknowledgment that these criteria are inappropriate. Further, an established paradigm will serve to block peoples' capability of appreciating perspectives inconsistent with that paradigm (see Levinthal, Chapter 10 in this volume). At Harrison, the strategic value of flexibility and vastly foreshortened response time – only a portion of which could be readily captured by such cost-reduction items as lowered inventory holding or obsolescence costs – was essentially invisible to existing assessment systems.

These limitations are especially likely where new technological capabilities emerge: indeed, as von Hippel (1988) and Henderson & Clark (1990) have noted, it is difficult indeed to see beyond in-place interpretive paradigms for technology. New technology often provides its advances because it transcends the limitations of past practice, so its capability to do what is "impossible" under older assumptions is to be expected – yet that offers managers little guidance for assessing new technological capability. Moreover, once adopted, it is not enough to set the new technology to doing what the old already accomplished (Goldhar & Jelinek, 1983; Jaikumar, 1986). Examples abound of failure to appreciate the potentials of new technology; yet this difficult task is precisely what effective technological entrepreneurship requires.

Cognitive change is an essential aspect of technological entrepreneurship, because conflicting paradigms can simply make communication, as well as assessment, impossible. To argue that a technological endeavor makes sense from one paradigm, while listeners are interpreting from another, different, and inappropriate paradigm, is folly. Discussions of technology may go so far as to address different criteria – recognizing, say, technological versus economic criteria – but fail to appreciate the importance of potential paradigm conflict, contradictory assumptions, or criteria that distort the dimensions of understanding by forcing consideration into inappropriate channels.

Innovation involves system change

Harrison's experience also suggests that even technologically competent practitioners of an old technology face orders-of-magnitude complexity increments in moving to new technology. Although only a portion of the Harrison story has been told here, enough is visible to hint not only at the difficulties its employees had to overcome, but also at the difficulties its managers encountered in trying to assess progress toward a goal they could not even fully articulate. Were the two project efforts being effectively run? In former times, on former projects, cost reduction numbers and direct comparisons with comparable existing activities could help assess project activities. Typically, visible increments of successful accomplishment could be sequentially tested out as, piece by piece, the work was finished.

On the new lines, although some incremental progress was visible – as individual elements of the equipment were put into position, for instance – a large fraction of the real difficulties involved each project as a system. Unlike every prior project, this time, until the whole system was up and running, nothing worked. Indeed, any partial product was useless: it couldn't be completed manually, as the new system was designed to accomplish tasks manual technology could not. Managers and peers outside the projects, long used to milestones and checkpoints that could assure them of progress, had none. When they sought to drive team members, the pressure itself became a major obstacle faced by project teams. Inappropriate measures – seniority, familiarity, visible stacks of output, status within the strong corporate culture, or even cost-reduction criteria – emerged to bedevil the technology entrepreneurship process. All suggest that technological entrepreneurship can seem highly illegitimate within even technologically competent organizations, where new technology is "different."

Cognitive commonalities

Two points stand out. First, old benchmarks don't work on a new technology. Incremental measures are inappropriate, and may be dysfunctional because they force efforts to accomplish what the new technology is not suited to achieve, or subvert attention from crucial other targets, or simply waste time and increase stress levels. Even those who support a project, if they seek to apply inappropriate old rules and criteria, can subvert development efforts. In short, technological entrepreneurship needs appropriate assessment, not merely naive "support."

Second, much missionary or consulting work may be required, to generate new paradigmatic thinking and comprehension in important decision makers. Older paradigms do not yield easily, even after initial agreement. Draco confirms many of the earlier insights, and offers several more. Old paradigms do indeed endure, and can be usefully called upon to revive the spirit of technological entrepreneurship – although a helpful external context might have provided still more support. The Draco CEO's awareness of how the missing supplier-industry support discouraged his company's technological entrepreneurship efforts speaks loudly to contemporary discussions of how industrial strength can erode, providing a highly suggestive link to (Porter, 1990).

Existing schema can be profoundly affected by strategic context, including senior managers' strategic moves, whether through "distractions" introduced by efforts to sell existing business lines, or the refocus of recommitment. Similarly, if the strategy is that cost-cutting is all that matters, technological entrepreneurship is unlikely to succeed, for innovation requires resources. New schema gain power when they find receptive audiences – at multiple levels of the organization. Senior level support, or at least "benign neglect," can be essential to support at the grass roots that produces technological entrepreneurship in bootleg projects that ultimately provide the stuff of official projects.

But this does not mean that any and every idea must be accepted as is. "Receptive" audiences need not be mere cheerleaders: they can challenge, expand, amend, and develop new ideas as well. Indeed, the data here suggest that cooperative challenge to test and strengthen and improve ideas is essential to their success in the marketplace: Denby's choice of new industry, Harrison's projects, and Draco's new tool all benefited by substantive interaction. (Again, Van de Ven and Grazman, Chapter 15 in this volume, provide detailed discussion.) In turn, if ideas are to be bettered, persistence despite failure must be supported. The importance of continued effort is also not a new finding (see, for example, Jelinek, 1979; Jelinek & Schoonhoven, 1994; Quinn, 1979), but its importance in mature industries is little appreciated, and perhaps more counter-cultural in the efficiency-dominated atmosphere of long-established and thus traditional firms.

Finally, these varied episodes underline the social, interactive nature of the technological entrepreneurship process. Innovation-initiating information is enigmatic, and many more than a single champion or entrepreneur must come to understand it. Cognitive explanations of how people jointly make sense of ambiguous stimuli are vastly more important than we may have thought in the past. If organizations are in any sense to become technologically entrepreneurial, there must be broad support for innovation efforts (Jelinek & Litterer, 1994), even (or perhaps especially) in mature-industry firms. Creating new shared interpretations lies the heart of the task, the sine qua non of organizational entrepreneurship so essential if technology is to succeed.

Cognitive approaches offer a valuable tool for understanding and analyzing into behavior and decisions within organizations that profoundly affect technological entrepreneurship. The perspective of the practitioners – and their cognitions and responses – are the appropriate focus for understanding the origins of innovation or its absence, the encouragement of entrepreneurship or its squelching, the welcoming or rejection of technological possibilities, and thus the success or failure of technological efforts.

These insights can be summarized around three cognitive innovation elements. Successful innovation in each of the three disparate instances reported here depended upon *the willingness of persons not formally charged with innovation, to undertake it.* At Denby, a sales executive pushed his growing recognition of impending disaster up through senior management above him to the board. At Harrison, junior level engineers persisted in championing projects they saw as strategically imperative in the face of their seniors' efforts to apply inappropriate criteria. At Draco, an engineer and a metallurgist combined forces to bootleg their new product amidst major cost-cutting and restructuring efforts. Willingness to share in these traditionally managerial decisions, and to insist upon being heard, is an essential first element to entrepreneurship and innovation.

Each case also illustrates *mindful alertness to anomalous data* that extant paradigms would rule out. Denby's industry had always been cyclical, yet the innovators eventually saw beyond cyclicality to structural change. Moreover, they saw beyond their industry to possibilities in a wholly different line of business into which they moved their firm. At Harrison, innovators moved from cost-cutting and efficiency as boundaries for thinking, to product-process redesign as a source of qualitative advantage – the very characteristics and activities excluded by strict cost-cutting views embedded so pervasively and successfully in the firm.

Finally, in each instance, *group effort was central* in moving the organization. The initial innovators enlisted others, used varied perspectives to make sense of data that did not fit in existing organizational paradigms, and finally brought their insights into good organizational currency. Often, the move into organizational currency involved negotiating a difficult liaison between "illegitimate" activities that might be rejected outright by simple application of existing paradigms, and long-held organizational values. Finding means to absorb the incongruity and restructure organizational shared cognitions enabled innovation efforts to proceed.

Three major mature industry innovations have been described here – each initially appearing very different from the others. Yet deeper analysis reveals that all contended with basic variables: cognitive phenomena involving shared understanding, interpersonal interaction to (re)create that shared understanding, and the need to adapt or restructure existing concepts against a backdrop of broader organizational meanings and paradigms. Exiting old technology, as at Denby; changing successful technology before its success has eroded into disaster, as at Harrison; and entrepreneuring into new technology within a current product and market context when no innovation has taken place for a long while, as at Draco, only seem very different.

Across industries and organizational levels, commonalities emerge. In each case, change in organizational cognitive context was central to action. In these accounts, traditional organizational means for dealing with uncertainty emerge as unhelpful at best, actively dysfunctional at worst. In each case, a cognitive explanation provides important insight into the nature of the organizational, managerial task at hand.

Acknowledgment

Support for this research was provided by the Center for Innovation Management Studies at Lehigh University, whose assistance is gratefully appreciated.

Note

1   Data are drawn from field interviews at three companies requesting anonymity, which shall be identified herein as "Denby," "Harrison," and "Draco." Company data drawn from public sources is suitably disguised, although crucial relationships are preserved.

References

(1984). Quality goes in before the name goes on. *Automotive Industries*, November, 51–52.

(1994). The siege of Intel. *Economist*, 330, 63–64.

Abernathy, W. J. (1978). *The Productivity Dilemma: Roadblock to Innovation in the Automobile Industry.* Baltimore: Johns Hopkins University Press.

Barnett, D. F., and Crandall, R. W. (1986). *Up From the Ashes: The Rise of the Steel Minimill in the United States.* Washington, D.C.: Brookings Institution.

Barr, P. S., Stimpert, J. L., and Huff, A. S. (1992). Cognitive change, strategic action, and organizational renewal. *Strategic Management Journal*, 13(1), 15–36.

Bartunek, J. M. (1984). Changing interpretive schemes and organizational restructuring: The example of a religious order. *Administrative Science Quarterly*, 29(l), 355–372.

Baumol, W., Blackman, S. A. B., and Wolff, E. (1989). *Productivity and American Leadership.* Cambridge, MA: MIT Press.

Berger, P. L., and Luckman, T. (1966). *The Social Construction of Reality.* Garden City, NY: Doubleday.

Bruner, J. S., and Postman, L. (1949-1950). On the perception of incongruity: A paradigm. *Journal of Personality*, 18, September 1949–June 1950), 206–223.

Cameron, K. S., Sutton, R. I., and Whetten, D. A. (Ed.). (1988). *Readings in Organizational Decline.* Cambridge, MA: Ballinger.

Chandler, A. D., Jr. (1990). The Enduring Logic of Industrial Success. *Harvard Business Review*, 69(2), 130–140.

Cohen, S. S., and Zysman, J. (1987). *Manufacturing Matters.* New York: Basic Books.

Dougherty, D. And Heller, T., (1994). The illegitimacy of successful product innovation in established firms. *Organization Science* 5(l).

Ettlie, J. (1988). *Taking Charge of Manufacturing.* San Francisco: Jossey-Bass.

Fiske, S. T., and Taylor, S. E. (1991). *Social Cognition* (2nd ed.). New York: McGraw-Hill.

Foster, R. (1986). *Innovation: The Attacker's Advantage.* New York: Summit Books.

Galambos, J. A., and Rips, L. (1982). Memory for routines. *Journal of Verbal Learning and Verbal Behavior*, 21, 260–281.

Goldhar, J. D., and Jelinek, M. (1983). Prepare for economies of scope. *Harvard Business Review*, 61(6), November –December, 141–148.

Hayes, R. H., and Abernathy, W. J. (1980). Managing our way to economic decline. *Harvard Business Review*, 58(4), July–August, 67–77.

Hayes, R. H., and Wheelwright, Steven C. (1984). *Regaining our Competitive Edge.* New York: Wiley.

Hedberg, B. (1981). How organizations learn and unlearn. In D. Nystrom & W. Starbuck (eds.), *Handbook of Organizational Design: Adapting Organizations to their Environments* (pp. 3–27). Oxford: Oxford University Press.

Henderson, R. M., and Clark, K. B. (1990). Architectural innovation: The reconfiguration of existing product technologies and the failure of established firms. *Administrative Science Quarterly*, 35(l), 9–30.

Huff, A. S., and Schwenk, C. (1990). Bias and sense making in good times and bad,. In A. S. Huff (eds.), *Mapping Strategic Thought* (pp. 89–108). Chichester: Wiley.

Jaikumar, R. (1986). Postindustrial manufacturing. *Harvard Business Review*, 64(6), November–December, 69–76.

Jelinek, M. (1979). *Institutionalizing Innovation*. New York: Praeger.

Jelinek, M. (1987). Production innovation and economies of scope: Beyond the 'technological fix'. *Engineering Costs and Production Economics*, 12, 315–326.

Jelinek, M., and Goldhar, J. D. (1983). Manufacturing technology and corporate strategy: Critical interface for the 1980s. *Columbia Journal of World Business* (Spring).

Jelinek, M., and Litterer, J. A. (1994). Organizing for technology and innovation. In W. Souder and D. Sherman (eds.), *Handbook on Technology Management*. Beverly Hills, CA: Sage.

Jelinek, M., and Schoonhoven, C. B. (1990). *The Innovation Marathon*. Oxford, UK Cambridge, MA: Basil Blackwell.

Jensen, M. C. (1993). The modem industrial revolution, exit and the failure of internal control systems. *Journal of Finance*, 48(3) July, 831–880.

Johnson, H. T. (1992). *Relevance Regained*. New York: The Free Press.

Johnson, H. T., and Kaplan, R. S. (1987). *Relevance Lost: The Rise and Fall of Management Accounting*. Boston: Harvard Business School Press.

Keene, P. G. (1991). *Every Manager's Guide to Information Technology*. Cambridge, MA: Harvard Business School Press.

Keisler, S., and Sproull, L. (1982). Managerial response to changing environments: perceptions on problem solving from social cognition. *Administrative Science Quarterly*, 27, 548–570.

Kuhn, T. (1972). *The Structure of Scientific Revolutions* (2nd ed.). Chicago: University of Chicago Press.

Lakoff, G. (1987). *Women, Fire, and Dangerous Things: What Categories Reveal About the Mind*. Chicago: University of Chicago Press.

Langer, E. (1988). *Mindfulness*. Reading, MA: Addison-Wesley.

Langer, E. J., and Piper, A. I. (1987). The prevention of mindlessness. *Journal of Personality and Social Psychology*, 53(2), 280–287.

Lynn, L. H. (1982). *How Japan Innovates: A Comparison with the U.S. in the Case of Oxygen Steelmaking*. Boulder, CO: Westview Press.

Miller, D. and P. Friesen (1980). Momentum and revolution in organizational adaptation. *Academy of Management Journal* 23(4), 591–614.

Mokyr, J. (1990). *The Lever of Riches*. New York: Oxford University Press.

Nelson, R. R. (ed.) (1993). *National Innovation Systems: A Comparative Analysis*. New York, Oxford University Press.

Petersen, D. E., and Hillkirk, J. (1991). *A Better Idea: Redefining the Way Americans Work*. Boston, MA: Houghton Mifflin.

Peterson, P. G. (1993). *Facing Up: How to Rescue the Economy From Crushing Debt and Restore the American Dream*. New York: Simon & Schuster.

Porter, M. E. (1980). *Competitive Strategy*. New York: The Free Press.

Porter, M. E. (1985). *Competitive Advantage*. New York: The Free Press.

Porter, M. E. (1990). *Competitive Advantage of Nations*. New York: The Free Press.

Prestowitz, C. V., Jr. (1988). *Trading Places*. New York: Basic Books.

Quinn, J. B. (1979). Technological innovation, entrepreneurship, and strategy. *Sloan Management Review* 20(3), 19–30.

Reich, R. B. (1983). *The Next American Frontier*. New York: The Times Books.

Reich, R. B. (1991). *The Work of Nations: Preparing Ourselves for 21st Century Capitalism*. New York: Alfred A. Knopf.

Reutter, M. (1988). *Sparrows Point*. New York: Summit Books.

Rogers, E. M. (1983). *Diffusion of Innovations* (3rd ed.). New York: The Free Press.

Silverman, D. (1971). *The Theory of Organizations*. New York: Basic Books.
von Hippel, E. (1988). *The Sources of Innovation*. New York: Oxford University Press.
Walton, R. E. (1987). *Innovating to Compete*. San Francisco: Jossey-Bass.
Whetten, D. A. (1980). Sources, responses, and effects of organizational decline. In J. R. Kimberly, R. H. Miles, et al. (eds.), *The Organizational Life Cycle: Issues in the Creation, Transformation, and Decline of Organizations* (pp. 342–374). San Francisco: Jossey-Bass.
Womack, J. P., Jones, D. T., and Roos, D. (1990). *The Machine that Changed the World*. New York: Rawson Associates.

12 Minimizing technological oversights: A marketing research perspective

Jehoshua Eliashberg, Gary L. Lilien, and Vithala R. Rao

I. Introduction

. . . if the weight of invention or discovery is one, the weight to bring it to actual development should be ten and the weight to produce and market it should be one hundred.

Masru Ibuka
President of Sony

Despite increasingly experienced management, the majority of new products fail to achieve their anticipated level of success in the marketplace. The causes for that lack of consistent market success have been the subject of much academic study (Lilien & Yoon, 1989). That literature is consistent with the results of a recent survey by a consulting firm, Ltd., that reports that among 154 senior marketing officers of U.S. corporations:

- 79% believe the new product development process could be improved
- 58% do not rate R&D as a successful source of new products
- 46% do not rate R&D's contribution to new product development as significant.

As for the reasons for their perception of why this process is less than ideal, consistent with the findings of Booz, Allen, and Hamilton (1982) they report:

- Products don't offer a competitive point of difference (52%)
- Product doesn't deliver as promised (43%).

In addition, 61% of the respondents expect that 30% or more of their sales will come from new products within the next 3–5 years. Finally, EFO reports that they have conducted this research periodically and the companies are getting more concerned: firms see new products as a source of hope, but they are showing ever more frustration over their internal processes for developing successful new products.

The literature on new product development going back to Mansfield and Wagner (1975) has consistently identified the radically new product as the riskiest type to develop, but at the same time, the type of product, that, if it succeeds, yields the largest gain. This result is intuitively clear – a slight improvement in an existing product is likely to be well received by the marketplace, but hardly likely to be a runaway winner; those "big hits" come from more visionary, dramatic innovations.

Thus, new technologies often provide *opportunities* for significant market successes, but such success is realized much less frequently than firms might like.

In this chapter, we will look at marketing research methods, both traditional and nontraditional, as ways to improve our ability to transform new technologies into products and services that "win" in the marketplace. In other words, we look to marketing research to limit technological oversights.

We proceed as follows. The next section provides a brief conceptual overview of the new product development process and the types of oversights that can occur. We then discuss the role that marketing research has traditionally played in improving new product success rates. We then provide a taxonomy of product/technology types and the sort of market research information that is most appropriate for each of those types. That taxonomy highlights the role that traditional and nontraditional market research needs to play to prevent technological oversights. We then discuss the need for a broader portfolio of marketing research methods to fill the gaps we have identified earlier. We conclude with an assessment of the potential and the limitations of marketing research to address the prevalence of technological oversights. A closely related topic that we do not address in this chapter – the fostering of creativity in new product development: increasing foresights – uses many of the same research methods. For an extensive review of the idea generation literature, see Urban and Hauser (1993).

II. New product development and technological oversights

The aim of Marketing is to know and understand the customer so well that the product or service fits him and sells itself.

Peter Drucker

The factors that emerge as being the most important to success of a technological innovation are those related to the importance of need satisfaction.

Rothwell

. . . but always, regardless of the amount, R&D money has gone to the development of instruments for which there was a real need.

Hewlett-Packard

The three quotes above put a market or customer orientation on the new product development process. In these days of "customer satisfaction," "delighting the customer," "total quality management," and the like, the focus is squarely on the customer as the final arbiter of market success. This is as it should be (at least according to marketers in a free market economy). And the various models for successful new product development put the customer at the core of the process. For example, Cooper (1986) recommends a seven stage "game plan" for new product development:

1. Idea generation
2. Preliminary assessment
3. Concept definition
4. Product development
5. Testing
6. Trial
7. Launch

Using this framework (other texts, like Urban & Hauser, 1993, provide similar structures), we consider below the role of customer input to avoid oversights. But first we must distinguish between two classes of oversights.

Oversight class 1: Radically new product market "disappointments." There is an extensive literature on new product successes and failures, but that literature is quite ambiguous on what "failure" means. For the discussion here, we use the rather vague term *disappointment* to refer to the two situations that are most commonly deemed "failures" in the literature: (a) the actual *rate* of penetration into the market is significantly lower than what the organization had expected or planned for OR (b) the ultimate *level* of penetration (sales, market share, or a similar measure) is significantly below the level anticipated. Note, then, that this disappointment is situation- and firm-specific: a penetration rate that satisfies firm A may not satisfy firm B. Note also that by the term "radical" we mean a product whose use or function is new or uncertain to the customer. By this definition, a new technology that is hidden from the customer (a RISC chip versus a 486 chip that can run the same software) is not radical from the customer's perspective, whereas a technology like interactive television that is functionally new to the customer would be radical.

Oversight class 2: Technology missing new product opportunities. For this type of oversight, a "potential" successful new product exists, but marketers ignore or overlook the opportunity. This is not a failure or "disappointment," except perhaps in retrospect; it is an opportunity loss in some sense, however.

Table 12.1 summarizes these two classes of oversights and their relationship to the new product performance of the firm. As the table indicates, introducing high potential products effectively and eliminating market failures is where marketing research can contribute. Correct decisions that

TABLE 12.1. Relationship between market potential and firm's marketing actions

Expected market potential for the new product	Firm's marketing actions with respect to the new product	
	Pursue the project (introduce, etc.)	Ignore the idea
High	(1) Success, or good foresight	(2) Oversight class 2: Lack of foresight or sin of omission
Low	(3) Oversight class 1: Market disappointment or sin of commission	(4) No disappointment: Good foresight

emerge from Cells 1 and 4 in the table represent good foresight, often resulting from effective marketing research. The other two cells reflect the two oversight cases we will focus on: Cell 2 misses an opportunity and is a *sin of omission*, whereas Cell 3 reflects introduction of a losing product and is a *sin of commission*.

Note that Class 1 and Class 2 errors here correspond to the false positives and false negatives in Garud, Nayyar, and Shapira (1994). The role of the marketing research methods that we develop here is to shrink both types of error probabilities – i.e., to increase the correlation between actual and predicted market performance.

How then do our two classes of oversights intersect with the seven-stage game plan above? Oversight Class 1 produces products whose market assessments are too optimistic in one way or another. Stages 2, 5, and 6 represent increasingly detailed attempts at market assessment. Oversights in this class must have been associated with overly optimistic market research assessments in one of those three stages.

Oversight Class 2 is relatively easy: as no product is developed, there is either a flaw in the idea generation process or the product is screened out as unworthy of launch during one of Stages 2 to 6. Note that an error in Stage I is an oversight of ignorance; an error in Stages 2 to 6 is a market misassessment on the low side.

In order to address these two classes of oversights, we must understand why they occur. There is an extensive literature on new product successes and failures (Booz, Allen, & Hamilton, 1971, 1982; Duerr, 1986; Cooper & Kleinschmidt, 1987; De Brentani, 1989; Yoon & Lilien, 1985, Lilien & Yoon, 1989; Rothwell et al., 1974; and Cooper, 1975) that provide some consistent clues. For example, for oversight Class 1, when market assessments are too optimistic, nine of the reasons that emerge are:

01.1 Lack of customer learning. By our definition, radically new products often require customers to change some of their consumption behavior. Even if the end seems clearly desirable, inertia often plays a key role in thwarting radically new product acceptance. Note that after a century, the QWERTY keyboard, originally developed to retard the typing speed of moveable typesetters (to avoid type-jams), is still the standard in spite of many attempts to introduce more sensible alternatives.

01.2 Lack of complete solution.   The penetration of the PC was considerably accelerated by the development of associated word processing and spreadsheet software. Note that these developments came from different organizations, so that each innovation was an incomplete solution to a customer need.

01.3 Early bugs.   Many organizations underestimate the power of negative word-of-mouth. A classical example involves the early field problems with heat pumps introduced in the early '50s. Those problems poisoned the market for heat pumps until the next generation of heating and cooling contractors emerged almost two decades later.

01.4 Value misassessment.   When solar heating systems were first introduced, early customer surveys showed high interest and high intention to buy. Most market forecasts from those data were much too high: as customers learned more about the real, total system costs (including initial costs, system lifetime, system maintenance, likelihood of fire damage due to system failure, etc.), their likelihood of purchase decreased. Realistic economic calculations early on would have provided more pessimistic forecasts (Lilien & Johnston, 1980).

01.5 Technology choice confusion.   Customers often do not choose the "best" alternative in isolation if that alternative must fit into a system. Many people believed that the Beta format was superior technically to the VHS tape format. However, the penetration of associated software in video rental stores for VHS made VHS players more attractive. Beta lost. Similar arguments hold for the penetration of Macintosh versus the PC.

01.6 Initial cost too high.   When energy efficient refrigerators, air conditioners, and the like emerged, manufacturers assumed that consumers would buy them because their life cycle savings would more than compensate for the higher initial cost. Hausman (1979) has shown that consumers use much higher implicit discount rates than manufacturers normally expect; market penetration for energy-efficient appliances was much slower than anticipated.

01.7 Short lifecycles and leapfrogging.   If customers have been taught to expect a new technology to arrive on a regular basis, they may delay purchase indefinitely. Many consumers who considered buying fax machines were put off by the frequent changes in options and configurations. Some have now bypassed the fax option completely, using alternatives that are completely electronic.

01.8 Channel resistance.   In many markets, new product plans require cooperation from the salesforce and/or distributors. If existing products are easier to sell and if the salesforce is compensated on a fixed percent of sales basis, the salesforce or other intermediaries will allocate less time to selling the new product than is in the best long term interest of the firm (Dearden & Lilien, 1990).

01.9 Wrong target market.   A radically new product often provides little real benefit to the original target market, but may have benefit in other markets. Video conferencing was originally thought to provide large potential advantages to multi-location organizations. It turns out that many types of interaction and communication take place face-to-face that cannot be accommodated in a video-conference – that market did not embrace the innovation. The same technology has been quite successful among networks of medical schools, where rare cases or new medical procedures can be shared with students and colleagues at remote locations.

Now let us consider Class 2 oversights, those where a market opportunity actually exists that is being ignored by potential firms. Note that the evidence in this area contains sample selection bias: we only learn about such oversights if, after the fact, someone does take advantage of the technological opportunity. The patent office may be full of latent opportunities, and new product texts recommend that firms make regular use of patent searches. For example: ". . . a highly successful entrepreneur in a Canadian firm conceded that most of his successful new product ideas were the result of a regular review of patents . . . " (Cooper, 1986, p. 77). Thus the evidence about the second type of oversights emerges only ex-post, if at all. Some of the most common reasons for such oversights are:

02.1 Lack of efficient or effective search.   Most of the failures of this type are due to lack of vision or imagination. Somehow, the early developers simply did not "know what they had." Why didn't Xerox's Palo Alto Labs see the potential in the operating system that eventually became the heart of the Macintosh? What did Apple see that Xerox didn't?

02.2 No customer understanding.   A technology may be developed by an R&D lab in a market that differs from the market in which a need exists. Indeed, Lee and Na (1994) show that radically new products are most likely to emerge from outside the industry – those with the technology often do not understand the full range of possible market needs they might serve.

02.3 Lack of imagination.   Many technological innovations represent the "potential" to produce new products. The accidental development of a "not-so-sticky" adhesive at 3M led to the market for the Post-It notes. How many other organizations have similar "opportunities" that they are simply ignoring?

02.4 Lack of resources/competencies.   If a firm develops a radically new product but lacks access to channels (access to shelf space in supermarkets, for example) a major potential success may be missed.

02.5 Missing value in synergies.   This is related but slightly different from the above. When videotex was introduced in areas of Florida by U.S. Knight Ridder in 1983, there was not enough software on the system to justify the customer investment in the hardware. With the range of information available today on private computer networks and on the Internet, customer investment in technology is now justifiable.

02.6 Technology changes customer behavior.   Radical innovations may not simply substitute for existing products, they may make wholesale changes in the ways consumers operate. When xerography was introduced, IBM turned down the technology, assuming it would merely substitute for carbon paper. And the original estimate for the market potential for digital computers worldwide was far fewer than ten. These are two technologies that have changed the way business is done.

What are the implications of the above from the standpoint of marketing research? First, we take as given that the customer is the final arbiter of product value. Thus, an exchange will take place if a customer finds the new product "worth the money." Hence, understanding how customers are likely to act – the focus of much of marketing research – is central to redressing the oversights we have identified above. Within the framework of radically new (to the customer) products, we must consider how the portfolio of existing marketing research tools can be used and what needs exist for other forms of marketing research.

In the next section we review the current portfolio of marketing research procedures aimed at developing and assessing the market for *radically* new products. Most new products are *NOT* radically new; rather, they allow customers to do things a bit better, faster, or cheaper or add some variety to an existing product mix. Customers can generally give reliable assessments of their likely behavior if the situation (new product) presented to them is within their realm of previous experience, i.e., what we refer to as *marginally new*. Most of us (except for a few visionaries) have difficulty imagining well outside that realm, suggesting that we may need other sources of market information to overcome the oversights outlined here.

More precisely, and always taking the customer's perspective, we call a new product *marginally new* if a close substitute to it exists in the marketplace. A new color copier that is a bit faster in its output, can easily be evaluated by a customer because it is similar to products that the customer is familiar with; a color copier with both fax and personal computer printing capabilities would be more difficult to evaluate because it does not fall into any established current category and combines several technologies not currently available together. These two types of new products are also called evolutionary innovations and revolutionary innovations, respectively.

III. Research methods for new product development

There is a vast literature (Urban & Hauser, 1993; Cooper, 1986) that indicates that new products have higher success rates and better returns on new product investment when their development and evolution follow a systematic procedure of research and testing. New product research methods track the new product development process stages we highlighted above and generally address the issues that arise in idea generation, preliminary assessment, concept definition, and testing. In general, the most widely used methods are geared toward marginally new products.

Table 12.2 provides a taxonomy of methods, classified by type of product and research method type. The traditional methods used for marginally new products (box 3) are:

Concept testing methods, used to get an early idea of how the target market responds to the "idea" of the new product. Early concept tests use informal focus groups for qualitative evaluations; later in the screening procedure, more formal preference and intent-to purchase measures are used amongst a sample of target customers (Urban & Hauser, 1993).

Product design methods, used to determine those features that should be included most cost effectively in the new product. Conjoint analysis is the most frequently used method for this purpose (Wittink & Cattin, 1989).

Product testing methods, used to see how customers react to the actual product, usually in the laboratory. For the most part, small groups of customers or prospects are used for product testing (Urban & Hauser, 1993).

Benefit segmentation analysis, used to determine segments of customers that have similar needs so that their preferences can be matched with appropriate new products (Haley, 1968; Kamakura, 1988).

Pretest market assessment methods, usually used as an intermediary step between product testing and test marketing. Here, several hundred customers are usually recruited or intercepted and put through a simulated shopping situation to provide an early indication of likely test market results (Silk & Urban, 1978).

Test marketing methods, used for evaluating the market response to a new

TABLE 12.2. A taxonomy of marketing research methods for new product development

	Nature of research method	
Type of new product	Traditional	Nontraditional
Radically new	(1) • Market definition and market structure analysis methods • Forecasting methods using analogy • Value assessment technique • Morphological analysis	(2) • Brainstorming methods • Lead user research technique • Information acceleration methods • Virtual reality-based research methods
Marginally new	(3) • Concept testing methods • Product design methods • Product testing methods • Benefit segmentation analysis • Pretest market assessment methods • Test marketing methods	(4) New techniques yet to be developed*

*Traditional methods provide adequate solutions to new product development for marginally new products.

product by introducing it locally, in one or more market areas, and carefully tracking the results (Blattberg & Golanty, 1978).

These methods all assume that customers are familiar with the product category and do not have to make any major modifications to their choice processes when considering the new product.

To see more clearly where problems with existing methods arise, let us focus on concept testing methods and the research decisions that are associated with them. We deal with two issues that arise in attempting to apply concept testing methods to radically new product. Specifically we focus on (A) describing new product concepts to subjects effectively (with related data collection issues), and (B) choosing an appropriate sample.

In describing new product concepts (issue A) we see three main subissues: (1) whether or not any comparative information is to be provided (or, indeed, is relevant), (2) what type of information (factual or emotional) we should try to obtain, and (3) what the effect of the subject's knowledge is on the quality of the response.

Issue A.1: Stand alone or competitive test. There are two popular types of test-designs: 1) *Monadic*, and 2) *Competitive*. In a monadic design, a subject is given only one concept to be evaluated. In a competitive design, the new concept being tested is presented along with those of some present brands. Summarizing previous use of these two techniques, Moore (1982) notes that both methods have had considerable successes in predicting trial. Admitting a lack of any serious research to compare these two methods, he hypothesizes that monadic tests are preferable when it is hard to identify direct competitors or when there is little search prior to purchase. In radically new products context, it appears that monadic tests might be more appropriate.

Issue A.2: Rational answers or 'emotional' answers from subjects. Axelrod and Wybenga (1985) argue that it is not enough just to know the rating (or ranking) of a product concept; it is equally important to know why the subject likes (or dislikes) that concept. Evaluative questions, such as *what* rating will give you this product concept? are good for getting only a rational response from the subject. To obtain subjects' emotional reasons for preferring a product concept alternative, more perceptual questions, such as *how* does this product concept differ from the others, should be asked. Radically new products may require subjects to change their method of evaluation dramatically and, thus, normally require perceptual questions.

Issue A.3: Concept evaluation result-sensitivity to subject knowledge. In concept testing it is generally assumed that subjects understand the product concept they are evaluating. The evaluation of a concept can be severely affected by level of the respondent's knowledge of the product concept. In the absence of full knowledge, the subject will augment the information with his prior experiences and subjective judgments. Thus, the researcher cannot be sure whether the subject is giving his true preferences or providing biased responses based on his augmentation of the information provided (Reidenbach & Grimes, 1984). For radically new products, the level of information that the subjects have about the product and the competitive environment must be carefully controlled for results to be valid. Note that subjects vary in degree of product knowledge. Knowledgeable subjects tend to give more valid responses; less knowledgeable subjects rely on reference groups (what he/or she believes to be the right answer within his or her group of peers) and core values (generic rather than specific product choice variables). Finally, different subjects have different information processing capabilities and may need different amounts of time to understand a new product idea (Berning, Kohn, & Jacoby, 1974). Based on such a premise, Tauber (1981) suggests that, like for advertising copy testing, new product concepts should be comprehension-tested before administration.

Issue B: Choosing a sample. Although the literature on concept testing suggests that the sample should be drawn probabilistically to be able to project to the market, it is not clear that such a random sample can give sound evaluations for radically new products. The points raised above about the effect of knowledge level on concept evaluation are also valid for the purpose of choosing a sample. If the concept test is for a complex product such as a CD-ROM, then knowledgeable people would be able to give more valid evaluations of the features of the new product than less knowledgeable individuals.

Thus, we see that with a radically new product, the rules of the research game are quite different than the rules for marginal products (see Table 12.3). First, the competitive set to be used for evaluating the radically new product either does not exist or is not easy to define for conducting evaluative research. Further, the researcher may find it hard to create and accurately describe an environment to the respondent about the use situation. Also, it is not clear whether the researcher can identify an appropriate group of respondents who can assimilate the information presented and provide accurate evaluations required for assessing the new product.

IV. Research tools for radically new products

Some "traditional" marketing research tools have been able to provide some limited success for the market assessment for radically new products (Table 12.2, box 1). They are:

Market definition and market structure analysis methods, which attempt to map customer attitudes or behaviors against the position of competitive brands. Such methods usually focus on either the clustering of customer-at-

TABLE 12.3. Some factors inhibiting the direct application of traditional new product development methods for radically new products

Phase of NPD process solutions	Factors	Potential solutions
Idea generation	• Thinking limited by available technologies.	• Need to consult visionaries and experts.
Preliminary assessment	• Limited by a lack of understanding of the customer's choice process. • Customer limited by lack of appreciation of the potential of the new product.	• Study of choice process under conditions of expected availability of the new product among expert users.
Concept definition and testing	• Limited by ability to define the new concept.	• Need to utilize better methods to communicate the new product concept.

titudes (as in benefit segmentation, above) or determining the substitution between products (Urban & Hauser, 1993).

Forecasting methods using analogies, where a product is matched (either physically or through its customer-benefit characteristics) with another similar product in order to assess both the rate of market penetration and the ultimate market potential for the product (Fisher & Pry, 1971; Choffray & Lilien, 1986).

Value assessment techniques, usually applied in nonconsumer markets. Here, interviews are conducted at customer firms to determine a comprehensive listing of cost elements associated with the usage of radically new product offering compared with the current operation (i.e., life cycle costing). Values are then associated with the cost elements to estimate the overall value to the customer of the new product (at a specific price) in that application. Alternatively, a full simulation model of the customer's operation can be developed (Anderson, Jain, & Chintagunta, 1993).

Morphological analysis, a method for new product idea generation, where a product is decomposed into its attributes and all possible combinations of those attributes are evaluated as possible "new products" (Adams, 1972).

Although these methods have been used with some success for radically new products, a number of nontraditional tools have emerged recently due, primarily, to two reasons: (1) limitations in the ability of the researcher to realistically present information on the characteristics and use of the new product to the potential user, and (2) limitations in the ability to identify the "appropriate" group of potential customers for eliciting reaction to the new product idea. To address the first issue requires an accurate conceptualization of a new product's features as well as a clear, comprehensible way of presenting them to respondents. In this respect, technological developments in the area of virtual reality have been used in a few cases. A technique called information acceleration based on virtual reality is discussed below.

The second issue – identifying the appropriate respondent group – is a continuing challenge. One must identify visionaries, experts, or innovators for eliciting responses. Also, statistical forecasting methods using representative samples may need to be replaced by "biased" – leading edge individuals – in order to review the new product under the most favorable circumstances. Thus, researchers must be creative, identifying visionaries or perhaps acting as visionaries themselves.

We suggest four nontraditional methods that may have some value for radically new products: brainstorming methods, the lead user technique, information acceleration, and methods based on virtual reality.

Brainstorming methods. These methods involve discussion among a group of appropriate respondents on the radically new product. Such discussions are typically conducted under the direction of an experienced moderator. The basic idea has been implemented in a variety of ways (Arnold, 1962; Prince, 1972).

Lead user technique. This technique involves studying the viability of a new product using a sample of current users of a firm's products whose present specific needs will become general in the marketplace months or years in the future. By studying such a group, the firm may identify the characteristics of the innovation to be developed as well as the potential of a new product under consideration. This technique may be more advantageous than a traditional focus group method because members of a focus group are generally constrained by current experience with existing products. Lead users, on the other hand, are those who have developed solutions to problems encountered with existing products (von Hippel, 1986; Urban & von Hippel, 1988).

Information acceleration. This method recognizes that a customer will be considering a new product in a "future world," whereas the testing is being conducted in a current world. The technique is designed to place the individual in the information-base of the future world. Thus, information acceleration attempts to create a simulated environment for assessing the effects of future information that can be made available via various media to consumers. Hauser, Urban, & Weinberg (1993) implemented this method to assess the demand for a new automobile using the format of a multimedia personal computer. Various visual and verbal information on the new product was stored on a video disk. The consumer (respondent) accessed this information from the computer's keyboard, mouse, or other input device by pointing to and choosing an icon or picture representing the information source. In one study, consumers had four types of information on the vehicle: advertisements, unrehearsed interviews with actual consumers to simulate word-of-mouth effects, articles on the product published in such magazines as *Consumer Reports* and trade publications such as *Car and Driver*, and a showroom encounter. In the showroom encounter, the respondent could have interactions with a salesperson, walk around the automobile, look at the manufacturer's price sticker, or look at a brochure on the automobile. The authors collected data on purchase intentions after exposure to any information source as well as at the end of the session on information gathering in the multimedia laboratory. Urban, Weinberg and Hauser (1996) provide a more complete description of the uses and limitations of the procedure.

Virtual reality-based research. The information acceleration method described above is but one technique based on the emerging field of virtual reality-based research. This technology goes by several names including multimedia, hypermedia, intermedia, and compact disc-interactive. It is difficult to predict where this technology will go, but it has many practical uses. In particular, it offers innovative ways of presenting new product concepts to potential users for eliciting their reactions. These methods are reported to have been employed in such projects as the development of theme parks (*Economist,* 1993), development of "new" credit unions (Pels & Merrick, 1993), and the design of magazines (Crispell, 1993). Various advantages and potential of virtual reality are described by Goerne (1992).

V. Conclusions

In this chapter we have suggested a number of reasons why radically new products fail to achieve full market success and how marketing research methods can (or might) be used to increase the rate of success. We suggest that a firm's failure to exploit a new technology can be largely attributed to its inability to match appropriate marketing research methods with the specific new product assessment problem. We have identified two major problem sources: a developer's inability to communicate or define the new product concept in a meaningful way, and inappropriate selection of potential evaluators of the concept. Solutions to these problems – such as testing among experts or visionaries, indirect customer value assessment procedures, the use of information acceleration concepts and the use of virtual reality technology for describing the new product – have the potential to address many of these problems.

We have proceeded in this chapter under the assumption that neither the technology (radically new vs. marginally new), nor the type of customer (consumer vs. industrial), nor the type of innovation (product vs. service, for example) affects the appropriateness of the market research method one might employ. As there are horses for courses, there are market research methods more appropriate for some of the situations above than for others. Although we do not have any global guidelines in mind, we suggest the following:

A. The technology is *not* critical in determining a research method; it is the consumer's response to the technology that matters.

B. Services need to be experienced; here traditional product testing methods (based on product use) should be considered as well as virtual reality-based research.

C. Process innovations, particularly in nonconsumer markets, can provide economic value (cost reductions) without changing functionality. Hence, value assessment methods are most appropriate here.

D. Also, in those business markets where organizational needs emerge at different times for different customers, the lead user method would appear apt.

E. Finally, consumers reduce adoption risk by acquiring information. The information acceleration method appears most apt for use in the consumer durables marketplace, where adoption risk is higher than for consumables.

We believe that new ideas and techniques are needed to adapt the existing array of new product development methods to radically new products. For example, marketing researchers need a theory of customer behavior under conditions of new product unavailability: this situation arises when a firm announces that a radically new product will be launched at a future time. Similarly, our methods assume a static set of preferences or needs among customers; radically new products are likely to change "needs" as customers build an understanding of "what might be." Dynamic customer preference models and new, associated research methods are likely to be needed here.

There is also a clear need to scan the scientific laboratory or R&D environment to determine what "best practices" are in selecting radically new product development projects to pursue. Such a study could assess the extent to which firms are missing opportunities for new technological products as well as determine what firms have been doing that has worked for them – i.e., what have they done that has made them successful in realizing the potential of a radically new product. Such a best-practices study could result in formal codification of those practices and become a rule-based or expert system method for radically new product market assessment.

In sum, existing marketing research methods have much to offer in addressing technological oversights, especially when those methods are carefully tuned to the problems that radically new products evoke. However, there are some exciting challenges and opportunities to move the field forward significantly, and we expect important advances in this area in the years to come.

References

Adams, L. (1972). *Conceptual Blockbusting*, Stanford, CA: The Portable Stanford.

Anderson, J. C., Jain, D. C., and Chintagunta, P. K. (1993). Customer Value Assessment in Business Markets: A State-of-Practice Study, *Journal of Business-to-Business Marketing*, 1, 1, 3–29.

Arnold, J. E. (1962). Useful creative techniques. In *Source Book of Creative Thinking*, S. J. Parnes and H. F. Harding (eds.). New York: Scribner.

Axelrod, J. N. and Wybenga, H. (1985). Perceptions that motivate purchase, *Journal of Advertising Research*, 25, 2, 19–21.

Berning, C., Kohn, A. and Jacoby, J. (1974). Patterns of Information Acquisition in New Product Purchases, *The Journal of Consumer Research*, 1, 2, 18–22.

Blattberg, R., and Golanty, J. (1978). Tracker: An early test market forecasting and diagnostic model for new product planning, *Journal of Marketing*, 44 (Fall), 59–67.

Booz, Allen, and Hamilton (1971). *Management of New Products* New York: Booz, Allen, and Hamilton.

Booz, Allen, and Hamilton (1982). *New Product Management for the '80s* New York: Booz, Allen, and Hamilton.

Brockoff, K. and Rao, V. R. (1993) Toward a demand forecasting model for preannounced new technological products, *Journal of Engineering Technology Management*, 10, 12, 211–228.

Choffray, J.-M. and Lilien, G. L. (1986). A decision support system for evaluating sales prospects and launch strategies for new products. *Industrial Marketing Management*, 15, 2, 75–85.

Cooper, R. G. (1975). Why new industrial products fail" *Industrial Marketing Management*, 4, 2, 315–326.

Cooper, R. G., and Kleinschmidt, E. J. (1987). New products: What separates winners from losers? *Journal of Product Innovation Management*, 4, 169–184.

Cooper, R. G. (1986). *Winning at New Products*. Reading, MA: Addison Wesley.

Crispell, D. (1993). Virtual Reality Meets Do-It-Yourself, *Folio: The Magazine for Magazine Management*, 22, 9 (May 15), 25–26.

De Brentani, U. (1989). Success and failure in new industrial services, *Journal of Product Innovation Management*, 6, 4, 239–258.

Dearden, J. A. and Lilien, G. L. (1990). "On optimal salesforce compensation in the presence of learning effects, *International Journal of Research in Marketing*, 7, 2, 179–188.

Duerr, M. G. (1986) *The Commercial Development of New Products*. New York: The Conference Board.

Economist (1993). Theme parks: Heart, brains, jobs, 328, 7827 (September 4), 33.

EFO (1995). *Innovation Survey Report on New Products*. Connecticut: Weston.

Fisher, J. C., and Pry, R. H. (1971). A simple substitution model for technological change," *Technological Forecasting and Social Change*, 2, 5, 75–88.

Goerne, C. (1992). Visionary marketer shape for concrete gains from the fantasy of virtual reality, *Marketing News*, 26, 25, 2.

Garud, R., Nayyar, P. R., and Shapira, Z (1994). Technological choices and the inevitability of errors, NYU Conference on Technological Oversights and Foresights, 11–12 March.

Haley, R. I. (1968). Benefit segmentation: A decision oriented research tool, *Journal of Marketing*, 32, 7, 30–35.

Hauser, J. R., Urban, G. L., and Weinberg, B. D. (1993). How consumers allocate their time when searching for information, *Journal of Marketing Research*, 30, 11, 452–466.

Hausman, J. A. (1979). Individual discount rates and the purchase and utilization of energy-using durables, *Bell Journal of Economics*, 10, 1 33–54.

Kamakura, W. A. (1988). A least squares procedure for benefit segmentation with conjoint experiments, *Journal of Marketing Research*, 25, 5 157–167.

Lee, M. and Na, D. (1994). Determinants of technical success in product innovation when innovative radicalness is considered, *Journal of Product Innovation Management*, 11, 1, 62–67.

Lilien, G. L. and Yoon, E. (1989). Determination of new industrial product performance: A strategic reexamination of the empirical literature, *IEEE Transactions on Engineering Management*, 36, 2, 3–10.

Lilien, G. L. and Johnston, P. E. (1980). *A Market Assessment for Active Heating and Cooling Products*, DOE Contract AC03-79CS-30209, September.

Mansfield, E. and Wagner, S. (1975). Organizational and strategic factors associated with probabilities of success in industrial R&D, *The Journal of Business*, 48, 4, 179–198.

Moore, W. L. (1982). Concept testing, *Journal of Business Research*, 10, 279–294.

Pels, M.-A. and Merrick, B. (1993). 2001: A credit union odyssey," *Credit-Union Magazine*, 59, 7, 40–45.

Prince, G. M. (1972). *The Practice of Creativity*, New York: Collier Books.

Reidenbach, E. R. and Grimes, S. (1984). How concept knowledge affects concept evaluation, *Journal of Product Innovation Management*, 4, 255–266.

Rothwell, R. et al. (1974). Sappho updated: Project sappho phase II *Research Policy*, 3, 258–291.

Silk, A. J. and Urban, G. L. (1978). Pre-test market evaluation of new packaged goods: A model and measurement methodology, *Journal of Marketing Research*, 15, 2, 171–19 1.

Tauber, E. M. (1981). Utilization of concept testing for new product forecasting: Traditional versus multiattribute approaches, in Y. Wind, V. Mahajan, and R. N. Cardozo (eds.), *New Product Forecasting*. Lexington, MA: Lexington, pp. 169–178.

Urban, G. L. and Hauser, J. R. (1993). *Design and Marketing of New Products*, 2nd ed. Englewood Cliffs, NJ: Prentice Hall.

Urban, G. L. and von Hippel, E. (1988). Lead user analysis for the development of new industrial products, *Management Science*, 34, 569–582.

Urban, G. L., Weinberg, B. D., and Hauser, J. R. (1996). Premarket forecasting of really new products, *Journal of Marketing* (forthcoming).

von Hippel, E. (1986). Lead users: A source of novel product concepts, *Management Science*, 32, 791–805.

Wittink, D. R., and Cattin, P. (1989). Commercial use of conjoint analysis: An update, *Journal of Marketing*, 53, 7, 91–96.

Yoon, E. and Lilien, G. L. (1985). New industrial product performance: The impact of market characteristics and strategy, *Journal of Product Innovation Management*, 3, 9, 134–144.

Section V
(S)Top management and culture

13 Firm capabilities and managerial decision making: A theory of innovation biases

Janet E. L. Bercovitz, John M. de Figueiredo, and David J. Teece

There is no reason to suppose that large firms are any less (or more) innovative than small or new organizations. What may be true is that the type of entrepreneurship differs. The best entrepreneurial opportunities for large organizations may be those based on the redeployment of the firm's resources and the extension of its competitive positions. Those most attractive to individuals and small firms may be based on new opportunity and the creation of new markets (Rumelt 1987, 151–152)

I. Introduction

Schumpeter's evolutionary theory of innovation suggests that the "gales of creative destruction" brought about by radical innovation will allow some organizations to gain competitive advantage and result in " . . . old concerns and established industries . . . perish[ing] that nevertheless would be able to live on vigorously and usefully if they could weather a particular storm [of this creative destruction]" (Schumpeter, 1942, 90). Although Schumpeter's argument does not specifically identify the organizational locus of the innovation, it does note that "new concerns or industries that introduce new commodities or processes" are likely to displace older industries (Schumpeter, 89).

Radical innovation and its organizational foundations became an important area of study in subsequent academic inquiry on innovation. Many commentators have highlighted the advantage small and de novo firms have over incumbent firms in generating and incubating radical innovations (Foster, 1986; Jewkes et al., 1958; Tilton, 1971; Abernathy & Utterback, 1978; Mitchell, 1989; Henderson & Clark, 1990).[1] This suggests two key research questions. Why do we observe many large firms eschewing radical, competency-destroying innovation in favor of incremental, competency-enhancing improvements to existing products and processes? How can we better understand the underlying determinants of the advantage that small and de novo firms might possess in developing these same radical innovations?

We argue that the failure to introduce competency-destroying innovations may be better understood as a product of the decision-making biases of some, but not all, large firms. That is, large firms tend to lose their ability and desire to engage in competency-destroying innovative activities as they grow because of decision-making biases associated with their size, asset base, business practices, and organizational structure.[2] Specifically, two main behavioral factors drive limited and biased decision making in organizations. These are (1) bounded rationality and cognitive decision-making frames, and (2) "inconsistent" risk aversion. It is the *interaction* of these behavioral features with the established capabilities, complementary assets, and/or administrative routines of incumbents that serves to *intensify* decision-making biases and, thus, limit radical innovation.

The existence of specialized, difficult-to-market assets intensifies bounded rationality decision-making biases by constraining the evolutionary contours a firm may pursue in two ways. First, by focusing the search for innovation opportunities on those solutions that employ the firm's asset base as currently contoured, the incumbent ties itself to current products and, more importantly, to the pursuit of incremental, competency-enhancing innovations and improvements. Second, even when potential innovations and research and development opportunities are encountered, they are explored using the cognitive methods that are consistent with the current routines of the firm. Thus, the incumbent may misperceive opportunities readily apparent to others.

Inconsistent risk preferences due to inadequate risk pooling, multilevel decision-making, and certainty effects, are further intensified by the existence of a current asset base and hierarchy. Hence, incumbent firms will be excessively risk-averse as compared to their unencumbered de novo counterparts, and thus, will be less likely to pursue competency-destroying radical innovations. Bold forecasting acts to reinforce these effects. It results in large firms pursuing bold forecasts along their current technological trajectory while small firms display bold forecasting along competency-destroying paths. Thus, incumbents will tend to produce incremental innovations to current technologies while smaller, de novo firms, not tied to current assets and routines, are more likely to embrace radical innovations.

These conjectures have deep strategic implications for the theory of the firm. Large firms must design strategies and decision-making procedures that allow them to balance the benefits associated with established assets and routines against possible negative effects on decision making. That does not mean that the days of the large firm are limited. To the contrary, we argue that Fortune 500 firms play a continuing and vital role in economic growth by channeling current technologies along competency-enhancing innovation paths.

In this chapter we explore the possibilities of integrating the core concepts of behavioral decision theory with the resource-based, strategic management theory of the firm, with special reference to technological innovation. To our knowledge, the literature on this area is quite sparse. Thus the theoretical formulation in this chapter should be considered preliminary and exploratory, and suggestive of the possible synergies between the two fields. The chapter is organized as follows. In Section II, we provide an overview of the literature on firm capabilities and complementary assets and illustrate the singular importance of investments in these arenas. In Section III, we review the behavioral decision-making literature and detail the behavioral factors that underlie biased decision making. Then, we explore how these key behavioral factors and established assets interact with each other to intensify biased decision making and constrain radical, competency-destroying innovative developments by large firms. In Section IV, we summarize the theoretical results and examine the cumulative effect of the decision-making biases. Section V begins by discussing the organizational implications of these decision-making biases. It then examines the popular management literature on strategic innovation and explores the underlying behavioral assumptions from management guidelines implicitly derive. On the whole, we find this literature goes too far in calling for downsizing. Finally, we consider how managers can pursue strategies that balance the positive rents from the current asset base with the costs of decision-making biases.

II. Theoretical foundations: Firm capabilities and complementary assets

Recent academic literature has highlighted the benefits firms may derive from holding, augmenting, and exploiting established capabilities, complementary assets, and/or administrative routines. These assets and routines may provide isolating mechanisms that allow firms to earn above normal economic rents. In-place assets may enhance a firm's ability to (1) efficiently deploy incremental innovations; (2) create distinctive competences and strategic advantage; (3) commercialize both in-house and third-party innovations; and (4) reduce systematic or undiversifiable risk.

In general, technologies evolve in an evolutionary fashion (Kuhn 1970). For example, advances in memory devices have been cumulative along a particular technological trajectory, from 1K to 4K to 64K to 256K to 1 megabyte, and so on (Teece, 1996). Given the tacit and cumulative nature of knowledge, experience with previous generations of a technology is often essential for future innovative success (Dosi, 1982, 1988; Cohen & Levinthal, 1990). Incumbent firms, having an established set of capabilities, complementary assets, and administrative routines, that are tailored to a specific technological paradigm, are generally able to capitalize on these established assets and "win" in the development of incremental innovations.

Further, idiosyncratic and difficult-to-replicate, established assets can be integrated to form firm-specific competences (Dierickx & Cool, 1989; Teece, 1988; Teece & Pisano, 1994).[3] Competences, comprised of both technical and organizational/economic dimensions, underlie and define the competitive strength of a particular firm. In essence, the firm's ability to solve both technical and organizational problems reside in its set of established assets and routines. As such, firms are encouraged to cultivate these capabilities/assets, especially those that are difficult to replicate, in order to insure a continuing stream of rents.

Established assets are also key in determining which firms "win" in the commercialization of innovations. Teece (1986) noted that one of the main factors that determines who wins from innovation is related to the positions of the leader and follower firms in what he terms "complementary assets." Complementary assets is defined as those capabilities or assets that are required to be utilized in conjunction with a specific innovation so that it is valuable to the user. In weak appropriability regimes, firms that control the necessary specialized assets – such as marketing, distribution, manufacturing, and/or after-sales service technologies – will be in a position to leverage these assets to capitalize on another firm's innovation and gain a dominant position in the market (Teece, 1986; Mitchell, 1989; de Figueiredo & Teece, 1996). Examples of incumbent firms that have successfully pursued this strategy are numerous and include General Electric (diagnostic imaging), Matsushita (VHS video recorders), and Seiko (quartz watch).

Finally, there is some evidence that firms can reduce their levels of systematic or undiversifiable risk by vertically integrating into key complementary assets (Helfat & Teece, 1987). Because uncertainty is a fundamental problem for complex organizations, organizational forms, and administrative routines that increase a firm's ability to minimize the effect of unanticipated events will improve long-run performance. Helfat and Teece show that integration into vertically-related activities provides an advantage of this type, as it enables firms to reduce both secondary uncertainty and behavioral uncertainty. Secondary uncertainty, the uncertainty arising from the lack of communication between decision makers (Koopmans, 1957:163), is attenuated by vertical integration that improves information flows through the removal of proprietary boundaries. Further, the cost of identifying and transferring relevant information is expected to decrease as communication codes and routines emerge within a unified organization (Armour & Teece, 1978; Williamson, 1975; Nelson & Winter, 1982). Behavioral uncertainty, uncertainty arising from the opportunistic behavior of economic actors (Williamson, 1985, 58–59), is also attenuated, as vertical integration significantly reduces the incentives for strategic distortion and nondisclosure of information.

Integration economies and strategic advantages cause firms to build and maintain established assets. However, ownership of dedicated assets can also intensify decision-making biases and thus impede a firm's ability to successfully engage in radical innovations. It is these consequences that we explore below.

III. Theoretical foundations: Behavioral underpinnings of "biased" decision making

A. Bounded rationality

One basic assumption of the behaviorist school is that individuals are boundedly rational. In contrast to the strong or hyperrationality assumptions of neoclassical economics, individuals are assumed to be "intendedly rational, but only limitedly so" (Simon, 1961, p. xxiv). Boundedly rational players have limits on their ability to comprehend, evaluate, and process information. To cope with these limitations, and to economize on scarce cognitive capabilities, individuals and organizations adopt heuristic problem-solving or decision-making routines (Nelson & Winter, 1982). A firm's routines guide behavior by defining "a list of functions that determine (perhaps stochastically) what a firm does as a function of various external variables (principally market conditions) and internal state variables" (Nelson & Winter, 1982, 16).

Unfortunately, adoption of these routines is not costless. Reliance on problem-solving routines effectively reduces the span of problemistic search and tends to produce strong path dependencies (Dosi, 1988; Nelson & Winter, 1982). Specifically, an organization's future behavior is narrowly constrained by its past behavior. Because the range of search is determined in large part by the firm's current routines, the perceived "viable" technological choice set is generally limited to alternatives "close-in" to the firm's current activities.[4] Nelson and Winter (1982, 134) conclude:

As a first approximation, therefore, firms may be expected to behave in the future according to routines they have employed in the past . . . it is quite inappropriate to conceive of firm behavior in terms of deliberate choice from a broad menu of alternatives that some external observer considers to be "available" opportunities for the organization. The menu is not broad, but narrow and idiosyncratic; it is built into the firm's routines, and most of the "choosing" is also accomplished automatically by those routines.

In general, attractive alternatives that are distant from the firm's current activities will be overlooked. Theoretically, firms could capture "distant" opportunities through broad-scan search routines. However, in practice, successful implementation of such routines has proven to be both difficult and costly. In order to reap the benefits of broad-scan search processes, the firm already must possess a significant knowledge base.

Further, a number of theoreticians contend bounded rationality tends to generate conservative behavior on the part of managers (see, for example, Kuran, 1988). To economize on cognitive powers, managers will tend to select options that are highly dependent, in a dynamic sense, upon decisions made previously (Day, 1987). Moreover, because behavioral rules are employed, the greater the complexity and uncertainty of a situation, the more likely the manager is to pursue conservative and incremental decision making (Heiner, 1983). In sum, inefficient decisions and decision-making biases that ultimately lead to limited search horizons and excessive conservatism may result from bounded rationality and the path dependencies bounded rationality generates.

Interaction of bounded rationality and established assets. The existence of established capabilities, complementary assets, and/or administrative routines of incumbents can exacerbate bounded rationality-based decision-making biases by further constraining search. Organizational scholars argue that incumbent firms, relying on "routines, assets, and strategies" developed to cope with existing technologies, are handicapped in making and/or adopting radical, competence-destroying, noncumulative innovations (Nelson & Winter, 1982; Tushman & Anderson, 1986; Henderson & Clark, 1990). Established assets affect decision-making competencies in two distinct, but related, ways.

First, incumbent firms with a base of established assets will further limit their search space to potential solutions and innovations that are "close-in" to these assets. Incumbent firms tend to narrowly focus problem-solving activities to exploit established technological and organizational trajectories and to enhance the future utility and value of existing assets. This first effect makes it difficult for these firms to see potential radical innovations. Second, incumbent firms tend to frame new problems in a manner consistent with the firm's current knowledge base, asset set, and/or established problem-solving heuristics. This second effect means that managers may not successfully address opportunities or potential innovations, even when they do see them. Thus, managers now face two constraints – cognitive limitations and framing biases generated from established assets.

Assets and close-in search

Although the incumbent firm's capability and asset base may be developed and refined over time (i.e., through organizational learning), in general, innovative change is incremental, cumulative, and path-dependent. The asset domain of the incumbent firm influences decision making. Teece and Pisano (1994), note a particular firm's path dependencies are not just technologically determined. Paths are identified by technological paradigms and trajectories (Dosi, 1982) and constrained further by the complementary assets the firm has already built or can readily acquire. Established assets directly affect the decision-making calculus by reducing the actual or perceived relative costs of "close-in" innovation alternatives. These assets serve to raise perceived and actual costs of a broader search in two ways: 1) they cause firms to focus search on competence-enhancing innovations, and 2) they cause firms to guard against competence-destroying innovations.[5]

Managers of firms with established assets may have incentives to pursue innovative alternatives that build on current assets and knowledge, and to ignore innovative alternatives unrelated to the firm's current assets. The marginal cost of gaining additional knowledge in a known area is often much less than innovation in a new, unrelated field (Cohen & Levinthal, 1990). The "switching costs" or the cost of changing trajectories and acquiring knowledge unrelated to the asset base can be quite high. Also, decision-makers tend to have strong aversions to losses and, as such, seek to avoid any situations or actions that have the appearance of causing financial setbacks (Kahneman & Tversky, 1979; Kahneman & Lovallo, 1993). This can create "status quo biases" where programs exploiting established assets are favored over more distant alternatives, even if they have higher expected values. Although past investments in specialized assets are sunk – the investment costs incurred to create these assets cannot be recouped – managers often perceive there to be incremental losses associated with writing off an established asset, despite the fact that rational economic logic suggests that "bygones are bygones."[6]

The relative advantage that de novo firms, unconstrained by assets and routines, possess in adopting radical innovations has been documented in numerous studies. Jewkes et al. (1958) concluded that a majority of seventy major twentieth-century inventions were made outside the R&D departments of large firms. Tilton (1971), studying the evolution of the semiconductor industry, provides evidence that in the early days of the industry, new enterprises led existing firms in the application and commercialization of certain semiconductor technology. These findings are further supported by Foster (1986).[7] Buzzell and Nourse (1967), tracing innovations in the processed foods industry, show that the majority of the new product innovations between 1954 and 1967 came from small organizations. A more recent empirical study providing support for this hypothesis is Henderson and Clark's (1991) study of the photolithographic alignment equipment industry.[8]

Framing

Equally important phenomena are cognitive limitations flowing from problem-framing. The existence of established assets shapes decision making by supporting limited search heuristics. In general, when an incumbent is faced with a new or different problem or opportunity, the search for solutions is framed by past experience and limited by established problem-solving routines.[9] As a result, incumbents often have distorted perceptions of innovation opportunities; incumbents may be unable to identify new opportunities and/or successfully operationalize new ideas. Adopting the framebreaking perspective required to overcome narrow search horizon is extremely difficult and costly for many boundedly rational actors tied to established problem-solving competences.

Henderson (1994, 101) notes that GM, IBM, and DEC have recently encountered difficulties because they have become, "prisoners of the deeply ingrained assumptions, information filters, and problem-solving strategies that make up their world views, turning the solutions that once made them great into new problems to be resolved." Specifically, GM's experience with the J-car is illustrative of the inability to break frames. Confronted with a strong Japanese import threat, GM set out to design a new and revolutionary car as an import fighter. However, when the engineers came together to design the new J-car, they relied heavily on the previous design of the X-car – engaging in "badge engineering" – changing the nameplate and a few decorative features. As Keller (1989) notes, the J-car was effectively a repackaging of the X-car. The design staff of GM may have been a victim to X-car cognitive frames, as well as extremely tight budgetary constraints of the GM cost accountants, and was unable or unwilling to accept the challenge and costs of frame-breaking.

B. Inconsistent risk aversion

Two main phenomena drive inconsistent risk aversion and lead to biased decision-making. They are (1) certainty effects; and (2) isolation effects. Prospect theory, an alternative to traditional utility theory in economics, has found that decision makers underweigh outcomes that are merely probable in comparison with outcomes that are obtained with certainty – the certainty effect. This effect contributes to excessive risk aversion in choices involving sure gains, and excessive risk seeking in choices involving sure losses (Kahneman & Tversky, 1979).[10] Further, to simplify choices between alternatives, individuals generally evaluate options in isolation. Viewing each alternative as unique leads decision makers to frame decisions in terms of perceived abilities and resources and ignore or undervalue possibilities for risk pooling. This "isolated" approach to decision making may produce inconsistent preferences and decision biases (timid choices and/or bold forecasts) that lead to inefficient outcomes (Kahneman & Tversky, 1979; Kahneman & Lovallo, 1993).

March and Shapira (1987, 1992) confirm and refine the main finding of Kahneman and Tversky: managers rarely behave in a manner consistent with classical decision-making theory. They model the processes of decision making and find managers are rather insensitive to the probabilities attached to outcomes. Thus, they conclude that "the behavioral phenomenon of risk taking in organizational settings will be imperfectly understood within a classical conception of risk" (March & Shapira, 1987, 1404) and thus, requires a theory that is able to incorporate the idiosyncracies that exist in executive risk-taking behavior.

Interaction of "inconsistent" risk aversion and established assets. The existence of established assets and routines exacerbates problems of excessive risk aversion. Specifically, both the isolation effect and the certainty effect may be intensified by the existence of established assets, causing incumbent firms to become comparably more risk averse than unencumbered de novo firms. In terms of innovative activity, this excessive risk aversion may lead to biased decision making, and may limit the probability that incumbent firms will explore risky, radical innovations.

Isolation errors

Temporal and cross-divisional risk pooling isolation errors

Although there are numerous theories of risk and risk aversion within the economics literature, this chapter highlights three models that are particularly relevant to the risk comparison conducted below. The first of these models is the capital asset pricing model (CAPM).[11] CAPM argues that the risk of any investment can be broken into two types: systematic (market) risk stemming from variations in the market as a whole, and unsystematic (unique) risk arising from a particular investment.[12] Because the market (shareholders) can diversify away all unsystematic risk, CAPM implies that if firms are managed to benefit shareholders, then on average there ought be no difference in the level of risk aversion between small and large firms in similar industries.[13] Expectations are that ρ_i, the level of risk aversion of the incumbent, will be equal to ρ_e, the level of risk aversion of the entrant firm; $\rho_i = \rho_e$.

The second model, the portfolio selection model (PSM), operates on the hypothesis that firms concern themselves with total investment risk. A firm can choose from a menu of innovation projects, each of which has an associated risk and return. In the standard Tobin-Markowitz portfolio selection model, a financial investor minimizes the variance of the return on his portfolio of risky assets subject to an expected return constrain.[14] Specifically, the portfolio selection model (PSM) suggests that because large firms generally hold a broader "portfolio" of projects, they have greater ability and opportunity to diversify away total risk. Thus, PSM predicts that ρ_i will be less than ρ_e; that is, $\rho_i << \rho_e$.

The focus of this section is a third model of risk aversion proposed by Kahneman and Lovallo (1993) based on prospect theory. They argue that decision makers tend to adopt narrow decision frames, focusing on the unique features of problems and therefore making decisions in isolation. When managers of incumbent firms evaluate potential innovative projects in isolation, they overlook many possibilities for pooling risks between projects and across time.[15] This has two related effects. First, not engaging in all available risk pooling opportunities causes the incumbent firm to be overly risk averse in pursuing innovative prospects than the optimal (nonbias) risk preferences would dictate. Second, the prevalence of this isolation error effectively negates some of the distinction in risk preferences between incumbent firms and de novo firms predicted by PSM. Therefore, the result of the Kahneman and Lovallo framework is intermediate to CAPM and PSM. That is, unlike CAPM, prospect theory would predict that there will be some risk pooling advantages associated with large firms, but these advantages will not be as great as PSM predicts.

In her study on the petroleum industry, Helfat (1983) provides empirical support for the assertion that large firms do engage in risk pooling, although suboptimally. That is, oil company investment portfolio alterations occur in the direction predicted by PSM, but are actually smaller than predicted by the PSM model (Teece, 1989). Although Helfat does not examine the internal decision-making mechanisms of the firm, we hypothesize that one source of suboptimal risk pooling is the decision-making biases noted by Kahneman and Lovallo. As such, the empirical evidence suggests that there may be support for prospect theory in predicting the cumulative risk aversion effect of the risk pooling errors would still be $\rho_i < \rho_e$.

Multilevel decision-making isolation errors

The incumbent firm's expected level of risk aversion is further influenced by the interaction of the isolation effect with the firm's established assets. In particular, incumbent firms with established organizational routines may encounter multilevel decision-making isolation errors that intensify tendencies toward excessive risk aversion. In complex organizations, key decisions are often evaluated sequentially at numerous levels throughout the firm. Although "cognitive" efficiency gains may be attained by parceling out first-line decision-making responsibilities to specialists, fragmented and sequential decision-making compounds risk biases (Kahneman & Lovallo, 1993).

To illustrate, lower and middle managers in different functional areas may be asked to evaluate different aspects of alternative innovation possibilities. These managers, each operating in isolation, will lack the means to aggregate risk possibilities. Further, if managers are evaluated in terms of short-run performance (budgets) with division losses weighed more heavily than division profits, managers will have additional incentives to take excessively risk-averse positions and thus exacerbate the isolation problem (Caves, 1970; Winn, 1977). As such, lower-level managers will present excessively risk-averse options to the upper level managers (Rumelt, 1987). Faced with a portfolio of excessively risk-averse options, upper level managers, who may be better able to aggregate the risk, will necessarily select an excessively risk-averse portfolio of innovations. Thus, risk-aversion biases are compounded with each additional level of decision making. This effect will be exacerbated if innovation agenda setting begins at lower levels in the organization *and* occurs through a "bottom-up" process. Keller (1989, 46) documents the decision-making process in General Motors where both incidents occurred. She found that the management incentive and bonus programs were two of the key factors that precluded GM management from taking the necessary risks. Managers were reluctant to forgo profits in the short term, thus inhibiting decisions to innovate that may have helped the firm in the long term. Keller also documents that oversight by GM top management was pervasive and most decisions went almost to the top of the organization before they could be resolved.

If, in general, incumbent firms with established administrative routines are organized in a more hierarchical fashion than de novo firms, they will be comparably more prone to these multilevel decision-making isolation errors than entrants. Under such conditions, $\rho'_i > \rho'_e$; the marginal effect on risk aversion of the incumbent becomes greater than the marginal effect on risk aversion of the entrant firm.

Bold forecasting

Kahneman and Lovallo have argued isolation errors may not only lead to excessive risk aversion, but also to bold forecasting. Bold forecasts are generated when firms take the inside view and focus on the abilities and resources of the particular group, consider the plan and the obstacles to its completion, construct scenarios of future progress, and extrapolate current trends. The inside view tends to produce excessive optimism in planning because managers anchor predictions on plans and scenarios.

Although both incumbents and de novo firms are susceptible to bold forecasting biases, these biases affect firms in different ways. In general, incumbents are optimistic about opportunities along the technological trajectory on which they currently operate and innovate. Incumbents will project rent streams for future innovations with reference to current product profits and the expected future benefits derived from the existing complementary asset base and established capabilities. As such, they tend to be overly optimistic about the innovative potential of incremental improvements to current technologies and practices.

Entrants, too, are optimistic about prospects along their technological trajectory. However, because entrants' technological trajectories are usually not congruent with incumbents' trajectories, their bold forecasts have a differing effect. Entrants normally excel at innovation along competence-destroying paths and, thus, they will be overly optimistic about the success of radical innovations. Hence, although both incumbents and entrants boldly forecast along their technological trajectories, the outcomes will be different because their technological trajectories are not the same.

In their contribution to this book, Dosi and Lovallo (1997) take a viewpoint that is complementary to ours. Whereas this chapter stresses the relative risk aversion and misframing of problems by asset-rich firms, Dosi and Lovallo argue that entrants are overconfident about success when they enter. They view entry as individually detrimental, but collectively beneficial, because of the learning externality that takes place. As small firms fail, other firms in the industry and potential entrants learn what does not work and what techniques and products are not effective (Mitchell, 1989). The theory being proposed here and the Dosi and Lovallo argument are complementary and mutually reinforcing. Both theories claim similar results: larger firms are more tied to current cognitive problem solving frames than are smaller, de novo firms when pursuing radical innovation. Whereas we examine the problem from the incumbent perspective, Dosi and Lovallo analyze the question from the perspective of smaller firms.

Certainty effects

The incumbent firm's excessive level of risk aversion is further accentuated by the interplay between the certainty effect and the firm's established assets. In most instances, existing complementary assets and administrative routines provide incumbent firms with relatively certain short-run cash flows. The certainty/established asset effect has two related strategic implications. First, it may increase the incumbent's desire to avoid competence-destroying innovations. When faced with a choice between innovative strategies that allow exploitation of these established assets and strategies that have some competence-destroying characteristics, most incumbent firms will choose the former strategy. Second, the "sure" returns associated with incremental (or established-asset exploiting) strategies will often be overvalued as compared to the "risky" expected returns of more radical (established-asset destroying) strategies. As such, decision makers will tend to require the expected returns of the "competence-destroying" strategy provide a substantial premium before such transactions are undertaken (Rasmussen, 1992).

One manifestation of the certainty/established assets effect is the avoidance of cannibalism by incumbent firms. As noted by Rumelt (1987), fear of cannibalizing existing profitable product lines reduces the incumbent's incentives to radically innovate. In general, the larger the "certain" rent stream, the weaker the incumbent's incentive to pursue radical innovations. For example, Xerox was slow to respond to the threat of low-priced Japanese plain-paper copiers because it was apprehensive of possibly cannibalizing its very profitable line of high volume machines (Jacobson & Hillkirk, 1986).

Additional evidence abounds that supports this certainty/established asset bias. Foster (1986) details how Du Pont failed to make the transition from nylon tire cords to polyester tire cords. Du Pont focused on improving its existing technology to protect "certain," but diminishing, returns on established assets (including a new nylon tire cord manufacturing facility) rather than pursuing a "riskier" innovative opportunity. As a result, the company's rival, Celanese, was able to capture over 75% of the polyester tire cord market.

Foster (1986) also documents NCR's oversight in "clinging" to its established line of business – electromechanical cash registers – and delaying the move to electronic machines to protect the base of NCR's revenues. In four years, from 1972 to 1976, eighty percent of the market for cash registers was lost to manufacturers of electronic products. In overvaluing the "certain" returns from its established assets, NCR was slow to adopt "competence-destroying" innovations.

More recently, the Wall Street Journal[16] noted that the woes of IBM and Digital Equipment were due to their reluctance to cannibalize their own assets and product lines. Because they relied so heavily on the certain rent streams from their current product lines, "they weren't aggressive [in] developing machines that would render their mainframes obsolete." Likewise, Keller (1989) shows that GM was reluctant to design and build good compact cars for fear it would take away from their big-car business.

In a broader empirical analysis of the petroleum industry, Greene (1985) found that oil companies allocated investment expenditures in a manner so as to reinforce past successes. Although the strategies employed differed across firms, each firm's strategy was developed early in its history and proved resistant to change. This finding supports the certainty effect hypothesis that incumbents often overvalue assured returns associated with the established asset base.

The certainty effect, best typified in the popular management literature as the "bird-in-the-hand" philosophy, strongly interacts with established assets to accentuate decision-making biases. This effect causes incumbent firms with established assets to be more risk-averse than de novo firms with few or no assets in place; $\rho_i > \rho_e$.

IV. Summary of theoretical considerations

Theoretical results

Table 13.1 summarizes the risk discussion we have put forth. We have presented four main behavioral (cognitive) factors that underlie inconsistent risk preference[s] and promote excessive risk aversion and decision-making biases. These are (1) risk-pooling isolation errors; (2) multilevel decision-making isolation errors; (3) bold forecasting errors; and (4) certainty errors. First, the empirical evidence supports the existence of risk-pooling isolation errors leading to an intermediate level of risk aversion (which is consistent with prospect theory). When large incumbent firms neglect some internal opportunities for risk pooling across divisions and across time, these firms reduce their ability to diversify risk internally. Because some (but not all) opportunities for risk pooling are taken by large firms, we would expect these firms to be less risk averse than small and de novo firms.

The second type of error differentially affects incumbent firms and de novo firms. Risk-aversion biases are intensified in organizations that rely on complex, hierarchical administrative routines. Generally, multilevel decision-making isolation errors cause incumbent firms with established administrative routines to become, on the margin, more risk averse than unen-

Table 13.1. Relative risk aversion biases for competency-destroying innovations in incumbent and entrant firms

Decision-making biases	Marginal effect	Expected cumulative effect
Isolation errors	$\rho_i' > \rho_e'$	
• Risk Pooling*		
Capital Asset Pricing Model (CAPM)	None	$\rho_i = \rho_e$
Portfolio Selection Model (PSM)	$\rho_i \ll \rho_e$	$\rho_i \ll \rho_e$
Prospect Theory	$\rho_i < \rho_e$	$\rho_i < \rho_e$
• MultiLevel Decision-Making	$\rho_i > \rho_e$	$\rho_i = \rho_e$
• Bold Forecasting[28]	$\rho_i > \rho_e$	$\rho_i > \rho_e$
Certainty effects	$\rho_i > \rho_e$	$\rho_i > \rho_e$
Bounded rationality / framing	$\rho_i > \rho_e$	$\rho_i \gg \rho_e$

*All risk pooling isolation errors marginal effects are relative to CAPM.

cumbered de novo firms. Managerial incentives may further accentuate these biases toward excessive risk aversion.

Third, both incumbents and entrants are susceptible to bold forecasting biases, although these biases are played out differently across firms. In general, asset rich firms tend to be overly optimistic with regard to incremental innovations, whereas unencumbered de novo firms tend to be overly optimistic about the potential of radical innovations. As such, the marginal effects on relative risk aversion is dependent on the type of innovation contemplated. With respect to radical innovation, bold forecasting biases will lead small firms to become, on the margin, relatively more risk-loving than their incumbent counterparts and, thus, more willing to engage in risky innovation. The risk-aversion differential between incumbent and de novo firms is further exacerbated by a fourth type of error. The certainty effect associated with established assets strongly accentuates the incumbent's level of risk aversion as the incumbent favors rent streams from current assets rather than uncertain returns from risky drastic innovations.

The final behavioral factor leading to decision-making biases is bounded rationality that manifests itself through the cognitive frames in which we think about problem solving. Bounded rationality discourages incumbent firms from pursuing drastic innovations in two ways. First, bounded rationality combined with established assets severely limits the firm's search horizon for new innovations. This, combined with conservative behavior rules for managers, generally results in excessive risk aversion for incumbents. Second, because problem solving is generally a local competence, new problems or potential innovations that are confronted will be framed in a manner consistent with the firm's current assets, routines, and assets. This will cause large firms to overlook frame breaking opportunities in favor of more incremental innovations.

Note that Table 13.1 reflects only the biases associated with risk aversion for competency-destroying innovations, and not those associated with limited search horizons or competency-enhancing innovations.

Although we have attempted to detail the marginal effects of each of the decision-making biases, these are only very rough predictions. It is difficult to make definitive statements about the cumulative effect of these biases on the relative level of risk aversion between large and small firms. Nevertheless, Table 13.1 summarizes our hypotheses on the cumulative effects. Only the risk-pooling isolation errors will cause the incumbent firm to be, on the margin, less risk averse than the entrant. So the direction of absolute risk aversion rests on whether the other isolation errors, bold forecasting errors, certainty effect, and bounded rationality effect are strong enough to overcome the risk pooling advantage incumbents possess. The empirical evidence indicates that the certainty/established asset effect is quite potent and, alone, will usually dominate all of the other effects. We therefore suggest that the cumulative effect of decision-making biases will cause large incumbents to be more risk averse in innovation policy than small and de novo firms. Keller (1989, 21) summarized the relative risk aversion. "To avoid a superficial conclusion, the point is not that small is necessarily better than big. But GM's complacent bigness reflects a fundamental risk-averse philosophy that is apparent in much of big business." Therefore, we expect small and de novo firms, on average, to be more likely to pursue breakthrough, competency-destroying innovations than large and incumbent firms.

V. Implications for the strategy of the firm

A. Organizational considerations and isolation errors

Isolation errors seem to have differential effects across organizational forms. For simplicity, we illustrate the effects of risk pooling and multilevel decision making on two stylized organizational forms: centralized and decentralized. Decentralized firms are more prone to risk-pooling isolation errors than centralized firms. Management in separated and distant divisions may not be fully informed of the activities of other divisions. Thus, managers will be less likely to exploit risk-pooling opportunities between projects in different divisions, especially when autonomy of the divisions is high. Conversely, managers of centralized firms connected through a hierarchical decision-making structure will be more aware of risk-pooling opportunities. Neither organizational form will be able to pool risk perfectly because of persistent isolation errors. Temporal risk pooling will continue to be a prima facia problem independent of organizational form selected.

Multilevel isolation errors have the opposite outcome for the two organizational forms. Decentralized divisions that do not labor under a hierarchical and bureaucratic organizational structure are able to bypass much of the multilevel decision-making isolation errors pervasive in centralized firms. Although decentralized firms are better positioned to cope with multilevel decision-making errors than centralized companies, they are not immune to the effect, because sequential decision-making still occurs. Table 13.2 summarizes these results.

If the goal of organizations is to minimize isolation errors and thus align

Table 13.2. Differential effects of isolation errors by organizational form

Organizational form	Risk pooling isolation errors	Multi-level isolation errors
Decentralized	High	Moderate
Centralized	Moderate	High

risk preferences with minimal bias, then firms should organize the boundaries and internal structures of the firm so as to best capture the benefits of the two organizational forms.[17] This is a challenging balancing act that becomes particularly important when firms make innovation decisions. The rest of this section reviews the implications of the theory outlined for the innovation and organizational strategy of the firm and provides examples of firms that have attempted this balancing act.

B. A response to the popular strategic management literature

The cry "innovate or die" has become a recurring theme in the recent popular management literature. Many articles, books, and seminars have focused on innovation, detailing the experiences of both innovative winners and losers. This literature argues that many of the United States' largest firms are inept at successfully innovating.

Responding to this perception, several well-known management "gurus" have sought to explain innovation pitfalls and propose viable innovation strategies for established firms. In general, they call upon managers of large and incumbent organizations to adopt radical, nonformulaic strategies to overcome the inertia that inhibits breakthrough innovation (Peters, 1990, 1991; Davidow & Malone, 1992, Handy, 1990). Motivating these frameworks is one key proposition: in order to maintain competitiveness, firms need to adopt innovation strategies that *force* change.[18] Specifically, the strategies they advocate encourage change through three basic mechanisms: (1) increasing exposure to ideas and approaches external to the firm; (2) designing organizational structures and incentives to catalyze and reward creative action; and (3) promoting the continual shedding of established assets and routines.

Seemingly superficial, these strategies have received little serious attention from academics. However, employing the theoretical framework posited in this chapter, it becomes clear that these recommendations are really organizational and strategic mechanisms to mitigate decision-making biases discussed in Section III. First, strategies that increase exposure to external ideas serve to widen the firm's problemistic search space and thereby attenuate the biases of bounded rationality-based decision making. For example, Peters calls for firms to actively pursue joint development projects with "lead" customers and vendors in order to forcibly inject an outsider's views into the firm's development process at an early stage.

Second, strategies that provide structures and incentives to catalyze and reward creative action serve to attenuate problems of excessive risk aversion. For example, strategies that call on the firm to "get lean" and "increase divisional authority" are really designed to reduce the number of management layers of the firm and to push decision making down to lower levels to minimize the inherent isolation errors through multilevel, hierarchical decision-making processes.

Third, and perhaps most importantly, Peters and others implicitly acknowledge the interaction effect between established assets and decision-making biases. Many of their recommended strategies (such as cannibalizing profitable product lines and licensing your most advanced technology) call for the shedding of established capabilities, complementary assets, and/or administrative routines to reduce the intensity of bounded-rationality based and inconsistent risk aversion decision-making biases. By jettisoning existing assets, the firm no longer has an asset base with reliable sources of short-run positive gains. This will, in turn, reduce the certainty/established assets effect and thereby reduce overall levels of risk aversion. Further, these strategies indirectly reduce bounded rationality-based decision-making biases. In abandoning assets, the firm frees itself of those routines and constraints these assets impose on the innovation search process.

C. Balancing strategies

Based on a reinterpretation of the popular literature using the theoretical lens developed in this chapter, it would seem that there is some underlying justification for the recommendations being suggested: they mitigate decision-making biases in the innovation decision. *Nevertheless, it is our contention that most of the recommendations in the popular literature go too far.* Although the firm should attempt to mitigate decision-making biases and cognitive misframing, it must recognize that the same routines and complementary assets that accentuate biases also convey numerous benefits and rent streams to the firm.

There are two ends to the asset/bias continuum. At one endpoint resides the traditional hierarchical firm that obtains substantial rents from its current established assets. However, this same firm encounters huge biases in decision making. Many of the largest hierarchically-organized U.S. firms have floundered in exploring radical innovative opportunities, which has resulted in performance failure. At the opposite end of the spectrum lies what has become popularly known as the virtual corporation, lauded by Peters and others. Virtual corporations rely on the market to provide competencies. This organizational form certainly breaks down the decision-making biases identified earlier, but fails to reap substantial benefits from tangible and intangible assets.

It is our contention that as a general rule, both of these endpoint strategies are extreme and will work in only special circumstances. Rather, we argue for a middle-ground approach where managers balance and attempt to neutralize the biases that complementary assets support against the competitive advantages the assets convey.

Some firms have developed structures and incentive schemes to achieve this balancing act. Minnesota Mining & Manufacturing (3M), for example, has a corporate policy that encourages scientists and engineers to use 15% of their time on projects and ideas of their own choosing. This, combined with 3M's program that, according to Ronald Mitsch, Senior Vice President of Research and Development at 3M, "continually reassesses the barriers to innovation that tend to develop over time"[19] is designed to confront the problems of bounded rationality, framing, and isolation errors. Further, 3M regularly partners with other companies to obtain complementary assets for its research and development. In order to overcome certainty effects, 3M has a formal goal of having 30% of its sales derived from products that are new or have been substantially modified in the past 4 years. Although 3M has encouraged these frame-breaking activities, Mitsch notes that the company "continues to expand and build on two dozen core technologies. . . ."[20] He concludes that 3M always keeps "one foot in the 'comfort zone' [to enable] us to compete more successfully."[21]

Another example of a firm breaking down the biases that affect innovation while still balancing its competitive and complementary assets is Hewlett Packard (HP). Pursuing some of the same structures and strategies common to 3M, but with even more vigor, HP has quickly become one of the fastest growing giant computer companies. Seventy percent of sales is represented by products introduced or substantially modified in the past 2 years. CEO Lewis Platt notes, "Most companies our size that have been very successful got themselves in deep difficulty – IBM, DEC, General Motors, Sears Roebuck. The only mistake they made is, they did whatever it was that made them leaders a little too long. I worry every morning that I, too, will be party to holding on too long."[22] Indeed, Platt says, "We have to be willing to cannibalize what we're doing today in order to ensure our leadership in the future."[23]

Motorola provides a final example of the type of balancing strategy we suggest. In order to eliminate the decision-making biases we have elucidated in this chapter, Motorola engages in two specific strategies. First, like HP, it constantly seeks methods of self-obsoleting its current technology in order to continually push the innovation envelope of its technical assets. This strategy is deeply ingrained in the corporate philosophy and stretches back to the days when Motorola opted to cannibalize its position in AM radio by developing FM transmission techniques. Self-obsoleting continues even today with the development of the Motorola Integrated Radio Service (MIRS) that is projected to effectively supplant Motorola's lucrative cellular handset business.[24] A second strategy Motorola pursues is to decentralize decision making at the team and divisional level, and encourage spin-off projects (similar to 3M's policy). Although these two strategies are designed to overcome certainty effects, multilevel decision-making biases, and bounded rationality and framing biases, Motorola also recognizes that some of its strength lies in exploiting current assets and pursuing incremental innovation along current technology contours. Thus, in the paging business, a business that was supposed to have died years ago, Motorola continues to pursue policies to enhance product quality and improve production processes.[25]

Clearly, 3M has adopted a more conservative balancing strategy than HP and Motorola. Although all three corporations are currently quite successful, 3M is focusing more on leveraging its complementary assets, whereas HP and Motorola are pursuing structures and strategies that are more focused on breaking down innovation biases. There is no general "correct" balance point. Rather, the appropriate mix that firms should achieve along the asset-bias spectrum will depend on the nature of the industry, the characteristics of the technology, and the goals of the firm. Indeed, Chesbrough and Teece (1996), in a viewpoint consistent with this chapter, have identified the conditions under which the virtual approach to business organization is a sensible strategy. They find the characteristics of the technology and the capabilities of the firm under consideration determine the efficacy of adopting a virtual corporate form as compared to adopting alternative organizational strategies.

In some instances, gains may be derived from adopting a set of strategies that favor abandoning assets to focus on eliminating decision-making biases. For example, if complementary assets are generic, widely available in the market, and provide very low rents, firms may benefit substantially from divesting these assets. The firm will no longer be constrained to search horizons limited by those assets. Likewise, there are instances when firms may wish to ignore the decision-making biases and, instead, focus on the building, maintaining, and exploiting of established assets. This might be a particularly successful strategy in stable or regulated industries with limited entry, or where assets are highly specialized.

Throughout this chapter, we have cited examples of firms that have been afflicted with decision-making biases to the point where they lost competitive advantage. However, this condition need not be permanent. Xerox provides a good example of how a firm can rebalance its strategy and thus turnaround its operations to gain a competitive edge.

In 1974, Xerox held back from adopting a "radical" product strategy when it decided not to introduce the Alto personal computer for fear of cannibalizing the certain rents of its other word processing products (Smith & Alexander, 1988; Teece, 1992). In essence, Xerox decided to select a strategy that favored current assets. Moreover, when Xerox developed the Star personal computer in 1981, it suffered from classic framing problems in it sales force as they tried to sell the new product as a "box" (as Xerox was accustomed to) rather than a "system." Repeated incidents such as these resulted in the exit of numerous managers and subsequent leakage of innovative technology from Xerox.[26]

However, with this evident leakage of technology, partially due to current routines and biases of executives and managers, several people within Xerox responded to the situation with experimental action that led to a de facto program of technology spin-outs and internal business ventures. Under the direction of Bill Spencer, a number of companies "spun out" of PARC, where the larger firm's decision-making biases were not encountered. The research developments in these spin-outs were not strictly along the technological trajectory of the Xerox Corporation, but the technologies were nonetheless important.

Clearly the transformation of Xerox from the days of Alto and Star to its direction under Spencer resulted in a new view of the corporation toward innovation. In overcoming biases that plagued the firm in the 1970s, Spencer was able to create organizational structures, such as the spin-out program and intrapreneurship, that allowed innovators to avoid the biases of the larger corporation while still taking advantage of the complementary assets Xerox had to offer.

VI. Conclusion

This chapter has examined the underlying behavioral factors that lead to decision-making biases and suboptimal selection of innovation alternatives by the firm: bounded rationality and cognitive problem frames and inconsistent risk aversion. In bringing together perspectives from four streams of literature – behavioral decision theory, dynamic capabilities, evolutionary economics, neoclassical risk theory – we have been able to offer new insights into the innovation policies of small and large firms. In integrating the micro-organizational behavior literature into broader strategic and organizational concerns of the firm, we have sought to expand a new interdisciplinary frontier for research.

We believe that this chapter could serve as a starting point for additional work in theory of the firm. One method in which this framework could be powerfully employed is in examining the costs of bureaucracy. Many researchers have suggested that bureaucratic costs increase with corporate size. We posit here that one primary cause of the increasing costs of bureaucracy is biases in decision making. We have argued that large firms are more subject to decision-making biases due to inadequate risk pooling, multilevel decision making, certainty effects, and bounded rationality. These problems, in turn, may increase with the size of the firm and the entrenchment of established assets. This chapter suggests bureaucracy will lead to biases that move the firm away from efficient solutions to more costly ones. The ideas in this chapter may help to address the Coasian question and unpack the bureaucratic costs of markets and hierarchies.

A second direction for future work is toward a more thorough empirical examination of the relation between organizational form, firm capabilities, and decision-making biases. Firms must often select strategies that balance mitigating one bias and incrementing another. Measuring the relative impact of these biases in different organizational forms may lead to a better understanding of the merits and demerits of hybrid forms of organization.

More generally, it would be fruitful to more systematically integrate behavioral decision theory with theories of innovation. We have moved the theory forward to incorporate the implications of decision-making biases with the theory of the firm to produce initial results. Pushing this line of thinking would not only enhance our understanding of the boundaries of the organization, but might also help in comprehending the underlying decision biases that result in firm inefficiencies and technical oversights.

Acknowledgment

Helpful comments have been received from Giovanni Dosi, Raghu Garud, Rebecca Henderson, Jim March, Praveen Nayaar, Zur Shapira, Barry Staw, and participants at the New York University Conference on Technological Foresight and Oversight.

Notes

1 In this chapter, we use the terms "large" and "incumbent" interchangeably and "small," "de novo," and "entrant" interchangeably. The large firm can be thought of as a Fortune 500 or multinational firm already in the industry. The small firm can be thought of as a new entrant to, or small firm already in, the industry.

2 Notable exceptions are 3M, Sun Microsystems, Motorola, AT&T, Xerox, and Hewlett-Packard. Some of these are discussed in Section V.

3 Teece (1988) defines a firm's competence as the set of differentiated technological skills, complementary assets, and organizational routines and capacities that provide the basis for a firm's strategic advantage.

4 As Cohen and Levinthal (1990, p. 131) note, "the ability to assimilate information is a function of the richness of the pre-existing knowledge structure: learning is cumulative, and learning performance is greatest when the object of learning is related to what is already known."

5 To a lesser extent, established assets skew managerial incentives toward narrower search horizons. Incentives tied to innovation budgetary and time constraints may make the narrow search horizon which utilizes the current asset base more "profitable" for individual managers than the wider search horizon that ignores this advantage.

6 In some firms, this mistaken perception is reinforced by incentive schemes that evaluate managers with respect to return-to-assets.

7   After reviewing the effect of technological discontinuities in several industries, Foster, a Director at McKinsey & Company (1986, p. 116) concludes, "I don't know of any comprehensive statistics that would stand up to academic scrutiny, but my feeling is that leadership changes hands in about seven out of ten cases when discontinuities strike. A change in technology may not be the number-one corporate killer, but it is certainly among the leading causes of corporate ill health."

8   This does not necessarily mean that all small firms will develop radical innovations. Rather, most small firms that attempt radical innovation will fail. But radical innovation will more likely be generated from small firms than larger firms.

9   As a firm moves along a given technological and organizational trajectory, it generally becomes more and more competent in solving problems of a particular nature. However, that competence comes at cost to the firm as it creates barriers to adopting innovative, off-trajectory problem-solving routines.

10 Loss aversion is one variant on this theme that has been identified. Kahneman and Lovallo (1993, p. 18) note, "Loss aversion . . . favors inaction over action and the status quo over any alternatives, because the disadvantages of these alternatives are evaluated as losses and are therefore weighted more than their advantages. Loss aversion strongly favors the avoidance of risks." This may reinforce the excessive risk aversion noted later in this chapter and result in more incremental innovation for the incumbent firm.

11 In this analysis, we have omitted consideration of the arbitrage pricing model (APT) because the predictions for risk pooling will be similar to CAPM.

12 The literature on the CAPM model is vast. For a more comprehensive discussion of the CAPM model, see Sharpe (1964), Lintner (1965), Jensen (1972), and Modigliani and Pogue (1974).

13 Helfat (1988, p. 1) points out that the CAPM may not be a realistic model, noting, "It may be unrealistic, however, to assume that firm managers do not also have attitudes toward risk of their own; specifically, it seems unrealistic to think that as stock market investors people are risk averse, but as firm managers they are not. Firm managers may find it difficult to diversify the risk that the returns to their human capital, in the form of salary, bonuses, stock options, and so forth, are tied at least in part to the fortunes of the firm, causing managers to concern themselves with total firm risk."

14 Papers further explicating this theory include Markowitz (1952), Sharpe (1971), and Brealey and Myers (1984). For a further treatment of the implications for decision making, see Helfat (1988).

15 Kogut and Kulatilaka (1994, pp. 55, 54) note that "today's heuristics are biased toward the short-term due to the evolution of particular institutions, ways of organizing, and rules developed during this century. Consequently, they ignore or undervalue platform investments. . . . Such undervaluations are to be expected when the investments are in new ways of doing things."

16 Rigdon, Joan E. (1994). "Cannibalism is a virtue in computer business, Tandem's CEO learns," *Wall Street Journal*, 131, 38, p. 1 (August 24, 1994).

17 We also expect differential bias effects across industries. Those industries with firms heavily reliant upon a large asset base will be more susceptible to asset interaction biases than firms in low asset intensive industries.

18 These strategies include, but are not limited to, the following: "License your most advanced technology; cannibalize your most profitable products, sell off/split off new units, sell off old winners to force dependence on the new, fund kin, sell on the outside market to show fitness, purchase on the outside market to encourage fitness, subcontract anything and everything, and create numerous joint ventures and alliances."

19 Three roads to innovation, *Journal of Business Strategy*, September/October 1990, p. 18.

20 Ibid, p. 19.

21 Ibid, p. 21.

22 How H-P continues to grow and grow, *Fortune*, May 2, 1994, p. 90.

23 Ibid.

24 Keeping Motorola on a roll, *Fortune*, April 18, 1994, pp. 67–78; The company that likes to obsolete itself, *Forbes*, September 13, 1993, pp. 139–144.

25 Ibid.

26 Some of the managers and innovators that left Xerox went on to found very successful high technology companies such as 3Comm, Adobe Systems, Metaphor Computers, FileNet, and GRID Systems.

27 We obtain the marginal and cumulative risk-aversion effects predicted only with respect to radical innovations. That is, the incumbent will be relatively more risk averse than entrants with respect to competence destroying innovations. Moreover, these same incumbents will be more risk-loving than entrants along competence enhancing innovations.

References and bibliography

Abernathy, W., and Utterback, J. (1978). Patterns of industrial innovation, *Technology Review*, 80, 97–107.

Armour, H., and Teece, D. (1978). Organizational structure and economic performance, *Bell Journal of Economics*, 9, 106–122.

Brealey, R., and Myers, S. (1984). *Principles of Corporate Finance*, 2nd ed. New York: McGraw-Hill.

Buzzell, R., and Nourse, R. (1967). *Product Innovation in Food Processing: 1954–1964*. Boston: Division of Research, Harvard Graduate School of Business Administration.

Caves, R. E. (1970). "Uncertainty, Market Structure, and Performance: Galbraith as Conventional Wisdom," in *Industrial Organization and Economic Development*: In Honor of E. S. Mason. J. W. Markham, and G. F. Papanek (eds.) Boston: Houghton Mifflin.

Chesbrough, H. and Teece, D. J. (1996). When is virtual virtuous? Organizing for Innovation. *Harvard Business Review*, 74, 1, 65–73.

Cohen, W., and Levinthal, D. (1990). Absorptive capacity: A new perspective on learning and innovation. *Administrative Science Quarterly*, 35, 128–152.

Davidow, W., and Malone, M. (1992). *The Virtual Corporation: Structuring and Revitalizing the Corporation for the 21st Century*. New York: Harper Business.

Day, R. H. (1987). The general theory of disequilibrium economics and economic evolution, in *Lecture Notes in Economics and Mathematical Systems*. D. Batten, J. Casti, and B. Johansson (eds.) Berlin: Springer-Verlag. 46–63.

de Figueiredo, J. M. and Teece, D. J. (1996) Mitigating procurement hazards in the context of innovation. *Industrial and Corporate Change*, 5(2), 537–559.

Dierickx, I. and Cool, K. (1989). Asset stock accumulation and sustainability of competitive advantage. *Management Science*, 35, 1504–1511.

Dosi, G. (1982). Technological paradigms and technological trajectories, *Research Policy*, 11, 3, 147–162.

Dosi, G. (1988). Sources, procedures, and microeconomic effects of innovation, *Journal of Economic Literature*, 16, 1120–1171.

Dosi, G. and Lovallo, D. (1997). Rational entrepreneurs or optimistic martyrs? Some considerations on technology regimes, corporate entries, and the evolutionary nature of decision-making biases. Chapter 4, this volume.

Foster, R. (1986). *Innovation: The Attacker's Advantage*. New York: Summit Books.

Greene, William N. (1985). *Strategies of Major Oil Companies*. Ann Arbor: University of Michigan Research Press.

Handy, C. (1990). *The Age of Unreason*. (Boston: Harvard Business School Press).

Heiner, Ronald. (1983). The origin of predictable behavior, *The American Economic Review*, 73, 4, 560–595.

Helfat, C. (1988). *Investment Choices in Industry*. Cambridge: MIT Press.

Helfat, C. and Teece, D. J. (1987). Vertical integration and risk reduction, *Journal of Law, Economics, and Organization*. 3, 47–67.

Henderson, R. (1994). Managing innovation in the information age. *Harvard Business Review* (1-2), 100–105.

Henderson, R. and Clark, K. (1990). Architectural innovation: The reconfiguration of existing product technologies and the failure of established firms, *Administrative Science Quarterly*, 35, 9–30.

Jewkes, J., Sawers, D., and Stillerman, R. (1958). *The Sources of Invention*. New York: Macmillan (rev. ed. 1969).

Jensen, M. C. (ed.) (1972). *Studies in the Theory of Capital Markets*. New York: Praeger.

Kahneman, D. and Lovallo, D. (1993). Timid choices and bold forecasts: A cognitive perspective on risk taking, *Management Science*, 39(1) 17–31.

Kahneman, D. and Tversky, A. (1979). Prospect theory: An analysis of decision Under risk, *Econometrica*, 47-2, 263–291.

Keller, M. (1989). *Rude Awakening: The Rise, Fall, and Struggle for Recovery of General Motors*. New York: William Morrow.

Kogut, B. and Kulatilaka, N. (1994). Options thinking and platform investment: Investing opportunities, *California Management Review* 36, 2 (Winter), 52–71.

Koopmans, T. C. (1957). *Three Essays on the State of Economic Science*. New York: McGraw-Hill.

Kuhn, T. S. (1970). *The Structure of Scientific Revolutions*. (2nd Edition). Chicago: University of Chicago Press.

Kuran, T. (1988). The tenacious past: Theories of personal and collective conservatism, *Journal of Economic Behavior and Organization*, 10, 143–171.

Lintner, J. (1965). The valuation of risk assets and the selection of risky investments in stock portfolios in capital budgets, *Review of Economics and Statistics*, 47, 13–37.

March, J. G., and Shapira, Z. (1987). Managerial perspectives on risk and risk taking, *Management Science*, 33, 1404–1418.

March, J. G., and Shapira, Z. (1992). Variable risk preferences and the focus of attention, *Psychological Review*, 99, 172–183.

Markowitz, H. M. (1952). Portfolio selection, *Journal of Finance*, 7, 79–91.

Mitchell, W. (1989). Whether and when? Probability and timing of incumbents' entry into emerging industrial subfields, *Administrative Science Quarterly*, 34, 208–230.

Modigliani, F. and Pogue, G. A. (1974). An introduction to risk and return, *Financial Analyst Journal*, 30, 68–80.

Nelson, R. and Winter, S. (1982). *An Evolutionary Theory of Economic Change*. Cambridge, MA: Harvard University Press.

Peters, T. (1990). Get innovative or get dead: Part I, *California Management Review*, 33, 1, 3–26.

Peters, T. (1991). Get innovative or get dead: Part II, *California Management Review*, 33, 2, 9–23.

Rasmusen, E. (1992). Managerial conservatism and rational information acquisition, *Journal of Economics and Management Strategy* 1, 1, 175–201.

Rumelt, R. (1987). Theory, strategy, and entrepreneurship, in *The Competitive Challenge: Strategies for Industrial Innovation and Renewal*. D. Teece (ed.) New York: Harper & Row.

Russo, J. E. and Shoemaker, P. (1989). *Decision Traps: Ten Barriers to Brilliant Decision-Making and How to Overcome Them*. New York: Simon & Schuster.

Schumpeter, J. A. (1942). *Capitalism, Socialism, and Democracy*. New York: Harper.

Sharpe, W. F. (1964). Capital asset prices: A theory of market equilibrium under conditions of risk, *Journal of Finance*, 19, 425–442

Sharpe, W. F. (1971). *Portfolio Theory and Capital Markets*. New York: McGraw-Hill

Simon, H. A. (1961). *Administrative Behavior*. 2nd Ed. New York: Macmillan. Original Publication, 1947.

Smith, D. and Alexander, R. (1988). *Fumbling the Future: How Xerox Invented, Then Ignored, the First Personal Computer*. New York: William Morrow.

Teece, D. J. (1986). Profiting from technological innovation: Implications for integration, collaboration, licensing, and public policy, *Research Policy*, 15, 285–305.

Teece, D. (1988). Technological change and the nature of the firm, in G. Dosi, et al. (eds.), *Technical Change and Economic Theory*.

Teece, D. J. (1989). Book review of Helfat: Investment choices in industry, *Journal of Economic Behavior and Organization*, 11, 448–449.

Teece, D. J. (1992). *Xerox Parc and the Personal Computer (A and B)*, University of California at Berkeley Case Study.

Teece, D. J. (1994). Strategies by which technological importers can profit from innovation, University of California at Berkeley working paper.

Teece, D. J. (1996). Firm organization, industrial structure, and technological innovations, *Journal of Economic Behavior and Organization*, in press.

Teece, D. J. Rumelt, R., Dosi, G., and Winter, S. (1994). Understanding corporate coherence: Theory and evidence, *Journal of Economic Behavior and Organization*, 23, 1–30.

Teece, D. J., and Pisano, G. P. (1994). The dynamic capabilities of firms: An introduction, *Industrial and Corporate Change*, 3(3), 537–556.

Tilton, J. E. (1971). *International Diffusion of Technology: The Case of Semiconductors*. Washington, D.C.: Brookings Institution.

Tversky, A. and Kahneman, D. (1986). Rational choice and the framing of decisions, *Journal of Business*, 59, S251–S278.

Tushman, M. and Anderson, P. (1986). Technological discontinuities and organizational environments, *Administrative Science Quarterly*, 31, 439–465.

Williamson, O. E. (1975). *Markets and Hierarchies*. New York: Free Press.

Williamson, O. E. (1985). *Economic Institutions of Capitalism*. New York: Free Press.

Winn, D. (1977). Relations between rates of return, risk, and market structure, *Quarterly Journal of Economics*, 91, 157–163.

14 Organization responsiveness to environmental shock as an indicator of organizational foresight and oversight: The role of executive team characteristics and organizational context

Johann Peter Murmann and Michael L. Tushman

I. Introduction

What makes firms successful over long periods of time? Many organizational theorists have argued that organizational environments evolve through long phases of incremental change, punctuated by radical transformations. Because changing environments can dramatically alter the basis of competitive success, organizations need to transform their mode of operation to enhance their prospects of future success. Change by itself, however, is not sufficient to deal with shifting criteria of market success: organizations have to change in a speedy manner in order to avoid losing their business to incumbent rivals or new entrants who are able to offer better, cheaper, or radically new products. If organizational decision makers cannot react with sufficient speed to new competitive challenges, attempts to align the organization with a changing environment may come too late and be entirely fruitless.

A large amount of empirical evidence has demonstrated the difficulty of firms to correctly foresee technological developments or even discern these shifts while they are occurring (Maclaurin, 1949; Tushman & Anderson, 1986; Henderson & Clark, 1990). As a result, the speed in which organizations adapt to major environmental changes can represent a crucial factor in reducing or amplifying the negative impact of a lack in technological foresight. The same is true for the case of technological oversights: the faster an organization can correct its failure to ascertain shifts in the environment, the better are its chances to limit the damage such oversights can have on the future success of its business.

One of the greatest challenges for organizations is to adapt to major environmental discontinuities in a speedy manner. Reorientations are one vehicle through which organizations adapt to environmental discontinuities. The environment cannot be controlled by the organization and thus is a source of uncertainty for organizational decision makers. Organizational environments become particularly unpredictable when they undergo radical transformations often caused by legal or technological discontinuities (Meyer, Brooks, & Goes, 1990). Because many organizations are caught by surprise by these dramatic environmental changes, organizational scholars have characterized these events as environmental jolts. According to Meyer (1982), "environmental jolts are transient perturbations whose occurrences are difficult to foresee and whose impacts on organizations are disruptive and potentially inimical" (p.515).

In order to assure survival in turbulent environments, organizations often need to change radically to adapt to new environmental requirements. Because organizations consist of sets of interconnected routines (Nelson & Winter, 1982), dramatic reorienting changes are a very difficult process for an organization and thus require a mode of operation that many scholars have called second-order learning (Lant & Mezias, 1992). Tushman and Romanelli (1985) have developed the following criteria for identifying such dramatic reorientations of the organization: "Reorientations are defined by simultaneous and discontinuous shifts in strategy (defined by products, markets and/or technology), the distribution of power, the firm's core structure, and the nature and pervasiveness of control systems" (p. 147).

Although previous research has argued that reorientations affect the life chances of organizations (Haveman, 1992; Lant & Mezias, 1992; Virany, Tushman, & Romanelli, 1992), this chapter explores one of the most important factors determining the success of organization change in competitive environments, namely, the speed of organizational adaptation. Because turbulent environments are often difficult to foresee, it is important for the organization to quickly take corrective action once it becomes clear that the old organizational strategy and structure are no longer aligned with the demands of a new environment. To date, no study has examined how quickly organizations respond to environmental discontinuities. Filling this gap in the literature appears very urgent, since Bourgeois and Eisenhardt (1988) have already provided evidence that successful organizations do make decisions quickly.

The present chapter is designed to begin a line of research on organization responsiveness by examining how top management team characteristics affect the speed in which organizations initiate a major reorientation after an environmental jolt. After developing hypotheses about the effects of top management team characteristics, we examine the impact of two organizational context variables, performance and size, on the speed of reorientation. We then test these theoretical arguments on a longitudinal data set (1909–1986) of 104 firms from the U.S. cement industry.

II. Theoretical background and hypotheses

Executive team characteristics and organizational responsiveness to environmental jolts

Difference in CEO and average team tenure   One important indicator of top management team (TMT) propensity to initiate a major organizational reorientation is the average tenure of its executive members (Ancona, 1989; Katz, 1982). As the average tenure of the executive team members increases, the group becomes more set in its ways to solve problems. In addition, an older group becomes more averse toward taking the risks that reorientations in turbulent environments entail. Longer-tenured executive groups have more to lose and less to gain from risky and painful changes because their expected additional tenure at the organization is shorter than for young executives. Shorter-tenured executives also have the advantage of possessing contacts in the environment and information about the environment that is likely to be less dated than in the case of longer-tenured executives. As a consequence, longer-tenured executives may lack the skills for adapting the organization to the new organizational requirements. In terms of the process leading from sensing the environmental turbulence to carrying out a reorientation, older executive groups are likely to be characterized by lower quality of information scanning, limited or distorted perception of the objective changes in the environment, the generation of fewer responses, and the selection of preexisting response patterns that may not be appropriate for the new environment. Longer-tenured executive teams are also more likely to be committed to the status quo, resisting a fundamental change in the organization's orientation (Staw & Ross, 1978).

Focusing on the entire executive group as proposed by the upper echelon perspective (Hambrick & Mason, 1984) tends to overlook the special role of the CEO in the decision-making process of the group (Jackson, 1992). Many studies have pointed out the disproportionate, often dominating, influence of the CEO (Haleblian & Finkelstein, 1993). A CEO can initiate and block many actions taken by the team. If the CEO has a shorter tenure than the team, he/she might effectively cancel out the inertial effects associated with older teams, forcing the team to respond quickly to a changing environment. Conversely, if the CEO has a long tenure, a more vigorous, shorter-tenured team might be stalled by an inert CEO who is not capable of sensing the need for a radical change in organizational orientation. Trying to capture these internal dynamics of the executive team, we propose the following relationship.

Hypothesis 1: The lower the CEO tenure compared to the average Top Management Team tenure, the less time will elapse between environmental discontinuity and reorientation.

Heterogeneity in team tenures and functional backgrounds

The literature on groups and top management teams is marked by a long controversy about the effects of heterogeneous groups on group and organizational outcomes. A number of researchers have discovered evidence that heterogeneity hurts group performance. O'Reilly, Snyder, and Boothe (1992) showed that homogenous TMTs are better able to implement adaptive changes and to avoid political shifts. Similarly, O'Reilly and Flatt (1989) found that homogeneity is related to innovation. Other studies, however, indicate that heterogeneity leads to better outcomes. Janis's (1972) seminal research on groupthink showed that group homogeneity leads to inferior decision making. Hoffman and Maier (1961) also demonstrated that heterogeneous groups come up with better solutions to problems. Finally, heterogeneity was linked to higher levels of diversification (Wiersema & Bantel, 1992).

Team heterogeneity in terms of team tenure and functional background leads to a larger pool of cognitive resources, different skill sets, and better collective identification and utilization of the threats and opportunities in the environment. As a result, heterogenous groups are more likely to exhibit organizational learning that Levinthal's Chapter 10 identifies as an important factor in organizational success. On the other hand, team members' proposals for organizational actions in heterogeneous teams are likely to clash because of a lack of a shared language and solution set. Furthermore, rivalry for power and status between various functions (finance, marketing, engineering, etc.) with different perspectives on how to run the organization effectively will reduce consensus and potentially hinder quick decision making (Dearborn & Simon, 1958).

Because group heterogeneity was clearly shown to have conflicting effects on group performance, a more differentiating approach is called for which takes into consideration the task environment and the time horizon of the decision-making process. Filley, House, and Kerr (1976) have already proposed that routine problem solving is best handled by homogenous groups, whereas ill-defined, novel problem solving is best handled by a heterogeneous group with a diversity of opinion, knowledge, and background. The amount of time that is available for making a decision is also an important variable. In the case of operational decisions, which have to be made in a matter of minutes or hours, homogenous teams with shared outlooks will perform better and faster. However, when the group has weeks or months to decide on a course of action (which is the case in major reorientation decisions after an environmental jolt) heterogeneous teams will perform better. In Chapter 15, Van de Ven and Grazman provide compelling evidence that heterogeneous teams bring about more innovation in turbulent environments. Heterogeneous teams in turbulent environments will sense more quickly the need for an organizational reorientation and collect the information about the appropriate response. As Garud and Shapira argue so persuasively in their contribution to this book, technological choices are inherently risky and teams will sometimes make the wrong decisions. Heterogeneous teams are more capable of tolerating these inherent uncertainties and commit themselves to a course of action relatively early. This allows heterogeneous teams to initiate faster a major reorientation. Thus we propose the following link connecting variation in team tenure and functional backgrounds with organizational responsiveness.

Hypothesis 2: The greater the variation in team tenure, the less time will elapse between environmental discontinuity and reorientation.

Hypothesis 3: The greater the heterogeneity in functional backgrounds of the team, the less time will elapse between environmental discontinuity and reorientation.

Turnover

Theorists of organizational adaptation have argued that a frame-breaking change is brought about by a new top management team (Tushman & Romanelli, 1985). Similarly, researchers on organizational demography have noted that change in organizational systems occurs primarily through the introduction of new individuals (Pfeffer, 1983). The entrance of new team members and the departure of old team members brings to the executive group individuals with different perspectives, perhaps because they arrive with experience in different industries. In addition, entering members enrich the team with skills and different cognitive and informational processes. Furthermore, they are likely to possess better knowledge of changes in the environment. Jelinek's chapter describes in great detail how cognitive schemas of stable teams make it very difficult for firms in mature industries to analyze and respond to threats to their business when the information is incongruent with schema that were appropriate for previous environments. New members are not committed to the status quo and thus are characterized by higher levels of motivation for change. Hambrick, Geletkanycz, and Frederickson (1993) have empirically demonstrated that the exchange of key decision makers of the team reduces its commitment to the current course of action. Consequently, if old members want to pursue the old course, they have to justify or at least explain the organization's strategic orientation to new members. This process by itself can lead to a reexamination of the organization's orientation. In addition, a new set of players on the team forces the establishment of a new power equilibrium, potentially shifting the dominant coalition and opening up the possibility of moving the organization into a new direction. Individuals who have newly joined the organization tend to have a longer time horizon and thus a greater stake in the continued success of their organization. If these new members sense that a reorientation of the organization is necessary to ensure its future success, they are more likely to press for speedy realignment with new environmental requirements. All these factors lead us to hypothesize a positive association between turnover and organizational responsiveness.

Hypothesis 4: The greater the change in team membership, the less time will elapse between environmental discontinuity and reorientation.

CEO succession

CEO turnover has repercussions over and above the discussed effects of replacing a regular team member. Executive succession brings to the helm of the organization a completely new principal agent who has at least the formal power to initiate major strategic acts. He/she may be hired with the explicit instruction or agreement to change the entire direction of the organization. As a result, a new CEO is often granted a latitude of action and legitimacy to make radical changes that the old CEO did not enjoy (Finkelstein & Hambrick, 1990). In addition, organizations tend to give the new leader a honeymoon period during which he/she can initiate radical changes without having to convince all organizational stakeholders of the appropriateness of the action.

A number of researchers have empirically examined the effects of executive succession. As a CEO stays longer at the helm of an organization, performance tends to decline (Miller, 1991). Virany, Tushman, and Romanelli (1992) demonstrated that executive succession can reverse this trend and improve subsequent performance. This empirical evidence, together with theoretical arguments presented earlier with regard to turnover of team members and the CEO, leads us to expect a positive relation between executive succession and organizational responsiveness.

Hypothesis 5: CEO succession will be inversely associated with elapsed time between environmental discontinuity and reorientation.

CEO experience with reorientation

Because the evolution of industries is generally marked by several environmental discontinuities, CEOs with long tenures have potentially taken their organization through previous reorientations. CEOs who have guided their organization through a reorientation after a discontinuous change may develop cognitive schemas for change that will enable them to react faster to the next environmental shock.

Kiesler and Sproull (1982) have noted that "if people expect and predict change, they are likely to notice its occurrence and incorporate its implications" (p.564). CEOs who have led their organizations through risky reorientations will learn a great deal about how such a process is effectively managed. As a result, they are more able to recognize the threats and opportunities imposed by another environmental jolt. As they have developed cognitive schemas and skills for changing the organization, their own psychological barriers to initiating another reorientation may be reduced, motivating them to make a quick reorientation after a jolt. By having initiated previous reorientations, the CEO has gained the confidence and trust of the executive team and the other organizational stakeholders, making it easier and quicker for the CEO to gain agreement on the necessity of another reorientation. CEOs who have initiated previous reorientations may have created an organizational culture that regards reorientations as normal events in the institutional life of an organization. Finally, a CEO experienced with reorientations is in a better position to predict what likely resistance is going to come from the organization as a whole. As a result, prior reorientation experience of the CEO should increase the responsiveness of the organization.

Hypothesis 6: The greater the CEO's experience with reorientations, the less time will elapse between environmental discontinuity and reorientation.

Executive team context and organizational responsiveness to environmental jolt

Performance   Whether or not the top management team will sense the need and feel the pressure to align the organization with the changed environment and whether it is capable of initiating a reorientation will be influenced to a great extent by the context in which the team operates. Although performance is often a dependent variable in organizational research, few studies have examined performance as an important independent measure for explaining organizational outcomes. A few researchers (Hambrick, Geletkanycz, & Frederickson, 1993) have begun to uncover the importance of performance as a catalyst for organizational decision making.

Because reorientations are consequential strategic acts, high organizational performance has a tendency to act as a blinder and cover up dangers coming from a changing environment. High-performing organizations are likely to have slack that buffers them against environmental changes; members of the organization will realize much later that the organization is no longer properly adapted to the environment. In a study of publicly held firms of the furniture and computer software industries, Lant, Milliken, and Batra (1992) have found that poor performance leads to a higher likelihood of organizational reorientation. Poor organizational performance and the threat of failure provide the executive team with legitimacy to try new courses of action and reorient the organization. More organizational stakeholders are willing to give up some of their dearly held prerogatives and turfs when the future existence of the organization is at risk, creating the sociological impetus and political room to change the basic orientation of the organization.

In addition, negative performance induces greater risk-taking behavior by organizational decision makers. Kahneman and Tversky (1979) presented persuasive evidence that decision makers take greater risks in connection with negative outcomes. Such psychological processes should increase the likelihood of quick reorientation for low performing organizations. All these psychological and sociologicàl factors suggest:

Hypothesis 7: The higher an organization's performance, the more time will elapse between environmental discontinuity and reorientation.

Size   The process of carrying out a reorientation in large organizations creates different dynamics and forces than in small organizations. Large organizations are typically regarded as inert things, incapable of changing their orientation in a speedy manner. Not surprisingly, organization theorists have long linked organizational size with bureaucratic inertia. Our final hypothesis specifies the relationship between size and reorientation speed.

Hypothesis 8: The smaller the organization , the less time will elapse between environmental discontinuity and reorientation.

III. Methods

Sample

The current study draws from a population of 291 firms that constituted the United States cement industry between 1909 and 1986. A total of 104 firms were selected in a two-stage process to reduce the cost of data collection, while ensuring a representative sample. Half of the firms were chosen through a random stratified sample for the purpose of identifying cohorts. The other half of the firms were selected because their long life-spans made them particularly suitable to study adaptive processes over time. While this nonrandom half of the sample may introduce a bias toward successful long-living firms, it provides us with the opportunity to test our hypotheses with a longitudinal research design. The data were collected on a yearly basis for the 104 firms from the *Annual Cement Directories* (1901–1986), published by Bradley Pulverizer, and from two technical journals, *Rock Products* and *Pit and Quarry*. Every firm in the sample is surveyed each year until it ceases producing cement, was sold, merged, or went bankrupt, or until the end of the data collection period.

Dependent variable

We measured responsiveness of organizations to major environmental jolts as the number of years that elapse between a jolt and reorientation. The evolution of the cement industry was shaped both by legislative/regulatory and by technological discontinuities. An analysis of the cement industry found that cement firms faced legislative/regulatory jolts in the years 1909, 1917, 1923, 1948, 1956, 1967, and 1969. In addition, technological discontinuities jolted cement firms in 1960 and 1972.

Reorientations were coded when an organization changed its strategy (adding cement types and brands, adding cement plants, and/or distribution centers) and its structure (divisionalizing, adding functions, adding and/or consolidating senior positions) over a maximum period of 2 years. The history of the cement industry was divided into 9 jolt periods that start in the year of a legislative/regulatory jolt or technological jolt and come to end in the year before the next jolt. For every one these jolt periods, we counted how many years after the jolt a firm would go through a reorientation. When an organization had not initiated a reorientation in the year the next jolt occurred, the value of the dependent variable for this particular jolt period was identified as a censored data point.

Independent variables

Executive team characteristics

Difference between CEO tenure and average team tenure   (CEO tenure minus team tenure). The distance in terms of tenure between the CEO and the team was measured as the number of years the CEO was already in his/her position minus the average number of years all team members were on the team.

Variation in team tenure.   We employed the standard measure for calculating a coefficient of variation in team members' tenure by taking the standard deviation of team tenure and dividing it by the mean.

Heterogeneity in functional backgrounds.   The functional categories were finance and accounting; production and operations; research and development; special services (such as transportation, public relations, and distribution); marketing; and general management or not otherwise classified. The functional category for each individual was identified by the associated title. If no function was identified (e.g., simply VP is listed), the executive was placed in the general category. The measure for functional heterogeneity was calculated by using the Gibbs-Martin Index, where p_i equals the proportion of team members in each functional category (Blau, 1977). Higher numbers of the index indicate more functional heterogeneity.

$$\left(FH = 1 - \sum_{i=1}^{n} p_i^2 \right)$$

Change in team membership.   We operationalized the turnover in the team as the sum of the number of executives who entered in a given year and the number of executives who left the team in a given year. This total fluctuation measure was standardized by team size in order to control for purely size effects.

CEO succession.   CEO succession was measured as a dummy variable. If a new person was listed as the CEO in a given year, the variable was coded as a one. When no CEO was listed for a firm, the variable was coded as a one when the chairman of the board left the firm. If for a given firm neither a CEO nor a chairman was listed, the CEO succession variable was coded as a one when the president left. Otherwise, it was coded as a zero.

CEO experience with reorientations.   We measured the experience of a CEO with reorientations as the number of times he/she was present and in the CEO position as the firm went through a reorientation. A CEO's experience with reorientation in other firms was not counted because such data was not obtainable.

Organizational context

Performance.   We operationalized performance as return on assets. Other performance measures were explored and yielded similar results

Size.   Size was measured as the total production capacity of the firm. Production capacity is a particularly good measure of firm size because it is not sensitive to changes in labor or capital intensity that occurred over the period studied.

Model specification

Because our model attempts to predict the length of time it will take an organization to initiate a reorientation after a jolt, the explanatory variables have to be measured at the jolt. In order to obtain more reliable estimates of the top management team and context variables at the jolt, we measured explanatory variables for each organization as the average of the values at the jolt year and its previous year.

Because many organizations do not initiate a reorientation in a given jolt period,[1] it was necessary to employ an accelerated event-time model. Unlike regular regression techniques, accelerated event history models as the failure time procedure in SAS (Proc Lifereg) are capable of estimating the effects of unobserved reorientations on the model. Thus the model takes into account the right censoring of the data that occurs when the dependent variable is measured before all firms had sufficient time to initiate a reorientation.

The Lifereg procedure requires the specification of an underlying distribution (Mitchell, 1989). We selected the loglogistic distribution because it seemed most appropriate for the underlying data. To test the stability of our models, we estimated the same models with an exponential distribution and a gamma distribution, obtaining very similar results.

Because a preliminary analysis suggested that the context variable size had a particularly strong effect and some executive team characteristics seemed to have little effect, we estimated four models to isolate the explanatory power of some particularly interesting variables. Model 1 contains all variables except size. Model 2 is the full model with all variables. Model 3 drops the CEO succession and change in team membership variables from Model 1, because they do not add to the explanatory power of the model. Model 4 adds the size variable to Model 3. Table 14.2 presents the numeric results of all four models. The highest correlation between any of the explanatory variables was 0.341 (Table 14.1 presents all correlations along with other descriptive statistics).

Time until
reorientation = f (CEO tenure minus average team tenure, Variation in team tenure, Heterogeneity in functional backgrounds, Change in team membership, CEO succession, Performance, Size)$^2_{\{Mean (Jolt Year, Jolt Year - 1)\}}$

IV. Results

Hypothesis 1 predicted that when the CEO has a shorter team tenure than the average team member, the organization will respond more quickly to a jolt. The hypothesis was confirmed at the 0.10 level when change in team membership and CEO succession, two variables that did not add to the explanatory power of the model, were dropped (Models 3 and 4). Models that include the two variables (Models 1 and 2) do not provide significant confirmation of the hypothesis, although the sign of the relationship is in the predicted direction.

Hypothesis 2 examined the effect of variation in team tenure on organizational responsiveness. As predicted, we found that teams with heterogeneous tenures are more capable of initiating a quick reorientation than homogeneous teams. The strongest support for this hypothesis comes from Model 3, which is significant at the 0.01 level.

Hypothesis 3 linked the top management team's heterogeneity in functional backgrounds to the responsiveness of the overall organization. It was predicted that greater functional diversity in the team will make it more capable of initiating a quick response to dramatic environmental changes. Strongly supporting evidence (at the 0.01 significance level) emerges from Model 3, whereas Model 1 provides marginally significant support at the 0.10 level. When the size variable is included in the models, we do not find

Table 14.1. Descriptive statistics (mean, standard deviation, range, and Pearson correlation for data set entering into the Lifereg Analyis)

	Mean	Std dev	Range	Correlation coefficients											
				2.	3.	4.	5.	6.	7.	8.	9.	10.	11.	12.	13.
1. Mean team tenure	9.31	5.10	1–29.5	0.435	−0.309	0.256	−0.102	−0.372	−0.087	0.107	0.063	0.153	−0.259	0.354	0.039
2. CEO tenure	7.00	7.01	0–46.5		0.721	0.100	0.070	−0.182	−0.342	0.067	−0.153	0.194	−0.193	0.070	0.109
3. CEO tenure minus team tenure	−2.3	6.41	−19.8 – 29.75			−0.091	0.004	0.069	−0.294	−0.011	−0.210	0.090	−0.02	−0.0174	0.085
4. Variation in team tenure	0.54	0.32	0–1.42				0.224	0.217	−0.182	0.305	0.467	−0.162	0.251	0.532	−0.119
5. Heterogeneity in functional backgrounds	0.47	0.15	0–0.781					0.104	0.056	0.200	0.215	−0.128	0.168	−0.219	−0.146
6. Change in team membership	0.19	0.23	0–1.4						0.341	0.031	0.145	0.004	0.185	−0.093	−0.021
7. CEO succession	0.10	0.22	0–1							0.057	0.350	−0.208	0.263	0.016	−0.018
8. CEO experience with reorientations	0.34	0.61	0–3.5								0.362	−0.322	0.324	0.333	−0.176
9. Number of organization reorientations	1.29	1.8	0–8									−0.389	0.623	0.458	−0.242
10. Performance	0.16	0.09	−0.03 – 0.34										−0.293	−0.200	−0.021
11. Size	7M	8.7M	0.36M–41.5M											0.185	−0.253
12. Age	36	23	1–97.5												−0.279
13. Time until reorientation	5.68	5.93	0–25												

Note: N ranges from 271 to 373. All correlations whose absolute value is below 0.09 are not significant; All correlation whose absolute value is above 0.16 are significant at 0.01 level; M = Million.

Table 14.2. Accelerated event-time estimates (dependent variable = time until reorientation)

Independent variables (Average of the jolt year and its prior year)	Model 1 (N = 257)	Model 2 (N = 232)	Model 3 (N = 261)	Model 4 (N = 242)
CEO tenure minus team tenure	0.015	0.019	0.022*	0.022*
	(0.013)	(0.014)	(0.013)	(0.013)
Variation in team tenure	−0.818**	−0.639*	−0.902***	−0.624*
	(0.335)	(0.379)	(0.3 35)	(0.359)
Heterogeneity in functional	−1.140*	−0.599	−1.370***	−0.644
backgrounds	(0.642)	(0.646)	(0.628)	(0.639)
Change in team membership	0.096	0.178	(0.493)	(0.513)
CEO succession	−0.426	−0.273	(0.411)	(0.439)
CEO experience with	−0.472***	−0.415**	−0.467***	−0.403**
reorientations	(0.152)	(0. 165)	(0.152)	(0.163)
Performance	2.944**	2.270**	3.146***	2.375**
	(1.184)	(1.182)	(1.183)	(1.167)
Size		−3.82E−8***		−3.88E−8***
		(1.105E −8)		(1.079E−8)
Intercept	2.983***	2.920***	3.117***	2.919***
	(0.443)	(0.441)	(0.493)	(0.440)
Scale	0.723	0.693	0.728	0.694
	(0.057)	(0.057)	(0 .057)	(0.057)
Model loglikelihood	−240.8	−211.6	−242.9	−211.7
No-covariate loglikelihood	−317.3	−317.3	−317.3	−317.3
Loglikelihood chi-squared	153.0***	211.4***	148.8***	211.2***
Pseudo r-squared	0.219	0.308	0.219	0.314

$^{***}p<0.01$, $^{**}p<0.05$, $^{*}p<0.10$ (standard errors in parentheses).

significant evidence for the hypothesis, although the sign of the relationship is in the predicted direction.

Hypothesis 4 examined the impact of change in team membership on the organization's speed of reaction. Neither Model 1 nor Model 2 provides significant evidence in favor of the prediction that higher levels of change in the top management team will lead to quicker organizational reorientation. The exact same result emerged with respect to Hypothesis 5. We did not find evidence that CEO succession will make the organization more capable of a quick reorientation.

Hypothesis 6 predicted that a CEO who has prior experience with reorientations will lead the organization more quickly to another reorientation in the wake of an environmental jolt. All four models provide strong support for the hypothesis.

Hypothesis 7 investigated whether high performance slows down the process of organizational reorientation. Again, all four models provide significant support for the hypothesis that high performance creates inertia, making the organization less capable of responding quickly to environmental discontinuities.

The final hypothesis (8) argued that smaller organizations will go through a reorientation faster than large organizations. Both models that included the size variable (Models 2&4) provide highly significant evidence that larger size—not smaller size as predicted—is an advantage in bringing about a quick response to environmental discontinuities. This unexpected result will be examined in greater detail in the discussion section.

In order to assess the explanatory power of all covariates in the model, we compared each of the four covariate models to a model without covariates. This comparison makes it possible to estimate the increase in the explanatory power of the models with covariates. As shown in Table 14.2, all four models lead to a highly significant increase in the loglikelihood chi-squared statistic. Pseudo r-squared statistics based on the loglikelihood statistic indicate that the models explain between 0.219 percent and 0.314 percent of the variance. Adding the change in team membership and the CEO succession variables (Models 1&2) does not improve the fit of the model.

An evaluation of all four models, in addition to a supplementary analysis not shown in the tables, indicates that the executive team variables and the context variables as groups account approximately for half of the explained variance. With four executive teams variables displaying roughly the same amount of explanatory power as two context variables, the models suggest that each context variable has more explanatory power than each executive team variable taken individually.

V. Discussion

This study, to our knowledge, represents the first attempt to link executive team characteristics and context to organizational responsiveness. We have consciously started the investigation of reorientation speed by focusing on directly observable executive team demographics and critical context variables. We found strong support for most of our hypotheses concerning the executive team characteristics and all of our context variables. Greater difference in CEO tenure compared to team average, greater variation in team tenure, higher functional heterogeneity, CEO experience with reorientations, poor organizational performance and, surprisingly, larger size were associated with short response times as predicted. To our knowledge, this is the first time in the organizational literature that a measure of the difference between the CEO tenure and average team tenure has been used to capture the dominating influence of the CEO while not neglecting the important role of the entire executive group in organizational decision making. Previous studies typically have either argued for the dominating influence of the CEO and left out the important role of the team as a whole, or they have argued for the importance of the entire team without taking into consideration the special role of the CEO on the team (Miller, 1991; Halebian & Finkelstein, 1993). Our measure of the difference in tenure of the CEO and the average team tenure is one way to account better for the internal dynamics on top management teams that help shape organizational outcomes.

Contrary to our hypothesis, we found that not smaller but larger organizational size leads to a quicker organization reorientation. The surprising result that small organizations appear to be characterized by more inertia than large organizations makes it necessary to reconsider our theoretical reasons for predicting that large organizations are less responsive. It appears that size represents more than complicated ways of communication and a multitude of levels in organizational decision-making processes. Size may also be a function of past organizational success that does not show up in the current performance measures at the time of the jolt. Organizations may have become large because they have during an earlier stage in their life successfully delivered an important output, creating further demand for their products and services. In addition, organizations that have previously learned to deal with environmental turbulence may tend to grow larger as other organizations fail. In a detailed case study on how hospital organizations reacted to an environmental jolt, Meyer (1982) found that large organizations, indeed, adapted more successfully to an environmental jolt. Similarly, Haveman (1993) furnished evidence from the savings and loan industry that large organizations are often more likely to change their strategies than small organizations. This evidence, along with the present findings, suggests that some organizations may learn to institutionalize routines for organizational reorientations and subsequently thrive and become large. Another important factor may be that large organizations more often have strategic departments whose specific goal it is to monitor threats and opportunities in the environment and propose organizational responses. As a result, large organizations may tend to be responsive to major environmental changes despite their complexity. The present findings clearly call for a reexamination of the inertia arguments in organizational theory.

With regard to executive team turnover and CEO succession, we found no significant relationship to organizational responsiveness. To explore these results in greater detail, we compared the levels of our independent variables at the jolt and at the time of reorientation. The goal was to ascertain whether organizations have changed their team characteristics since the time of the jolt in order to be capable of bringing about a reorientation. We found statistically significant evidence that organizations, at the moment they go through a reorientation, display more CEO succession, more top management team turnover, more heterogeneity in functional backgrounds, lower performance, and bigger size compared to the jolt year (For the numerical results, see Table 14.3.) These additional pieces of evidence lend further support for our hypotheses linking top management team and context variables to the ability of carrying out reorientations. The levels of executive team turnover and CEO change are both higher when the organi-

Table 14.3. *T-test comparison of independent variables at jolt year and the reorientation year*[1]

	Mean at jolt	Mean at reorientation	Mean difference	Std dev	T-value	Prob>|T|
Ceo tenure minus team tenure	−3.280	−3.678	0.397	0.505	0.786	0.433
Variation of team tenure	0.679	0.711	−0.032	−0.021	−1.498	0.137
Heterogeneity of functional backgrounds	0.501	0.522	−0.021**	0.008	−2.519	0.013
Change of team membership	0.221	0.267	−0.047**	0.022	−2.090	0.039
Ceo succession	0.180	0.240	−0.060*	−0.273	−1.804	0.074
Ceo experience with reorientations	0.634	0.888	−0.254***	0.035	−7.127	0.0001
Performance	0.156	0.135	0.016*	0.008	1.989	0.050
Size	10,438,621	11,003,650	−81 0470***	251207	−6.789	0.001

***$p<0.001$, **$p<0.05$, *$p<0.10$.
N ranges from 81 to 108.
[1]T-tests are based on the average of independent variables at jolt year and its prior year *minus* the average of independent variables at the reorientation year and its prior year.

zation goes through a reorientation in contrast to when the jolt surprises the organization. Evidently, old executive teams adapt to environmental turbulence by recruiting new members and new CEOs in order to regain the ability to initiate organizational orientations.

VI. Conclusions

This study represents the first systematic examination of speed of organizational responsiveness and has yielded important results for thinking about organizational foresights and oversights. We have uncovered evidence that both executive team characteristics and context have an impact on organizational responsiveness. We have found that shorter CEO tenure compared to team average, greater variation in team tenure, greater functional heterogeneity, CEO experience with reorientations, larger size, and poor performance are associated with faster reorientation speeds. Applying the upper-echelon perspective and organizational demographics as a first approach to identify the factors that influence organizations' speed of reorientation has proved to be very fruitful and promising for future research.

Our arguments relating observable executive team demographics to the speed of organizational reorientation are largely based on assumed but unobserved cognitive processes. Jelinek's Chapter 11 complements our research as it focuses on cognitive factors in explaining organizational outcomes by interviewing key decision makers. The evidence provided by these interviews with incumbent management teams shows in a direct way how important it is to maintain an appropriate pool of cognitive resources and fresh perspectives at the highest level of the organization. When executive groups are not rejuvenated with new members who bring a different set of beliefs, cognitive skills, and experiences into the team, organizations may not be able to overcome the inherent inertia that is associated with schemas and routines that were created in different environmental conditions.

The next step in this line of research would be to design an empirical study that would test in more detail the connection between response speed and organizational foresight and oversight. Our understanding of the significance of response speed for organizational success would be greatly enhanced if we had a more precise assessment as to what extent the speed of organizational adaptation determines how costly oversights can be for organizations. Similarly, whether an organization is capable of acting with foresight may depend to a large degree on how fast it can implement a decision. A foresight not acted upon with sufficient speed can very well end up being a dramatic oversight!

Notes

1 Many organizations in our sample never went through a reorientation in their lifetimes, making a statistical procedure for estimation right censored data imperative.
2 The number of previous reorientations of an organization and organizational age were excluded as control variables because of high multicollinearity with our explanatory variables.

References

Ancona, D. (1989). Top management teams: Preparing for the revolution. In J. Carroll, (ed.). *Social Psychology in Business Organizations*. New York : Erlbaum.
Blau, P. M. (1977). *Inequality and Heterogeneity*. New York: Free Press.
Bourgeois, L. J. and Eisenhardt, K. M. (1988). Strategic decision processes in high velocity environments: Four cases in the microcomputer industry. *Management Science* 34, 7, 816–835.
Dearborn, D. C. and Simon, H. A. (1958). Selective perception: A note on the departmental identification of executives. *Sociometry* 21, 2, 140–144.
Filley, A. C., House, R. J., and Kerr, S. (1976). *Managerial Process and Organizational Behavior*. Glenview, IL: Scott Foresman.
Finkelstein, S. and Hambrick, D. C. (1990). Top-management-team tenure and organizational outcomes: The moderating role of managerial discretion. *Administrative Science Quarterly* 35, 484–503.

Haleblian, J. and Finkelstein, S. (1993). Top management team size, CEO dominance, and firm performance: The moderating roles of environmental turbulence and discretion. *Academy of Management Journal* 36, 4, 844–863.

Hambrick, D. C., Geletkanycz, M. A., and Frederickson, J. W. (1993). Top executive commitment to the status quo: Some tests of its determinants. *Strategic Management Journal* 14, 401–418.

Hambrick, D. C., and Mason, P. A. (1984). Upper echelons: The organization as a reflection of its top managers. *Academy of Management Review* 9, 193–200.

Haveman, H. A. (1992). Between a rock and a hard place: Organizational change and performance under conditions of fundamental environmental transformation. *Administrative Science Quarterly* 37, 1, 48–75.

Haveman, H. A. (1993). Organizational size and change: Diversification in the savings and loan industry after deregulation. *Administrative Science Quarterly* 38, 1, 20–50.

Henderson, R. M. and Clark, K. B. (1990). Architectural innovation: The reconfiguration of existing product technologies and the failure of established firms. *Administrative Science Quarterly* 35, 9–30.

Hoffman, L. R. and Maier, N. R. F. (1961). Quality and acceptance of problem solutions by members of homogeneous and heterogeneous groups. *Journal of Abnormal and Social Psychology* 62, 2, 401–407.

Jackson, S. E. (1992). Consequences of group composition for the interpersonal dynamics of strategic issue processing. *Advances in Strategic Management*. Greenwich: JAI Press, pp. 345–382.

Janis, I. L. (1972). *Victims of Group Think*. Boston: Houghton Mifflin Company.

Kahneman, D., and Tversky, A. (1979). Prospect theory: Analysis of decision making under risk. *Econemetrica* 47, 262–291.

Kiesler, S., and Sproull, L. (1982). Managerial responses to changing environments: Perspectives on problem sensing from social cognition. *Administrative Science Quarterly* 27, 371–381.

Lant, T. K., and Mezias, S. J. (1992). An organizational learning model of convergence and reorientation. *Organization Science* 3, 1, 47–71.

Lant, T. K., Milliken, F. J., and Batra, B. (1992). The role of managerial learning and interpretation in strategic persistence and reorientation: An empirical exploration. *Strategic Management Journal* 13, 8, 585–608.

Maclaurin, W. R. (1949). *Invention and Innovation in the Radio Industry*. New York: MacMillan.

Meyer, A. D. (1982). Adaptation to environmental jolts. *Administrative Science Quarterly* 27, 515–537.

Meyer, A. D., Brooks , G. R., and Goes, J. B. (1990). Environmental jolts and industry revolutions. *Strategic Management Journal* 11, 93–110.

Miller, D. (1991). Stale in the saddle: CEO tenure and the match between organization and environment. *Management Science* 37, 1, 34–52.

Mitchell, W. (1989). Whether and when? Probability and timing of incumbents' entry into emerging industrial subfields. *Administrative Science Quarterly* 34, 2, 208–230.

Nelson, R. R. and Winter, S. G. (1982). *An Evolutionary Theory of Economic Change*. Cambridge: The Belknap Press of Harvard University Press.

O'Reilly, C. A. and Flatt, S. (1989). *Executive Team Demography, Organization Innovation and Firm Performance*. Working paper, University of California, Berkeley.

O'Reilly, C. A., Snyder, R. C., and Boothe, J. N. (1992). The effects of executive team demography on organizational change. *Organizational Change and Redesign: Ideas and Insights for Improving Managerial Performance.* New York : Oxford University Press.

Pfeffer, J. (1983). Organizational demography. *Research in Organizational Behavior.* Greenwich, CT: JAI Press, pp. 299–357.

Staw, B. M. and Ross, J. (1978). Commitment to a policy decision: A multi-theoretical perspective. *Administrative Science Quarterly* 23, 40–64.

Tushman, M. L. and Anderson, P. (1986). Technological discontinuities and organizational environments. *Administrative Science Quarterly* 31, 439–465.

Tushman, M. L. and Romanelli, E. (1985). Organizational evolution: A metamorphosis model of convergence and reorientation. *Research in Organizational Behavior.* Greenwich, CT : Jai Press, pp. 171–222.

Virany, B., Tushman , M. T., and Romanelli, E. (1992). Executive succession and organization outcomes in turbulent environments: An organizational learning approach. *Organization Science* 3, 1, 72–91.

Wiersema, M. F. and Bantel, K. A. (1992). Top management team demography and corporate strategic change. *Academy of Management Journal* 35, 91–121.

15 Technological innovation, learning, and leadership

Andrew H. Van de Ven and David N. Grazman

Introduction

In keeping with the theme of this book on technological oversights and foresights, this chapter examines the forms of intelligence that can guide the process of developing and commercializing technological innovations. The innovation process is an ambiguous and uncertain journey in which entrepreneurs, with financial support and approval from top managers or investors, undertake a sequence of events to develop and transform a vague novel idea into a concrete implemented reality. Several years of intensive investment and effort are often required to develop an innovation to the point where its end results can be determined. As a consequence, much of the innovation journey involves an adaptive learning process to deal with conditions of *ambiguity* (i.e., where it is not clear what specific preferences or objectives should be pursued to reach a vague superordinate goal) and *uncertainty* (i.e., where it is not clear what means of actions will achieve desired outcome goals).

However, two prior field studies of learning processes during innovation development by Van de Ven and Polley (1992) and Garud and Van de Ven (1992) found no evidence of trial-and-error learning during the initial pre-market period of innovation development, but clear evidence of it during the ending market-entry period when the specific innovations were being commercialized and introduced in the market. *Trial-and-error learning* is an adaptive process in which entrepreneurs continue with their course of action if the outcomes associated with it are positive, and they change their course of action if the associated outcomes are negative. In both studies, the initial period of innovation development began when an entrepreneurial team was formed and funded to explore an innovative idea, and ended 4 to 6 years later when innovative products were developed and ready for market introduction. This period was characterized by high ambiguity on which of several possible technical designs should be pursued for development. The ending market-entry period lasted another 3 to 4 years, and dealt with uncertain but less ambiguous problems of scale-up manufacturing, marketing, and market introduction of the technical designs that were developed in the earlier period.

The failure to find evidence of trial-and-error learning during the beginning premarket period was examined in subsequent studies of the patterns of events that unfolded during this initial period of innovation development by Cheng and Van de Ven (1995) and Polley and Van de Ven (1995). These studies empirically found that the actions taken by innovation units and the outcomes they experienced reflected a seemingly random, chaotic pattern during the beginning premarket period, and a more orderly pattern of trial-and-error learning during the ending market-entry period of innovation development.

This prior research raises more questions than it answers. Why did the top managers who invested in and periodically reviewed innovation progress not provide order to the seemingly random behaviors of their innovation teams? Why did their innovation teams not engage in a process of trial-and-error learning during the premarket period of innovation development? Do these prior studies suggest that the innovation teams and their leaders learned nothing during their initial 4 to 6 years of innovation development? Or do the findings mean that the innovation units and leaders engaged in some other type of knowledge acquisition that was not captured by the model of trial-and-error learning examined by the researchers? This chapter addresses these questions in an inductive way by describing and analyzing the behaviors and perceptions of top managers as they conducted periodic administrative reviews of their innovations.

Part I of this chapter describes three common patterns in the behaviors of top managers that were observed in real time during the beginning and ending periods of innovation development: (1) many (not one or a few) top managers at different hierarchical levels were actively involved in the development of innovations within their organizations; (2) these top managers typically did not reflect unified and homogeneous perspectives; instead, they held opposing views and performed roles that served as checks and balances on each other in making innovation investment decisions; and (3) over time, the top managers made pragmatic decisions in response to changing innovation conditions and perspectives held by other top managers, rather than according to a planned course of action.

These observed patterns provide the key ingredients for proposing a dynamic view of innovation leadership in Part II of the chapter. This view departs from popular treatments of leadership by arguing that in uncertain and ambiguous situations, organizational learning and adaptability are enhanced by achieving balance between diverse, opposing, and conflicting views among top management decision makers. The common quest for consensus and support among top managers to a single strategic vision of a leader at the top of the pyramid is not effective for dealing with highly ambiguous and uncertain situations. Instead, these situations call for a pluralistic power structure of leadership that incorporates the requisite variety of diverse perspectives necessary to make uncertain and ambiguous innovation decisions. Although a homogeneous structure of power and leadership is efficient for well-understood tasks, it tends to squelch consideration of diverse and opposing viewpoints inherent in ambiguous tasks. Thus, pluralistic leadership increases the chances for technological foresights and decreases the likelihood of oversights. However, such a pluralistic structure does not ensure intelligent leadership. Instead, it emphasizes that the odds of organizational learning and adaptability increase when a balance is maintained between dialectical leadership roles throughout innovation development.

I. Observed behaviors of innovation leaders

The Minnesota innovation studies

The data on which this chapter is based come from the Minnesota Innovation Research Program (MIRP). As described by Van de Ven, Angle, and Poole (1989), this program consisted of longitudinal field studies undertaken during the 1980s by 14 different research teams (involving over 30 faculty and doctoral students) who tracked the development of a wide variety of product, process, and administrative innovations from concept to implementation or termination. Although the research teams adopted different methods and time frames that fit their unique circumstances, they adopted a common conceptual framework. This framework focused on tracking changes in five concepts that were used to define innovation development. The process of innovation was defined as the development of new *ideas* by *people* who engage in *transactions* (or relationships) with others within a changing environmental *context* and who change their behaviors based on the *outcomes* of their actions. Comparisons of innovations in terms of these five concepts permitted the researchers to identify and generalize overall process patterns across the innovations studied. Many of these patterns are discussed in Van de Ven, Angle, and Poole (1989).

More specific evidence for some of these developmental patterns was limited to a few innovations that were studied using detailed real-time observations of the developmental process. In particular, in this study of innovation leadership we will focus on two such fine-grained studies undertaken by Polley and Van de Ven (1989) of the development of therapeutic apheresis and by Garud and Van de Ven (1989) of the development of cochlear implants. The cochlear implant program (CIP) ran from 1977 to 1989 as an internal corporate venture to create an implanted device allowing profoundly deaf people to hear. The therapeutic apheresis program (TAP) existed between 1981 and 1988 as a joint venture of three corporations

to create a biomedical technology that treats autoimmune diseases by removing pathogenic blood components. Using event sequence methods described in Van de Ven and Poole (1990), both studies consisted of longitudinal field studies of the events that occurred in the development of the two
biomedical innovations from the time funding and efforts began to initially
develop the innovation until the innovations were commercially implemented in the market. Using the five core MIRP concepts, events were defined as instances when changes were observed in the development of the
innovation idea, the innovation managers, the transactions or relationships
they engaged in with resource controllers and other organizational units,
the external context beyond the control of the innovation team and judgments of positive or negative outcomes associated with these events. Van de
Ven and Polley (1992) and Garud and Van de Ven (1992) describe how these
events were further coded and analyzed to examine the model of trial-and-
error learning referenced in the introduction.

Based on the overall patterns identified across the MIRP innovations, and
detailed study of these patterns in the CIP and TAP innovations, we will
now describe the common behaviors of top managers or resource controllers regarding the innovation projects in which they invested.

Active and collective leadership

In a comparison of the innovations studied by MIRP researchers, Schroeder
et al. (1989) report that top management teams exercised very active
"hands-on" leadership roles. These managerial roles appeared to vary as
different problems or opportunities unfolded for an innovation. Leadership
involvement did not appear to diminish over the life cycle of innovation development; it remained relatively constant over time of innovation development from concept to implemented reality.

Statistical evidence of the active involvement of leaders in the innovation
process is shown in Figure 15.1. The backgrounds of the graphs plot the total number of events that were observed in the development of the TAP and
CIP innovations. The shaded time series in Figure 15.1 indicate the number
of times that the top managers were directly involved in the total events: 49
of 325 events in TAP, and 81 of 719 events in CIP. As we will see below (Figures 15.3 and 15.4), these events involved many (not just one or a few) top
managers located at different hierarchical levels in the development of CIP
and TAP.

These data remind us of an important distinction made by Baveles (1960)
between the idea of leadership as a personal quality and the idea of leadership as an organizational function. The first continues to be the dominant
view of leadership, and leads us to look at the qualities, abilities, or behaviors of the individual leader at the top of the organizational pyramid. The
second, which is more congruent with our data, refers to the distribution of
decision-making power and influence throughout an organization. It leads

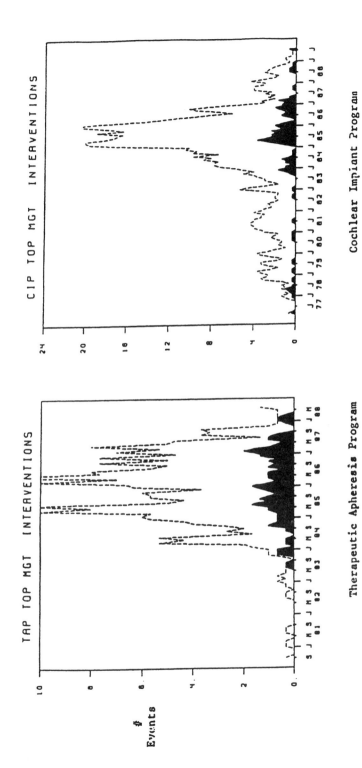

Figure 15.1. Number of events involving top managers of TAP and CIP innovations.

us to look at the patterns of influence and power exercised by organizational participants, and the specific conditions or situations when they exercise leadership.

> In these terms we come close to the notion of leadership, not as a personal quality, but as an organizational function. Under this concept it is not sensible to ask of an organization, "Who is the leader?" Rather we ask "How are the leadership functions distributed in this organization? The distribution may be wide or narrow. It may be so narrow – so many of the leadership functions may be vested in a single person – that he [she] is the leader in the popular sense. But in modern organizations this is becoming more and more rare (Baveles, 1960, 494–495).

This point of view is consistent with that of Katz and Kahn (1978, 571) who define leadership as acts of influence (beyond mechanical compliance with routine directives) on organization-relevant matters by any member of the organization. It suggests that almost any individual in an organization may act as a leader, and that different persons may contribute in different and diverse ways to the leadership of the organization. Indeed, in their review of leadership research, Katz and Kahn (1978, 572) linked the distribution or sharing of leadership behavior with organizational effectiveness. Because the sharing of influence increases the quality of decisions and the motivation of organizational participants, Katz and Kahn proposed that the more influential (i.e., leadership) acts are widely shared in an organization, the more effective the organization.

What are these leadership acts? Baveles suggested that they consist of influential behaviors that reduce an organization's uncertainty in making decisions and achieving objectives. Because our topic deals with innovation leadership, we can take a more concrete and restricted view by focusing on the behaviors of individuals in managerial positions that influence the commitment of organizational resources (money, personnel, and ideas) to the development of innovations. This limits our examination to the behaviors of upper echelon executives who, by virtue of their organizational positions, have legitimate authority to influence innovation investment decisions.

Innovation leadership roles

Angle and Van de Ven (1989) examined the behaviors of top managers or investors in the innovations studied by the researchers. They report that top managers at different levels in the organizational hierarchies did not reflect unified and homogenous perspectives; instead, they often expressed opposing views and performed roles that served as checks and balances on each other in directing the innovation developmental process within their organizations. As Figure 15.2 illustrates, Angle and Van de Ven (1989) identified four different kinds of leadership roles: sponsor, critic, institutional leader, and mentor. Whereas the corporate sponsor or champion role is well known (see the seminal article by Schon, 1963), the roles of critic, mentor, and institutional leader have not received adequate attention. Much of the innovation literature has focused too exclusively on the champion/sponsor role (see review in Howell and Higgens, 1990), and this inhibits theory building because any role logically assumes a counter-role.

A role is an expected set of behaviors of persons occupying an organizational position (Graen, 1976, 1201). Roles are what actors in positions do (Stryker and Statham, 1985, 323). Roles are both socially constructed (through interactions) and institutionally prescribed by the structure of rules and responsibilities of actors in positions vis a vis other organizational positions. When an actor assumes an organizational position, we expect certain behaviors from the actor in relation to other actors. On the part of the role incumbent, certain behaviors become extensions of the role itself, influenced by the ongoing interactions between the role occupant and others in the role set. Based on these expectations, we behave differently toward that actor in comparison with actors in other positions.

An important implication of this view of role relationships is that any role assumes a counter role; each role is dependent on others in its constellation or role set. Conceptual myopia occurs when one focuses exclusively on a single position without reference to other interdependent positions. (Stryker and Statham, 1985, 323). Thus, just as it is incomplete to discuss a leader without a follower, a plaintiff without a defendant, or a proponent without an opponent, it is equally incomplete to examine an innovation

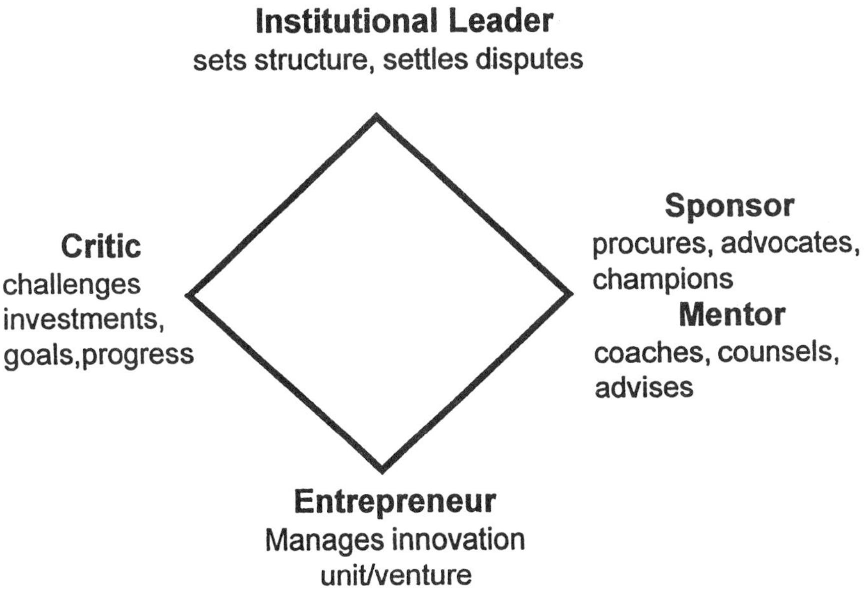

Institutional Leader
sets structure, settles disputes

Sponsor
procures, advocates, champions
Mentor
coaches, counsels, advises

Critic
challenges investments, goals, progress

Entrepreneur
Manages innovation unit/venture

Figure 15.2. Leadership roles involved in innovation development. *Source:* Angle and Van de Ven (1989), p. 681.

champion or sponsor without explicit reference to the other roles it juxtaposes. Empirically, there may be unbalanced situations where only one role, such as a champion, is dominant or evident. These situations are unbalanced not because of the exercise of one role, but because of the lack of exercise of other roles in the set. In these and other situations, explanations of how and why a champion behaves are usually found in the relative influence and behavior of other roles in the organization. Indeed, the success or failure of an innovation champion is more often produced by the behaviors of other interdependent role actors (such as the entrepreneur, critic, or institutional leader) than it is by the actions or intentions of the champion role actor.

In the innovations studied by the MIRP researchers, Angle and Van de Ven (1989) observed that the sponsor or champion role was typically performed by a manager sufficiently high in the organizational hierarchy to command the power and resources to push an innovation idea into good currency. This sponsor was an advocate for the innovation and its entrepreneur in corporate and investor circles where investment decisions were made. The sponsor, also "ran interference" within the corporation for the innovation. Like all the leadership roles, the sponsor role could be performed by more than one person.

Closely related to the sponsor role was a mentor role, which could be distinguished in some organizations through a division of labor. Whereas the sponsor role involved activities of procuring, advocating, representing, and championing an innovation at upper-echelon executive levels, the mentor role entailed coaching, counseling, and advising activities with innovation entrepreneurs on a more direct and daily basis. The mentor role was typically performed by an experienced and successful innovator, who was assigned or assumed managerial responsibility to coach (and perhaps supervise) the innovation manager or entrepreneur. Mentors served as role models for the innovation team leader and, in combination with innovation sponsor, provided encouragement, guidance, and other types of support to the entrepreneur.

In the interest of checks and balances, the role coalition represented by innovation sponsor and mentor was often counterbalanced by a critic role. This role was performed by a "devil's advocate," who applied dispassionate "hard-nosed" business criteria to the innovation, and forced the corporate sponsors and entrepreneurs to reexamine their assumptions and alternative courses of action to develop their innovations. The critic role was evident in administrative review meetings when certain top managers challenged and questioned entrepreneurs about innovation project investments, goals, or progress. Perhaps more than any other role, the critic's role was likely to be shared by several persons.

Balancing these opposing roles was the role of institutional leader, which was often performed by an executive who was removed from the "battlefield," as it were, and therefore less subject to the partisan myopia that afflicted those closer to the innovations. The institutional leader maintained a balance of power between the pro-innovation influences of the sponsor–mentor coalition and the reality-testing influences of the critic, so that conflicts could be solved based on the merits of the case, rather than on power alone. In addition to settling disputes, the institutional leader role was also evident when organizational structures and arrangements were established or modified to enable and constrain innovation activities.

In visualizing the power dynamics among these leadership roles, one is drawn to Davis and Lawrence's (1977) analogy of a diamond of relationships among the general manager, project manager, functional manager, and "two-boss" manager in a matrix organization. As illustrated in Figure 15.2, at the top of the diamond is the institutional leader role – performed by a person who is concerned with the innovation as only one of a family of responsibilities. This psychological distance from the innovation, per se, allows a breadth of perspective not easily attained by the more immediate actors. In the middle of the diamond are the two opposing liberal and conservative forces: (1) the champion-mentor coalition, and (2) the critic. At the bottom of this diamond is the entrepreneur or innovation project manager, who is exposed to this dialectical field of forces.

The top of Figures 15.3 and 15.4 plot the cumulative frequencies in which these leadership roles were exercised during the development of the TAP and CIP innovations, respectively. In both figures, the total leadership events are the same as the cumulative numbers of events involving top managers shown in Figure 15.3. These leadership events were classified into sponsor, critic, and institutional leadership roles according to the definitions stated above for these roles. Two researchers coded these events; they agreed on 93% of the cases, and disagreements were resolved by mutual consent. Figures 15.3 and 15.4 combine mentor events with sponsor events because there were too few mentoring events in the TAP and CIP cases to warrant a separate breakout.

As might be expected by the extraordinary energy necessary to mobilize resources and support for launching new ventures, Figures 15.3 and 15.4 show that in both innovations, the corporate sponsor role was performed almost twice as often as the critic role. In the case of TAP, being a joint venture among three organizations, the cumulative occurrence of the institutional leadership role exceeded that of the sponsor role, whereas in the CIP internal corporate venture, the institutional leader role was as prevalent as the critic role. This indicates that a joint interorganizational venture requires greater involvement of an institutional leader to create new enabling structures and arrangements between organizational partners for an innovation than is required for an innovation undertaken within an organization.

The bottom half of Figures 15.3 and 15.4 show the number (and percentage) of times that individual executives – identified by the positions they occupied in their organizational hierarchies – performed in the roles of sponsor, critic, and institutional leadership for the TAP and CIP innova-

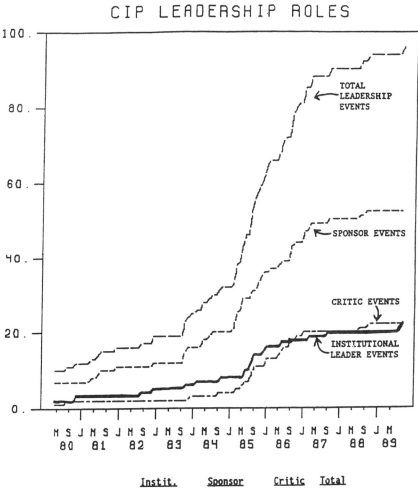

Figure 15.3. Frequencies of leadership roles and executives performing them in CIP.

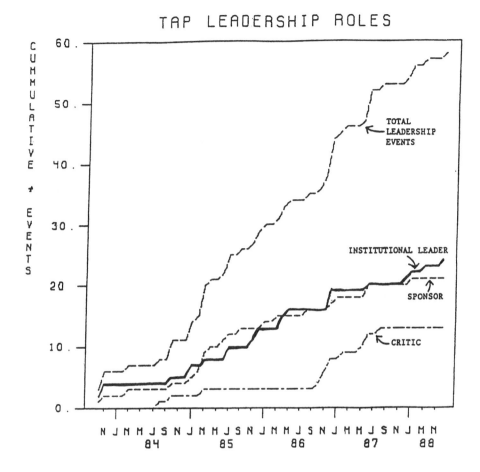

Figure 15.4. Frequencies of leadership roles and executives performing them in TAP.

tions, respectively. In the case of TAP, ACO, BCO, and CCO are the fictitious names of the three organizations involved in the joint venture, and the most active Group VP is a senior executive of ACO. In the case of CIP, the executives are listed in hierarchical order. In both cases, the committee is a corporate-level resource allocation board comprised of the executives listed plus other top managers.

The data in Figures 15.3 and 15.4 clearly show that each individual executive who was involved in more than one event performed at least two or more of the leadership roles. Contrary to popular notions that executives are consistent in their role behaviors (Meindl, Ehrlich, & Dukerich, 1985), the data show a surprising flexibility in which each executive shifted roles or performed multiple leadership roles over time with respect to the TAP and CIP innovations. These data support the notion of examining leadership as the distribution of roles in an organization, rather than as a characteristic of the person at the top of the pyramid.

Relationships among leadership roles

Across the innovations studied by the Minnesota researchers, Angle and Van de Ven (1989) observed that innovations encountered significant hurdles in cases where one or more of these leadership roles were absent. For example, a new company startup did not enjoy the umbrella of legitimacy and credibility provided by an institutional leader, nor was the counsel of a mentor available. Both deficits significantly hindered the ability to engage in business transactions with large customers and distributors. In addition, the board initially consisted only of inside directors, which limited the exposure of company principals to the kinds of divergent perspectives provided by critics in the corporate settings.

Angle and Van de Ven (1989) note that these leadership roles also serve as checks and balances on each other in guiding innovation development. For example, the innovation sponsor ran interference for the project at corporate levels, while a mentor provided direct supervision, coaching, and counseling to the innovation unit. The counterbalancing role to this coalition was the critic, which was often expressed by challenging and questioning the reality or wisdom of an innovation's goals, budgets, and schedules in terms of "bottom-line" business criteria and priorities. Without this role, the propensity of innovation sponsors to delude themselves and others by seeing ambiguity through rose-colored glasses might exhaust organizational resources by investing the corporate treasury "down a rat hole." On the other hand, were the critic to be able to run unchecked, no venture might be allowed a chance to succeed, because innovation is an inherently risky undertaking. Thus, the institutional leader's role is that of a power broker, ensuring that supports and restraints for the innovation are reasonably well balanced.

These patterns of checks and balances among the leadership roles were not immediately evident in the event sequence data, which show that managers encountered numerous issues, distractions, and "noise" in real time from one event to the next. Decision-making patterns became apparent by undertaking two steps. First, from the database we selected only those events that pertained to a substantive issue or debate that was known in retrospect to have occurred during the CIP or TAP innovation journeys. Then we examined the leadership roles and interactions among top managers that unfolded in the event stream on a given substantive issue or debate.

We will now exemplify how relationships among the leadership roles unfolded over time with a brief examination of an important debate in each of the CIP and TAP cases. However, we place a caveat on the analysis that follows. While it was difficult for us as nonpartisan real-time observers and as analyzers of recorded transcripts to detect the patterns of leader interactions and their effects, we speculate that it is highly unlikely that these processes were apparent to the participants involved in the issue streams. In other words, the reconstructions that we present here appear logical and knowable only in retrospect; in real time, the decision-making processes were probably neither.

II. CIP single versus multiple channel technology debate

One issue stream that influenced the development of CIP related to the question of whether to pursue the development and commercialization of a single or multiple channel technology for cochlear implants. In lay terms, the issue dealt with whether to surgically implant one or many electrodes deep inside the cochlea of the ear of profoundly deaf people so they could hear. The CIP story begins at the time when a single-channel device was available and clinical trials found it to be safe. Multichannel devices were not yet available for clinical trials, but otologists were claiming that this more sophisticated but unproved device would be safe and provide more efficacious hearing. Throughout the course of the CIP program, its managers were engaged in discussions about which technology would be the more prudent to pursue. Table 15.1 presents the chronological sequence of events on this issue, coded in terms of the dominant leadership roles exercised in each event, and a characterization of their content. We will briefly summarize the events below; Garud and Van de Ven (1992) and Van de Ven and Garud (1993) describe the events in greater detail.

During the initial uncertain and ambiguous period of CIP's gestation, the distribution of leadership roles among managers was skewed towards sponsor behaviors, with little influence of either institutional or critic roles. Because top corporate managers each participated in multiple innovation projects simultaneously, those who chose to act as cochlear implant (CI) sponsors[1] encountered little criticism for their pursuit, nor was there significant institutional scrutiny of the project for almost 3 years. This period of high ambiguity and uncertainty about CIs continued until late in 1980,

Table 15.1. CIP leadership role events (pertaining to the single (SC) versus multiple channel (MC) issue stream)

Date	Leader Code	Activity
03/02/78	S	SC/MC technologies explored with external organizations
03/02/78	S	SC technology explored with external organization
02/02/79	S/I	Commitment made to acquire SC technology
07/31/79	S	Goals communicated internally
08/15/80	C	Doubts expressed about program goals
11/01/80	I	Central group organized to consolidate operations
04/17/81	S	Internal justification of pursuing both SC and MC devices
07/21/81	S	Strategic plan authored for three generations of devices
12/01/81	S	Agreement made to pursue SC technology with external organization
12/02/82	S/I	CEO visits other organization to show commitment
10/21/83	I	Agreement altered to reflect focus on MC
12/06/83	C	Joint venture agreement for MC device rejected
02/24/82	I	Funds allocated internally for SC and MC development
04/20/84	S	Sector Review: Additional funds requested, SC device supported
06/18/84	S	Need for leadership in MC technology recognized
09/04/84	C	Funding levels for SC questioned, MC development encouraged
02/11/85	S	Funding levels for MC placed under scrutiny
05/06/85	S	Sector Review: MC technology favored
10/11/85	S	Clinician writes letter in support of SC pursuit
10/20/85	S	In response to letter, CIP sends letter to clinician emphasizing MC
12/17/85	S	CIP team awaits additional funding for MC
01/16/86	C	SC viability questioned; various concerns expressed
05/11/86	S	Sector Review: General funding levels for CIP lowered
06/20/86	I	Executive Committee approves involvement in hearing aid market
07/15/86	C	Portion of CIP program sold to outside organization
10/21/86	I	Acquisition of small organization
01/22/87	C/S	Pressure increased to shift focus from cochlear implants to hearing aids
03/01/87	S	MC technology receives renewed focus
09/15/87	I/C	SC technology sold off; development on MC postponed
09/14/88	S	Clinician attempts to revive SC efforts of CIP

Totals: 20 (55.9%), Sponsor, 6 (20.6%), Critic, 7 (23.5%), Institutional Leadership Role Events

when corporate sponsors began to consolidate company CI-related activities by establishing the CIP as a formal innovation unit. By this time, sponsor behaviors had succeeded in developing a number of external relationships with research institutes that were involved in the development of single-channel CIs. Beginning in 1981, corporate executives acting as institutional leaders became involved in agreeing to these interorganizational relationships and in setting the organizational structures and operating parameters of the CIP. To legitimate these agreements, the CEO of the corporation visited a venture process, and by doing so increased his familiarity with the details of the CI technology and program.

The critic role surfaced in response to these changes and increasingly visible activities by institutional and sponsor role behaviors. In December 1983, critics prevented a joint venture agreement that would have pushed the multiple-channel device as a clear priority. They believed that the technology was not yet clinically proven and were unwilling to support the heavy R&D that such a task would require. Critics had called into question the legitimacy of pursuing both single and multiple channel CI technologies. In February 1984, institutional leaders decided to fund the development of both technologies, but in a sector review held in April 1984, sponsors were able to obtain support for accelerating the single channel program to "neutralize" the threat of multiple-channel devices in the marketplace. By May 1985, the apparent threat had disappeared and with continued critic involvement countering sponsors' activities, institutional leaders began to question the single channel device's market potential. After reviewing funding levels for both technologies, the institutional sector review committee determined that developing the multiple channel device was now the preferred course of action.

During the ensuing year critics and sponsors were actively involved in debates over which device had the most market potential, which device would be safer in patients, and appropriate funding levels allocated by the organization. An atmosphere of uncertainty characterized the CIP program team as it sought to define conclusively the mission it had set for itself. In May 1986, institutional actors again became involved during the annual sector review. However, instead of settling the debate between sponsors and critics, the review committee lowered overall funding levels for the project and suggested that managers more activity pursue the hearing aid market. Critics seized upon this lack of institutional support for the CIP, and advocated dismantling the program altogether. However, corporate sponsors generated sufficient support in the spring of 1987 to continue the pursuit of a multiple channel device. But these efforts did not materialize, as the corporation divested the CIP by selling its CI technology, patents, and assets to a former competitor in September 1987.

III. Defining the TAP joint venture agreement

The TAP innovation venture was the product of an agreement among three organizations to combine their technological, research, and business capabilities to develop a blood filtration device that could separate pathogenic substances from a patient's blood to treat a variety of autoimmune diseases. However, even with careful contracting and due diligence, the definition of the relationship between the organizations became a source of ongoing confusion and misinterpretation. We therefore chose to focus on this issue stream of defining the joint venture agreement among the three parent organizations. See Table 15.2 for a listing of the chronological events and leadership roles relevant to this debate, Polley and Van de Ven (1995) describe these events in greater detail.

Because TAP was an interorganizational joint venture, the institutional leader role was called upon to lay the framework in which the coventuring organizations would perform their respective portions of the project. Talks between the organizations began in January 1981, by executives acting as

Table 15.2. TAP leadership role events (pertaining to the defining of the TAP joint venture agreement issue stream)

Date	Leader code	Activity
01/01/81	I	ACO and BCO discuss apherisis cooperation
03/01/83	S	ACO and BCO begin formal joint venture discussions
06/01/83	I	ACO executives intervene to assist joint venture discussions
11/16/83	I	ACO and BCO sign joint venture agreement; SBU formed.
03/01/84	S	Confusion expressed concerning responsibilities
10/29/84	S	ACO managers discuss expanding scope of ACO/BCO joint venture
03/12/85	S/C	BCO accuses ACO of changing philosophies about the agreement
07/15/85	I/S	ACO manager visits BCO to renegotiate joint venture agreement
11/13/85	I	BCO reorganizes along business lines
03/26/86	S	ACO discusses dropping BCO as venture partner
04/05/86	I	BCO managers, including CEO, killed in plane crash
10/01/86	C	ACO manager suggests looking outside BCO for manufacturing function
12/01/86	I	TAP reorganizes business and marketing teams; CCO becomes subsidiary of ACO
12/10/86	S	Discussions of synergies between TAP and CCO
12/11/86	I/C	BCO manager agrees to forego 50% of next year's royalty income
12/11/86	I/C	BCO funding levels fall due to financial problems
02/09/87	C	BCO management unhappy with TAP delays
06/01/87	I/C/S	ACO discusses imbalance of spending levels and proposes an adjustment
06/25/87	S	Joint ACO/BCO review of TAP; BCO dissatisfied with ACO's commitment
12/29/87	I	ACO terminates agreement with BCO
01/18/88	I/S	ACO and BCO lawyers meet to unravel agreement
03/09/88	I	ACO and BCO lawyers continue to work through legal issues
06/16/88	I	Final agreement on asset distribution by ACO and BCO

Totals: 9 (31.0%) Sponsor, 6 (20.7%) Critic, 14 (48.3%) Institutional Leadership Role Events project sponsors primarily interested in sharing and combining technical and business capabilities to develop apheresis. However, no results materialized from these talks until the CEOs of the respective organizations met and informally agreed to promote the strategic alliance. This informal agreement legitimated and authorized entrepreneurs and sponsors to mobilize interest within and between their respective organizations. In November 1983, the agreement was signed and the institutional actor's role in the definition of the relationship disappeared until July 1985.

In the interim managers acted as sponsors and critics in propelling the project along. However, throughout 1984 and 1985, confusion continued to permeate the relationship. In March 1984, managers of ACO wrote an official memo outlining issues of misunderstanding related to the TAP agreement. Although there was uncertainty about the TAP venture, corporate sponsors indicated in this memo that, "The embryonic nature of this program, the investment risk, and the need to minimize the effect on our existing business dictate this unique structure." While trying to coordinate the efforts of scientists and engineers involved in developing the blood filtering device, managers, acting as both sponsors and critics, were still trying to establish the precise form the agreement would take. Sponsors advocated exploring more cooperation among the organizations during October 1984, while critics questioned the levels of commitment of each party. Executives and entrepreneurs from each organization expressed concern in March 1985 that the other party was "backing off' from the original philosophy of the joint venture agreement and that goals were being redefined through objection rather than strategic action.

Leadership roles in 1986 remained relatively balanced. After a reorganization by one of the partners, managers seemed to enjoy a bit more clarity into the nature of the relationship. Although other partners were considered for additional funding to the joint venture during the autumn of 1986, significant problems arose in the relationship when one partner experienced internal financial problems and expressed discontent with the delays in commercializing the TAP device. With financial difficulties a reality for one of the partners, more emphasis was placed on lowering the probability that any chosen action would make matters worse rather than better.

During 1987 sponsors and critics both within and between the coventuring firms countered one another's proposals on alternative courses of action and budget levels to commit to the program. During an administrative review meeting of the program in late 1987, a senior executive from one of the partners intervened by informing the other parties that his organization would make no further financial investments in TAP beyond December 1987, and that another investor should be found to join the venture. Failing several attempts to negotiate acceptable agreements with potential investors, executives of the sponsoring organizations agreed to terminate the TAP joint venture. For the next 18 months, the TAP entrepreneurial unit occupied itself by solving technical design problems at a significantly reduced budget level with the diminishing hope that a new investor would be found at the last minute, while institutional leaders and their lawyers deconstructed the legal relationship, distributed assets, and formally terminated TAP in June 1988.

IV. Balance and timing of leadership roles

A normative implication from the foregoing description of the TAP and CIP innovation journeys is that the balance and timing of different leadership roles are related to an organization's capability to manage uncertainty and ambiguous processes. Specifically, *we propose that the likelihood of organizational learning and adaptability increase when the temporal order and degrees of involvement of the leadership roles occur in the manner illustrated in Figure 15.5.*
The rationale for this proposition is as follows. The entrepreneurial role represents the major source of energy for developing an innovation, and its exercise is therefore expected to be a relatively constant upper bound on the involvement of alternative leadership roles during innovation development.

In the CIP and TAP innovations, we observed that the critic role did not emerge with sufficient strength to counter the sponsor role until late in the developmental period and after the entrepreneurial venture had already encountered significant mistakes and setbacks that were, perhaps, avoidable. We believe that the timing of the critic's role came too late, and tended to increase the odds of terminating (rather than correcting) an innovation venture. We propose that the critic role is most constructive in the initial period of innovation development, because it forces sponsors and entrepreneurs to

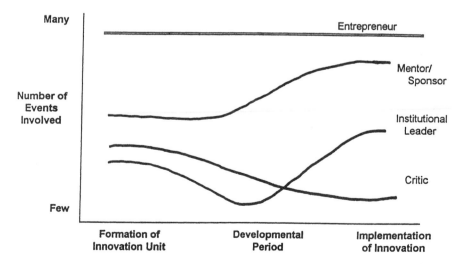

Figure 15.5. Timing of leadership roles during successful innovation development.

rethink and explore alternative plans and budget requests for launching their innovation.

In both CIP and TAP, the roles of innovation sponsor and mentor were observed dominant during the first half of the innovation development period, but then tended to subside when innovation development problems could not be adequately addressed in response to the questions by critics, which gained strength and legitimacy among top managers. These observations suggest that following the support needed to make an initial investment decision, the roles of innovation sponsor and mentor become increasingly important over time. This is especially true in the middle of the innovation journey, when entrepreneurs most need support and coaching to correct mistakes. The sponsor's role is also critical during the implementation period, when managers make key decisions to integrate and link the innovation with the strategic directions of the firm.

As stated before, the role of the institutional leader is critical in balancing the often opposing views of the critic and sponsor or mentor. With timing, the institutional leader's role appears most critical at the very beginning of an innovation to legitimate the venture's initial formation and investment, and at the implementation period when institutional established to diffuse and adopt the innovation are built. During the middle period of innovation development, exercise of institutional leadership is necessary only to the extent of intervening in irreconcilable conflicts that may surface between opposing critic and sponsor/mentor coalitions and result in stalemates that impede further innovation development.

The pluralistic structure of leadership roles described here comes close to the strategy initially proposed by Thompson and Tuden (1959) for inspirational decision making. According to Thompson and Tuden (1959, 504) the ideal structural design for making decisions under conditions of uncertainty (disagreement on means) and ambiguity (disagreement on goals or ends) is the following:

(1) the individuals or groups must be interdependent and thus have some incentive for collective problem-solving, (2) there must be a multiplicity of preference scales and therefore of factions, with each faction of approximately equal strength, (3) more information must be introduced than can be processed, and it must be routed through multiple communication channels, and (4) each member must have access to the major communication networks, in case [or in the hope that] inspiration strikes.

This pluralistic structure for inspirational decision making represents a significant departure from popular treatments of leadership, which emphasize unity and consensus among the top management team members to a single strategic vision of the leader at the top of the pyramid. A unified homogeneous leadership structure is effective for routine trial-and-error learning by making convergent, incremental improvements in relatively stable and unambiguous organizational situations. However, this kind of learning is a conservative process that serves to maintain and converge organization-al routines and relationships toward the existing strategic vision. As Levinthal discusses in Chapter 12, although such learning is viewed as wis-dom in stable environments, it produces inertia and competency traps in changing worlds.

Highly ambiguous, uncertain, and changing situations, such as innova-tion development, require a more pluralistic leadership structure that en-courages the requisite variety of diverse perspectives needed for learning by discovery (Polley & Van de Ven, 1995). This type of learning entails mindful alertness to anomalies (Jelinek & Litterer, Chapter 13) a shift in core assumptions and decision-making premises; the development of new inter-pretive schemes (Bartunek, 1993) and unlearning prior premises and estab-lished routines (Viraney, Tushman, & Romanelli, 1972). Whereas routine tri-al-and-error learning reduces variety by focusing on a singular vision, learning by discovery increases variety and diversity of perspectives from which new understandings and objectives can emerge (Hedberg, Nystrom & Starbuck, 1976). Thus, a pluralistic leadership structure increases the chances for technological foresights and decreases the likelihood of over-sights.

However, a pluralistic structure does not ensure intelligent leadership. Instead, it emphasizes that the odds of organizational learning and adapt-ability increase when a balance is maintained between dialectical leadership roles throughout innovation development. Such a structure places tremen-dous strains on the institutional leadership role in preventing the upper echelon executive team from flying apart into a state of anomie. Philip Selznick (1957) understood this precarious situation by emphasizing that one of the key functions of institutional leadership is to order internal and external conflict.

Interest groups form naturally in large-scale organizations, since the total enterprise is in one sense a polity composed of a number of suborganizations. The struggle among competing interests always has a high claim on the attention of leadership. This is so because the direction of the enterprise as a whole may be seriously influ-enced by changes in the internal balance of power. In exercising control, leadership has a dual task. It must win the consent of constituent units, in order to maximize voluntary cooperation, and therefore must permit emergent interest blocs a wide de-gree of representation. At the same time, in order to hold the helm, it must see that a balance of power appropriate to the fulfillment of key commitments will be main-tained (Selznick, 1957, 63–64).

Achieving such internal diversity is difficult to maintain. Perhaps, this is why organizations with executive teams that value contradictory perspec-tives and keep them in balance are seldom observed. However, studies of these exemplary outliers provide some useful clues. First, Levinthal (in Chapter 12) discusses structural mechanisms for maintaining diversity within the firm by establishing multiple sources of resources and bases of legitimate authority that promote multiple communities of practice or learning groups.

Second, Bartunek (1993) points out that achieving balanced internal diversity requires strong institutional leadership to tolerate the ambiguity of holding multiple perspectives, to be able to truly balance the power between managers with different perspectives, and to enable their interaction toward a creative outcome. In the cases where she observed such balanced internal diversity, institutional leaders used a negotiation approach to issue management, like that described by Ury, Brett, and Goldberg (1988). She notes that where this negotiation style was used, the eventual resolution of conflicts brought about a more complex and creative understanding than had been present before. The outcomes occurred in part because powerful people were able to hold and respect different perspectives, both their own and that of others (Bartunek, 1993, 343). Whenever conflicting positions exist, Bartunek (1993, 337) warns that a cooperative, facilitative style that assumes shared interests is more likely to increase the underlying conflict and the possibility of significant oversight, whereas a negotiation approach that consciously builds on different perspectives is more likely to succeed.

The demographic composition, experience, and turnover of top management team members represent a third set of factors related to achieving balanced internal diversity. Empirically, Sutcliffe (1994) found that accuracy of environmental perceptions by top management teams is a function of the diversity of experiences and intensity of organizational scanning by top managers. In addition, Tushman and Murmann (in Chapter 11) show that heterogeneity in functional backgrounds of executive teams is related to shorter response times to initiate a strategic reorientation after an environmental jolt. However, conflicting evidence comes from a study of 85 Fortune 500 firms by Wiersema and Bantel (1993), who found that heterogeneity in educational backgrounds or tenure of top management teams were unrelated to firm strategy, performance, and environmental conditions. Instead, they found that environmental instability and resource scarcity were directly related to top management team turnover and firm strategic change.

Complementary with the findings of Wiersema and Bantel, a longitudinal study of 59 minicomputer firms by Virany, Tushman, and Romanelli (1992) discovered two modes of successful organizational adaptation in this turbulent industry. The most typical mode combined sweeping CEO and executive team turnover and strategic reorientations. A more rare, and over the long-term more effective, adaptation mode involved strategic reorientations and moderate executive team changes, but no CEO turnover. Virany, Tushman, and Romanelli (1992) state that this rare set of extraordinarily successful organizations had relatively stable executive teams that initiated reorientations to stay ahead of turbulent environmental conditions:

[They] were able to balance relative stability in the senior team along with fundamental organization change. These executive teams initiated second-order learning not through sweeping executive-team and/or CEO change, but through reorientations in the context of executive-team stability. These unique executive teams seem to possess an ability to learn not through executive-team change, but through changes in how they work together. (p. 89)

The typical mode of organizational reorientations through sweeping top management turnovers either indicates an unusually high rate of "bad luck" or a common failure within top management teams to maintain the requisite internal diversity of perspectives and learning processes necessary to deal with environmental ambiguity and change. This typical mode supports Virany, Tushman, and Romanelli's conclusion (1992, 89) that "executive succession can be a powerful lever for improving organizational performance." However, this lever also admits to a learning failure by the top management team, and must therefore be pulled again when the next environmental jolt occurs, if the organization is to retain its ability to adapt.

V. Concluding discussion

Managers of multiyear innovation development projects, such as TAP and CIP, hope to achieve ultimate project success by making periodic investments in a learning process that reduces the uncertainty and ambiguity of an innovative idea into a concrete implemented reality. The downside risks of this process are the possibilities of making Type I and II errors. As Chapter 18 by Garud, Nayyar, and Shapira discusses, Type I errors, or "false positives," consist of investing in innovation projects that turn out to be unsuccessful, whereas Type II errors, or "false negatives," are decisions not to invest in projects that eventually achieve success elsewhere. The likelihood of making Type I and II errors is a function of the (1) the *uncertainty*, or predictive validity of the relationship between ex-ante project investment decisions and ex-post project success, (2) the *ambiguity* of knowing what investment decision hurdles to use and what specific performance targets or outcomes should be pursued to achieve a vague superordinate goal, and (3) the *risk aversion* of decision makers.

Project uncertainty may be described by the correlation between the ex-ante investment decision and ex-post project success or failure. This correlation tends to be low (near zero) when making an initial investment in an inventive idea, and to increase over time as a result of what is learned through trial and error between periodic continued investments in the project. Only by increasing the predictive validity of this relationship can both types of errors be simultaneously minimized. As the correlation between project selection decisions (x) and outcome success (y) increase along the range of $0.00 > r_{xy} > 1.00$, the likelihood of Type I and II errors decrease while the probability increases of accepting successful projects and rejecting projects that turn out to be failures.

However, Shapira (1995) points out that having criteria for project selection and performance outcomes are necessary preconditions for establishing the predictive validity of this relationship. In this sense, reducing project ambiguity is a precondition for reducing project uncertainty. The ambiguity of knowing what criteria to use for project selection and what desired performance outcomes to target can only be learned through discovery. This discovery process is largely dependent on the repertoire of experiences and perspectives of decision makers. The broader and more diverse this base of experience among decision makers, the lower the ambiguity in knowing what specific decision hurdles and outcome targets to apply to multiyear investment projects.

Finally, the risk aversion of decision makers is a key factor because it is widely recognized that greater returns often come from projects associated with higher levels of ambiguity and uncertainty. Depending on the risk orientation of managers and the salience of the particular rewards and penalties associated with errors of omission or commission, costs associated with any entrepreneurial decision must implicitly include a willingness to err either toward a Type I or Type II error.

Viewing leadership as a set of interdependent roles for guiding periodic investment decisions in the development of innovations has important implications for understanding the likelihood of Type I and II errors. The relative balance and timing of the leadership roles shown in Figure 15.5 proposes a leadership structure that is highly pluralistic when beginning the innovation development stage and increasingly unified at the innovation implementation stage. During the initial period of innovation development, we argued that a pluralistic structure encourages the surfacing of multiple and diverse perspectives that are needed to reduce innovation ambiguity and uncertainty. When this diversity and conflict is kept in balance through institutional leadership, such a pluralistic structure should increase the chance of technological foresights and reduce the likelihood of oversights. As levels of project ambiguity and uncertainty decrease, the likelihood of Type I and II errors decreases. In these cases a more traditional homogeneous structure of leadership is appropriate for mobilizing a unified and efficient organizational implementation effort of the innovation.

We conclude by discussing the likely consequences of imbalances in the exercise of sponsor, critic, and institutional leadership roles. Of the four leadership roles considered, the sponsor is more actively involved in an innovation than the critic or institutional leader, only the entrepreneur is a more active participant. The appropriate proportion of involvement on the part of the sponsor, as illustrated in Figure 15.5, was greater than the other two roles with an increased prevalence later during the development period and the implementation of the innovation, as a sponsor's involvement helped pave the way for the successful commercial introduction of the new technology.

An imbalance in the sponsor role, however, can result in both Type I and Type II errors. When sponsors are too actively involved early on, perhaps to a level more likely associated with the entrepreneur who enjoys day-to-day involvement in a project, errors of commission (Type I errors) are likely to occur as a result. Excessively enthusiastic efforts on the part of the sponsor can trigger initial investments, that through a recurrent cycle of sensemaking and justification (Weick, 1993) can lead to an escalation towards those courses of action later determined commercial or technological failures. The opposite situation is not enough involvement or a lack of willingness of any leader to take up the role of the sponsor. Low levels of sponsor involvement, especially early in the ambiguous and uncertain formation of the innovation unit, are likely to result in Type II errors, as no innovation project is likely to gather enough momentum or guidance to surmount inertial organizational barriers.

Imbalances in the critic role relative to sponsors and institutional leaders are likely to result in both types of errors as well. We proposed that the critic role is essential in the early period of innovation development, when highly ambiguous and uncertain characteristics of an innovative idea are not surfaced or addressed. When the initial phase of an innovation does not include sufficient critic involvement, poor decisions and incorrectly chosen courses of action are likely to go unchallenged, and Type I errors are likely to occur. Too much of the critic's role, however, can cause Type II errors when the critic becomes too aggressive in challenging assumptions and refocusing each debate during the initial stages of an innovation. Unless the critic allows some projects to progress past the formation stages, very few investment commitments will continue on towards commercialization. Furthermore, if the critic remains excessively active in later periods of innovation implementation, such repeated criticisms will likely prevent any project from successful introduction.

The institutional leader role is important at the earliest stages of an innovation during the formation of the innovation team and later on when an innovation moves from development to implementation and market introduction. As resource controllers and agents of legitimacy, an institutional leader's involvement constructs the infrastructure need for a successful innovation. As with imbalances in the involvement of sponsor and critic, too much or too little involvement by institutional leaders is dysfunctional to the innovation process either through oversights by commission (Type I errors) or emission (Type II errors). When the institutional leadership role is not adequately exercised in the early stages of an innovation, investment decisions are likely to be made that do not enjoy an umbrella of legitimacy with top management in an organization or with other actors external to the firm. Type I errors are likely when institutional leadership is not present to referee debates between sponsor and critic. Type II errors arise when institutional involvement becomes excessive, and sponsors, critics, and entrepreneurs find themselves entangled in a web of bureaucratic and institutional controls and restrictions.

In summary, technological foresights are more likely to occur when a proportional temporal balance of all four leadership roles is exercised during the development of an innovation. Unbalances in any of the leadership roles increase the likelihood of Type I and II errors, which in turn may accumulate to prevent successful development of innovations that are the basis for organizational reorientations to changing environmental conditions. The view of leadership proposed here departs from popular treatments that emphasize unity and consensus among top managers to the strategic vision of the CEO. This homogeneous structure of power and leadership is effective for managing relatively well-understood tasks and making convergent, incremental organizational improvements under stable environmental conditions. However highly ambiguous, uncertain, and rapidly changing environmental situations call for a pluralistic power structure of leadership that incorporates diverse perspectives that tend to be squelched in an elite power structure. Pluralistic leadership increases the chances for technological foresights and decreases the likelihood of oversights. However, such a pluralistic structure does not ensure intelligent leadership. Instead, it emphasizes that the odds of organizational learning and adaptability increase when a balance is maintained between dialectical leadership roles throughout innovation development.

Acknowledgments

We are grateful to our colleagues in the Minnesota Innovation Research Program for assistance in collecting the data on which this chapter is based. In particular we recognize Raghu Garud and Douglas Polley for extensive assistance in collecting the longitudinal data on the development of the CIP and TAP innovations. We also appreciate useful suggestions on an earlier draft of this report from John Seely Brown, Robert Burgelman, Diana Day, Carolyn Egri, Raghu Garud, Zur Shapira, Kathleen Sutcliffe, Michael Tushman, Marrgarethe Wiersema, and other colleagues during presentations at the Strategic Management Research Center of the University of Minnesota and at the NYU Stern School Conference on Technological Oversights and Foresights.

Note

1 As discussed earlier, references to managers as "sponsor," "critic," or "institutional leader" are references to the exercise of a particular role, not to any particular individual.

References

Ancona, D. (1993). The classic and the contemporary: A new blend of small group theory, Chapter 11 in J. K. Murningham (ed.), *Social Psychology in Organizations*. Englewood Cliffs, NJ: Prentice Hall.

Anderson, P. A. (1983). Decision making by objection and the Cuban missile crisis. *Administrative Science Quarterly*, 28, 201–222.

Angle, H. L. and Van de Ven, A. H. (1989) Suggestions for managing the innovation journey, Chapter 21 in A. H. Van de Ven, H. L. Angle, and M. S. Poole (eds.), *Research on the Management of Innovation*. New York: Harper & Row, 663–697.

Argyris, C. and Schon, D. (1978). *Organizational learning: A theory of action perspective*. Reading, MA: Addison-Wesley.

Bartunek, J. M. (1993). Multiple cognitions and conflicts associated with second order organizational change. Chapter 15 in J.K. Murningham (ed.), *Social Psychology in Organizations*. Englewood Cliffs, NJ: Prentice Hall.

Baveles, A. (1960). Leadership: Man and function. *Administrative Science Quarterly*, 4, 491–498.

Brickman, P. (1987). *Commitment, Conflict, and Caring*. Englewood Cliffs, NJ: Prentice Hall.

Brunsson, N. (1982). The irrationality of action and action rationality: Decisions, ideologies, and organizational actions. *Journal of Management Studies*, 19, 29–34.

Chakravarthy, B. S. (1984). Strategic self renewal: A planning framework for today. *Academy of Management Review*, 9, 3.

Cheng, Y. and Van de Ven, A. H. (1996). Learning the innovation journey: Order out of chaos? *Organization Science*, 6, (November–December).

Daft, R. L. and MacIntosh, N. B. (1981). A tentative exploration into the amount and equivocality of information processing in organizational work units. *Administrative Science Quarterly*, 26, 207–224.

Davis, S. M. and Lawrence, P. R. (1977) *Matrix*. Reading, MA: Addison-Wesley.

Eisenhardt, K. (1989). Making fast strategic decisions in high velocity environments. *Academy of Management Journal*, 32, 543–576.

Garud, R. and Van de Ven, A. H. (1993). Thoughts on internal corporate venturing. Chapter 21 in H. E. Glass and B. N. Cavan (eds.), *1994 Handbook of Business Strategy*. New York: Faulkner & Gray.

Garud, R. and Van de Ven, A. H. (1992). An empirical evaluation of the internal corporate venturing process. *Strategic Management Journal*, 13, 93–109.

Gersick, C. J. G. (1994). Pacing strategic change: The case of a new venture. *Academy of Management Journal*, 37:1, 9–45.

Gerth, H. and Mills, C. W. (1946). In Max Weber (ed.), *Essays in Sociology*. New York: Oxford University Press, 236–244.

Graen, G. (1976). Role-making processes within complex organizations. Chapter 28 in M. D. Dunnette (ed.), *Handbook of Industrial and Organizational Psychology*. Chicago, IL: Rand McNally.

Howell, J. M. and Higgins, C. A. (1990). Champions of technological innovation. *Administrative Science Quarterly*, 35, 317–341.

Katz, D. and Kahn, R. L. (1978). *The Social Psychology of Organizations*. New York: Wiley.

March, J. G., Sproull, L., and Tamuz, M. (1991). Learning from samples of one or fewer. *Organization Science*, 2, 1–14.

Meindl, J. R., Ehrlich, S. B., and Dukerich, J. M. (1985). The Romance of leadership. *Administrative Science Quarterly*, 30, 78–102.

Mintzberg, H., Raisinghani, O., and Theoret, A. (1976). The structure of unstructured decision processes. *Administrative Science Quarterly*, 21, 246–275.

Polley, D., and Van de Ven, A. H. (1996). Learning by discovery during innovation development. *International Journal of Management*, in press.

Ross, J., and Staw, B. (1986). Expo 86: An escalation prototype. *Administrative Science Quarterly*, 31, 274–297.

Schroeder, R. G., Van de Ven, A. H., Scudder, G. D., and Polley, D. (1989). The development of innovation ideas. Chapter 4 in A. H. Van de Ven, H. L. Angle, and M. S. Poole (eds.), *Research on the Management of Innovation*. New York: Harper & Row, 107–134.

Selznick, P. (1957). *Leadership in Administration*. New York: Harper & Row.

Shapira, Z. (1995). *Risk Taking: A Managerial Perspective*. New York, NY: Russell Sage.

Sitkin, S. (1992). Learning through failure: The strategy of small losses. In L. Cummings and B. Staw (eds.), *Research in Organizational Behavior*, 14, 231–266.

Stryker and Statham (1985). Symbolic Interaction and Role Theory. Chapter 6 in Lindzay and Aronson (eds.), *Handbook of Social Psychology*, 3rd ed. New York: Random House.

Sutcliffe, K. M. (1994). What executives notice: Accurate perceptions in top management teams. *Academy of Management Journal*,

Thompson, J. and Tuden, A. (1959). Strategies, structures and processes of organizational decision. In J. Thompson et al. (eds.), *Comparative Studies in Administration*, Pittsburgh, PA: University of Pittsburgh Press.

Van de Ven, A. H. and Garud, R. (1993). Innovation and industry development: The case of cochlear implants. In R. Burgelman and R. Rosenbloom (eds.), *Research on Technological Innovation, Management and Policy*, vol. 5. Greenwich, CT: JAI Press, pp. 1–46.

Van de Ven, A. H., Angle, H., and Poole, M. S. (1989). *Research on the Management of Innovation*. New York, Harper & Row, Ballinger Division.

Van de Ven, A. H. and Polley, D. (1992). Learning while innovating. *Organization Science*, 3, 1, 92–116.

Virany, B., Tushman, M. L., and Romanelli, E. (1992). Executive succession and organizational outcomes in turbulent environments: An organizational learning approach. *Organization Science*, 3, 72–91.

Weick, K. E. (1993). Sensemaking in organizations: Small structures with large consequences. Chapter 2 in J. K. Murningham (ed.), *Social Psychology in Organizations: Advances in Theory and Research*. Englewood Cliffs, NJ: Prentice Hall.

Wiersema, M. F. and Bantel, K. A. (1993). Top management team turnover as an adaptation mechanism: The role of the environment. *Strategic Management Journal*, 14, 485–504.

16 Risky lessons: Conditions for organizational learning

Baruch Fischhoff, Zvi Lanir, and Stephen Johnson

Introduction

For both individuals and organizations, most behavior is habitual. In a given situation, people do what they have usually done. When their behavior changes, it is often gradual, as behavior patterns are shaped by the feedback that they evoke. Producing good outcomes increases a behaviors' chance of being performed again, whereas unpleasant outcomes increase the search for alternative behaviors. Learning may be defined as appropriate change or consistency (Levitt & March, 1988).

The learning process involves a series of decisions, where one option is business as usual and the other options constitute changes – either innovations or reversion to earlier behavior. Whenever learning is possible, each option must be evaluated in terms of the outcomes it can cause and the lessons it can teach. For example, a short-term loss might be weighed against the chance to learn something generally useful (e.g., passing up a favorite watering hole in order to try a new restaurant, pulling one's best sales rep off solid accounts in order to test a new territory) (Einhorn, 1986).

Decision theory provides a set of well-articulated analytical methods for making such choices (Kleindorfer, Hershey, & Kunreuther, 1992; Raiffa, 1968; Watson & Buede, 1986; von Winterfeldt & Edwards, 1986). It can incorporate both an action's direct impacts and its informational value. The value of information can be both instrumental (through improving future decisions) and intrinsic (through satisfying curiosity, reducing the aversiveness of uncertainty, or providing the "thrill value" of trying something different).

As a formalization, however, decision theory is necessarily mute regarding substantive aspects of this learning process. It cannot provide behavioral alternatives, nor instruct one in their implementation, nor extract their lessons, nor determine the latent potential for identifying new hypotheses.[1]

These vital functions require individuals who can identify opportunities and understand their implications, as well as settings that allow them to act on these beliefs and absorb the lessons that follow. The remainder of this chapter begins by developing a general framework for predicting when organizations can experiment effectively. The framework is then illustrated in the context of one organization that is frequently challenged to experiment: the operational military. The chapter concludes by discussing the practical and scientific implications of this perspective, including whether the threats to innovation identified in this case study apply to other introductions of advanced information technologies.

The framework: A synopsis

Our analysis begins by discussing briefly when experimentation might be needed. It then advances three necessary conditions for effective experimentation. These are: (1) *competence*, defined as the ability to execute routine behaviors and preset plans; (2) *insight*, defined as the ability to identify potentially useful alternative behaviors; and (3) *initiative*, defined as the ability to act on these possibilities, both to try them out and to implement those that seem to work.

We hold these to be necessary conditions for both individuals and organizations. Having more people involved increases the challenge of coordinating their experimentation. Such coordination is needed not only for the actual act of decision, but also for its precursors (e.g., deciding how to interpret a complex reality and how to weight different outcomes) and its consequents (e.g., deciding what lessons to learn and how to implement them).

One common form of coordination is across the levels of a hierarchical organization. It must accommodate the conflicting desires for central control and local autonomy. In the context of experimentation, this tension revolves around who gets to decide that it is time to try something different: Those at the top or those at the bottom? Those with the big picture or those with the local details? Those at headquarters or those in the field? Our framework addresses these issues by considering the opportunities available to those at different levels in an organization for meeting the three conditions for effective experimentation. Whether these opportunities are realized depends on how well the organization manages its human and material resources.

Our analysis finds no simple and universal prescription for balancing centralization and autonomy. Rather, it points to a constant adjustment process, as the people in an organization create the informal arrangements needed to make its formal procedures work. Changed circumstances may destabilize this balance. Those changes could be exogenous, such as new competitors, shifting consumer tastes, or regulatory reform. Or, the changes could be endogenous, such as new personnel, "reengineered" work relations, or increased telecommuting. If changes come too fast, an organization may never regain its equilibrium. As a result, effective experimentation may be most difficult where it is most needed.

Conditions for experimentation

Planning and its limits

In all but the simplest environments, effective operations require a mixture of planning and improvisation. The former creates the basic structure of an organization, designed to ensure that it begins an action with the best strategy that can be determined in advance. The latter allows it to respond to surprises, exploiting opponents' unanticipated weaknesses and its own unrealized potential. Experimentation can keep plans from becoming straightjackets, whereas plans can provide clear, shared points of departure for improvisations. This need for balance applies to high-tech startups, manufacturers of consumer products, and university capital campaigns. Planning can be seen explicitly in standard operating procedures, contingency plans, employee handbooks, and training exercises. It can be seen less explicitly in equipment specifications, personnel selection procedures, and incentive schemes.

Despite the extraordinary efforts invested in plans, they have inherent (and familiar) limits. One is the difficulty of ensuring that plans are executed as drafted. Will equipment perform as vendors have promised? Can operational units stay coordinated? Will people stay the course under pressure? Plans are limited, too, by the intellect of those who are making them. Plans are imagined descriptions of future states. If the imagination is wanting, then critical situations may be overlooked or oversimplified. If the imagination is adequate, then there may be too many possible contingencies for each to receive adequate attention. Even if the plans are there, it may be hard to master them all or access the right one when contingencies arise.[2] In competitive situations, further limits arise from planners' attempts to render their opponents' plans irrelevant. Those who plan surprises must be ready for surprises.

Under these constraints, planning can fall prey to systematic biases (Armstrong, 1986). The best known of these might be, in military parlance, "fighting the last war," not realizing how conditions have changed (May, 1973). Others include exaggerating how well a situation has been understood (Fischer, 1983), how much one holds the initiative (Dawes, 1988), or how quickly tasks can be completed (Kidd, 1970). Plans may also have to protect myths, such as the prowess of top management, the self-image of participating units, and the performance of vendors' products. Although such myths may keep an organization going, they render its plans suspect. Indeed, all of these limits create a place for experimentation, perhaps recognized, perhaps not.

Three capabilities

Given these limits to planning, an organization becomes vulnerable if it sticks rigidly to even the best plan. Its personnel may become demoralized as well as immobilized, if they cannot exercise control over their environment. Its predictability may embolden opponents to improvise. As a result, plans should be treated as useful fictions, allowing one to get started, but requiring adaptation if things begin to go awry. At that point, improvisation is needed. In order to answer that need, decision makers must be able to generate potentially useful experiments, evaluate their results, and act on those evaluations. Those three abilities might be called competence, insight, and initiative.

Competence. Successful planning makes experimentation possible. Plans create the expectations needed to identify surprising developments and prompt the search for additional alternatives. Mastery is needed to devise elaborations that preserve a plan's strengths, while correcting its weaknesses. Competence creates a common perspective, allowing initiatives to be communicated and justified. It can help people manage the emotional load of action, as well as the cognitive load. A feeling of mastery can strengthen morale, by inspiring confidence in a plan and those who produced it. It can reduce complacency, by clarifying opponents' capabilities and one's own vulnerabilities. The process of mastering plans can create cohesive units, willing to follow their leaders in both the original plan and the improvisations based on it.

Insight. Innovations resemble challenges to a scientific paradigm (Kuhn, 1962; Lakatos, 1970). Legitimate ones come from individuals who have pushed the paradigm as far as it could go and found it lacking. Having exhausted their ability to resolve discrepant results, they can innovate without seeming disloyal. Taking that step requires the independence of spirit and mind needed to come up with viable alternatives. It means overcoming the inertia (or even self-censorship) that comes from realizing how difficult it is to do things differently. Realizing this potential still requires some luck and genius.

Initiative. One necessary ingredient in taking action on good ideas is competence, providing familiarity with the human and material resources that must be used differently. Executing an innovation requires willingness to assume responsibility for its consequences, recognizing that failures may be punished more severely than equivalent mishaps with routine actions (Landman, 1987). Indeed, even novel successes may evoke suspicions of disloyalty. Organizations must achieve the right balance between rewarding fidelity and initiative. They also must provide the "slack" resources needed to implement an initiative. Individuals who are already stretched to their limits intellectually are less able to generate and elaborate new plans. Organizations stretched to their material limits, or individuals stretched to their physical limits, cannot set off in new directions even if they can see them.

Loci of experimentation in hierarchical organizations

The two logical policy extremes are to let experimentation be the exclusive province of those at the top of a hierarchical organization or of those at the bottom. The two following sections discuss, in turn, the conditions favoring experimentation at each locus, including the roles and consequences for individuals elsewhere. For example, those at the bottom will often have to implement experiments designed at the top; those at the top will often have to capitalize on the lessons learned from experiments initiated at the bottom. Top managers can often create risks for their subordinates, while insulating themselves from consequences; on the other hand, they may be surprised by their exposure to the losses (or embarrassments) created by local initiatives.

Top-down experimentation

The general case for letting top managers experiment rests on their roles in shaping the initial plan and guiding its implementation. These roles confer advantages in competence, insight, and initiative – and corresponding disadvantages.

Competence. Top managers should have the fullest understanding of the current plan's overall logic. As a result, they should be in the best position to evaluate its success in practice. Knowing which alternative plans were rejected in the planning process should keep them from prematurely abandoning a plan that is encountering difficulty. On the other hand, their public commitment to a plan may make them reluctant to acknowledge problems, even if they overcome their private commitment to it.

Inight. Knowing when and even what to change need not confer knowledge of how to change. Because they have been around longer, top managers should have a larger repertoire of possible solutions. Those who have risen through the ranks should understand the small picture at the bottom better than those in the lower echelons could understand the big picture at the top. Senior managers should have a broader range of possible resources on call. Only they can consider experiments with multiple units.

Those at the top may even be in the best position to evaluate experiments conceived at the bottom. For example, they may have the best guess at how an initiative proposed by one unit would affect others. Will it use a disproportionate share of resources? Will it remove the experimenting unit from a vital support role? They may even evaluate those experiments more accurately than the units involved in them. For example, senior staff may be better able to tell whether an initiative has succeeded because of a particularly gifted local leader, a particularly clumsy opposing response, some unusual local conditions, or an unrepeatable element of surprise.

On the other hand, senior staff may be too rooted in the current plan to produce useful innovations. They have, after all, put their best thinking into the very plan whose failings have prompted the search for experiments. Their familiarity with "life in the trenches" may be dated, perhaps without their realizing it – creating an illusion of competence.

Initiative. However good the new ideas, top managers should be in the best position to implement them. Their basic responsibility is, after all, to develop coordinated plans (e.g., avoiding "friendly fire"), to communicate plans to local units, and to ensure adherence that should apply to new plans as well as old ones. They should have the legal authority for ordering experiments to be taken. If they understood the original plan's limits (a question of competence), then they should have ensured the needed slack resources.

On the other hand, a top-down initiative may be the most difficult to implement, insofar as it requires redirecting a complex organization in real time. Its details must be specified for and communicated to all local units. That communication must not only convey information, but also inspire confidence – at the same time as the same leaders' previous plan is being abandoned. It means shifting from the plan with the highest probability of success to one with some chance of having a higher probability. Often, a top-down experiment that might beat the odds on an original plan might also place the entire organization at risk.[3]

Bottom-up experimentation

Alternatively, lower-level personnel can initiate experiments, with higher-level personnel reviewing their efforts. Successful initiatives can be disseminated to others in the organization, whereas failures are discarded with localized damage. Whether unsuccessful experimenters are censored or forgiven will depend on (a) whether a case can be made that the initiative might have succeeded, (b) whether the experiments threaten the authority of higher echelons, and (c) whether the innovators have suffered enough already.

Competence. Those in the lower levels of an organization have less to learn, hence a better chance to master their part of the plan completely. They may benefit from repeated practice and, through it, understand the weaknesses and fictions in the official plan. Many organizations survive even routine operations only because of jerry-rigged local solutions (Perrow, 1984). On the other hand, local competence need not confer understanding of the overall plan nor the local unit's exact place in it.

Insight. Although they lack the big picture, lower echelons do have direct contact with their small segment of it. They know what can be known about what opponents are doing, how their own people are responding, how their equipment works, and how much sense the general plan makes for their particular situation. They are in a unique position to spot unexpected vulnerability and unrealized potential (e.g., Brokensha, Warren, & Werner, 1980). They have concrete, hands-on knowledge, unlike big-picture knowledge, which is necessarily synthetic and aggregated. Those details can provide the raw material for creative, practical solutions. Higher echelons may demand getting more out of a situation; only local personnel can produce it. Remoteness from headquarters may reduce pressure to document nascent plans prematurely, while their specifics are still being worked out.

Unfortunately, local successes may be so specific that they teach few general lessons. They may drain resources needed elsewhere. They may pull the system in conflicting directions, undermining the possibility of immediate and coordinated responses. In such situations, an organization is more than the sum of its parts. It no longer makes sense to take limited gambles with loosely coupled local units in hopes of discovering some useful new ideas.

Initiative. Wherever a good initiative is generated, it must still be implemented locally. Being on the scene, local leaders should be in the best position to inspire others with their mastery of the new plan, and to make midcourse corrections. Exposing themselves to similar dangers should help them to send subordinates into unknown situations.

Lower-level experimentation may also be more affordable. An organization can allow one local unit to experiment, in part, because it has other local units. If the damage from an ill-conceived initiative is limited to that unit, then remaining units can still implement the original plan or try other experiments. On the other hand, one successful experiment can provide a solution applicable to many such units (if it can be spotted, generalized, and disseminated by an alert headquarters).

Realizing this potential for lower-level risk taking requires enough independence of thought to ensure that different initiatives are generated and tried. If everyone thinks alike, similar experiments will be tried repeatedly, in effect, putting many eggs in one new basket. However, divergent thinking should not mean divergent loyalty. Lower-level initiatives necessarily violate the "letter" of the central plan. If they also violate its spirit, they may threaten the organization's viability. If criticism drifts toward irreverence and impatience, it can undermine confidence and morale. If the drift is detected, local units may be denied the right and resources to experiment.

The following sections apply this general framework to the specific context of military operations, a domain known for elaborate planning followed by fevered improvision. The concluding section considers the generality of the issues shown in the sharp relief of this particular context.

Military risk taking

Taking risks is essential to the success of military operations. It involves both putting lives on the line, with acts entailing physical danger, and putting careers on the line, with needed improvisations. Risking lives effectively requires courage, commitment, maturity, and leadership. Armies train their soldiers emotionally to control instinctive fear responses, socially to create a unit and cause worth fighting for, and cognitively to analyze risky situations (e.g., when does risking one's life in the short run, by abandoning a seemingly safe position, increase the chances of preserving it in the long run'?) (Cushman, 1983; Helmsley, 1982; McCormick, 1983).

Recognizing the limits to planning, the fundamental doctrines of most armies assign an explicit role to initiative.[4] Doing so means finding a way to distinguish improvisation from insubordination. One such conceptualization argues that all soldiers share a common world outlook, so that the experimenters are doing what the planners would have done in their stead (i.e., had the planners had the information available locally). That logic is strained when the "surprising facts" about local conditions are ones that, in the lower level's estimation, the higher echelons should have anticipated.

A second doctrinal formulation for allowing experimentation is claiming to have an incentive structure that ensures common interests throughout the organization. Commanders worry about their soldiers; soldiers work for the general cause – each party confident that the other will take risks on its behalf.[5] Situations demanding experimentation can strain this logic, too. When plans are failing, lower echelons may not feel that their concerns are being understood, much less protected, when higher echelons improvise. Conversely, their experiments may look like attempts to save themselves in deteriorating situations, with little concern for the common good.

A primary vehicle for creating a stable role for experimentation is training. It can create the personal relations needed for subordinates to trust their leaders' improvisations and the shared outlook needed for them to grasp a sketchy and evolving idea. Hard training can reassure superiors that experiments are faithful to the spirit (and creators) of the original plan – not acts of rebellion, by subordinates who never really accepted the plan, nor acts of desperation, by subordinates who never could execute it. This clear doctrine and solid training are necessary, but not sufficient conditions for effective experimentation. The potential still must be realized in the behavior of specific individuals facing particular circumstances. Inevitably, that requires an adjustment process, balancing the pressures for centralized control and local autonomy. If conditions change, that process must begin again. The following sections consider how a balanced situation would be affected by a specific change, common to military and other organizations: advances in technology.

The nature of modern C³I

The demand for C³I

Command, control, communications, and intelligence systems (C³I) are the lifeblood of a military organization, tying together its pieces, allowing equipment and training to be used most effectively. As a result, there is continuous pressure for better C³I, whose general directions have not changed since antiquity. The desire is for more and better information, delivered more quickly, and in more usable form. In the service of these goals, the US C³I budget had grown to $36 billion for FY85 (e.g., Buckingham, 1980; Department of Defense, 1984; Everett, 1982; Hwang, Schutzer, Shere, & Vena, 1982; Zraket, 1984).

Although some responses are automated, ultimately the system must serve human beings (if only to enable them to change the automation).[6] Nonetheless, it is much easier to measure the quantity and speed of the information being delivered than its quality and usefulness. As a result, the surest trends in C³I are increased volume and timeliness (Brewer & Bracken, 1984; Welch, 1982). The ultimate goal is for headquarters (a) to know at all times the position and movement of every soldier and piece of equipment and (b) to download all available information relevant to local units' missions. That information should help local units to act when forced to go it alone (Brodsky, 1982; Coulam & Fischer, 1985; National Research Council, 1990).

Pressures of C³I

Any C³I system needs a protocol for formulating, transmitting, combining, interpreting, and storing messages. Increasing the volume and speed of communications creates pressure to automate these processes. That may, in turn, place a premium on messages in standardized formats, particularly those with quantitative information that is readily combined and compared.

Standardization may reduce the opportunities to send or receive unusual messages. It may bring into contact units that have had little opportunity to develop communication patterns. As a result, there will be little context for the highly stylized messages that they receive. In effect, the system acts as though the interoperability of equipment ensures the interoperability of its human operators. The change may also emphasize the intelligence function of local units, so that headquarters increasingly views them as information nodes rather than action nodes. It may promote technical specialists over other kinds of leaders (e.g., Kiesler & Sproull, 1991; Malone, 1985; Perrow, 1983; Seminara & Parsons, 1982; Sheridan, 1980).

In addition to these general pressures, the impact of C³I will depend on a variety of specific system-design choices. For example, the system might use a party-line approach (Metcalf, 1986), providing everyone with access to every message, in the hopes of creating a widely shared mental model of the system's status and operation. Conversely, the system could use a need-to-know approach, in hopes of minimizing distractions (by reducing the number of messages) and increasing candor (by reducing the number of listeners). The format and even vocabulary of verbal messages might be fixed in order to avoid informality, but at the price of reducing nuance and improvisation.

These design decisions can affect not only the quality of communications, but also the nature of the social relations within the system (Kiesler et al., 1984, 1985; Spencer & Ekman, 1988; Sproull & Kiesler, 1986). Knowing people through electronic messages is different than knowing them face to face or over the phone. Different still is getting to know people through one medium and then transferring to another. Some people talk fluently, but stumble at writing; others would much rather be pen pals than phone pals. It may be hard to lead through electronic mail, but frustrating to play telephone tag for routine communications. Some observers report that electronic communications are much more likely to escalate in hostility than direct conversations.

Table 16.1 summarizes these general changes in the operating environment created by advanced C³I systems. The precise impact of any specific system will depend on its design details and on users' opportunities to master it. The following section considers the effects of changes in C³I on military risk taking.

Possible effects of C³I on experimentation

On the lower levels

Competence. In some ways, advances in C³I should help local units to master their original plan. Training should be improved by commanders' increased ability to monitor performance and to provide feedback. Computer programs might show how the plan applies to specific situations. Sharing

Table 16.1. Behavioral properties of C³I systems

- high volume of information flow
- automation of information processing
- standardization of communications
- reliance on formal representations
- distancing of units
- flexibility in networks

information efficiently should make plans easier to execute. Preserving a record of each unit's actions and communications might help evaluate its experiences and refine the plan (Pew, Miller, & Feeher, 1982).

On the other hand, the new systems may greatly complicate the plans that must be mastered. A promised (even vaunted) advantage of the emerging technology is allowing much greater flexibility in configuring units. That ability is, arguably, essential in a hostile and unpredictable environment. However, it means that much of the plan exists only at a high level of abstraction, namely, the rules for generating possible variations on its general conception. Inevitably, some features of these variations will become apparent only when they are actually implemented. For example, communication channels are partly defined by their actual users, including what they decide to say, what they leave unsaid, and who gets to share their communications. Until these human relations are in place, a plan has not been mastered (Hiltz, 1984; Hirokawa & Poole, 1986). Under these circumstances, rather than being the basis for improvisations, the original plan is itself something of an untried (and perhaps unwitting) experiment.

Especially in the operational military, a workable plan requires commitment to people as well as principles. Without mutual trust, lower echelon experiments may seem like insubordination, whereas upper echelon orders may seem like unreasonable demands for obedience and endangerment. C^3I systems may reduce the level of trust not only by patching unfamiliar units together, but also by reducing the intimacy of communications among units with continuing relations.

Finally, C^3I systems are a technology under rapid development. As a result, there is constant temptation to tinker with them, as opportunities arise for improving hardware or software. However, each such change requires some getting used to, as operators learn how the system behaves (and misbehaves). As a result, mastery will decrease during transition periods.

Insight. Having more of the big picture might help local units to interpret their own situations. That should, in turn, promote the insight needed for successful experimentation. Improved access to other local units might do the same. Knowing more might counterbalance the tendency to overinterpret anecdotal information about local conditions (Kahneman et al., 1982).

On the other hand, an emphasis on synoptic information may suppress the telltale clues that could suggest experiments (and the need for experimentation). Standardization can limit what information local units collect, what issues dominate their deliberations, and what kinds of expertise they value. These tasks could further distance local commanders from their immediate environment (and its potential insights). A job description that emphasizes providing timely reports in standard format may generally encourage routinization over innovation.

C^3I systems may also diminish insight by requiring technical expertise in order to understand how the system itself works, what quirks it has, what problems it might be hiding, and what additional performance might be wrung from it. Those abilities may be vested in technicians rather than in the commanders who understand the substantive side of military operations.[7] Generating insights would, then, require coordinating the knowledge of rather different people, often under realtime pressures.

Initiative. C[3]I systems are often described as allowing "distributed decision making," by conveying headquarters' perspective everywhere. If local units interpret situations in the way that headquarters would, then doctrine allows them to take initiatives (in the way that headquarters would) (Fischhoff & Johnson, 1990; National Research Council, 1990). Although shallow, this sharing of responsibility could expand the range of actionable initiatives.

On the other hand, the system may create an irresistible temptation for headquarters to want to know more about local activities simply because it can know more. Should things go poorly, headquarters may be held accountable for knowing everything that it could have known. Such constant surveillance may preclude initiatives that challenge conventional wisdom or develop over time. By keeping headquarters distant and impersonal, the system will further restrict lower echelon's opportunities to describe insights and negotiate permissions. Even if initiatives are feasible logistically, it may not be possible to justify them analytically in real-time. Eventually, local units may censor what they say – and think. Why make plans that can't be executed?

Technically oriented systems may also encourage technically oriented plans. It is much easier to create a tidy picture of plans when they emphasize machines rather than people (Swain & Gutman, 1983). Given the great expense of military personnel and material, there is a ready market for optimistic expectations of efficiency in planning and coordination. As a result, units may operate with a bare minimum of resources, leaving little slack for initiatives.

On the upper levels

Competence. In low-tech hierarchies, orders pass through many hands on their way down from the top. Along the way, they evolve from general directives to specific instructions. Often involving consultation and negotiation, this process extracts the local meaning of the general plan. A parallel process transfers field reports upward, through successive stages of clarification and aggregation. These are social processes requiring individuals sensitive to one another's situation and idiom. Without them, headquarters cannot make its plans understood, nor understand how they are being executed. C[3]I systems can transmit orders and reports more quickly and reliably, increasing the chances that the precise words will reach their targets soon enough to be relevant. However, headquarters' competence will be undermined if it takes transmission as a guarantee of comprehension.

Higher echelons will, naturally, attempt to read between the lines of field reports. However, like any other endogenous change, C^{3}I may erode this ability. The competence of those at the top comes, in part, from their having once been at the bottom, giving them some idea of what it is really like down there. However, changing technologies may mean that it is no longer the same "down there" as it was during their tenure in the ranks.

Insight. Those in command have gotten there, in part, by virtue of their past successes in evaluating communications – as a function of who sent them, from which situations, and for what purpose(s). They have had to be able to tell when senders are hiding or overlooking something, or just not speaking clearly enough. That close reading provides clues to when experiments are needed and what they might be.

C^{3}I systems can threaten this critical source of insight by reducing commanders' ability to read between the lines. Stylized reporting protocols can eliminate the contextual cues needed for effective interpretation. They may even preclude certain kinds of information, such as "psychological" descriptions of soldiers' morale and beliefs or qualifications, expressing residual doubts and worries about a plan and its evolution. If commanders recognize the limits, then they can respond with appropriate caution. If not, then C^{3}I systems may create an illusion of insight, by providing easy access to situations that outsiders cannot really understand. As a result, commanders may be tempted to give orders where they should be taking instruction. For example, a contributing factor in the failure of the Iran hostage rescue mission was President Carter's ability to wield a "6000-mile-long screwdriver," as a result of having direct contact with forces in the field (Lanir et al., 1988, and references therein).

Initiative. C^{3}I systems are designed to help headquarters put its initiative into action. It is intended to locate the resources (people, equipment) needed for implementation, to disseminate the relevant orders, and to monitor their execution.

Getting orders out is not, however, the same as getting them accepted. Whatever the official rules say, obedience is often negotiated between subordinates and their immediate superiors, through disciplined questioning and clarification. Some feeling of being misunderstood, misdirected, and misused is the lot of foot soldiers. Reducing direct human contact should just exacerbate it.

Unless recognized, this distancing can add a fictive element to the implementation. Headquarters can imagine having won subordinates' respect just as it might imagine commanding units that no longer exist or that never operated according to the plan. If C^{3}I erodes credibility, it might also be exploited for new opportunities to hide infidelity – especially if a computer or radio check replaces the traditional surprise visit to the trenches.

Summary

Taking risks means doing things that are not in the plan, perhaps elaborations on it, perhaps deviations from it. Although essential to military success, such improvisations occupy a delicate role in proceduralized, hierarchical organizations. Military doctrine affords them a formal role, which must then be realized in the lives of the individuals who must accomplish them. The impact of C^3I will depend on how it affects these formal and formal relationships. Providing improved communications and intelligence should help local commanders to identify and investigate initiatives. However, unless they can act on promising initiatives, the net result may be increased frustration and decreased interest in exploring options. Local units may even focus their ingenuity on developing high-tech ways of defeating high-tech constraints on (what they see as) their essential freedom of action.

If this speculative account is accurate, then one must ask how C^3I systems could backfire in this way. One possible cause is that the technical difficulties of making these systems work at all leave little room for human issues in the C^3I design process (Perrow, 1983; Reason, 1990). There might be some concern about computer interfaces. However, it is likely to come after the fundamental design is set and, with it, the impacts on social relations and shared beliefs.

A second possible cause of a reduced ability to experiment is an inevitable price of meeting the challenges of the modern battlefield. Many military operations occur so quickly that information flows must be standardized and automated, for both attackers and defenders. It is unfortunate if human relations get cramped. However, at least the humans will have a chance of surviving. If they do, then they can try improvising.

A third possible cause is the trend toward increased reliance on specialized units which are then combined for specific missions. As a result, military operations are increasingly likely to involve units with little common language or history. Although such combined forces may have more latent flexibility, it may be harder for commanders to identify those initiatives and rally troops behind them. C^3I is one such specialty, with its own skills and culture. It is simultaneously necessary for experimentation and frustrating to it. The need to coordinate diverse and unfamiliar forces requires commanders to keep close tabs on local units, at the risk of engaging in suffocating surveillance.

Conceivably, today's battlefield has actually reduced the importance of experimentation. With extreme time compression, there may be no time to ponder initiatives nor share experiences with those that have been tried. However, concern for extreme circumstances may have diverted attention from the routine ones that still dominate many military operations and the preparations for them. The challenge is to prevent the need to program actions for fast wars from reducing the ability to fight protracted conflicts that allow (and require) experimentation.

Conclusion

Successful organizations must achieve a balance between authority and autonomy. Any significant change in an organization's circumstances can disrupt this balance. As described here, advances in C^3I are one such exchange that seem to strengthen authority. If time and experience allow, the forces of autonomy may reassert themselves. However, where a system must work right the first time, imbalances need to be addressed early in the design process. If not, they will be resolved by institutional factors, such as who controls the budgets, what training designers have, and which temptations technology vendors offer. The analytical perspective developed here is intended to provide partial guidance for that design process.

Applying this perspective elsewhere involves identifying: (a) the organization's need and opportunity to experiment, (b) the potential loci of its experimentation decisions, and (c) the challenges to coordinating their respective strengths and weaknesses. That analysis could be used either to predict an organization's performance or to improve it, by creating designs that facilitate learning from risky lessons.

The conclusions of this specific analysis should generalize most readily to settings that resemble the operational military in these three respects. For example, it might be particularly relevant to other organizations in fast-changing competitive environments (e.g., high-tech computer or drug firms). Indeed, it might be more relevant to them than to the peacetime, waiting-for-something-to-happen military. This analysis should be particularly relevant to other rule-bound organizations, and to ones in technological flux. Speculatively, the sometimes limited contribution of technology to office productivity may reflect an inability to resolve this tension between new and old work relations.

Of course, advances in C^3I are not the only contemporary change that could affect experimentation. One logical extension of this analysis would be to other changes, such as reengineering, downsizing, and increased reliance on outsourcing. Another extension would be to examine the effects of the same changes in other organizations, varying in their complexity, internal heterogeneity, environmental uncertainty, and slack resources. The case study focused on transition periods, both because they are practically important and because they may reveal processes that are less visible in steady state.

The present analysis makes various empirical claims regarding the behavioral properties of C^3I systems. These are based, in varying degrees, on anecdotal observation of such systems (in part, as participant), experimental evidence (using laboratory analogs of related systems), and general behavioral principles. These claims are interpreted within an analytical framework specifying the conditions for effective experimentation. These issues were thought through, rather than modeled formally. Our goal was conceptual integration of diverse perspectives from cognitive psychology, human factors engineering, decision theory, and organizational science. If this seems like a potentially useful juxtaposition, then the serious work of elaborating this perspective could begin by examining other contexts, constructing formal models, and conducting behavioral observations.

Acknowledgments

We thank the following individuals for their thoughtful comments on previous drafts of this article: John Dockery, Oscar Grusky, Kenneth Mackenzie, Tom Sheridan, Zur Shapira, Ola Svenson, and two anonymous reviewers. This research was sponsored by the Office of Naval Research and the National Science Foundation, whose support is gratefully acknowledged. The opinions expressed are those of the authors.

Notes

1   These formal limits to decision theory are in addition to its empirically demonstrated limits as a descriptive account of how decision theories are actually made (Kahneman, Slovic, & Tversky, 1982; von Winterfeldt & Edwards, 1986). Herrnstein (1990) and Thaler and Shefrin (1981) provide specific discussions of deviations from the theory in balancing short-term and long-term objectives.

2   A contemporary approach to managing complexity is to program a set of "rules of engagement," then compute the implied response to specific circumstances. The idea is that decision makers will thoroughly understand those few rules, which the computer will then efficiently combine. This approach assumes a deep understanding of the rules and leaves little place for learning or experimentation (J. Metcalf, personal communication).

3   In decision theoretic terms, the *expected value* of such an innovation would be less than that of the original plan. However, it has a broader distribution of outcomes, including some consequential "upside" risk. Choosing a more uncertain option makes one *risk seeking* – unless the expected informational value of the experiment is enough to compensate for the reduced expectation of the direct outcomes.

4   For example, two of von Clausewitz's (1976) thoughts are, "the higher up the chain of command, the greater is the need for boldness to be supported by a reflective mind, so that boldness does not degenerate into purposeless bursts of blind passion" (p. 190) and ". . . great strength of character, as well as great lucidity and firmness of mind, is required in order to follow through steadily, to carry out the plan, and not to be thrown off course by thousands of diversions." (p. 78)

5   For example, Huntington (1964) describes German doctrine on these points as having "on the one hand subordinated the individual to the collective will and intelligence of the whole and yet guaranteed to the individual wide freedom of

action so long as he remained upon his proper level and within his sphere of responsibility."(p. 51)

6   For example, according to former Secretary of Defense Caspar Weinberger, "The central feature of any C^3I system is the human decision makers – the commanders plus their various staffs and others. These decision makers operate within a framework of established doctrine, strategies, tactics, and procedures, supported by an array of sensors, computers, communication links, command facilities, and other equipment. Through these interlinked C^3I systems, our command authorities seek in both peace and war to accomplish military missions directed by civilian authorities. Force capability is inextricably related to the quality of C^3I components and to the manner in which they are integrated with associated weapon systems and decision makers." (Department of Defense, 1984, p. 241)

7   One chilling example was related to me by a colleague working for NASA. He reports accompanying the chief pilot for a major airline and the chief pilot for a major airframe vendor as the latter transferred a new model of plane to the former. Toward the end of their flight, the plane responded in a totally unexpected way. Both were baffled. Eventually, the problem was identified as a bug in the plane's computerized controls. The collective experience of the two pilots left them completely unprepared to diagnose this problem.

References

Armstrong, J. S. (1986). *Long-range planning* (3rd ed.). New York: McGraw-Hill.

Brewer, G. D., and Bracken, P. (1984). Some missing pieces of the C^3I puzzle. *Journal of Conflict Resolution, 28,* 451–469.

Brodsky, S. L. (1982). Control systems aspects of command and control. In J. Hwang, D. Schutzer, K. Shere, and P. Vena (eds.) *Selected Analytical Concepts in Command and Control* (pp. 41–60). New York: Gordon and Breach.

Brokensha, D. W., Warren, D. M., and Werner, O. (1980). *Indigenous Technical Knowledge*. Baltimore: Associated Universities Press.

Buckingham, C. T. (1980). Lifeblood of full combat power. *Army,* 20, April.

von Clausewitz, C. (1976). *On War.* (M. Howard and P. Paret, eds. and trans.). Princeton, NJ: Princeton University Press.

Coulam, R. F., and Fischer, G. W. (1985). Problems of command and control in a major European war. In R. F. Coulam and R. A. Smith (eds.), *Advances in Information Processing in Organizations,* vol. 2. Greenwich, CT: JAI Press.

Cushman, J. H. (1983). *Command and Control of Theater Forces: Adequacy.* Washington, DC: AFCEA International Press.

Dawes, R. M. (1988). *Rational Choice in an Uncertain World.* San Diego: Harcourt Brace Jovanovich.

Department of Defense. (1984). *FY 1985 Report of Secretary of Defense Caspar W. Weinberger.* Washington, DC: Department of Defense.

Einhorn, H. (1988). Accepting error to make less error. *Journal of Personality Assessment,* 50, 389–395.

Everett, R. R. (1982). Yesterday, today, and tomorrow in command, control, and communications. *Technology Review,* 84, 1, 66–68.

Fischer, G. W. (1983). Conceptual models and military threat assessment. *Journal of Social Issues,* 39, 1, 87–116.

Fischhoff, B., and Beyth-Marom, R. (1983). Hypothesis evaluation from a Bayesian perspective. *Psychological Review*, 90, 239–260.

Fischhoff, B. and Johnson, S. (1990). The possibility of distributed decision making: Appendix to B. Fischhoff, *Distributed Decision Making: Workshop Report* (pp. 25–58). Washington, DC: National Academy Press.

Helmsley, J. (1982). *Soviet Troop Control: The Role of Command Technology in the Soviet Military System*, New York: Brassey's Publishers.

Herrnstein, R. (1990). Rational choice theory. *American Psychologist*, 45, 356–367.

Hiltz, S. R. (1984). *On-line Communities: A Case Study of the Office of the Future*. Norwood, NJ: Ablex.

Hirokawa, R. Y. and Poole, M. S. (eds.) (1986). *Communication and Group Decision-making*. Beverly Hills, CA: Sage.

Huntington, S. P. (1964). *The Soldier and State*. New York: Vintage.

Hwang, J., Schutzer, D., Shere, K., and Vena, P. (eds.). (1982). *Selected Analytical Concepts in Command and Control*. New York: Gordon and Breach.

Kahneman, D., Slovic, P., and Tversky, A. (eds.) (1982). *Judgment under Uncertainty. Heuristics and Biases*. New York: Cambridge University Press.

Kidd, J. F. (1970). The utilization of subjective probabilities in production planning. *Acta Psychologica*, 34, 338–347.

Kiesler, S., Siegel, J., and McGuire, T. W. (1984). Social psychological aspects of computer-mediated communication. *American Psychologist*, 39, 1123–1134.

Kiesler, S. and Sproull, L. (1991). *Connections: New Ways of Working in the Networked Organization*. Cambridge, MA: MIT Press.

Kiesler, S., Zubrow, D., Moses, A. M., and Geller, V. (1985). Affect in computer- medicated communication: An experiment in synchronous terminal-to-terminal discussion. *Human–Computer Interaction*, 1, 77–104.

Kleindorfer, P. R., Kunreuther, H. C., and Schoemaker, P. J. H. (1992). *Decision Sciences*. New York: Cambridge University Press.

Kuhn, T. (1962). *The Structure of Scientific Revolution*. Chicago: University of Chicago Press.

Lakatos, I. (1970). Falsification and the methodology of scientific research programmes. In I. Lakatos and A. Musgrave (eds.), *Criticism and the Growth of Scientific Knowledge*. Cambridge: Cambridge University Press.

Landman, J. (1987). Regret and elation following action and inaction. *Personality and Social Psychology Bulletin*, 13, 524–536.

Lanir, Z., Fischhoff, B., and Johnson, S. (1988). Military risk taking: C³I and the cognitive functions of boldness in war. *Journal of Strategic Studies*, 11, 1, 96–114.

Levitt, B. and March, J. G. (1988). Organizational learning. *Annual Review of Sociology*, 34–40.

Malone, T. B. (1985). Human factors in early system development. *Proceedings of the Human Factors Society Annual Meetings*, 29, 1156–1160.

May, E. (1973). *The Lessons of History*. Cambridge: Harvard University Press.

McCormick N. J. (1983). *Reliability and Risk Analysis*. New York: Academic Press.

Metcalf, J. (1986). The Grenada mission: A commander's report. In R. Weissinger-Baylon and J. G. March (eds.), *Decision Making in Military Organizations*. New York: Pitman.

National Research Council. (1990). *Distributed Decision Making*. Washington, DC: The Council.

Perrow, C. (1984). *Normal Accidents*. New York: Free Press.

Perrow, C. (1983). The organizational context of human factors engineering. *Administrative Science Quarterly*, 28, 521–541.

Pew, R., Miller, D. C., and Feeher, C. E. (1982). *Evaluation of Proposed Control Room Improvements through Analysis of Critical Operator Decisions*. EPRI NP-1982. Palo Alto, CA: Electric Power Research Institute.

Raiffa, H. (1968). *Decision Analysis*. Reading, MA: Addison-Wesley.

Reason, J. (1990). *Human Error*. New York: Cambridge University Press.

Seminara, J. L. and Parsons, S. O. (1982). Nuclear power plant maintainability. *Applied Ergonomics*, 13, 177–189.

Sheridan, T. D. (1980). Human error in nuclear power plants. *Technology Review*, 82, 4, 23–33.

Spencer, K. and Ekman, P. (eds.) (1988). *Handbook of Nonverbal Behavior*. New York: Cambridge University Press.

Sproull, L. and Kiesler, S. (1986). Reducing social context cues in electronic mail in organizational communication. *Management Science*, 32, 1492–1512.

Swain, A. and Gutman, H. C. (1983). *Handbook of Human Reliability Analysis with Emphasis on Nuclear Power Plants*, NUREG/CR-1278. Washington, DC: Nuclear Regulatory Commission.

Thaler, R. and Shefrin, H. H. (1981). An economic theory of self-control. *Journal of Political Economy*, 89, 392–406.

Watson, S. and Buede, D. (1986). *Decision Synthesis*. New York: Cambridge University Press.

Welch, J. A. (1982). C³I systems: The efficiency connection. In J. Hwang, D. Schutzer, K. Shere, and P. Vena (eds.), *Selected Analytical Concepts in Command and Control* (pp. 3–130). New York: Gordon and Breach.

von Winterfeldt, D., and Edwards, W. (1986). *Decision Analysis and Behavioral Research*. New York: Cambridge University Press.

Zraket, C. A. (1984). Strategic command, control, communication and intelligence. *Science*, 1306–1311.

17 Exploiting enthusiasm: A case study of applied theories of innovation

Gideon Kunda

Introduction: Bureaucracy and innovation

Social scientists have long attempted to understand the social and organizational forces that enhance or undermine innovation in corporate settings. The products of such investigations, their proponents claim, may be implemented by managers in order to enhance corporate performance (Kanter, 1988). In particular, many programmatic texts on the nature of R&D and other organizations have claimed that "bureaucracy" undermines the conditions necessary for individual and organizational innovativeness (Ritti, 1971; Rothman & Perucci, 1970; Shenhav, 1988). In this view, widely propagated by both academics and popular writers, and supported by broadly held commonsensical beliefs, rigid hierarchical structures bolstered by rules and regulations, formalized procedures, and "red tape," constrain the social environment of professional work and suppress the intrinsic motivation (Deci, 1975; Shapira, 1989) and innate capacity for creativity (Amabile, 1988) that individuals are capable of bringing to it. Bureaucracy, the argument goes, encourages conformity and particularism and discourages playfulness, exploration, and risk taking. Such environments produce cautious, conservative, and uninspired "organization men" for whom "playing it safe" and "cover your ass" are the primary rules of organizational survival, whereas innovation and its consequences pose a continuing threat (see Perrow, 1986). These pathologies of bureaucracy are particularly detrimental to the performance of R&D organizations in which technological foresight and oversight are crucial factors (see Garud, Nayyar, & Shapira, this volume, chapter 1): bureaucratic culture enhances the probability that technological foresights are suppressed and facilitates those processes that encourage oversight and allow it to become the norm; anything else, in this view, threatens the stability of the existing order and the particular interests that support it.

This critique of bureaucracy has historically been accompanied by a stream of ideas – ranging from utopian visions to pragmatic recommendations – concerned with reforming organizations (see Barley & Kunda 1992; *Business Week*, 1993). The prescriptions that flow from this view all point to what may be called *debureaucratization* as a solution to the problem of innovation. Freedom from bureaucratic constraint, in this view, is a crucial factor in the successful performance of technical organizations. Thus, in the more platitudinous "let-a-thousand-flowers-bloom" version, managers are urged to do away with the various types of rigid hierarchical and rational controls associated with bureaucracy, and to experiment instead with alternative types of flexible, nonbureaucratic organizational forms which, presumably, will tap their intrinsic motivation and innate innovative capacities (Kanter, 1988). For more cautious, and perhaps more realistic, reformers like Schoonhoven and Jelinek (1990), innovativeness hinges on the ability to create what they call a "dynamic tension" between chaos and structure, mixing freedom with tight controls. Rejecting "unstructured adhocracy," they call for a "hybrid situation": "systematic approaches but not bureaucratic rigidity, authoritarian management, or overemphasis on the 'forms.' Open tolerance of individuality and initiative are crucial but not at the price of lack of system . . ." (p. 80). Whatever else one makes of such advice, it is immediately apparent that the various images of the "debureaucratized organization" border on the oxymoronic and threaten implementers with a seemingly insurmountable set of practical contradictions. Aware of this, Schoonhoven and Jelinek, like others, attempt to find a way out of the impasse by adopting the terminology of "corporate culture": the threat of chaos found in even a partial elimination of bureaucracy can be contained, they claim, if managers gain control of the underlying order of cultural rules.

Culture and organization

Culture as a conceptual lens for understanding and shaping organizational phenomena gained considerable popularity over the last decade (Barley et al., 1988). Although no longer in possession of the glamor associated with "hot topics," and suffering from the kinds of conceptual confusion that come with this particular terrain, the cultural perspective has nevertheless been established as a legitimate framework for organizational analysis (Trice & Beyer, 1993). According to this perspective, most of its adherents would agree, organizations are best seen as rule-governed systems of meaning with, or against which, members define themselves and carry out and make sense of their activities.[1] It is these shared rules, many of them informal, some perhaps implicit, not to say unconscious, that are seen as a crucial defining feature of organizational life. Bureaucracy, in this sense, is associated with one particular configuration of cultural rules; other forms, more or less conducive to managerial interests, are possible.

So defined, culture has been offered to the managerial community as a management tool of considerable importance (Barley et al., 1988). Understanding, shaping, and controlling the implicit rules that guide employees' everyday organizational life, managers are repeatedly told, is a prerequisite for the optimization of corporate performance. It is this line of reasoning that leads to the prescriptive view of the nonbureaucratic culture: cultural control, the argument goes, makes bureaucratic procedures of control redundant, thus removing impediments to innovation associated with them, while maintaining control through other means. For example, a culture in which demonstrations of motivation and hard work are highly valued, requires less formal supervision; a culture in which open "bottom-up" communication and debate is the norm removes the need for mechanisms for unilateral managerial decision making, and so on. Thus, under "appropriate" cultural conditions, some, if not all, of the barriers to innovation associated with bureaucracy can be removed. The problem for managers, then, is one of cultural design.

The managerial literature abounds with prescriptions for what innovative nonbureaucratic work cultures should look like, with unsubstantiated promises of their results, and with lists of various techniques for bringing them about (see Schoonhoven & Jelinek 1988). There is considerable doubt, however, about the extent to which such rhetoric is taken seriously by the managerial community. Students of the history of managerial ideology have suggested that the link between discourse and practice has been tenuous at best: some assume it is empty rhetoric that disguises or justifies unchanging managerial practice; others claim that changing managerial fads – from Taylorism and on – have rarely been implemented (Barley & Kunda, 1992). In both cases, there is little if any data on the relationship between theory and practice at the point of production: everyday corporate life. In this chapter, I use ethnographic data and a cultural perspective to examine what happens when the idea of an innovation-enhancing nonbureaucratic culture is actually implemented. The chapter is based on the empirical materials documented in *Engineering Culture* (Kunda, 1992) – an ethnography of a large high-tech corporation well-known for its long standing, theory-informed efforts to design and build a culture that promotes technological innovation. The case-based ethnographic perspective does not allow a direct comparative test of the success of managerial efforts to enhance creativity and promote innovation; rather, it places these efforts in a broader perspective by providing an in-depth critical analysis of the ideas that underlie them and their relation to practice. Thus, the chapter documents the development of the founder's beliefs about the relationship between bureaucracy and innovation into a managerial ideology of control, describes management's efforts to implement the ideology in order to create and maintain an innovative culture, and examines some of the unanticipated consequences of the practical implementation of managerial ideas for the organization and for the people involved.

Tech: A brief history

Tech[2] was founded in the years following World War II in the first spate of foundings that set the stage for the so called high-tech revolution. Sam Miller, the founder, recognized the innovative potential of a technical idea he was helping develop, with government funding, at a prestigious technological institute. With a few partners, a small investor, and a working prototype, he founded Tech. The company was built around both a technical and a social vision. The technical vision, although regarded by many at the time as overly ambitious, soon proved itself quite feasible. The company successfully met the first challenge facing all start-ups: its product was greeted with apparently deserved enthusiasm in the market place. The second, more significant challenge – creating an organization capable of generating a stream of innovations – was also overcome: the products that followed seemed to fulfill the promise of the first and met with a similar reception. The company grew rapidly around its technological prowess. Despite periodical setbacks typical of the high-tech industry, Tech emerged as one of the leaders in its field, known in particular for its strong and innovative R&D orientation and its "cutting edge," "state of the art" technologies.

The social vision that drove Miller was no less ambitious. Like many of his contemporaries in the mid-century managerial world, he was aware of the rapid bureaucratization of work in the United States, concerned, like many of them, with the threat this posed to "traditional American work values," and worried that the evils of bureaucracy would undermine Americans' innate capacities for hard work and for technological innovation. This, he feared would sap America's military, political, and moral power in the midst of a highly threatening, technology-driven cold war. Armed with an amalgamation of his religious convictions (a personalized version of the Protestant Ethic) and the then popular Human Relations rhetoric (a secular version of the religious dogma), Miller set out to create a company that would do away with the evils of bureaucracy and allow American workers once again to find personal fulfillment and collective creativity in their work. In Miller's retrospective words, the company had "almost a moral obligation to society." "When we started Tech," he recalls, "the business fad was McGregor and theory X and Y. Some tried and said: I knew it wouldn't work. We made it work. . . . We were masters at exploiting the enthusiasm that comes from an independent spirit" (Kunda, pp. 61–62).

Unlike many senior managers, however, Miller was not satisfied with remaining a visionary. Following is a brief review of the ways in which he attempted to translate his ideas into reality.

Designing the innovative organization

Tech's formal policies governing its employees' work lives were a direct outgrowth of Miller's ideas. These policies, implemented from above at his insistence (occasionally against the better judgment of his advisors and managers), came to be regarded as mainstays of Tech's emerging corporate culture, a culture regarded by many employees, as well as outside observers, as unique. The essence of Miller's principles, and his main concern during the three decades he controlled the company, was the promotion of individual initiative and the encouragement of risk taking: he wanted to create an environment in which talented engineers, driven by what he assumed was their natural proclivity for heavy investment in their work, would feel free to pursue their technical visions unencumbered and unconstrained by unnecessary bureaucratic procedures.

First, and considered most crucial by Miller, was a policy of "no layoffs." Despite recurring external and internal warnings that such a policy was too costly, not to say downright un-American, the company managed, by and large, to maintain its commitment over the years and through a number of rather severe crises.[3] Guaranteed employment – and the various types of retraining and education programs associated with it – was presented as a "security net" that would, in the long run, encourage innovativeness by allowing engineers to experiment with new technologies, to take risks without fear of the consequences of becoming obsolete, and to challenge prevailing directions without fear of retribution. Moreover, it would presumably elicit the engineers' best efforts by enhancing their sense of obligation to their enlightened employer. These efforts would undoubtedly produce the many options from which the company's managers could then choose its technical directions. In the long run, Miller promised his critics, "short-sighted bean-counters" in his view, that such a technical and managerial workforce would more than justify the cost of maintaining it.

Second, to complement the effects of the no-layoff policy, the company instituted an open internal labor market. All job openings in the company were publicly posted and all employees encouraged to attempt to fill positions through direct contact with those offering them. The personnel department's traditional control of "promotable pools" was not allowed, and hierarchical control of promotion opportunities was severely curtailed. This, it was believed, would release employees' innovative energies by freeing them from too much concern with satisfying and protecting their immediate superiors, and would prevent talented people from being held down or back by superiors fearful of criticism and competition, or dependent on their continued efforts in their current jobs.

Third, Miller attempted to do away with the reality and symbols of bureaucratic forms of control: the company was designed as a flexible network rather than a rigid hierarchy. The R&D division, in particular, was structured as a loose and very ambiguously defined "matrix" organization with vague boundaries, complex overlapping "dotted lines" of reporting, a dense network of informal relations, ambiguous definitions of authority and responsibility, frequently changing configurations, and much scope for entrepreneurship and competition. Competition, initiative, and "ownership" became key concepts. Miller believed that in such an environment, more like a market place than a mechanistic structure, his employees' commitment, motivation, and investment in work would be enhanced, the "good ideas" they develop would "bubble up," and the strongest ones would survive. This design was complemented by open office space architecture that removed physical and spatial barriers to communication (typically erected along lines prescribed by bureaucratic structures) as well as many of the accepted status symbols of organizational life: in their place employees were offered shared dining rooms, standardized office cubicles, open parking, and so forth. Similarly, an electronic network was developed to facilitate unmediated and unencumbered communication between all professional and managerial employees.

Finally, an effort was made to absorb employees' lives into an expanded organizational community within which many of their social and psychological needs could be fulfilled. For example, flexitime work arrangements enabled loosely defined working hours and self managed schedules, allowed work at home, and deemphasized traditionally enforced boundaries of time and space. In addition, heavy resources were invested in employees' well-being: various types of leisure and social activities were made available in the organizational context; a broad array of employee benefits – ranging from childcare to a credit union – were offered; an Employee Assistance Program provided free counselling; and so on. Tech, in short, set out to become a model employer.

In sum, Tech's policies reflected its founder's strong belief that an innovative organization must do away with the trappings – real and symbolic – of bureaucracy, relinquish some of the hierarchical methods of control it entails, and thus create for its engineers an open, competitive, and yet secure work environment that would leash and enhance their intrinsic motivation to work hard and long, elicit and facilitate their natural proclivities for experimentation, and encourage them to take risks and assume responsibility. This, he felt, would allow the organization as a whole to produce the kind of technological variation that would present management with numerous options and would, through a "survival of the fittest" model, facilitate its choices.[4]

In such a work environment, the metaphor of "culture" rather than of "structure" became a key organizing principle. Within the broad contextual parameters set down by company policy, few specific "bureaucratic" guidelines for behavior existed. The lack of clear organization charts and the absence of the standard hierarchically enforced "rules and regulations" left cultural rules as the main systematic guides for and predictors of behavior. Consequently, Tech management invested heavy efforts in developing and disseminating its managerial ideology – an elaborate specification of the culture – to the people expected to live by it. The next two sections offer a brief overview of the substance of the textual output of these efforts, followed by a discussion of the manner in which it was enacted in employees' lives.

Creating a codex

The founder's oft-repeated ideas concerning the nature of the company and the people who worked for it were developed and elaborated over time (with the help of a small army of hired consultants and academics) into a well documented codex. Textual representation of these ideas permeated the work environment: publications, booklets, manuals, videos, newsletters, brochures, research notes, literature summaries, and slogans form an ever-present backdrop of work. Consider, for example, the first ten minutes of an engineer's workday. The engineer

has been around the company for a while; like many others, he has definite ideas about "Tech culture" and what it takes to get things done in Engineering. But, as he is constantly reminded, so does the company. When he arrives at work each morning, he encounters evidence of a "company point of view" at every turn. First are the bumper stickers adorning many of the cars in the Lyndsville parking lot. "I LOVE TECH!" they declare, somewhat unoriginally, the words underscored by the ubiquitous little red heart designed into the company logo. "This shit is everywhere," he says; "I got it on my own car."

If the bumper stickers seem trivial, almost tongue-in-cheek, the short walk to his cubicle takes him past a plethora of more serious stylized references to his experience as a member of the organization. Inside the building, just beyond the security desk, a large TV monitor is playing a videotape of a recent speech by Sam Miller. As he walks by, he hears the familiar voice discuss "our goals, our values and the way we do things." "It's the 'We Are One' speech,'" he notes as he walks by, "nothing new." He has read the speech in a company newsletter and excerpts are posted everywhere. Turning a corner, he stops by a large bulletin board fixed to the wall next to the library. On one side is a permanent display including the well known statement of the "Company Philosophy" ("It's the Bible – the Ten Commandments for the Techie: make a buck and do it right"), and a selection of personnel policies titled "Your Rights and Obligations." On the other, clippings and copies of recent references to Tech in local, national, and trade newspapers are prominently posted. He glances at the latest addition, "High Motivation in High-Tech: The New Work Force"; an anonymous hand has highlighted the company name in bright yellow. By the cafeteria, where he stops for coffee, a flipchart calls attention to Dave Carpenter's presentation ("High Technologies' Strategy for the Future – How You Fit In. The talk will be videotaped"), and to a workshop on "Career Management at Tech: How to Make the Most of Yourself " Close by, piles of brochures are stacked on a table in front of the personnel office. Tom takes one, headed "If you are experiencing signs of stress, perhaps you should give us a call." Inside it offers some words of wisdom: "Everyone experiences stress at some time. . . . Stress isn't necessarily a bad thing. . . . You can do something about stress." He turns into the workspace labyrinth, picks up his mail, and enters his cubicle, where he plans to spend the morning.

Cultural commentary finds him also in the relative seclusion of his own space. As he sits down, he switches on his terminal in a practiced, smooth move, absentmindedly logs on, and turns to the screen. On his (electronic mail) he notices among the many communications another announcement of the afternoon events; a memo titled "How Others See Our Values" reviewing excerpts on Tech Culture from recent managerial bestsellers, a request to be interviewed by a consultant for a culture study; and the daily review of all references to Tech in the press. In his mail ("the hardcopy") he finds *Techknowledge,* one of a large number of company newsletters. On the cover is a big picture of Sam Miller against the background of a giant slogan – "We Are One." He also finds an order form for company publications including Ellen Cohen's "Culture Operating Manual." His bookshelf has mostly technical material, but also a copy of *In Search of Excellence* distributed to all professional and managerial employees, and a business magazine with a cover story on Tech's corporate culture, titled "Working Hard, Having Fun." For good measure, an "I LOVE TECH" bumper sticker is fixed to his filing cabinet. The day has hardly begun, yet Tom is already surrounded by "the culture," the everpresent signs of the company's explicit concern with its employees state of mind (and heart). (Kunda, pp. 50–52)

A few examples of the kinds of texts employees frequently encounter illustrate the systematic and repetitive nature of the managerial version of the culture. A typical description of the company's social attributes is found in a personnel publication:

People are really considered to be important to the company, they do not take a second seat to profits. The company has followed a tradition of full employment Employees are involved in Tech. Most individuals do not see a sharp demarcation between themselves and the company. . . . There is a great deal of drive and energy to keep decision making at the lowest possible levels . . . people have ownership in what they do . . . there are minimal formal processes. There is little bureaucracy compared to other places. Those processes in place are considered only guidelines. While these could be seen as motherhood statements, they truly appear to be part of the operating fabric of Tech. (Kunda, p. 70)

Another publication specifies the "mindset" required of employees:

A lot of people we hire into this company, at least the ones that stick around, have basically the same mind set. Someone who is innovative, enthusiastic, willing to work hard, who isn't hung up on structure, and who has absolutely no concern with educational background. They demand an awful lot from themselves. The harshest critic in the system is yourself and that drives you to do some terribly difficult things. You have to be a self-starter, an individual who takes chances and risks and moves ahead. The expectation is that everyone is going to work hard, not for hard work's sake, but for the fun of it, and enjoy doing what they are doing, and show commitment no matter what it takes. A core of the environment is individual commitment, a lot of integrity, and a very high level of expectations from yourself. Hassle is the price of the organizational structure. For those who don't like it, it's very frustrating. You can wrap those three or four things together (openness, honesty, success, fairness) and you can sum it all up in one word and that is caring. Caring about your job, the people who work for you, yourself (Kunda, p. 73)

As these brief examples suggest, the widely disseminated codex developed around the founder's ideas consists of two central themes, both of which resonate with conventional academic wisdom concerning sociological and psychological factors that enhance innovation. The social environment is described as informal, flexible, and relatively egalitarian. It is an environment in which motivation is founded on intrinsic standards enhanced by peer pressure rather than on a formal reward system and hierarchical supervision, and in which decisions emerge from the interactions of committed individuals willing to "take chances and risks and move ahead."

The second theme is an explicit articulation of the experiential rules of membership: what one is to think and feel if one is to become a full fledged, successful member. "Intrinsic motivation" is the key requirement. Behavioral rules are vague: individuals are told to be entrepreneurial, to "do the right thing" (the company slogan). Instead, the emotional dimensions of membership that supposedly drive behavior are articulated: loyalty, identification, "fun," and a deep commitment to the company, its technology and goals, to the point where the self becomes inseparable from the organizational community.

The managerial view of the culture – flexible environments, deeply committed and highly motivated individuals – exists not only in textual form. The ideas are dramatized and brought to life in the endless stream of interaction in which employees are forever participating. The following section offers an extended example.

Bringing the culture to life

"Tech," employees know, "is a group culture"; there are numerous occasions for structured face-to-face interaction, ranging from routine work group meetings through training groups to various encounters with managers. Whether designed for work or leisure, large or small, one-time or repetitive, these events are opportunities for members not only to enact but also to experience aspects of the managerial view of the culture. Space does not permit exemplification of all these issues, but the following excerpt suggests the flavor of these events. It is a description of the "Intro to Tech Orientation Workshop," also known as "Bootcamp," a two-day event designed to introduce new engineers to the company.

The module on Tech culture comes first. Ellen Cohen is the invited speaker. Introduction are made. The twenty five participants give brief descriptions of their organizational location and technology. Most of them are "new hires" three to six months out of school; some have transferred from other companies. One or two have vaguely defined jobs in Corporate, there is an older engineer from Manufacturing, a fairly senior finance manager from Engineering, and a technician from Field Service.

"Culture" is not a notion that engineers take to easily, and newcomers are often unfamiliar with the appropriate behavior in Tech training seminars; consequently, the module – designed as a series of interactive exercises – requires some goading. After passing out handouts summarizing the talk, Ellen writes the word "culture" on a large flipchart and says:

"The topic today is culture. We have a spectrum of people here from all over the company. Feel free to chime in. 'Culture' has become something of a fad. First, what is 'culture?' What do you think?"

A young engineer slouching in the corner answers: "Fungus. I had a culture for my senior science project. But my dog ate it." Some laugh. Ellen smiles too, but continues undaunted. "We're looking at behavior, at people. What is the characteristic of people at Tech?" She waits, marker in hand, with a warm, inviting looking smile, nodding in anticipation, perhaps indicating the signs of affirmation she is looking for. Her question hangs. No answers. Some coffee sipping. "You feel like you've all been chosen, right?" she says, nodding her head more vigorously and still smiling. Still no replies. The stony silence highlights the incongruity of her demeanor, but she persists. "What else? what are people like at Tech?" Some volunteers speak up, drawn in by discomfort, if nothing else: "Friendly." "Amicable." She writes it all on the flip chart. The tempo picks up: "Individual- and teamwork." "I'm expected to be a good corporate citizen." "Strong customer orientation." "People tend to like Tech no matter how confused," she says, and adds: "How do you feel?"
Some of the participants raise their hands. She calls on each in turn.

"I like it here. I hope for profit. I respect Sam Miller a lot. Where I worked before you'd hope they fail! Here the executives aren't as ruthless as in other companies; they are more humane. I haven't met anyone here I don't respect. "

"I flash off on the (electronic mail) and get to people without them wondering why; they are open and willing to share information."

"People understand. There is tolerance for new people."

"There's a supportive atmosphere. . . ."

As they speak, Ellen makes encouraging sounds and lists key phrases on the chart: "profit; not ruthless; humane; respect; open; share info; tolerance-, supportive. "
When the sheet is full, she pulls it off the flipchart, pastes it to the wall and says: "This is what makes Tech a different kind of place. People are relaxed and informal. What else?" Someone says: "There is little difference between engineers and managers; it's hard to tell them apart." "Authority Not a Big Deal," she writes in bold letters on the flip chart. Then she adds: "In other places you're incompetent till proved otherwise; here it's the other way around, right?" Not waiting for an answer, she writes "Confidence in competence," and says: "They know what they are doing, or believe it." "A little too much," the guy sitting next to me whispers to his neighbor. . . .
Ellen turns to the flip chart, writes "We Are A Family," and says:

"This is the most important one. We have a no-layoff policy. It's the ultimate backup plan. It would break some people's hearts if we had to do it. We face it as a family: cutting costs, hiring freezes. Every member is asked to contribute."

A young woman from corporate who has been silent so far, bursts out in a concerned, almost angry tone:

"I work in corporate. A lot of the stuff is only a myth there. I see the very high up people fighting to the death. There is no clear person with the last word. They bounce responsibility around."

She starts to give an example from a well known failed project, but Ellen interrupts her rather brusquely:

"Tech isn't wonderful or glowing. It's not. It's human. But it's the best I've seen! I was a nomad before I came here. I'm sorry you haven't seen the rest of the companies so you can appreciate Tech. (Pause). That is another thing about Tech. People are quick to point out faults, as if they didn't have any. Where I worked before there was rampant empire building. Tech is much better. We are a state-of-the-art pioneer. There is great love and great criticism of the company."

The instructor wins more and more ground with every minute of the meeting. As the following excerpt suggests, the session ends with total success. The emotional intensity of the module's conclusion . . . seems to captivate all the participants. Ellen flips off the viewgraph, puts down the marker, and gives a short talk that sounds off-the-record, very personal, almost motherly:

"There is a downside to all of this! There can be a lot of pain in the system! Be careful; keep a balance; don't overdo it, don't live off vending machines for a year. (Laughter). You'll burn out. I've been there; I lived underground for a year, doing code. Balance your life. Don't say: 'I'll work like crazy for four years, then I'll get married.' I heard this from a kid. But who will he marry? Don't let the company suck you dry; after nine or ten hours your work isn't worth much anyway."

The sudden switch to a subversive sounding message creates the air of rapt attention. All eyes are on her as she walks slowly from the flipchart to the center of the room. After a brief pause, she adds the finishing touch; "What kind of company do you think allows me to be saying these things to you?" Nobody stirs for a few moments, and then a break is called. (Kunda, pp. 109–113)

The event, on the face of it, is a familiar scene to those aware of advances in techniques of corporate socialization. Yet it also exemplifies the elaborate, frequently occurring, and highly involving events through which the managerial ideology is brought to life. The event not only brings the substance of the ideology to participants' awareness in a persuasive fashion, it also allows them to experience the company's claims of openness, flexibility, and concern for employees; to publicly enact the roles it requires of them; and to observe and supervise their own and others' adherence to such cultural requirements. Cultural control, in short, has a pervasive presence in the everyday lives of employees. What is its impact?

Living with the culture

Tech's Engineering division is, by many, if not all, accounts a stressful environment. Like many of its kind, the organization is project based; and the stress typically associated with project management is exacerbated by the Tech style of management. Projects are allocated on a competitive basis.

Consequently time and budget commitments are overly optimistic at best, downright lies at worst. Slipping deadlines, budget crunches, ambiguous definitions of authority, and political moves by competing groups contribute to rising pressure, overwork, tension, and conflict. The relative freedom to move afforded by the internal labor market magnifies the problems as talented people "skip ship" during crises. Temporary resolutions are often the lull before the next storm.

Nevertheless, Tech Engineering is an environment perceived by many as conducive to professional creativity, at least in comparison to other companies. Many engineers are aware, indeed are even thankful, for the efforts gone into designing their work environment, often referred to as an "engineers' sandbox." A typical comment is offered by a young, recently hired engineer:

Tech has the best engineers. I'm an engineer, and I want state-of-the-art technology. At Chiptech they develop what Marketing tells them. I'm happy as long as you keep me away from marketing types. Tech caters to engineers. Its reputation in the industry is a country club for engineers. It's laid-back. Overall there are less fires, less stupid deadlines. They allow people to transfer freely, they put a lot of money into training, they give inexperienced people opportunity. Learning is the most important thing to me. If I gave it up I'd become comatose. Right now I'm learning chip design. A totally new area for me. Some engineers love houses, others cars; engineers like details, how things work. I like to learn. And the environment here is open enough to let you get involved in anything you like.

Once you've worked with Tech products in a Tech environment, it's hard to go to anything else. They are just so much better. It's an engineer's dream – if he is into technology. (Kunda, pp. 176–177)

For those who have been around for a while, life is a little more nuanced and perhaps not as optimistic. Those who survive and flourish in the Tech environment seem to incorporate – with various degrees of awareness – the rules of the culture. In their work lives, they appear to be manifestations of the founder's vision. Consider, for example, a consulting engineer recognized by many for his talent:

Tom . . . is hunched over his terminal, his back to the opening of his cubicle. He is wearing earplugs to close off the rest of the world. Things are going well, he would acknowledge, almost too well. His promotion just came through. He is now a "consulting engineer" – a title coveted by many Tech engineers. His contribution to a number of key projects is apparently being recognized by the faceless mass that seems to determine reputation in the "technical community," and he is getting more and more electronic mail from all over the company. In his group he is considered the resident expert on XYZ technology. This year he earned close to 60K, and for the first time he was given stock options – the secret sign of inclusion. His current role is rather vaguely defined, and he can get involved in almost anything. In fact he is expected to, and he is aware of the pressure to "make things happen" and how it works on him. "That's the culture – designed ambiguity. It sucks people in," he says. He has been invited to join a number of task forces, and is thinking of learning some of the business issues. ("A little night reading. And time out for some of the hoopla.

I'll go to Carpenter's presentation later. Once I'd have laughed, but when you start getting around you need to go.") He considers his position a good balance between remaining technical and getting into management. Recollections of his burnout episode a few years back and a brief and unsuccessful stint at a crazy start-up company have lost their painful edge. He is back with Tech. And he seems to have arrived.

Right now Tom is trying to understand the intricacies of a failing project. Rick Smith, the project manager, was finally removed and someone has to figure out what the hell was going on: the technical problems and also some of the people issues. ("A lot of egos involved!") Tom was the natural choice. It temporarily adds a few extra hours to the working day, but it's fun, it's a challenge, it's involving. Today he came in earlier than usual, and he will probably spend most of the weekend on it. "Boy, did they ever screw up," he says as he stares at the screen. Every now and then an audible beep announces the arrival of an electronic message. He fights the temptation to flip screens. "It'll take a while today just to go through the mail and stay current. Things sure pile up when you're riding the wave. That's the culture. You have to learn to work it. And to protect yourself. People can get swept away. It's great. Like the joke. You get to choose which 20 hours to work out of the day." (Kunda, pp. 17–18)

Tom's success story is a familiar tale. So, however, are the intimations of danger between the lines, and the sense of being engulfed and somewhat out of control. Although he currently experiences himself "riding the wave," for many others the dangers loom large: burnout, attributed to the particular qualities of Tech, is always close at hand.

This is a real seductive organization. You wanna do more and more. I work seventeen, eighteen hours a day. I get a few hours done in the early morning then I take the kid to school, spend the day here, and work in the evening. It's family and work. That is it. It's hard. A lot of burnout. Maybe because of 'he who proposes does.' Its not like Silicon or Chiptech. They say Tech encourages divorces. They promise you a lot, make it lucrative, give you more and more. It's not just Tech; it is this whole industry. People get addicted to work. I look around and I see weird things. I see screwed-up marriages, I see fucked-up kids. I thought Ben had problems: alcoholism, a depressed wife. So I found him another job. But now his replacement has just left his wife and kids himself. (Kunda, pp. 17–18)

Rick is a typical casualty:

Rick . . . – recently removed from his position – is slowly cleaning out his desk. He stops every now and then to light another cigarette. Mary, his secretary, is in the outer cubicle pretending to be occupied, even though the phones have stopped ringing. Like many other familiar and less familiar acquaintances of Rick's, she is behaving as if nothing has happened. He is not sure if he should be grateful for this studied "business as usual" demeanor, but he plays along with it. However, the large half-filled cartons on the table and the blank screen on his terminal – sure indications of a standstill – belie the signs of routine. Rick would acknowledge that he has burnt out. "I should never have taken this job. Can't quite figure out when things started to go wrong. Bastards just threw me into this damn project. No feedback, no guidance, no support, no warning. 'Its Tech culture,' they say. 'Do What's Right.' Some help! I was so busy with all the details, never had time to get deep enough into the technical stuff. Had to rely on the group members. And they wouldn't communicate. With each other. Or with me. And the schedules were unrealistic in the first place. Probably because of all the politics. When we started to slip, things just fell apart. Everyone was watching. Probably whispering. I found out later that my boss was checking who was logged on at night. They do that. This company's like an aquarium. And my problems at home didn't help. Drinking more and more. What comes first – sipping or slipping? It hit the fan when I told them I was taking two weeks to dry out again – right before the last schedule slip. Luckily the guys in process engineering up in Hanover were willing to take me. The EAP [Employee Assistance Program] advisor here helped – he's a company shrink. Contracted and sworn to secrecy. A real professional. They have a lot of experience with this type of thing. Finally found something for me. Had to do a lot of looking first. Maybe I should take it easy for a while. Or even reconsider this whole damn company! If I can afford to – there should be a warning out front: High Technologies – It's Hazardous to Your Health." (Kunda, p. 19)

One approach to these casualties is to consider them part of the professional hazards of engineering, not necessarily unique to Tech. Says an engineering manager:

I don't buy all that "we are unique" song and dance. There is nothing unique about Tech. Constant reorganization is a way of life in this industry. Everyone knows that – unless their head is up their butt. That is the way it is, particularly in this kind of changing technology.

That is the nature of the industry. Constant change, high pressure, motivation to achieve. It results in burnout. That is the "old Tech." Sam has one primary criterion: success in the marketplace. Nothing else counts, no institution at Tech is holy. We'll try different things. Sociologists tell us the price is high. Bullshit! Get people really involved and motivated and 20% burn out. But 80% work. And there are countless start-ups to employ people. I worked at Data Corp and it was exactly the same. (Kunda, pp. 172–173, 181)

An oft-encountered response to the demands of life at Tech, whether unique or not, is to view the culture as a managerial manipulation. Cynicism about the managerial rhetoric is frequently heard.

I've learned here that you can do your own job, but you have to let the waves flow over you; ignore them or you'll go crazy. There is a lot of shit coming down, people wandering around, consultants, studies; that's the way it is, but it isn't a bad place. On a scale of ten it's maybe a six or a seven; but they really stuff ten pounds of shit into five-pound bags. I have a Russian immigrant friend who says it reminds him of the USSR; all this shit about Big Brother. (Kunda, p. 184)

More crucially, many have developed a new twist to the age old worker response of alienation: alienation from the company's seductive pressure to express conformity to required standards of feeling, to become a Techie; alienation from the experiences the company prescribes and that one is often called upon to display. The only way to survive at Tech, it is often said, is to "learn to speak the culture" but to "depersonalize," to "develop a thick skin," to "remember it is all a game," not to let things get to you," to "never show what you are feeling," "not to believe the California bathtub crap," and to "always be suspicious of the motives and agendas of others."

Thus, intense managerial efforts to shape employees in the corporate mold produces a somewhat different outcome.

> If the attempts to engineer culture . . . are aimed at defining the members' self for them, this very attempt undermines its own assumptions. The engineers of culture see the ideal member as driven by strong beliefs and intense emotions, authentic experiences of loyalty, commitment, and the pleasure of work. Yet, they seem to produce members who have internalized ambiguity, who have made the metaphor of drama a centerpiece of their sense of self, who question the authenticity of all beliefs and emotions, and who find irony in its various forms the dominant mode of everyday existence. (Kunda, p. 216)

Conclusion

The sustained and concerted efforts to shape a "nonbureaucratic culture" had a significant impact on the company's way of life. The relaxation of bureaucratic controls was indeed experienced and appreciated by many engineers. The "corporate culture" was also recognized and publicized in the popular press; indeed, Tech was an oft used and much lauded exemplar of excellence during the peak of that particular fad in the eighties: the rather unique combination of freedom, commitment, and chaos, it was argued, were the source of the company's proven ability to tap and channel its employees' motivation, commitment, and abilities toward sustained organizational innovativeness.

To what extent can postbureaucratic corporate culture be credited with such magnificent accomplishments? How, in fact, if at all, are the company's successes – and failures – related to its self-conscious efforts to shape a culture of innovation? Such questions cannot be fully addressed with the type of data presented in this chapter. Indeed, the very notion of success and failure, particularly in the long run, is itself extremely complex and its various constituting elements are difficult – if not impossible – to unravel. However, it is worth pointing out that a cursory glance at Tech's record does reveal a more ambiguous reality than the proponents of postbureaucratic cultures of work would have us believe. Purely from a technical point of view there were a series of key successes. There is no doubt that, over the years, the company produced a steady stream of innovations, some of which set industry standards for years to come. However, there were also a number of major failures, one of which practically destroyed the company: the company's concerted attempt to move into a new and increasingly important market niche collapsed, and, more recently, the company, along with others of its class, has been floundering, both in terms of its technical direction and in terms of its financial performance. Analysts searching to establish the causes of these events would be hard pressed, I suspect, to isolate luck, randomness, technical leadership, the engineering personality, the technological imperative, or changes in the structure of the industry and the market, from organizational factors, without falling into one tautological trap or another. And even if such connections could be established, there is reason to suspect – so goes conventional industry wisdom – that the same organizational features that enhance technological innovation undermine other aspects of performance where planning and rationality are required, not the least of which is long term relations with markets, clients, and customers, where, in the final analysis, the criteria for the success or failure of innovation are ultimately determined.

Thus, debureaucratization might, as students of innovation predict, do away with those processes that cause oversight, and create an organization that produces a steady stream of innovative ideas. But the same factors might just exacerbate the problem of foresight: how to choose among ideas, and, ultimately, how to tailor them into useful and desirable products. Debureaucratization, then, might, if anything, produce too much of a good thing: the overinnovative organization, incapable of managing or directing the endless streams of ideas it produces.

These claims, however, must remain speculative at best. What is clear, however, is that innovation cannot and should not be considered in isolation: the attempt to institutionalize a "nonbureaucratic" culture that enhances innovation has much wider ramifications than the number and quality of new ideas or new products in a given period. Thus, the data indicate that the attempt to create a "nonbureaucratic" organization is riddled with paradox. Bureaucracy, ultimately, is a form of control founded on an institutionalization of rules of conduct. In an effort to do away with such rules, the company turned instead to a concerted effort to specify and enforce the rules of experience, or, in other words, to find a way to shape and control intrinsic motivation. The irony, of course, is that attempting to define and manipulate that which is "intrinsic" makes the target of these efforts quite extrinsic. As Kunda (1992, p. 220) argues, "the essence of bureaucratic control – the formalization, codification, and enforcement of rules and regulations – does not change in principle . . . it merely shifts its focus – at management's discretion – from the organizational structure to the organizational culture, from the members' behavior to their experience." Thus, despite claims to the contrary, such managerial attempts are part of the more traditional processes associated with bureaucratic control and subject to all its problems. In short, the organized efforts to do away with bureaucracy create a new and perhaps more virulent type of bureaucratic pathology, a form of well-disguised bureaucratic control in which employees are equally susceptible to the kinds of pressures bureaucracy produces, only more so: it is a form of control that denies its own existence and is thus resistant to management, both by managers and by those subjected to it.

It is clear, then, that applied theories of "innovation," which present it as the only dependent variable, one that we are asked to accept as unquestionably good, are used, in the process of their implementation, as ideologies of managerial control. This raises two types of concerns. First, it raises a serious moral question. Such an ideology provides the justification and legitimation for practices that should raise serious doubts among those concerned with the well being of people employed in industries driven by innovation. In particular, this chapter, and the material on which it draws, provide some insight into the processes of applying theories of innovation, expose the commercially driven shaping of the self in corporate settings that they disguise, and reveal the hidden or ignored costs behind the notion of "innovation at any cost." Second, for those for whom such moral concerns are not an issue, and for whom the success or failure of "innovation" (and presumably the profits associated with it) is the criterion of choice for evaluating organizational life, it is worth pointing out another danger of applied theories of innovation. To the extent that such an ineffable concept – owing as much or more to the vagaries of the human condition as to "social factors" – can be related in a causal fashion to specifiable organizational conditions, the engineers of culture might consider, using their own logic, whether they are helping to create the very conditions that endanger their own dependent variable: a new form of bureaucracy that undermines the personal and organizational prerequisites of morally driven professional practice.

Ethnographic evidence, readers accustomed to more traditional approaches to the study of innovation might claim, is at best a flimsy base for such sweeping statements. More might be needed to make a convincing case. But at the very least it is hoped that this chapter and the book from which it derives its data will provide an impetus for research that does not allow its assumptions to go unquestioned, that is sensitive to the ideological role managerially oriented research is often called upon to play, the biases this introduces into its findings and claims, and the price it entails, both for scientific inquiry and for its objects of study.

Notes

1 The nature of these rules, the extent to which they are clear cut as opposed to ambiguous and the degree to which they are – or need to be – shared by members is the subject of intense debate among scholars (who seem often to confuse empirical questions with axiomatic theoretical claims). See Martin (1993) for a review of these issues.

2 The name of the company is disguised, as are those of all people mentioned.

3 This policy did not survive the recent managerial succession forced by changes in the company's fortunes. Miller was forced out by his board of directors, and his successors decided to reduce the company's workforce rather significantly.

4 These ideas, developed and implemented as early as the 1950s, were not only precursors to later attempts to theorize innovation; the company (or at least an idealized version of it) also served as an empirical base for the claims of influential academics and popular management writers. See, for example, Kanter (1983) and Schein (1992).

References

Amabile, T. M. (1988). A model of creativity and innovation in organizations. *Research in Organizational Behavior*, 10, 123–167.

Barley, S. R.; Meyer; G., and Gash, D. C. (1988). Cultures of culture: Academics, practitioners and the pragmatics of normative control. *Administrative Science Quarterly*, 33, 24–60.

Barley, S. and Kunda, G. (1992). Design and devotion: Surges of rational and normative ideologies of control in managerial discourse. *Administrative Science Quarterly*, 37, 363–399.

Deci, E. (1975). *Intrinsic Motivation*. New York: Plenum.

Garud, R., Nayyar, P., and Shapira, Z. (1997). Technological innovation: Oversights and foresights. Chapter 1, this volume.

Jelinek, M. and Schoonhoven, C. B. (1990). *The Innovation Marathon: Lessons from High Technology Firms*. Oxford: Basil Blackwell.

Kanter, R. M. (1988). When a thousand flowers bloom: Structural, collective, and social conditions for innovation in organization. *Research in Organizational Behavior*, 10, 169–211.

Kunda, G. (1992). *Engineering Culture: Control and Commitment in a High-Tech Corporation*. Philadelphia: Temple University Press.

Perrow, C. (1986). *Complex Organizations: A Critical Essay*. 3rd ed. New York: Random House.

Ritti, R. R. (1971). Dual management: Does it work? *Research Management*, 14, 19–26.

Rothman, R. A. and Perucci, R. (1970). Organizational careers and professional expertise. *Administrative Science Quarterly*, 15, 282–293.

Shapira, Z. (1989). Task choice and assigned goals as determinants of task motivation and performance. *Organizational Behavior and Group Performance*, 44, 141–165.

Shenhav, Y. A. (1988). Abandoning the research bench: Individual, organizational and environmental accounts. *Work and Occupations*, 15, 5–23.

Trice, H. and Beyer, J. (1993). *The Cultures of Work Organizations*. New York: Walter de Gruyter.

Section VI
Clearing the fog

18 Beating the odds: Towards a theory of technological innovation

Raghu Garud, Praveen Nayyar, and Zur Shapira

At the Museum of Natural History in New York, a series of panels graphically depicts natural selection at work. In one panel, a fox runs after a rabbit. In another, a tiger is poised to kill a fox. And so on.

To survive, each animal must rely on the competitive advantages stemming from its own unique abilities. Nothing else matters. Ultimately, outcomes are inevitable and determined. There is no choice in such a world. All that animals have to rely on is what they do best. Pursued by a fox, it makes a lot of sense that a rabbit should run as fast as possible. In the circumstances, it is the best thing to do. Looking at the panel, though, it is not clear that running will be enough to save the rabbit.

The inevitability of outcomes in such a naturally selected world strikes home as one gazes at a magnificent display of dinosaurs. Despite their size, and indeed because of it, dinosaurs became extinct when the earth's atmospheric temperatures soared when either a volcanic eruption occurred or a meteorite hit the earth. Helpless to adapt, dinosaurs became extinct as a species, to be replaced by others better suited to survive the changed ambient conditions.

Subsumed in the natural selection process depicted in these panels are the four challenges to a theory of technological innovation that we articulated (Garud, Nayyar, and Shapira, chapter 1, this volume). These challenges stem from the inevitability of the occurrence of technological oversights and foresights. Oversights and foresights are inevitable because technological outcomes are *uncertain* and *contingent* upon a match between the internal capabilities of a firm and its external environments. Furthermore, oversights and foresights are inevitable because technological choices are *complex* even as they are *constrained* by the past. From the perspective of a natural selection process, uncertainty stems from random variations, contingencies arise as selection environments change exogenously, and constraints are created through an imprinting process where past experiences are retained. Needless to say, the complexity that is inherent in this natural selection process is dealt with without the presence of human intelligence (Figure 18.1).[1]

Progressing from the section displaying primates to the section displaying humans at the Museum of Natural History, one senses an important difference. The panels no longer suggest creatures trapped with only the competencies they were endowed with at birth. Rather, the panels imply that humans have the wherewithal to use technologies to extend their physical and cognitive abilities and accomplish tasks they have not achieved before. One gets the sense that humans can not only respond to the world or shape it in ways that match their competencies, but that they also have the ability to abandon their past and create a new future. This flexibility is hinted at, for example, in the contrasts between the panel displaying icemen wearing animal skins to protect themselves from the Arctic cold, and the adjoining panel featuring an aborigine wearing a loin cloth to help him survive the sweltering desert heat.

These images evoke thoughts about how humans adapt to different environments. They also remind us of the enormous impact humans have had in shaping the world as we now know it. Indeed, the world we interact with is, increasingly, not a natural one, but an artificially created one. In this constructed world, variations are not always random, nor do selection environments preexist. Moreover, humans are not relatively powerless, like animals, for they do not have to enact scripts based only on the past.

It is this proposition that we would like to develop in our attempts at developing a theory of technological innovation. Specifically, we would like to highlight a technologically created world; one where it is possible to prepare for serendipity, where fits can be tailored, and where individuals have the power to bring about change through continuity. Shaping this process are humans, who, through the use of their cognitive abilities, can manage the complexities associated with technological innovation (Weick, 1990) (see Figure 18.2).

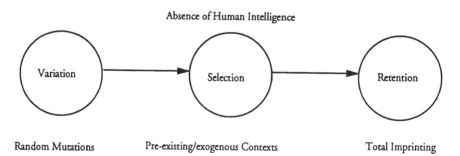

Figure 18.1. Challenges to the construction of a theory of technological innovation.

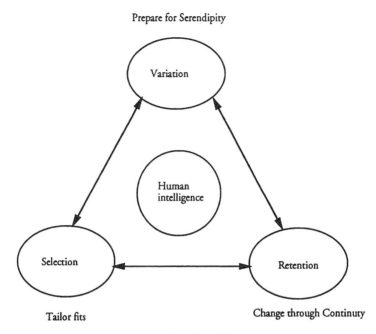

Figure 18.2. Toward a theory of technological innovation.

Innovation in a technological world

3M Corporation is most admired for its ability to sustain itself based on technological innovation. 3M's corporate aim is to generate 25% of its revenues from products introduced in the past 5 years. It appears that 3M has been able to meet this target regularly for over 20 years; a record that suggests that it might be possible for a firm to beat the "coin-flip" challenge offered by Barney (this volume).[2]

How can a firm such as 3M corporation systematically beat the odds associated with natural selection or subsumed in the coin flip analogy? An answer may lie in the now often repeated story of how "Post-it" notes were created (Nayak and Keteringham, 1986; Video on *In Search of Excellence*). It appears that an adhesive was created that was not appropriate for traditional purposes. Under most circumstances, such a product would have been considered a "failure." Not at 3M, however. Ever mindful of the problems of marking certain pages of the Bible, Art Fry, a research scientist at 3M Corporation, conceived of a use for the "failed" adhesive by conceptualizing a new product that was both "permanent and yet temporary." As told by Art and Lew Lehr (then CEO of 3M Corporation), this product was carefully introduced within 3M and in other institutional arenas before it was finally offered to the market.

The Post-it notes story suggests how individually and collectively humans can beat the natural selection process. Specifically, it suggests how creativity can be induced, how selection environments can be shaped, and how change can be accomplished even while maintaining continuity. It also suggests how a group of initiated managers can collectively shepherd the complex innovation process.

Preparing for serendipity

We all know of Louis Pasteur's famous adage "fortune favors the prepared mind." Such a statement is reminiscent of other moments of insight in the lives of individuals such as Newton and Archimedes. More generally, it appears that the notion of creativity can be a cultivated phenomenon (Amabile and Conti, this volume, chapter 7).

To appreciate how it might be possible to cultivate creativity, it is important to have a theory of change that goes beyond considering creativity as comprising acts of genius that occur in random. Usher (1954) offers such a theory. He suggests that the emergence of novelty is a cumulative syntheses of a number of steps that include "perception of a problem," the "setting of a stage," an "act of insight," and finally an "act of critical revision." Such a process is similar to Koestler's (1964) theory of "bisociation," a process whereby creative people associate ideas from unrelated fields to create a totally new one.

Cumulative synthesis is a process that has evolutionary antecedents but revolutionary consequences. This view underscores the potentially dysfunctional consequences of aiming for either evolutionary or revolutionary innovations. For instance, the dysfunctional aspects of adopting a "breakthrough" mentality are well documented by Rosenbloom and Cusumano (1988) in their study of the evolution of VCR technology. They show that early pioneers who embraced a breakthrough mentality lost out to others who adopted a more consistent and pragmatic approach that can best be described as a process of "learning-by-trial." The dysfunctional aspect of adopting only an evolutionary mentality is illustrated by the ways in which American firms got caught up within a given frame of thinking that can best be described as "just-in-case." Consequently, many American firms failed to recognize the benefits of adopting a "just-in-time" approach.

The cumulative synthesis approach requires a mindset towards innovation that is very different from a mindset traditionally adopted in industry. Specifically it requires individuals to continually experiment with old and new ideas, probing the world around them to learn which endeavors might be successful (Eliashberg, Lilien, & Rao, this volume, chapter 12), which may need to be shelved for the future, and which must be abandoned. Institutions are not mechanisms to sanction individuals for "failed" efforts, but are devices for the retention of knowledge from "experiments." In this way of thinking, initiatives, whether they lead to immediate successes or not, are neither oversights nor foresights, but are "probes" from which individuals can learn (Garud, Nayyar, and Shapira, chapter 3, this volume). Indeed, these initiatives create the very variations from which a larger collective can choose (Dosi and Lovallo, chapter 4; Levinthal, chapter 10, both this volume).

Tailoring fits

Unlike animals, humans are capable of "waiting" (Elster, 1983). Specifically, humans are capable of refusing favorable opportunities in the present in order to create even more favorable ones in the future. In the terminology introduced by March (1991), humans can forgo "exploitation" in the present in order to "explore" more favorable opportunities for the future.

An ability to wait and explore generates an "options value" to technological innovation (Kumaraswamy, 1996). Such an options value stems from the asynchronies that exist in the creation of ideas, markets, and institutions required for the successful implementation of technological innovations (Garud & Nayyar, 1994). As Cohen, March, and Olsen (1972) have pointed out in an organizational context, garbage can systems extract options value from innovations by facilitating the coupling of solutions with problems across time and space. Indeed, as Wilson and Hlavacek (1984) found, most innovations "unshelved" by firms were successful in comparison to a hit rate of two out of 10 that is typical of normal innovations (Mansfield, 1981).

Waiting and exploration also allows for the coevolution of firm capabilities, customer preferences, and institutional rules over time. Coevolutionary dynamics are necessary if we recognize that customer preferences are not given ex-ante, but can be institutionally shaped and molded (March, 1971). Similarly, markets and institutional infrastructures do not preexist, but must be created. Indeed, as Hirsch, (1975) has demonstrated, institutional environments can be coopted and shaped to create the appropriabilty regimes required to benefit from innovations (Teece, 1987).

From this way of thinking, the "temporary-permanent" attribute of Post-it is not given ex-ante, but one that is created. Similarly, the possibilities inherent in computer and information technologies do not preexist, but are continually shaped through a process of interaction between the providers, users and other institutional players. In this sense, innovation itself is a negotiated activity, where ideas, markets, and institutions coevolve. In such a world, fits just don't happen (Langlois, this volume), but must be tailored (Brown, this volume, chapter 6).

Change through continuity

The popular adage is that those who don't know the past are condemned to repeat it. Particularly in environments characterized by rapid change,

though, there may be virtue in not knowing the past so well. Path dependencies and an emphasis on maintaining internal consistency constrain future possibilities (Porac, this volume; David, 1985; Arthur, 1988; Utterback,
1994, Levitt & March, 1988). In turn, if left unchecked, such a momentum
may lead organizations to escalate their commitments to failing courses of
action (Staw, 1981).

Several chapters in this book provide the rationale and the means to attenuate links with the past (e.g. Levinthal, chapter 10; Jelinek, chapter 11;
Brown, chapter 6). However, the notions of cumulative syntheses (Usher,
1954) and bisociation (Koestler, 1964) suggest that it is important to go beyond the past even while building upon it. That is, we ought to think about
accomplishing revolutionary outcomes with evolutionary strands.

Cumulative syntheses and bisociation require linkages between two or
more seemingly unrelated ideas to create a new one. Such a process results
in new functionality and performance that would not have been possible if
the two dissociated ideas had not been associated. The act of creation and
novelty requires both an in-depth understanding of each strand of knowledge, as well as an ability to bring these knowledge strands together in a
powerful yet purposeful manner.

Such a process is best illustrated by the invention of the Sony Walkman
(Nayak and Ketteringham, 1986). Challenged to create a personal stereo
system, the engineering team, secluded from the rest, came up with many
"out of the box" solutions using their in-depth understanding of various
bodies of knowledge. The creation of a small set of speakers, however, was
one area that stymied the team. The solution looking for a problem was
identified by a "wandering chairman" who serendipitously discovered that
a different group had created a set of speakers for which they did not have
an immediate use. The act of creativity was one of coupling these two unrelated sets of activities.

A key lesson here is that what is considered possible is often institutionally and cognitively defined. These possibilities also become taken for
granted (Henderson, chapter 9, this volume). As Geertz (1973) suggests, we
become "creatures caught in webs of significance of our own making,"
thereby reducing chances of coming up with a true innovation.

Another lesson is that new ideas are generated by building upon the old,
thereby extracting the options value inherent in the innovation process.
Such a view is very different from the views that generally abound about innovations. Most think of innovations as representing a break from the past.
Such a perspective, however, creates a problem. A break from the past implies the creation of an idea that is "decontextualized" from existing knowledge streams and competencies, thereby increasing the likelihood of failure
(Garud & Nayyar, 1994). Indeed, as the "Post-it" notes case illustrates, both
continuity and change have been hallmarks of innovation at 3M and in the
occurrences of other "breakthroughs" (see Nayak & Ketteringham, 1986).

Seeing through the fog

Humans drive this process of innovation. On the one hand, the human brain is capable of very complex thoughts, including the envisioning of new phenomena. On the other hand, it also makes "Procrustean transformations" and then justifies them. Indeed, the human brain's brilliance can also be its undoing. No matter what the phenomena are, we can come up with explanations and justifications, even as we constantly fall into retrospective rationality traps. Confronted with contrary evidence, we can come up with more powerful explanations that incorporate or dismiss such evidence and serve, ultimately, to further narrow the mind. We are also subject to a number of cognitive biases of which vividness, availability and anchoring are but a few (Bercovitz, de Figueiredo, & Teece, this volume, chapter 13; Tversky & Kahneman, 1974). Often, these biases are further reinforced through social interactions that lead to conformity, focus, and the elimination of alternative views (Janis & Mann, 1977). Furthermore, these biases are exacerbated by incentives that affect decision processes (Shapira, 1995).

A recognition of this duality creates the need for mechanisms that can compensate and expand the role of humans as they engage in the innovation process. For instance, Van de Ven and Grazman (chapter 15, this volume) suggest dialectical processes that can be found in the roles inherent in 3M's innovation processes. Such a process operationalizes the notion of discrediting that Weick (1967) suggests – i.e., when we believe, we must disbelieve, and vice versa. Extending this perspective, Murmann and Tushman (chapter 14, this volume) suggest how cognitive limits can be extended through the collective mobilization of intelligence. These views acknowledge that creativity and cognition is as much an individual activity as it is a social one.

But the mobilization of collective intelligence comes at a price. Autonomous innovation can get dampened as induced and cultural processes take over (Fischhoff, Lanir & Johnson, chapter 16, this volume; Kunda, chapter 17, this volume). Consistent with the message that Bercovitz et al. (chapter 13, this volume) provide, it is therefore important to balance induced and autonomous sources of innovation (Burgleman, 1983).

Beating the odds

Challenges to a theory of technological innovation arise from the fact that outcomes are uncertain and contingent upon a match between internal capabilities and external environments, even as the process itself is complex and constrained by the past. An options value inherent in any creative act offers a way of addressing these challenges. Specifically, if we adopt an options perspective to technological innovations, it is possible to (1) reduce the downside uncertainties associated with innovation, (2) gain the time required to tailor fits, (3) build upon the past even while departing from it, and (4) revel in the complexity associated with innovation, thereby allowing for chance events to create new ideas.

Implicit in our views on how we might create a useful theory of techno-logical innovation is a perspective that variation, selection, and retention processes involve social and cognitive dimensions (Weick, 1979). Moreover, these processes coevolve (Figure 18.2). For instance, any innovation requires the creation of new technological, institutional, and marketing fields. In turn, these fields constrain future innovations. Successful firms such as 3M are able to convert such constraints into the very launching pads for future innovations. They use knowledge streams of the past to create new ideas for the future. Thus, continuity and change go hand in hand, tied together through a continual process of learning and unlearning.

The coevolutionary perspective draws attention to the fact that innova-tion is a process rather than an outcome. When considered as an outcome alone, the term innovation draws attention to concepts such as oversights and foresights that can be defined only in hindsight. However, as part of a larger process, these very outcomes become the bases by which technology entrepreneurs probe their worlds, create them, and decide on the time and place for the implementation of ideas. As Brown (chapter 6, this volume) noted: "You are forever aiming at targets you can't see, or you don't under-stand, or that change as a result of things you do." In such a conceptualiza-tion, one can see the makings of a theory of technological innovation where-in it is possible to "beat the odds."

Acknowledgments

We thank Roger Dunbar, Sanjay Jain and Arun Kumaraswamy for their in-puts at various stages of the development of ideas contained in this chapter. We thank the Center for Entrepreneurial Studies, Stem School of Business, New York University for providing us with administrative and financial support required to complete this chapter.

Notes

1   These issues can be mapped on to Van de Ven's (1986) categories codifying inno-vation. Specifically, Van de Ven and his colleagues conceptualized innovations as changes in ideas, people, transactions, and contexts, leading to certain outcomes. Outcomes correspond to the notion of oversights and foresights that we have used, changes in ideas are surrounded by uncertainty, the notion of contexts raise issues about contingencies between the internal capabilities of a firm and its ex-ternal environments, transactions evoke images of how the past can constrain the future, and, at the core of these processes are people who employ their cognitive abilities to either aid or abet the innovation process (see also Campbell, 1969).

2   Starting in 1993, 3M Corporation changed its goal to 30% of sales from new prod-ucts in the last 4 years. In 1993, they did not meet this goal (although they met

the 25% goal). They did accomplish the new goal in 1994 and expect to accomplish it for 1995 as well. Source: 3M Corporate Public Relations Department (1996).

References

Arthur, B. (1988). Self-reinforcing mechanisms in economics, in P. Anderson et al. *The Economy as an Evolving Complex System*. Reading, MA: Addison-Wesley.

Burgelman, R. A. (1983). A process model of internal corporate venturing in the diversified major firm. *Administrative Science Quarterly*, 28, 223–244.

Campbell, D. T. (1969). Variation and selective retention in socio-cultural evolution. *General Systems*, 16, 69–85.

Cohen, M. D., March, J. G., and Olsen, J. P. (1972). A garbage can model of organizational choice. *Administrative Science Quarterly*, 17, 1–25.

David, P. (1985.) Clio and the economics of QWERTY. *Economic History*, 75, 227–332.

Dosi, G (1982). Technological paradigms and technological trajectories. *Research Policy*, 11: 147–162.

Elster, J. (1983). *Explaining Technical Change: A Case Study in the Philosophy of Science*. New York: Cambridge University Press.

Garud, R. and Nayyar, P. (1994). Transformative capacity: Continual structuring by inter-temporal technology transfer. *Strategic Management Journal*, 15, 365–385.

Garud, R. and Rappa, M. (1994). A socio-cognitive model of technology evolution. *Organization Science*, 5(3), 344–362.

Geertz, C. (1973). *The Interpretation of Cultures*. New York: Basic Books.

Hirsch, P. M. (1975). "Organizational environments and institutional arenas" Adninistrative Science Quarterly, 20, 327–344.

Hughes, T. P. (1989).*American Genesis: A Century of Invention and Technological Enthusiasm, 1870–1970*. New York: Viking Press.

In Search of Excellence. (1985). Video. Waltham, MA: Nathan/Tyler Productions.

Janis, I. L. and Mann, L. (1977). *Decision Making*. New York: Free Press.

Jelinek, M. and Schoonhoven, C. B. (1990). *The Innovation Marathon: Lessons from High Technology Firms*. Cambridge, MA: Basil Blackwell.

Koestler, A. (1964). *The Act of Creation*. New York: Macmillan.

Kumaraswamy, A. (1996). *A Real Options Perspective of Firms' R&D Investments*. Unpublished Doctoral Dissertation, New York University.

Levitt, B. and March, J. G. (1988). Organizational learning. *Annual Review of Sociology*, 14, 319–340.

Mansfield, E.(1981). How economists see R&D. *Harvard Business Review*, November–December, 98–106.

March, J. G. (1971). The technology of foolishness. *Civilokonomen*, 4, 4–12.

March, J. G. (1991). Exploration and exploitation in organizational learning. *Organization Science*, 2, 1, 71–87.

Nayak, P. and Ketteringham, J. (1986). *Breakthroughs*. New York: Rawson Associates.

Powell, W. W. (1991). Expanding the scope of institutional analysis. In W. W. Powell and P. J. DiMaggio (eds.), *The New Institutionalism in Organizational Analysis*. Chicago: The University of Chicago Press, pp. 183–203.

Rosenbloom, R. S. and Cusumano, M. A. (1987). Technological pioneering and competetive advantage. The birth of the VCR industry. *California Management Review*, 29, 4.

Rosenberg, N. (1994). *Exploring the Black Box: Technology, Economics, and History*. New York: Cambridge University Press.

Shapira, Z. (1995). *Risk Taking: A Managerial Perspective*. New York: Russell Sage Foundation.

Smith, D. and Alexander, R. (1988). *Fumbling the Future: How Xerox Invented, then Ignored, the First Personal Computer*.New York: William Morrow.

Staw, B. M. (1981). The escalation of commitment to a failing course of action. *Academy of Management Review*, 6, 577–587.

Teece, D. J. (1987). Profiting from technological innovation: Implications for integration, collaboration, licensing and public policy. In D. J. Teece (ed.), *The Competitive Challenge: Strategies for Industrial Innovation and Renewal*. Cambridge, MA: Ballinger, pp. 185–219.

3M Corporation Public Relations Department communication, (1996).

Tversky, A. and Kahneman, D. (1974). Judgment under uncertainty: Heuristics and biases. *Science*, 185, 1124–1131.

Usher, A. (1954). *A History of Mechanical Inventions*. Cambridge, MA: Harvard University Press.

Utterback, J. M. (1994). *Mastering the Dynamics of Innovation*. Boston. Harvard Business School Press.

Van de Ven, A. H. (1986). Central problems in the management of innovation. *Management Science*, 32, 5, 590–607.

Weick, K. (979). *The Social Psychology of Organizing*. Reading, MA: Addison-Wesley.

Weick, K. (1990). Technology as equivoque: Sense-making in new technologies. In P. Goodman and L. Sproull (eds.), *Technology and Organizations*. San Francisco: Jossey Bass, pp. 1–44.

Wilson, T. L. and Hlavacek, J. D. (1984). Don't let good ideas sit on the shelf. *Research Management*, 27, 3, 27–34.

Author Index

Abernathy, W. J. 30, 149, 150, 152, 174, 206, 234
Abrahamson 189
Acs, Z. J. 61
Adams, L. 225
Adner, R. 176, 177
Aguilar, F. 33
Ahlstrom, D. 62
Alchian, A. 15, 167, 168
Aldrich, H. 61
Alexander, R. 3, 20, 252
Ali, A. 21
Allen, P. M. 62, 217
Alster, N. 3, 21
Amabile, T. M. 6, 112, 113 325, 348
Amit, R. 21, 23
Ancona, D. 262
Anderson, C. A. 142
Anderson, J. C. 225
Anderson, P. 30, 91, 149, 150, 152, 174, 238, 260
Andrews, E. L. 33
Andrews, F. M. 112
Andrews, P. 131, 135, 138
Angle, H. L. 279, 284, 285, 286, 290
Ansoff, H. I. 187
Aoki, M. 61
Appod, S. J. 62
Argote, L. 44, 168
Argyris, C. 168, 170, 188
Armour, H. 236
Armstrong, J. S. 308
Arnold, J. E. 225
Arnold, J. III 44
Arrow, K. J. 54, 72

Arthur, B. 4, 23, 141, 143, 174, 177
Ashford, S. J. 112
Audretsch, D. B. 61
Auster, E. 61
Axelrod, J. N. 223

Bacdayan, P. 168
Bailyn, L. 112
Baldwin, J. R. 57, 61
Bantel, K. A. 263
Barley, S. 326, 327
Barnett, D. F. 192
Barney, J. B. 3, 16, 18
Barr, P. S. 183, 188, 205, 206
Bartunek, J. M 183, 187, 206, 298, 299
Bashe, C. J. 92
Bateman, T. 43
Batra, B. 266
Baumol, W. 183
Baveles, A. 282, 284
Bazerman, M. H. 34, 43
Bercovitz, J. 4, 6, 59, 351
Berger, P. L. 187, 188
Berning, C. 223
Beyer, J. 326
Bianco, M. 61
Bijker, W. 130
Blackman, S. A. B. 183
Blais, R. A. 62
Blattberg, R. 222
Blau, P. M. 268
Bleakley, F. R. 20
Boden, M. 62
Boeker, W. 173

Boothe, J. N. 263
Bougon, M. G. 187
Boulding, K. E. 72
Bourgeois, L. J. 261
Bower, J. L. 28, 176
Brackfield, S. C. 113
Brealey, R. 2, 27, 28, 255
Brett 299
Brodsky, S, L. 314
Brokensha, D. W. 312
Brooks, G. R. 261
Brown, J. S. 5, 173, 175, 187, 349, 350, 352
Brüderl, J. 52
Bruner, J. S. 188
Buckingham, C. T. 314
Buderi, R. 35
Buede, D. 306
Burgelman, R. A. 134, 175, 177, 187, 351
Butcher, L. 90
Butos, W. N. 91
Buzzell, R. 239

Cable, J. 61
Callon, M. 62
Cameron, K. S, 183, 205
Campbell, D. T. 351
Carroll, G. R. 50
Carroll, P. 87, 91, 131, 142
Cascio, W. 25
Cattin, P. 221
Caves, R. E. 16, 17, 243
Chandler, A. D. Jr. 80, 81, 185
Cheng, Y. 280
Chesbrough, H. 252
Chiaromonte, F. 58
Chintagunta, P. K. 225
Choffray, J. M. 225
Chposky, J. 86, 87, 131
Christensen, C. M. 150, 176, 255
Clark, K. B. 51, 55, 81, 161, 187, 207, 234, 238,
    240, 260
Cohen, W. M. 30, 54, 76, 168, 169, 172, 173,
    236, 239, 254
Comroe, J. H. 22
Conner, K. R. 22, 34
Constant, E. W. 150
Conti, R. 6, 112, 1113, 118, 348
Cool, K. 236
Coon, H. M. 113
Cooper, R. G. 4, 23, 216, 217, 219, 221
Corrigan, B. 28
Coulam, R. F. 314
Crandall, R. W. 192

Crispell, D. 226
Cummings, L. L. 112
Cushman, J. H. 313
Cussumano 348
Cyert, R. M. 173, 176

Daft 187
David, P. 4, 23, 60, 350
Davidow, W. 249
Davis, S. M. 287
Dawes. R. M. 28, 308
Day, R. H. 238
De Brentani, U. 217
Dearborn, D. C. 188, 263
Dearden, J. A. 219
Deci, E. L. 113, 325
de Figueiredo, J. 4, 6, 59, 351
Demsetz, H. 16
Devadas, R. 168
Dierickx, I. 236
DiFillippi, R. 16
DiMaggio, P. 174
Dosi, G. 4, 5, 23, 30, 44, 51, 53–58, 61, 62, 78,
    141, 149, 235, 237, 239, 244, 349
Dougherty, D. 187, 189
Dripps, R. D. 22
Duerr, M. G. 217
Duguid, P. 173, 175
Dukerich, J. M. 290
Duncan 189
Dunne, T. 41, 50, 61
Dutton, 188, 189
Dyer, L. 44

Edelman, G. M. 74, 75, 91
Edwards, W. 306, 321
Egidi, M. 53, 61, 62
Ehrlich, S. B. 290
Einhorn, H. J. 29, 30, 34, 36, 61, 306
Einspruch, N. G. 151
Eisenhardt, K. M. 22, 261, 300
Ekamn, P. 315
Eliashberg 6, 348
Elster, J. 5, 349
Epple, D. 168
Ettlie, J. 184
Everett, R. R. 314

Farrell, C. 22, 174
Farris, G. F. 112
Feeher, C. E. 316

Ferguson, C. H. 82, 84, 86, 131, 134, 137, 144
Filley, A. C. 263
Finkelstein, S. 262, 265, 274
Fischer, G. W. 308, 314
Fischhoff, B. 6, 7, 29, 142, 317, 351
Fisher, F. M. 78, 79, 80, 84
Fisher, J. G. 225
Flamm, K. 79, 81, 91
Flatt, S. 263
Foster, R. 22, 149, 150, 152, 183, 234, 239, 245, 254
Fox, F. V. 43
Foy, N. 131
Freeman, C. 23
Freeman, J. 16, 50, 170, 171
Friesen, P. 181

Galai, D. 21, 33
Galbraith, J. R. 32, 187
Gale 16, 17
Gardiner, J. P. 149
Garen, G. 285
Garud, R. 4, 23, 59, 62, 85, 115, 130, 217, 279, 281, 282, 291, 325, 345, 349, 350
Geertz, C. 350
Geletkanyca, M. A. 264, 266
Georgious 187
Geroski, P. 49, 57, 61
Ghemawat, P. 30, 31, 168
Gitomer, J. 113
Glance, N. S. 62
Goerne, C. 226
Golanty, J. 222
Goldberg 299
Goldfarb, P 113
Goldhar, J. D. 184, 199, 207
Goreki, P. K. 61
Graham, M. B. W. 23, 31, 35, 36
Grazman, D. 6, 205, 209, 263, 351
Greene, D. 113
Greene, William N. 245
Greenwood, J. E. 84
Grimes, S. 223
Grossman, B. S. 113
Gryskiewicz, N. 116
Gryskiewicz, S. S. 114
Gutman, H. C. 317

Haleblian, J. 262, 274
Haley, R. I. 221
Hambrick, D. C. 262, 264, 265, 266
Hannan, M. T. 16, 50, 170, 171

Harrar, G. 88
Harrigan, K. 189
Harrison, B. 62
Hauser, J. R. 215, 216, 221, 225, 226
Hausman, J. A. 218
Haveman, H. A. 261, 274
Hayek, F. A. 73, 74, 90
Hayes, R. H. 183, 206
Hedberg, B. L. T. 170, 187, 298
Heiner, Ronald. 238
Helfat, C. 236, 255
Helmsley, J. 313
Henderson, R. M. 4, 6, 51, 54, 55, 81, 161, 165, 207, 234, 238, 240, 260, 350
Hennessey, B. A. 113
Hernstein, R. 321
Hershey, 306
Higgins, C. A. 285
Hill, C. W. L. 23
Hillkirk, J. 182, 184, 245
Hiltz, S. R. 316
Hinkle, D. E. 91
Hirokawa, R. Y. 316
Hirsch, P. M. 30, 349
Hitt, M. A. 23
Hlavacek, J. D. 349
Hoffman, L. R. 263
Hogarth, R. M. 29, 30, 36, 61
Hogg, T. 62
Holland, J. H. . 61, 168, 171
Hoskisson, R. E. 32
House, R. J. 263
Howell, J. M. 285
Huberman, B. A. 62
Huff, A. S. 183, 206
Hughes, T. P. 3, 20, 91, 130
Huntingon, S. P. 321
Hwang, J. 314

Jackson, S. E. 262
Jacobson, 245
Jacoby, J. 223
Jaikumar, R. 189, 207
Jain, D. C. 225
Janis, I. L. 43, 44, 188, 263, 351
Jelinek, M. 6, 184, 196, 187, 199, 207, 209, 276, 298, 326, 327, 350
Jensen, M. C. 182, 194, 206, 255
Jewkes, J. 243, 239
Johnson, H. T. 185, 199, 206
Johnson, L. R. 83, 92
Johnson, S. 6, 7, 317, 351
Jones, D. T. 182

Jovanovic, B. 61
Jurs, S. G. 91

Kahn, R. L. 284
Kahneman, D. 41, 43, 44, 239, 240, 241, 242, 243, 254, 267, 316, 321, 351
Kalwani, M. U. 21
Kamakura, W. A. 221
Kanter, R. M. 112, 325, 326, 341
Kaplan, R. S. 185, 199, 206
Katz, B. 78, 79, 262
Katz, D. 262, 284
Kay, N. M. 22
Kazanjian, R. 32
Kearns, D. T. 35, 189
Keisler, S. 183, 187, 188, 206
Keller, M. 62, 240, 243, 245, 247
Kerr, S. 263
Ketteringham, J. 3, 20, 347, 350
Kidd, J. F. 308
Kiesier, S. 265, 314, 315
Kim, L. 150
Kirchoff, B. A. 61
Klein, B. 61
Kleindorfer, 306
Kleinschmidt, E. J. 4, 217
Klepper, S. 50, 62
Koestler, A. 348, 350
Kogut, B. 255
Koopmans, T. C. 236
Koppl, R. G. 89, 91
Kovenock, D. 21
Kuhn, T. S. 91, 168, 170, 183, 206, 236, 309
Kulatilaka, N. 255
Kumaraswamy, A. 85, 349
Kunda, G. 6, 7, 102, 326, 327, 328, 332, 335, 336, 337, 338, 339, 340, 351
Kunreuther, H. 306
Kuran, T. 238

Lakatos, I. 309
Landman, J. 309
Langer, E. J. 185
Langlois, R. N. 188
Lanir, Z. 6, 7, 351
Lant, T. K. 266
Lave, J. 101
Lawrence, P. R. 287
Lazonick, W. 81
Lee, M. 219
Lenz 187

Leonard-Barton, D. 170, 199, 205, 207
Leonsis, T. 86, 87, 131
Lepper, M. R. 113
Levine, J. B. 36
Levinthal, D. A. 5, 6, 30, 53, 54, 58, 59, 61, 62, 76, 115, 169, 172, 173, 176, 177, 205, 207, 236, 239, 254, 263, 298, 349, 350
Levitt, B. 4, 306, 350
Liberman, M. 18
Lillien, G. L. 6, 214, 217, 218, 219, 225, 348
Lincoln 187
Lintner, J. 255
Lippman, S. 16
Litterer, J. A. 209
Litterer, J. A. 298
Loasby, B. J. 77, 83
Louis, 187
Lovallo, D. A. 5, 41, 43, 44, 47, 239, 241, 242, 243, 244, 254, 349
Luckman, T. 187, 188

Machlup, F. 72, 91
MacKay, D. M. 73, 90
Maclaurin, W. R. 260
Mahmood, T. 61
Maier, N. R. F. 263
Malerba, F. 51, 61
Malone, M. 249
Malone, T. B. 314
Mancke, R. B. 15, 16, 17, 79, 80
Manes, S. 131, 135, 138
Mann, L. 351
Mansfield, E. 4, 215, 349
Marais, M. L. 44
March, J. G. 4, 5, 24, 26, 36, 43, 57, 61, 168, 170, 171, 173, 175, 176, 178, 187, 241, 300, 306, 349, 350
Marengo, L. 144, 53, 54, 55, 61
Markoff, J. 136
Markowitz, H. M. 255
Martin 341
Mason, P. A. 262
May, E. 308
Maynard Smith, J. 91
McCormick 313
McGlade, J. M. 62
McGowan, J. J. 84
McKennsa, R. 133
McKie, J. W. 79, 80
McMurray, S. 36
Meindl, J. R. 290
Merrick, B. 226
Metcalf, J. 315

Metcalfe, S. 57, 62
Meyer, A. D. 261, 274
Meyerson 187
Miller, D. C. 181, 265, 274, 316
Miller, J. H. 50, 62
Miller, J. P. 33
Miller, K. L. 32
Miller, R. 62
Miller, S. S. 77
Milliken, F. J. 266
Misa, T. 62
Mitchell, R. 31
Mitchell, W. 51, 234, 236, 244, 270
Modigliani, G. 255
Montgomery, D. B. 18
Moore, S. D. 32
Moore, W. L. 223
Moritz, M. 86, 90
Morris, C. R. 82, 84, 86
Morrison, C. R. 131, 134, 137, 144
Murmann, J. P. 6, 124, 204, 299
Myers, S. 22, 27, 28, 255

Na, D. 219
Nadler, D. A. 35, 189

Postman, L. 188
Powell, W. W. 4, 23, 170, 174
Preisendorfer, P. 52
Prince, G. M. 225
Pry, R. H. 225
Pugh, E. W. 83

Quinn, J. B. 181, 209

Raff, D. 91
Rafiguzzaman, M. 61
Raiffa, H. 306
Rao, 6, 348
Rappa, M. 4, 23, 130
Rasmusen, 245
Ratti, R. R. 325
Reason, J. 319
Reed, R. 16
Reich, R. B. 183, 202, 206
Reidenback, E. R. 223
Reinganum, J. F. 54
Reinganum, J. J. 172
Rifkin, G. 88
Rigdon, Joan E. 255

Riggs, W. 61
Rip, A. 62
Robertson, P. L. 75, 83, 90
Rodgers, B. 131
Rogers, E. M. 183
Rogers, W. 131
Romanelli, E. 176, 261, 264, 265, 298, 299, 300
Romer, P. M. 174
Roos, D. 182
Rosenberg, N. 4, 23
Rosenbloom, R. S. 255, 348
Rosenkopf, L. 30, 149, 169
Ross, J. 43, 142, 168, 262
Rothman, R. A. 325
Rothwell, R. 217
Rumelt, R. 116, 17, 234, 243, 245
Ruskin, J. 110
Ryan R. M. 113
Ryle, G. 75

Sahal, D. 149, 152
Salancik, G. 173
Saloner, G. 174
Salvatore, R. 56
Samuelson, L. 41, 61
Saviotti, P. P. 57
Sawers, D. 234
Schein, E. 341
Scherer, F. M. 174
Schoemaker, P. J. H. 21, 23, 44
Schön, D. 109, 168, 170, 188, 284
Schoonhoven, C. B. 186, 209, 326, 327
Schot, J. 62
Schrader, S. 61
Schroeder, R. G. 282
Schuen, A. 61
Schumpeter, J. A. 35, 141, 175, 234
Schutzer, D. 314
Schwalback, J. 61
Schwenk, C. R. 23, 183, 206
Scott, W. R. 23
Sculley, J. 90
Seabright, M. A. 44
Selznick, P. 298
Seminara, J. L. 314
Senge, P. M. 167
Shapira, Z. 21, 24, 33, 36, 43, 59, 113, 115, 217,
    241, 300, 325, 345, 349, 351
Sharpe, W. F. 255
Shefrin, H. H. 321
Shenhav, Y. A. 325
Shere, K. 314
Sheridan, T. D. 314

Shuen, A. 236
Silk, A. J. 221
Silverman, D. 186, 187, 188
Simon, H. A. 168, 177, 188, 263
Sistitio, P. 61
Slovic, P. 321
Smith, D. 3, 20, 252
Smith, R. P. 61
Snyder, R. C. 263
Sobel, R. 131
Spencer, K. 315
Sproull, L S. 4, 183, 187, 188, 206, 265, 300, 314, 315,
Starbuck, W. H. 170, 298
Statham 285
Staw, B. M. 34, 43, 262, 350
Steffins, J. 131, 134, 140
Stillerman, R. 234
Stimpert, J. L. 183, 205, 206
Stinchcombe, A. L. 90
Stryker 285
Suarez, F. 55, 78
Sutcliffe, K. M. 299
Sutton, R. I. 183, 205
Swain, A. 317
Swaminathan, A. 50

Tamuz, M. 300
Tauber, E. M. 223
Teece, D. J. 4, 6, 30, 31, 44, 55, 59, 61, 75, 76, 81, 136, 144, 236, 237, 239, 242, 252, 254, 349, 351
Thaler, R. 321
Therrien, L. 31
Thompson, J. 297
Tiger, L. 60
Tilton, J. E. 176, 234, 239
Toberts, M. J. 41, 61
Trice, H. 326
Tuden, A. 297
Tushman, M. L. 6, 30, 91, 124, 149, 150, 152, 169, 174, 176, 204, 238, 260, 261, 264, 265, 298, 299, 300
Tversky, A. 23, 41, 43, 44, 239, 240, 241, 267, 321, 351

Urban, G. L. 215, 216, 221, 225, 226
Ury . 299
Usher, A. 1348, 350
Usselman, S. W. 81, 82
Utterback, J. M. 4, 7, 30, 55, 78, 149, 150, 152, 174 234, 350

Van de Ven, A. H. 4, 6, 62, 112, 205, 209, 263, 279, 280, 281, 282, 284, 285, 286, 290, 291, 294, 298, 351
Van Maanen, 187
Van Wyk, R. J. 147, 150
Vena, P. 314
Vincenti, W. G. 144
Virany, B. 261, 265, 298, 299, 300
von Clausewitz, C. 321
Von Hippel, E. 170, 207, 22
Von Winterfeldt, D. 306, 321

Wagner, S. 215
Walton, R. E. 188
Warren, D. M. 312
Watson, S. 306
Watson, T. J. 136
Watts, R. K. 151
Weber, M. 187
Weick, K. E. 5, 22, 173, 187. 302, 346, 351, 351
Weimer, W. B. 73
Weinberg, B. D. 226
Welch, J. A. 314
Wenger, E. 101
Wensley, R. 16, 17
Werner, 0. 312
Wheelwright, Steven C. 183
Whetten, D. A. 183, 184, 205
White, G. I. 23
Wiersema, M. F. 263, 299
Wilke, J. R. 20, 21, 33
Williamson, O. E. 28, 236
Wilson, T. L. 349
Winn, D. 243
Winter S. G. 16, 23, 31, 55, 56, 61, 75, 78, 136, 168, 169, . 170, 172, 173, 237, 238,261
Wittink, D. R. 221
Wlersma, W. 91
Wolff, E. 183
Womack, J. P. 182, 184
Wybenga, H. 223

Yelle, L. E. 168
Yoon, E. 217

Zajac, E. J. 34
Zangwill, W. I. 36
Zey 187
Ziegler, R. 52
Zietham, C. 43
Zysman, J. 61

Subject Index

Absorptive capacity, 54, 76, 169
Adaptation, x
Allen, Paul, 138
Ambiguity, 279
Anomoalous data, 209
Anthropology, contributions of, to research, 103
Apheresis, therapeutic, Minnesota Innovation Research Program study of, 281–282
Apple Computer, 86, 89, 134
    early failures of, 96
Argyris, Chris, 109
Arrow, Kenneth, 72
Aspiration level, 24
ATM manufacturing, patterns of entry, post-entry performance, and exit in, 50–51
Authority, 320
Autonomy, 320

Balancing strategies, 250–253, 296
Benchmarks, 208
Bold forecasting, 243–244
Boundary objects, 102, 104
Bootlegging, 28–29
Boulding, Kenneth, 72
Bounded rationality, 53
    as decision bias, 237–238
Breakdowns, 186
Bureaucracy, 325
Bureaucratic pathology, 340
Burnout, 7
Buying patterns, 98

Capital asset pricing model of risk aversion, 241, 255n
Capitalism, personal, cognition and, 88–90
Carlson, Chester, 97
Carroll, Paul, 142
Cary, Frank, 134, 137
CEOs, organizational responsiveness and, 262–263, 265–267
Certainty/established asset effect, 240, 244–246
Chance events, 15
Change, incremental, 260
Change, rapid, 34
Choice, rational, 41
Chandler, Alfred, 80, 86
C³I (command, control, communications, and intelligence), 322n
    demand for, 314
    effects on experimentation, 315–319
        on lower levels, 315–317
        on upper levels, 317–319
    pressures of, 314–315
Citicorp, 20
Cochlear implant program
    innovation leadership in, 282, 283f, 284, 287, 288f, 290–291
    Minnesota Innovation Research Program study of, 281–282
    single versus multiple channel technology debate in, 291–293, 292t
Cocke, John, 84
Co-evolution, 53
Cognitive schemes, 266

Cognitive structures, 130
Cognition, organization and, 75–78
Commitment, escalation of, 4
Communication, during downsizing, 121
Communities of practioners, 130, 173
Compaq, 141, 142
Competence, 307
Competence gap, 53
Competence trap, 52, 205
Competetive blind spots, 42
Complementary assets, 235
Computer industry, 71–94
  perception and misperception in,
    78–88
  by IBM, 78–82
  and IBM's system 360, 82–84
  and personal computers, 85–88
  and RISC architecture, 84–85
Computers
  distributed, early barriers to, 96, 98–99
  personal. See Personal computers
  shift from mainframe to distributed, 142.
    See also IBM, DOS transactions of
Core capabilities, 170
Core competences, 75, 195
Core rigidities, 170
Corporation(s). See also Firm(s); Organiza-
    tion(s)
  changing mental models of, 105–107
  developing new relationships and knowl-
    edge in, 100–101
Corporate entry, 41
Cospecialized assets, 30
Cray Research, 31
Creative destruction, 233
Creativity, 325
  cultivation of, 348–350
  defined, 111–112
  downsizing and. See Downsizing
  environmental determinants of. See
    Environmental determinants of
    work motivation, creativity, and in-
    novation
  extrinsic motivators and, 113
  fostering, 6, 129
  individual, in model of organizational in-
    novation, 112–113
  intrinsic motivation principle of, 113
  team, 112
Creeping determinism, 143
Culture, 326
Cumulative synthesis, 348–349
Customers, research and, 103–104
Cybernetics theory, 90n–91n

Darwinian Tolstoys, xi
DEC, 140
Debureaucratization, 326
Decision biases, 23, 41–68
  certainty/established asset effect and,
    244–246
  conclusions about, 58–60
  discussion of, 253
  evolutionary role of, 41
  in economic change, 52–59
  experimental design for, 45–47, 46t
  summary of, 47, 48t, 49
  firm strategy and, 248–253
    balancing approaches to, 250–253
    isolation errors and, 248–249
    popular strategic management literature
      and, 249–250
  individual, organizational errors and,
    42–45
  isolation errors and, 241–244
    bold forecasting and, 243–244
    multilevel decision-making isolation er-
      rors, 242–243
    temporal and cross-divisional risk pool-
      ing, 241–242
  learning and, 52–54
  optimism as, 41
  organizational reinforcement of, 43
  in patterns of entry, post-entry perfor-
    mance, and exit in manufacturing,
    49–52
  positive effects of, 52, 59–60
  theory of, 233–259
    assets and close-in search in, 238–239
    behavioral underpinnings of, 237–241
    bounded rationality in, 237–238
    firm capabilities and complementary as-
      sets in, 235–236
    framing and, 240
    inconsistent risk aversion in, 240–241
    summary of, 246t, 246–248
Decision criteria, 26
Decision making
  behavioral aspects of, 34–35
  local, 139–140
  risk aversive versus risk seeking,
    24–27
  rules of engagement and, 321n
Decision theory, 306–307
  limits of, 321n
Demming, W. Edwards, 182
"Devil's advocate," 286
Dialectical processes, 26, 28
Diebold, ATM manufacture by, 50–51

Digital Equipment Corporation, 87–88, 89
  certainty/established asset effect and,
  245
Distinctive competences, 236
Docutel, ATM manufacture by, 50–51
Dominant design, 148, 149
DOS operating system. *See* IBM, DOS transactions of
Downsizing
  avoiding or reversing negative effects of,
    122–123
  effect on innovation and creativity,
    118–123
  innovation and, 111
  mechanisms of psychological impact dur-
    ing, 120
  motivational and attitudinal changes due
    to, 122
  negative effects of, 112
  social changes due to, 121–122
  structural changes due to, 120–121
  Work Environment Inventory of,
    118–119
Duality, 20
Du Pont Corporation, certainty/established
  asset bias and, 245
Dynamic capabilities, 75
Dynamic tension, 326

Eckert, J. Presper, 79
Economies of scale, 15
Enactment, 5
Engineering Research Associates, 79
Entrepreneurship
  in mature-industry firms, 181–213
  and changes in basic production tech-
    nology, 196–199
  cognitive approaches to, 208–210
  cognitive theory and, 187–189
  data gathering and preparation in,
    189–190
  and difficulty of fundamental change,
    193–195
  and exit option, 195–196
  and fundamental market shifts,
    192–193
  and revival of innovation, 199–204
  technological, organizational incorpora-
    tion of, 204–206
Environment, work, during organizational
  change, 118
Environmental change, organizational entrepreneurship and, 181–183

Environmental determinants of work motivation, creativity, and innovation,
  111–125
  downsizing, 118–123. *See also* Downsizing
  individual creativity and, 112–113
  organizational innovation and, 113–116
  relationships among, 116–117
  summary of, 123–124
Environmental shock, organizational responsiveness to, 260–278. *See also* Organizational responsiveness
Equilibrium, x
Era of ferment, 30
Era of technological change, 30
Error, Type I and Type II, 22, 76, 300
Escalation, 43
Estridge, Donald, 135, 137
Evolution, x
Executive succession, 265
Exit option, 195
Experience, 168
Experimentation, 307. *See also* Technological
  innovation
  bottom-up, 311–313
  capabilities needed for, 308–309
  conditions for, 171, 308–310
  and limitations of planning, 308
  loci of, in hierarchical organizations,
    310–313
  risk taking and, 313–314
  summary of, 319–320
  top-down, 310–311
Exploitation, x, 34, 57–58, 178
Exploration, x, 5, 34, 57–58, 178

Failure, ix
False negatives, 25, 300
False positives, 25, 300
Firm(s). *See also* Corporation(s); Organiza-
  tion(s)
  de novo, radical innovation by, 239
  failure rates of, 41
  high-foresight, attributes of, 17, 18
  interindustry differences in performances
    of, 42
  intraindustry differences in performances
    of, 42
  large
    innovation difficulties of, 184–186, 185t
    innovation in, 239, 255n–256n. *See also*
      Decision biases, theory of
    and interaction of bounded rationality
      and established assets, 238

Firm(s) (*continued*)
  low-foresight, 17
  mature-industry
    barriers to innovation by, 183–186
    culture of, innovation and, 206–207
    innovation in, 181–183
    organizational entrepreneurship in. *See*
      Entrepreneurship, in mature-industry
      firms
    patterns of entry, post-entry performance,
      and exit in, 49–52
    resource-based view of, 18, 35
    theory of, innovation and, 234–235
Firm performance, luck hypothesis of, 15–16
Firm strategy
  balancing approaches to, 250–253
  isolation errors and, 248t, 248–249
  in popular strategic management litera-
    ture, 249–250
Flamm, Kenneth, 81
Foods, processed, innovations in, 239
Ford, 182
Forecasting, technological. *See* Technological
  forecasting
Foresight, 95, 129, 340
Frame breaking, 264
Framing effects, 43

Gates, Bill, 133, 135, 138, 143
GenCorp, and problems of fundamental
  change, 193–194
General Electric Corporation, 80
  incentive schemes of, 32–33
General Motors
  framing problems of, 240
  market losses by, 182–183
General Tire, 194
Good judgment, 101
Group mindset, fostering changes in,
  108–109
Groupthink, as cause of organizational opti-
  mism, 43–44, 263
Grove, Andrew, 133

Hayek, F.A., 72–73, 91n
Hazard rates, 52
Hewlett Packard, 86
  innovation strategy of, 251
High-Tech Electronics International, study of
  high- and low-creativity projects at,
  118–123
Hindsight, 4, 95, 143

Hitachi Corporation, bootlegging practices
  of, 28–29
Honda, 32, 182
Human judgment, 4

IBM, 31
  ATM manufacture by, 51
  case study of, 78–82
  certainty/established asset effect and, 245
  DOS transactions of, 131–143
    business and technological blunders re-
      lating to, 132–133
    local rationality and, 134–143
  personal computer manufactured by,
    86–87
  RISC technology and, 84–85
IBM 360 Series, case history of, 82–84
Illusions of control, 41
Improvisation, 309
Incentives, technological innovation and,
  32–34
Imperfect explorers, 54
Inertia, 172, 262
  dominant designs and, 174
  organizational, 170–173, 174
Information processors, 54
Initiative, 307
Innovation, 136, 204. *See also* Technological
  innovation
Innovation biases. *See* Decision biases
Innovative thinking, 117
Innovative yield, xi
Inside view, 44
Insight, 307
Institute for Research on Learning, 100–101
Intel Corporation, IBM transactions with,
  132
Intelligence, individual versus group, 101
Interaction analysis, 103
Internal rate of return, for evaluating pro-
  jects, 27
Intuition, 101
  pump, 108
Investment, inadequacy of, 182–183
Investment decision, 21
Irrationalities, 42
Isolation errors, 240–244
  bold forecasting, 243–244
  multilevel decision-making, 242–243
  relative risk aversion biases due to, 246t,
    246–248
  temporal and cross-divisional risk pooling,
    241–242

Jobs, Steven, 86, 89–90

Kay, Alan, 90
Know-how, 101
Knowledge, 8, 72, 130
  individual versus group, 100t, 100–101
  public good nature of, 173
  spillover, 173
  structure of, 72–75

Lamarckian Carlyles, xi
Lamarckism, xi
Latent opportunities, 219
Leadership
  balance and timing of roles of, 296f,
    296–301
  in cochlear implant program, 282, 283f,
    284, 287, 288f, 290–291
  defined, 284
  role in innovation, 284–291, 301–303
  in therapeutic apheresis program, 281–282,
    283f, 287, 288f, 289–291
  types of roles in, 284–285, 286f
  relationships among, 290–291
Leadership Through Quality, 103
Leapfrogging, 218
Learning, x, xiv, 7, 8, 42, 52, 57–58, 306
  adaptive, 53
  decision biases and, 52–54
  from mistakes, 29
  minetic, 174
  organizational. See Organizational learning
  trial-and-error
    defined, 279
    in technological innovation, 279–280
Learning curve, studies of, 168
Loasby, Brian, 83
Loci of experimentation, 320
Lotus Corporation, 141
Lowe, William, 86, 134, 137–138
Luck, 3, 14, 15

Macintosh computer, 90, 141
MacKay, Donald, 72–73
Management. See also Top management team
  cognitive function of, 76
  in theory of technological innovation, 6
  total quality, 102–103
Managerial ideology, 327
Manufacturing, patterns of entry, post-entry
  performance, and exit in, 49–52

Market analysis, for photocopiers, 97–98
Market perception, 76
Marketing research. See also Research and
    development
  anthropological approach to, 103
  changing game of, 95–110
  and collaboration with corporations, 99
  informal communications and, 102
  interaction analysis and, 103
  for new product development, methods
    for, 221–224, 222t
  methods, 215
  oversight, foresight, and hindsight in, 95
  priorities in, 32
  quality listening and, 102–103
  for radically new products, methods for,
    224t, 224–226
  and reframing world, 104–109
    by changing mental models, 105–107
    by fostering changes in group mindset,
      108–109
    by fostering organizational forgetting,
      107–108
  technological oversights and, 214–230
  tools, 6
  traditional relationship to corporation,
    99–100
  and working in fog, 95–99
Mauchly, John W., 79
McKenna, Regis, 133
Medical imaging industry, patterns of entry,
    post-entry performance, and exit in,
    51
Mental maps, 188
Mental models, changing, 105–107
Microprocessor, development of, 85–86
Microsoft Corporation, IBM's DOS transac-
    tions with, 131–133, 135. See also IBM,
    DOS transactions of
Mindful alertness, 209
Mindlessness, 185
Mindset, group, fostering changes in,
    108–109
Minnesota Innovation Research Program,
    studies of, 281–282
Minnesota Mining & Manufacturing Corpo-
    ration, 3, 21, 351, 352n–353n
  bootlegging practices of, 28–29
  innovation strategy of, 251
  technological innovation by, 347–348
Minnesota Research Innovation Program,
    leadership roles studied in, 286–287,
    288f, 289f, 290
Misperceptions, 76–77, 77t

Mistakes, 57
Mitsch, Ronald, 251
Money Machine Inc., 50
Monopoly power, 15
Motivation
    during downsizing, 122
    environmental determinants of. *See* Environmental determinants of work motivation, creativity, and innovation
    to innovate, 114–115
    intrinsic versus extrinsic, 113
Motorola, innovation strategy of, 251
Myers, Mark, 100

n-armed bandit problem, 171
National Cash Register
    ATM manufacture by, 51
    certainty/established asset effect and, 245
NCR. *See* National Cash Register
NEC, 140
Nelson-Winter framework, 75–76
Net present value, for evaluating projects, 27

Olsen, Ken, 87–88, 89
Operational perception, 76
Optical lithography
    data and methodology for study of, 165–166
    defining limits of, 154–158
        complementary technologies and, 162
        component performance and, 159–162
        forecast errors regarding, 158–159
        structure of debate about, 155–158
        and user needs and capabilities, 159
    evolution of, 151–153, 153f
    predicted limits of, versus realized performance, 147, 148f
    process of, 151, 152f
    technological forecasting applied to, 147–166. *See also* Technological forecasting
    uses and types of, 151
Optimism
    as decision bias, 41
    organizational, groupthink as cause of, 44
    in project evaluation, 44
Optimism hypothesis, 44–45
Options, 31
Organization(s). *see also* Corporation(s); Firm(s)
    and ability to recognize opportunities, 76–78

as cognitive structures, 75–78
and economic structure of opportunities, 88–90
culture and, 326–327
definitions of, 187
fostering forgetting by, 107–108
perceptual abilities of, 76
Organizational behavior
    knowledge-centered view of, 54–57
    psychological assumptions versus rationality and, 42–43
Organizational entrepreneurship. *See* Entrepreneurship
Organizationl innovation, 112
Organizational learning, 167–180, 187
    administrative capabilities and, 169–170
    codification of, problems with, 170
    collective discovery and, 175
    collective inertia and, 174
    as collective wisdom, 173–174
    competency traps in, 172
    conclusions about, 177–178
    conditions for, 306–324
    effect of successes and failures on, 56–58
    as facilitator of new insights and knowledge, 168–169
    false, 168
    inertia and, 170–173
    framework for, 307–308
    innovation and, according to conventional wisdom, mature-industry innovations, and Minnesota study, 191t
    levels of aggregation and, 175–177
    n-armed bandit problem and, 171
    need for unlearning of, 170–171
    political structures and, 173
    positive feedback cascades in, 177
    and suppression of discovery, 171–172
    technological innovation and, 279–305
    as wisdom, 168
Organizational perception, 71
Organizational responsiveness
    and CEO experience with reorientation, 265–267
    CEO succession and, 265
    and executive team working context, 266–267
    firm size and, 267
    and heterogeneous versus homogeneous top management teams, 262–264
    study of
        discussion of, 273–275, 275t
        methods for, 267–270
        results of, 270–273, 271t, 272t

top management turnover and,
264–265
Outcomes, 3
aggregate, 5
Outside view, 44
Overconfidence, 41
Oversights, 95, 129, 340
by commission, 23
by omission, 23

Paradigms, 78
Pasteur, Louis, 348
Path dependency, 4, 57
Penalties, 24
Personal capitalism, 88
Personal computers
case history of, 85–88
development of, 36n
IBM's loss of market leadership in, 131. *See
also* IBM, DOS transactions of
Xerox Corporation and, 96
Photocopiers
digital, 107
early market analysis of and barriers to,
97–98
Plans, 309
Playfulness, 171
Post-it notes, 347–348, 349, 350
Predictability, improving, 29–30
Predictive validity, 25, 29
Preparadigmatic structure, 78
Problem sensing, 183
Process, xiv
Products, new, 215, 216
customer orientation and, 216
development of, 215–221
lack of market success for, 214–215
literature on successes and failures of,
217–220
Products, finished, xiv
Prospect theory, 43

Radical innovation, 96, 108, 233
Radical transformations, 260
RCA Corporation, 3, 20, 36n, 80
Reality, 188
Reflective practioners, 109, 110
Remington Rand, 79, 80
Reorientation, 261
Research, marketing. *See* Marketing research

Research and development
downsizing in, impact on work environment for creativity and innovation,
118–123
effectiveness of, 35n
optimism and, 44
organizational receptiveness and, 76
Research methods, 221
Research tools, 224
Return on investment, for evaluating success, 27
Reynolds, A. William, 193–194
RISC chips, 3, 21
RISC technology, case history of, 84–85
Risk aversion, 253
capital asset pricing model of, 241
inconsistent
in biased decision-making, 240–241
established assets and, 241
portfolio selection model of, 241–242
prospect model of, 242
versus risk taking, 24–27
Risk-oriented thinking, 111
Risk taking, 117, 319
experimentation and, 319–320
military, 313–314
C³I in, 314–315
prospect theory of, 43
Role(s)
defined, 285
leadership, 284–290, 285f, 288f, 289f. *See
also* Leadership; Top management
team
Ruskin, John, 110

Sanyo Corporation, 140
Schön, Don, 109
Schumpeter, J.A., 141
Schumpeter's theory of innovation, 233
Schumpeterian economics, x, 54, 58
Selection criteria, 29
Self-renewal through innovation, 182
Sequential hurdles, 32
Serendipity, 56
Semiconductor industry
innovation in, 239
patterns of entry, post-entry performance,
and exit in, 51
Sin of commission, 217
Sin of omission, 217
Slack resources, 186
SmithKline Beecham PLC, 32
Sony Corporation, 3, 20–21

Sony Walkman, innovation in development of, 350
Sperry Rand, 80
Steel industry, market shift and, 192–193
Strategic criteria, 198
"Stickiness," 23
Stucky, Susan, 100
Sun Microsystems, 3, 21
  RISC technology and, 85
Superstitious learning, 168
Switching costs, 239
Synthesis, cumulative, 348–349
Systematic biases, 308

Team heterogeneity, 263
"Tech"
  brief history of, 328
  bringing culture to life in, 333–335
  creating a codex for, 331–333
  and design of innovative organization, 328–331
  living with culture of, 335–339
Technological change, 15, 21
  in large firms, 184–186
  role of incentives in, 32–34
Technological choice, 20–40
  biases in. See Decision biases
  boundaries of, 129–146
  constructionist approach to, 131–132
  IBM as example of. See IBM, DOS transactions of
  ex-ante versus post-ante criteria for, 28
  false negatives and false positives in, 23–29
  foresight in, 175–177
  improving predictability in, 29–30
  judgmental processes and cognitive biases and, 23–24
  learning from mistakes in, 29–30
  market-pull hypothesis of, 22
  model for, 27–29
  net present value and internal rate of return and, 27
  oversights in. See Technological oversight
  selection decision and outcomes in, 24–27, 25f, 26f
  technological, economic, and institutional perspectives on, 22–23
  technology-push hypothesis of, 22
  trade-offs between errors in, 30–32
Technological discontinuity, 261

Technological forecasting
  bold, 247
  isolation errors and, 243–244
  in optical lithography, 147–166
  technology life cycle as guide to, 147. See also Technological life cycle
Technological foresight, 3, 21
  inevitability of, 345
Technological innovation, xiv, 3–9. See also Experimentation
  beating the odds in, 351–352
  bureaucracy and, 325–326
  case study of applied theories of, 325–342
  challenges to developing theories of, 3–5
    complexity, 4–5
    constraints, 4
    contingency, 4
    uncertainty, 3–4
  competency-destroying, decision biases and. See Decision biases, theory of
  defined, 112
  developing theories of, 5–7
    by learning to flip coins, 5
    by reducing constraints, 6
    role of learning in, 7–8
    role of top management in, 6–7
    by tailoring fits, 5–6
  displacement effects of, 141
  downsizing and. See Downsizing
  environmental determinants of. See Environmental determinants of work motivation, creativity, and innovation
  at individual versus organizational level, 186
  in large firms, 184–186, 185f, 255n–256n
  leadership roles in, 284–290, 285f, 288f, 289f
    balance and timing of, 296f, 296–300
    learning and, 279–305. See also Cochlear implant program; Therapeutic apheresis program
    ambiguity and uncertainty and, 279–280
    concluding discussion about, 300–303
    introduction to, 279–281
  luck hypothesis of, 13–19
    objections to, 16–17
    rejection of, 17–18
  in mature-industry firms, 181–183
    barriers to, 183–186
    building technological entrepreneurship into, 204–206
    firm culture and, 206–208
    revival of, 199–204
  motivation for, 114–115

necessary conditions for, 307
observed behaviors of leaders in,
281–291
Minnesota Innovation Research Program studies of, 281–282
opportunity costs of, 172–173
options value and, 349
organizational
individual creativity in, 112–113
model of, 112–116
and organizational administrative capabilities, 169–170
organizational downsizing and, 111
past learning and, 168–169
radical
by de novo firms, 239–240
in small versus large firms, 233–234
Schumpeter's theory of, 233
as shapers versus responders to market, 130–131
skills in management of, 115
system change and, 207–208
in technological world, 347–348
top management behavior during process of, 280–281
top management involvement in, 282, 283f, 284
top management turnover and, 264–265
towards a theory of, 345–354
challenges to, 345–346, 346f
components of, 346, 347f
serendipity in, 348–351
Type I and I errors and, 300–303
University of Minnesota research project on, 190, 191t
Technological life cycle
dominant design and, 149–151
as forecasting tool, limitations of, 147–149, 150–151, 163–164
schematic of, 149, 150f
Technological outcomes, 3
Technological oversight, 3, 20–21, 175–177
class 1 (for radically new products), 216
reasons for, 217–219
class 2 (for missed new product opportunities), 216–217, 217t
reasons for, 219–220
conclusions about, 227–228
versus foresight, 132
inevitability of, 345
minimizing, 214–230
organizational correction of, 260–261
Technological communities, 42
Technological paradigms, 42

Technological tragectory, 140, 169
Technology, production, changes in, 196–199
Therapeutic apheresis program
innovation leadership in, 281–282, 283f, 287, 288f, 289–291
leadership in, joint venture agreement and, 293–296, 294t
Minnesota Innovation Research Program study of, 281–282
3M Corporation. See Minnesota Mining & Manufacturing Corporation
Timing, 296
Tire industry, changes affecting, 193–195
Top management team. See also Leadership
hetereogeneous versus homogeneous, and organizational responsiveness to environmental shock, 262–264
role in innovation, 282, 283f, 284
during technological innovation process, 280–281
Toshiba Corporation, 140
Total quality management, 102–103
Toyota, 182
Trade-offs, x, 34
Trajectories, 3, 95
technological, 6, 23
Treatment effect, 30
Trial-and-error learning, 279

UNIVAC, 79
Uncertainty, 21, 279
Unexamined assumptions, 188
University of Minnesota Innovation Research Project, 190, 191t
Unlearning, 6, 171
Useful fictions, 309
Usselman, Steven, 81

Variation–selection–retention, xi
Darwinian, xi
von Neumann, John, 79

Watson, Thomas, Jr., 80, 136
Watson, Thomas, Sr., 83, 137
Weinberger, Caspar, 322n
"White elephants," 26
Wisdom, 6, 168
Work environment, during organizational change, creativity and innovation and, 118

Work Environment Inventory, 116–117
Wozniak, Stephen, 86, 89

Xerography
    development of, 36n
    invention of, 97

Xerox Corporation, 3, 20, 140, 256n
    distributed computing and, 96
    innovation strategy of, 252–253
    Leadership Through Quality program of,
        103
    oversights of, 95–99
    research-corporation relations at, 99–101